15.13

The
Imperial
Years

Also by Alonzo L. Hamby

*Beyond the New Deal: Harry
S. Truman and American Liberalism*
*The New Deal: Analysis
and Interpretation*
*Harry S. Truman and the
Fair Deal* (Editor)

The Imperial Years

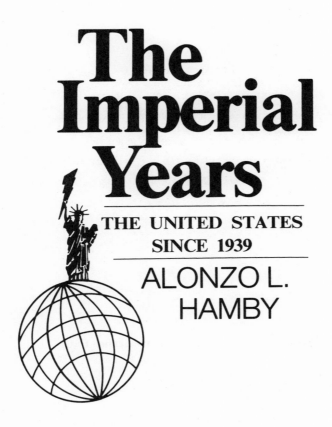

THE UNITED STATES SINCE 1939

ALONZO L. HAMBY

WEYBRIGHT AND TALLEY
New York

The Imperial Years:
The United States Since 1939
COPYRIGHT © 1976 BY ALONZO L. HAMBY

MANUFACTURED IN THE UNITED STATES OF AMERICA

Design by Bob Antler

SECOND PRINTING

Library of Congress Cataloging in Publication Data

Hamby, Alonzo L
The imperial years.

Bibliography: p.
Includes index.
1. United States—History—1945– 2. United States
—History—1933–1945. I. Title.
E741.H34   973.92   76-5799
ISBN 0–679–40131–8
ISBN 0–679–40135–0 pbk.

To My Mother
and to the
Memory of My Father

Preface

History is the collective memory of a society. A nation's conception of its past provides both a sense of identity and a point of departure for future actions. Social groups as well draw upon history, as they understand it, for self-comprehension, justification, and guides for present-day problems. Statesmen seeking vindication for their policies frequently invoke "the lessons of history" or "the logic of history" as if they were referring to an irresistible force which will dictate the future.

Actually, any memory is fallible, and a collective memory is especially open to dispute. Nations and groups attempting to employ the past for their own purposes arrive at diametrically opposed views of the same episode or problem. Academicians, presumably capable of greater objectivity, hurl conflicting interpretations at one another with an abandon that must bewilder laymen who come into contact with the world of scholarship. A welter of tangled events and uncertain facts, history yields few self-evident guides to the future.

The average person, easily and often justifiably bored and confused by learned controversy when he is even aware of its existence, tends to accept the popular mythology that appeals to him. Because of this, he may sidestep not simply pedantic argument but also verifiable fact. He may embrace dangerous and inaccurate simplifications—the belief, for example, that the Munich crisis provided the only guide for handling the Vietnam conflict. An understanding of the past is necessary in order to come to grips with the present, but it must be an informed understanding with a sense of the complexity of human affairs, not a popular mythology that provides simple answers for hard and complicated problems.

This book makes no claim to the discovery of some transcendent absolute truth. Nor is it a "text" in what has unfortunately become the commonly accepted sense of that term—a bland encyclopedic recitation of events with no apparent direction or purpose other than the negative goal of being inoffensive. It is an interpretation of American history in the contemporary age, directed not just to the college student who needs a reference book but to the informed American searching for perspectives with which to face the baffling and often frightening world of the 1970s.

Few countries have possessed a stronger sense of ideals than the United States. The experience of founding a new society in a new world, of escaping the tyranny and oppression of the old world, gave America a unique sense of destiny from the beginning. America at the least was a special land of opportunity with far more hope of happiness for the ordinary man than poverty-ridden Europe. America at the most was a utopia, a beacon light of inspiration that the rest of the world would someday emulate. The American Revolution both fulfilled and strengthened these aspirations. It established a federal republic, a free, representative government without the corrupt trappings of a monarchy or an aristocracy, practicing a simple, relatively equalitarian style of life, protecting the fundamental rights of all its citizens, standing apart as a light of hope in a misery-ridden world. Like most ideals, the American ideal was in some aspects inconsistent with reality—its most glaring contradiction was black slavery—still it was accurate enough to capture the imagination of many less fortunate peoples. Deeply imbedded in the national consciousness as a received truth beyond serious question, it gave the American republic a unique sense of mission.

This utopian impulse has its pitfalls; the millennium is perpetually elusive. The resolution of one crisis almost invariably brings forth new, unforeseen problems that come as a shock to a people conditioned to expect a total solution. The resulting frustration, as likely as not, stimulates a search for scapegoats and hinders rational understanding of the new dilemma that has emerged from the old. Americans have yet to learn that total success in any great endeavor, be it the establishment of international peace or the abolition of poverty, is unlikely.

Even America's most enduring success, the U.S. system of representative government, has been inconsistent with the utopian impulse. A monument to the wisdom of the eighteenth-century Enlightenment, the American system has fostered and preserved popular decision making and personal liberty over a longer period of time than can be claimed by any other major government in the world. Yet built on the principles of diffusion of power and checks and balances, it encourages the postponement of problems until they become crises, then rarely allows the imposition of the complex solutions that crises demand. And, while it necessitates imperfect, compromise policy decisions, it also rests on a voluntary popular support that practically forces political leaders to rally support with the millennial promises that seem to have such great appeal to the American character. Ramshackle answers to difficult public questions may be part of the price of representative government, but Americans traditionally have been unwilling to make such a concession.

Throughout its history, as the United States developed from a relatively homogeneous, agrarian-oriented society to a heterogeneous, urban-industrial society, the relevance of the old ideal and the utility of old techniques came into question. In the years after 1939, the American nation, at the zenith of its wealth and power, was plunged, irreversibly it appeared, into a world from which it had tried to maintain a chaste isolation. Suddenly, it seemed in danger of assuming the sort of identity that it always had abjured, that of a wealthy imperial nation. Mass affluence allowed most Americans to enjoy a degree of luxury and self-indulgence well removed from the simple life that the founding fathers had venerated as a source of civic virtue. The sheer fact of awesome power and the imperative of protecting vital national interests in a disordered world—not the expansionist tendencies of capitalism or some lust for power and glory—forced the United States to preside over an empire its citizens did not want. At the same time, the nation had to preserve the essential democratic-republican ideals that had made America different and valuable. The history of our own time is in large measure the story of this difficult and often poorly performed task. As the country reached its bicentennial, its founding ideals were recalled more frequently than ever, and the inevitable gap between aspiration and accomplishment was perhaps too often noted. Yet whatever the failures of its promise, the maintenance of the American ideal was more essential than ever in a world menaced not by flabby eighteenth-century monarchies but by ruthlessly efficient varieties of twentieth-century totalitarianism.

All writers of history, including those who try to conceal the fact from themselves, approach their topic from a personal viewpoint which provides an organizing principle for their work and strongly influences their conclusions. The historian, if he is honest, considers all the evidence, takes his own preconceptions into account, and avoids forcing facts into a straitjacket; but he cannot escape from his most basic beliefs. Facts are mute creatures incapable of speaking for themselves. My own viewpoint is that of an individual who came of voting age at the beginning of the 1960s and who finds the liberal-democratic tradition preferable to the modish strains of radicalism lumped together under the term "New Left."

Fad and fashion are as shifting and pervasive in the intellectual world as among the jet set. During the 1960s, events made radicalism, militance, and revolution seem chic. The liberal tradition, victimized in part by its own excesses and in part by a fate that destroyed its most attractive representatives, came to appear tired and excessively rational. Many of its spokesmen experienced a failure of nerve which led them into confessions of intellectual impotence. Yet their basic faith was a sound one. Its central elements—affirmation of human dignity, belief in equal opportunity, commitment to personal liberty, the need to achieve a balance between absolutist morality and crass self-interest—impress me as the best creed for living in an always imperfect world.

I have moved in other directions that are presently not fashionable in the intellectual-academic community. Believing that most of our national problems are met, if not always resolved, in the arena of politics, I have emphasized political history. Convinced that national leaders frequently possess considerable leeway in making decisions which affect our lives, I discuss important personalities at some length. Feeling that our Presidents do much to establish the tone of our politics and society, I employ the presidential synthesis as a basic organizing principle. I have sought to avoid the built-in obsolescence of a history dominated by the concerns of the moment and especially have attempted to refrain from the mode of analysis in which every past event or decision is examined from the perspective of Vietnam. I have tried to abjure both a morality-play narrative that presents issues in terms of a stark good vs. evil dualism and the style of relativism that refuses to make value judgments.

No society is perfect; it would be an exercise in foolish complacency to gloss over the injustices that exist in America. Still, the United States and the other liberal capitalist and democratic socialist states of the Northern Hemisphere have managed to achieve levels of human freedom and material well-being which amply justify their existence and refute leftist clichés about repression and imperialism. I believe unapologetically that the containment of the Soviet and Chinese varieties of communism or any other totalitarian system is a necessity, but one that can be achieved only through the renunciation of Messianism and the establishment of a diplomacy characterized by morality, flexibility, a sane balance of means and ends, an awareness of the limits of U.S. power, and a guideline of enlightened self-interest.

Ultimately, the purpose of historical literature should be less to convert than to inform. I hope that the reader, whether he finds my opinions prophetic or perverse, will maintain a critical, questioning attitude and that when he concludes this book he will feel better able to deal with the world around him.

No author can undertake a project of this magnitude without a great deal of help. I have of course drawn freely upon the work of many outstanding historians, whom I have attempted to acknowledge in the bibliographical essay. My colleague John L. Gaddis read chapter after chapter of frightfully rough draft with his usual intelligence and goodwill. Charles C. Alexander and George C. Herring criticized portions of the manuscript. As I possess what some would consider an above-average reserve of stubbornness, I did not always display my gratitude by acceding to their suggestions, and I alone am responsible for what follows. Mrs. Doris Dorr typed the manuscript with her customary cheerfulness, accuracy, and cryptographic skill. My wife, Joyce, gave me invaluable intellectual and emotional support.

Contents

The
Imperial
Years

ONE

America in 1939

CHRONOLOGY

1929–39

1929

OCTOBER   The Wall Street Crash; beginning of the Great Depression

1931

SEPTEMBER   Japan invades Manchuria

1932

NOVEMBER   Franklin D. Roosevelt elected President of the United States

1933

JANUARY   Adolf Hitler appointed chancellor of Germany
MARCH–JUNE   The First Hundred Days of the New Deal: establishment of Agricultural Adjustment Administration, National Recovery Administration, Public Works Administration, Federal Emergency Relief Administration, Home Owners Loan Corporation, Federal Deposit Insurance Corporation, Civilian Conservation Corps, Securities and Exchange Commission, Tennessee Valley Authority

1934

APRIL   Johnson Debt Default Act

1935

MAY   Italy invades Ethiopia; U.S. Supreme Court rules National Recovery Administration unconstitutional

JUNE–AUGUST   Second Hundred Days of the New Deal: Wagner Act, Social Security Act, Wheeler-Rayburn Holding Company Act, Banking Act, "Wealth Tax" Act, Works Progress Administration

AUGUST   First Neutrality Act

1936

JANUARY   U.S. Supreme Court rules Agricultural Adjustment Administration unconstitutional

FEBRUARY   Soil Conservation Act; extension of First Neutrality Act

MARCH   Hitler remilitarizes the Rhineland

JULY   Spanish Civil War begins

NOVEMBER   Roosevelt reelected in landslide victory

1937

FEBRUARY   Roosevelt proposes to pack the Supreme Court

MAY   Second Neutrality Act ("Cash and Carry")

JULY   Senate rejects Court-packing plan; Farm Security Administration established; Japan invades China

DECEMBER   Japanese planes attack U.S.S. *Panay;* House begins debate on Ludlow Resolution

1938

FEBRUARY   Establishment of second Agricultural Adjustment Administration

MARCH   Germany annexes Austria

JUNE   Fair Labor Standards Act; establishment of Temporary National Economic Committee

JUNE–NOVEMBER   Roosevelt fails in attempt to purge conservative Democrats in party primaries; Republican gains in midterm elections solidify conservative coalition in Congress

SEPTEMBER   Munich crisis; Czechoslovakian Sudetenland
             conceded to Germany

1939

MARCH   Germany absorbs remainder of Czechoslovakia
APRIL   Italy invades Albania
MAY   Italo-German alliance (Rome-Berlin Axis)
AUGUST   Nazi-Soviet alliance; Germany issues ultimatum to
         Poland

The 1930s were among the most traumatic years of modern history, frightening and disheartening to those who lived through them. The decade witnessed the collapse of the shaky world order erected by the statesmen at Versailles. A fearsome totalitarianism and aggressive militarism appeared to many to be the "wave of the future" for Europe and Asia. In the United States a special and uniquely American dream lay in ruins—the dream, fostered by Republican leaders in the 1920s, of ever-increasing abundance created by an enlightened corporate leadership which in turn drew support from government policies of dynamic conservatism. Indeed, by 1939, many Americans had experienced ten years of harrowing deprivation, and the United States had come close to social collapse. True, the most terrible days of the Great Depression were past, and the nation had reached an equilibrium of sorts. It was a distinctly unsteady, unprosperous equilibrium, however, and few dared to hope for much more than a somewhat lesser degree of austerity. Moreover, those who watched events across the oceans were beginning to realize that the United States faced new and greater trials.

HARD TIMES:
THE GREAT DEPRESSION AND AMERICAN LIFE

By the standards which prevailed a third of a century later, life in 1939 was simple, even for ordinary Americans who had escaped the worst impact of the depression. Luxuries that the middle class of the 1970s would take for granted were rare or simply not available. Depression or not, America was determined to be, as the phrase goes, a nation on wheels, but less than 60 percent of American families owned a car. Popularly priced automobiles, if advanced beyond the Model T, were still relatively

low-powered vehicles, and automotive designers had been able to give
little attention to comfort and ease of operation. (The first rudimentary
automatic transmission in a mass-produced passenger car appeared in the
fall of 1939.) The automotive culture of superhighways, elaborate camping facilities, and opulent motels was virtually nonexistent. Travelers slept
in unpleasant little tourist cabins, and in most parts of the country a
four-lane, limited-access expressway was considered an engineering
wonder as remarkable and remote as the Great Pyramids.

At home, air conditioning was not yet an essential of comfortable
living. Appliances common in today's kitchens—electric skillets, electric
can openers, ten-speed blenders—were not in use. About half of America's
housewives still did their cooking on coal or wood ranges. Of course, there
was no home television, but radio provided much the same sort of instant
information and popular entertainment; the movies and the newsreels
which invariably accompanied them added a visual dimension.

As always, rural life was harder. If by some miracle one could find a
prosperous farm, he would nevertheless be likely to find a dreary existence. Only about a quarter of the farms had electrical service; yet this
total, made possible largely by government underwriting of rural electrification cooperatives, represented a 250 percent increase over 1933.

For those who had been seriously affected by the depression, life was
extremely shabby and bleak. The statistics are overwhelming. Of a total
work force numbering about 50 million, unemployment had ranged from
13 million in early 1933 to 9 or 10 million in 1939. Even the ardent
reformer Harry Hopkins predicted a "recovery" in which the jobless
would still total 4 or 5 million. Earlier in the decade, before the institution
of federal deposit insurance, almost ten thousand banks had failed, wiping
out the savings of millions of persons. American manufacturing output,
which had increased by 364 percent over the thirty-year period from 1899
to 1929, rose by less than 3 percent during the 1929–39 decade. A third of
the nation's railroad mileage was in bankruptcy. American farmers no
longer faced what had been a very real threat of liquidation, but farm
prices averaged slightly less than two-thirds of the 1929 level and were at
just 77 percent of parity.*

The human costs, while intangible, were grimmer. If few persons
actually died of starvation, many suffered from malnutrition and fell
victim to diseases that strong bodies could have warded off. The psychic

---

* The parity index is a measurement of farm purchasing power. During the 1930s, its
base (100) was the buying power of basic commodity prices during the relatively prosperous years, 1910–14. A level of 77 percent of parity indicated that the average farmer received prices for his crops which enabled him to purchase only about 77
percent of the consumer goods he would have been able to buy in the years just before
World War I.

toll was formidable and widespread. Unemployment meant not simply a loss of income but of the occupation around which a man structured his life. The foreclosure of an individual's home or farm meant not simply a loss of shelter and property, as bad as this was, but of a man's stake in society. Prolonged joblessness could lead to the restructuring of lines of authority within a family, away from an unemployed husband toward a working wife or son. Families that were hit especially hard might disintegrate. During the worst days of the depression, at least a million men wandered about the country, ostensibly looking for work but in fact bumming around in boxcars because there was nothing else for them to do, no place for them to go.

The depression, in short, inflicted upon its victims feelings of helplessness, aimlessness, and alienation. Persons who had once felt themselves part of society found themselves outside of it, torn between feelings of personal guilt at their idleness or failure and a sense of anger at a system that seemed to have chosen them almost randomly for suffering. Those who escaped the worst, moreover, could not avoid being affected by those who were most unfortunate. Bread lines, apple sellers, reliefers, Okies making the long trek to California, wretched inhabitants of the Hoovervilles—all impressed a sense of economic insecurity upon an entire generation. The very rich may have escaped the effects of the depression, but most ordinary Americans were brushed in one way or another. Few did not have friends or relatives who had been hurt. Very few could feel optimistic about their future. The generation that came to maturity in the 1930s, having experienced terrible economic insecurity, wanted above all economic security. This desire would be one of the most basic factors of American life and politics for the next twenty years.

THE NEW DEAL: WHAT IT DIDN'T DO, WHAT IT MIGHT HAVE DONE, AND WHAT IT DID

A popular myth, until recently a staple of Democratic political rhetoric, states that the New Deal saved America, vanquished the depression, and restored prosperity. A less popular myth, counterproductive as political rhetoric but devoutly held by those who had strongly identified with the Republican governments of the 1920s, says that the New Deal blocked the return of prosperity and inflicted some species of socialism or communism on a once-free country. Neither myth enjoys a very intimate relationship with what actually happened.

The New Deal came to power at the worst point of the depression. Initially, its leaders were the beneficiaries of an intense mood of public desperation. They might well have been able to establish some sort of socialism (under a different name, of course) had they wished to do so. And the New Deal did engage in some experimentation which amounted to a type of socialism. It encouraged rural cooperatives and financed a few collective farm settlements; it stood for public ownership of electrical power; it created the Tennessee Valley Authority (TVA), one of the world's foremost examples of regional planning. All the same, the main thrust of the New Deal was in another direction.

Coming to office at a time when the banking system had collapsed, the New Dealers did not even consider the alternative of nationalization. Instead, they worked with financial leaders to hammer out legislation which essentially restored the old system on a sounder basis than before. Their first plan for industrial recovery, built around the National Recovery Administration (NRA), involved the organization of major industries around codes that regulated labor relations, production, pricing, and selling practices. The codes, however, had to be drawn up *jointly* by representatives of government and business; that is, industry had a veto power which it used to gain favorable provisions. Moreover, although each code was supposed to recognize the right of collective bargaining, the corporations usually succeeded in evading this requirement, thereby making the Wagner Act necessary. After the U.S. Supreme Court declared the NRA unconstitutional in 1935, the New Deal undertook an antimonopoly drive which curbed a few of the worst abuses of big business but achieved practically no success in breaking up economic concentration. The objective of the antimonopoly campaign, of course, was precisely the opposite of socialism; it was an effort to make private enterprise freer and more open. As it was, the New Deal subjected business and banking to some regulation but made little change in their fundamental structure. The years after 1939 witnessed the greatest corporate growth in American history.

The New Deal proceeded from two central convictions. One was the belief that large industry and finance had enjoyed dangerously excessive power and that this power had to be more equitably distributed throughout American society. In part, it was this effort at redistribution that the businessmen mistook for socialism. The other important conviction was the assumption that the government should make minimum provisions for the welfare of its citizens. In short, the New Deal was an attempt not to abolish American capitalism but to change it by redistributing the power within it and grafting a rather crudely developed welfare state onto it.

The New Deal brought important power and benefits to an agricultural economy that had been in a state of depression since it had overexpanded to meet the temporarily heavy needs of World War I. Through a variety of devices, including acreage allotments and commodity loans, the government pushed agricultural prices up beyond levels that the free market would have dictated. Mortgage-relief acts saved thousands of farms from ruin. In 1933, 54 of every 1,000 farms were going under the auctioneer's hammer in a forced sale; by 1940, the rate was down to 16 per 1,000, the lowest ratio since the early 1920s. Moreover, the New Deal greatly enhanced the quality of rural life through its rural-electrification program. No previous national administration had given so much recognition to agriculture or contributed so greatly to its welfare. Before the 1930s, farmers who produced basic commodities had fought a generally losing battle against the chaos of the free market. The New Deal programs brought a degree of organization to agriculture, and shifted the market odds in favor of the farmer. It is no exaggeration to say that rural America had been saved from disaster.

The New Deal brought equally great benefits to the labor movement. The National Labor Relations Act (the Wagner Act) guaranteed the right of collective bargaining and cleared the way for the organization of the most powerful labor-union movement in American history. Efforts to organize unskilled industrial workers had usually failed in the past, and during the 1920s even the established trade unions, represented by the American Federation of Labor (AFL), suffered serious membership losses. Under the New Deal the AFL recovered and began a period of growth. Moreover, an aggressive new labor federation, the Congress of Industrial Organizations (CIO), successfully established huge new unions in the great mass-production industries. In some instances, rebellious workers compelled management capitulation by occupying key plants and refusing to budge until their union obtained recognition. By 1939, more workers had been unionized than ever before in American history. The new unions were still shaky and had not yet proven that they could deliver substantial economic benefits to their members, but their size and their initial successes had already made them a powerful factor in American society.

With the passage of the Fair Labor Standards Act in 1938, the New Deal established national wage-and-hour standards and forbade the employment of child labor in interstate commerce. As originally passed, the law made many exceptions, and one congressman sarcastically proposed an amendment which would direct its administrator to report whether anyone was actually covered by it. Even so, the bill forced wage increases for millions of workers, and in subsequent years Congress steadily enlarged its coverage and tightened its loopholes. By 1939, whether because of the unions or wage legislation, the average production worker with a steady job in a major manufacturing industry worked 10.7 hours per week less than in 1929 but had greater purchasing power.

The Fair Labor Standards Act affected few unionized workers. It was one demonstration of the New Deal's determination to provide minimum benefits for the unorganized and underprivileged. The Social Security Act established a federal system of old-age and survivor's insurance and provided for federal contributions to state systems of unemployment compensation, old-age pensions, and welfare assistance. Other programs attempted to meet the immediate problems of the depression. Mortgage-relief statutes may have saved farms or homes for as many as a million people. Work-relief agencies provided jobs for millions of the unemployed, although they also paid substandard wages and did not provide work for a majority of the jobless.

The welfare measures aimed specifically at the depression helped many people, but the assistance was generally temporary and was neither a financial nor psychological substitute for regular gainful employment. The permanent programs did not compare favorably with those established in Germany a half century earlier by Otto von Bismarck, who was hardly a creeping socialist. Yet to Americans of the 1930s, the New Deal welfare effort was controversial and even revolutionary. The proclamation of a classless society probably would not have won the allegiance of the underprivileged so completely.

The welfare programs, the great assistance given to agriculture and labor, and the foolish accusations of socialism and communism all acted to obscure one central failure of the New Deal—it never ended the Great Depression. By 1939 the New Deal had reached its end as an ongoing program; the forces opposed to it had become strong enough to block significant new legislation, and indications are that it had lost its intellectual dynamism anyway. True, the country had achieved a partial recovery, and the apocalyptic sense of crisis which had been so widespread in early 1933 was long since gone. But over 17 percent of the labor force was still out of work; and few, if any, observers ventured to hope for much more than a halving of that rate. The New Deal may have saved America by instilling confidence in the government, but despite the oratory of political myth makers, it had not vanquished the depression.

The reasons for this failure are complex. For one thing, most leading businessmen and financiers, alienated from the New Deal and confused by it, developed a "depression psychology." Unable to foresee the return of boom times, they deferred expansion and new investment which could have been powerful stimuli to the economy. They demonstrated that in a capitalist society, a political movement cannot count on economic success unless it wins a measure of confidence from the capitalists. The New Deal contributed at least as much to the failure through its own internal contradictions and inconsistencies. The NRA, for example, may have failed because huge public works programs were not coordinated with it. The Social Security Act, while laudable as a welfare measure, imposed payroll taxes that took millions of dollars of purchasing power out of the economy.

The New Deal's opponents observed with alarm that its programs ran up large budget deficits, but the leading exponent of deficit spending, the English economist John Maynard Keynes, warned at the time that the federal expenditures were not nearly great enough to lift the economy out of the depression. In 1937 the administration actually cut back on relief spending and presented a balanced budget to Congress. The country plunged into a serious recession which wiped out much of the recovery that had been achieved. After months of indecision, the government returned to the old, inadequate levels of spending. Throughout the 1930s, New Dealers shrank from draconian budget policies which might have restored business confidence and at the same time refused to accept the huge deficits which probably would have led to recovery despite the qualms of the businessmen. The New Deal never attained a systematic grasp of the economy, never pursued a coherent recovery plan, and never ended the depression.

Nor, contrary to an impression which prevailed at the time, did the New Deal provide major assistance for those at the bottom of American society, the individuals who did not have to worry about a mortgage because they had never owned a farm or home, who had little or nothing in the way of marketable skills. Welfare programs provided a dole for the hard-core poor but did not give them the means to become independent, contributing members of society. The New Dealers were aware of the poor, spent time agonizing over their plight, and devised some attempts to improve their position. The most notable of these efforts was managed by the Farm Security Administration. FSA loans enabled sharecroppers and tenant farmers to buy their own small homesteads, and the agency instructed them in practical agricultural techniques. The FSA's concerns and objectives were laudable, and it succeeded in focusing national attention on the problem of rural poverty. But it could muster little political support and never received the massive financing necessary for a major war against agricultural poverty. Moreover, many of the small farms it did establish were economically untenable. Perhaps an attack on hard-core poverty was impossible as long as the depression and mass unemployment persisted. As it was, the New Deal lifted many small commercial farmers and blue-collar workers who had existed on the fringes of poverty securely into the middle class, but it could give the poor little except welfare.

With the possible exception of the Indians, politically invisible on their reservations, no group in American society was more under-privileged than the Negroes, who still struggled with little success against the vicious combination of racial prejudice and poverty. The New Deal advanced nothing that might be called a civil rights program. It opened the government to Negroes as never before, had an informal "black cabinet" which advised the administration on race relations, and displayed on the whole a genuine sympathy for Negro aspirations. At the same time, some federal agencies continued to practice discrimination, and the administration refused to support a measure as basic as anti-lynching legislation. American Negroes gave their overwhelming support to the New Deal because of the benefits they received from its relief programs, but the New Deal made no effort to cope with the special problems that grew out of being black.

To a later generation the New Deal racial policies seem to be token-ism at its most blatant and ineffective. In the 1930s, however, segregation had scarcely become a topic of political debate; most white Americans at least tacitly assumed black inferiority. The white image of the Negro found expression in "Amos 'n Andy," a radio show that ironically used white actors, and in the films of the shuffling comedian Stepin Fechit; such portrayals were good-humored, but they did not depict the Negro as a man with human complexities and ambitions. They both expressed and reinforced a national stereotype. Given this national mood and given the great economic difficulties of the 1930s, the New Deal concerned itself with priorities other than civil rights.

The New Deal thus was neither an initial stage of state socialism nor an all-conquering surge of liberal democracy. It set the stage for a more equitable distribution of social and economic power within American society and imposed the crude beginnings of a welfare state. It distributed great benefits to a middle class that had been seriously hurt by the de-pression, but it did much less for the poor. It did not achieve its central objective of ending the depression.

Some historians, mostly young and radical, have stressed the failures of the New Deal and made light of its achievements. It is natural for a young generation to patronize its predecessor; it is also true that historians with the perspective of thirty years can draw balanced assessments with greater accuracy than those involved in the political battles of the depression decade. All the same, one cannot ignore the fact that the New Deal seemed revolutionary to the people who lived through it. This impression cannot be dismissed as an illusion perpetrated by mass hypnosis; it was based solidly upon the great changes taking place in labor and agriculture and upon welfare legislation which may seem primitive and commonplace today but which was new and sweeping in the political milieu of the 1930s.

The New Deal was a blend of accomplishment and failure, but it undeniably changed American society.

FDR: THE PATRICIAN
AS DEMOCRATIC POLITICAL LEADER

The New Deal was a political success, and much of its popularity stemmed from the appeal of the man who presided over it. Franklin D. Roosevelt was the exemplar of democratic political leadership. No President since Andrew Jackson had won the allegiance of the common man so completely; yet Roosevelt was anything but a common man himself. He was an aristocrat, in the American sense of the word. He was born in 1882 at Hyde Park, New York. His family was old and well established, had something of a tradition of social leadership and responsibility, owned a substantial landed estate, and possessed plenty of money but was not among the vulgar rich. The Roosevelts were, as some described them, the "best people." Young Franklin was educated by tutors, learned such gentlemanly recreations as sailing, was sent to the exclusive Groton preparatory school, then to Harvard College and the Columbia University Law School. As a student, he generally received "gentleman's grades" of *C* or slightly better and never bothered to finish law school since it was not necessary to do so in order to take the New York bar examinations; despite this lackluster record, his family connections won him a comfortable place with a prominent New York City law firm. For a few years, he divided his time between his law practice and his role as a young country squire at his beloved Hyde Park.

Roosevelt's early life was that of many another young gentleman; he was well educated, well placed, comfortable, and, according to most accounts, something of a snob. He was, however, also coming to maturity in one of the most exciting epochs of American political history, the Progressive era. Early twentieth-century progressivism was an extremely complex movement. One of the impulses which went into it was the resentment felt especially by patricians such as Roosevelt against nouveau riche industrialists and financiers, who built their huge empires with no sense of social responsibility, and against political bosses, generally Irish-Americans, who manipulated immigrant voters and plundered the public treasury. Moreover, during the years that young Roosevelt was going to college and beginning his law career, his distant cousin Theodore Roosevelt was bringing the drab Presidency of the Hayes-to-McKinley era back to the center of American politics, fighting for conservation, denouncing trusts, advocating a Square Deal for all, and generally making reform fashionable and compelling. There can be little doubt that he was a great influence on his Hyde Park cousin.

In 1910 Franklin was offered a chance to run as a Democrat (the Hyde Park Roosevelts were Democrats; the Oyster Bay Roosevelts were Republicans) for the state legislature from his normally Republican home district. He promised to protect the interests of the local farmers, and he stood for a certain type of progressivism—denunciation of bosses in both parties and advocacy of clean government. By now, Theodore Roosevelt was out of office, and the uneasy unity he had managed to impose upon the Republican party had been irreparably shattered. The new excitement in Washington was being provided by a group of insurgent Republican progressives locked in bitter combat with the unfortunate President Taft and the regular party organization. Young Roosevelt based his appeal on the style of these insurgents; his name, energetic campaigning, and the demoralization which prevailed within the GOP provided him with his first political victory.

As a member of the legislature, he continued in this pattern of progressive insurgency. He quickly won national attention as a spokesman of a group of dissident Democrats who fought against the Tammany Hall candidate for the U.S. Senate. (The Seventeenth Amendment, providing for direct popular election of senators, did not become effective until 1913.) Roosevelt's insurgents tied up the legislature for weeks, but their battle was futile and a bit silly. In the end they had to compromise on a candidate who was equally acceptable to the machine politicians. The young legislator had won reams of favorable publicity, but he had also illustrated the shallow side of progressivism. Roosevelt soon learned that Tammany men were not ogres, that it was possible and even necessary to work with them on many matters, and that they numbered in their ranks individuals of the caliber of Alfred E. Smith and Robert F. Wagner, Sr. He began to discover that reform entailed welfare legislation as well as boss-baiting and started to vote for such measures. Nevertheless, he maintained his posture of insurgency, remained cool toward Tammany, and broke with the organization in 1912 to support Woodrow Wilson for the Democratic presidential nomination.

The dividend for this gesture was a large one. Upon winning the Presidency, Wilson appointed Roosevelt assistant secretary of the navy. In those days, the post was the number-two position in the department. Since Navy Secretary Josephus Daniels had but a meager knowledge of naval problems and concentrated on congressional relations, Roosevelt had great responsibility for the management and operations of the navy. He presided over a naval expansion program and a major war, demonstrated administrative ability, displayed imagination, learned about labor relations while trying to settle shipyard disputes, and developed a grasp of the political process in Washington. He made only one serious political mistake; in 1914 he allowed his name to be entered in the New York senatorial primary against that of a Tammany-supported but highly respectable candidate, and he was soundly defeated. After this incident, he realized that insurgency could limit as well as advance a political career and worked toward a reconciliation with the machine.

In 1920, the Democratic presidential candidate, James M. Cox, picked Roosevelt as his running mate. Cox never had a chance of victory, but the campaign was a great opportunity for his young vice-presidential candidate. Roosevelt toured the country, made hundreds of speeches and hundreds of contacts, learned the political topography of the entire nation, and in general made an excellent public impression. He profited enormously from the experience, and nobody blamed him for the Democratic defeat. It seemed that he had a brilliant political career ahead of him.

Then in 1921 he contracted a serious case of polio. For a while his public life appeared to be at an end, and his strong-willed mother urged him to return home to semiretirement. Yet whatever the initial shock, whatever his own uncertainties, he decided to remain in politics and undertook a strenuous, agonizing, and often frustrating program of exercise and therapy to regain the use of his paralyzed legs; after seven years, when he returned to full-time political life, he was improved but still unable to walk without assistance. Biographers will never cease to speculate about the effect this experience had upon Roosevelt. Some believe, perhaps a bit romantically, that it gave him a sense of identity with the underdog, thereby preparing him for greatness as a democratic leader; others doubt it. Certainly these hard years brought out qualities of courage and perseverance and forced him to develop a limitless and infectious optimism. These traits were an important part of his political success; it makes little difference whether he had possessed them before polio brought him down.

For all the suffering and heartbreak it involved, the polio attack was a politically fortunate event. It removed Roosevelt from politics at a time when his party was hopelessly divided and doomed to minority status. Torn by cultural hatreds which expressed themselves in debates over such issues as Prohibition, fundamentalism, immigration restriction, and the power of the Ku Klux Klan, the Democratic party was a poor vehicle for a politician with national aspirations. Roosevelt affiliated himself with the political ambitions of his fellow New Yorker, Governor Alfred E. Smith, and made memorable nominating speeches for Smith at the Democratic conventions of 1924 and 1928. But he never was caught up in the ethnic and religious animosities that swirled around Smith, and he carefully preserved his contacts with all factions of the party. He was largely successful in remaining above the battle, playing, as Frank Freidel has observed, the role of a young elder statesman concerned with the future of the party and not irrevocably committed to any group within it.

In 1928, Smith, making his tragic bid for the Presidency, persuaded Roosevelt to run for governor of New York. Roosevelt had some misgivings, but the pressure upon him was great and the opportunity tempting. He won a narrow victory while Smith was losing New York to Hoover. Roosevelt was a progressive and extremely popular governor who won reelection in 1930 by a convincing margin. Yet many perceptive observers considered him weak, indecisive, and superficial. He equivocated when serious scandals broke out in the administration of New York City's Democratic mayor, Jimmy Walker, engaged in fence-straddling on Prohibition, and backtracked on the League of Nations. The enormously influential columnist Walter Lippmann described him as a pleasant young man who wanted to be President—and was utterly without qualifications for the job. During his campaign for the Presidency in 1932, Roosevelt's speeches were confused and inconsistent, giving little hope to those who wanted him to outline a coherent and convincing plan of recovery from the depression.

Roosevelt's inconsistency reflected an almost compulsive experimentalism. Both as a politician and as a planner, he wanted as many options as possible. Especially in the early days of the New Deal, he welcomed advice from and sought the support of every social group. Disposed toward action rather than obsessed by coherence, he rarely worried about the internal contradictions that permeated the New Deal. He considered himself a breaker of outworn tradition but offered no real philosophy or overall program to replace the dogmas that he junked. He simply described himself as "a Christian and a Democrat." His admirers have labeled his outlook "pragmatism"; his critics decry it as a formless "opportunism." In fact, Roosevelt's experimentalism was both a strength and a weakness. It freed him from the binding concept of government which destroyed Herbert Hoover, but it precluded a total commitment to any overall recovery plan. It contributed to the early appeal of the New Deal, but perhaps also to the New Deal's ultimate failures.

Roosevelt quickly convinced most doubters that he could manage the Presidency. As a legislative leader, he displayed skill in manipulating congressmen, knowing when to press them, when to make deals, when to compromise on their terms. Critics asserted that he was a bad administrator, and in fact the lines of authority he delegated were frequently overlapping, shifting, and unclear. Preferring to make changes by indirection, he rarely fired an unsatisfactory subordinate; instead, he would shift the man to another job or perhaps leave him in his post and set up a new agency to assume part or most of his responsibilities. Such techniques quite naturally led to bureaucratic feuds and jealousies, some of them spectacular. But they also ensured that most major issues and decisions would come directly to Roosevelt for resolution; his "poor administration" was a way of keeping a grip upon the vastly expanding government he headed.

The real secret of Roosevelt's strength as President, however, was his appeal to the "common man," the ordinary American who had felt the brunt of the depression. In part, this appeal rested upon what some have called the Politics of the Deed, the actual acts of assistance to those who needed help. But it was also based upon an extraordinary mastery of the communications media. Roosevelt was the first President to institute a schedule of frequent, informal press conferences; he used the institution to develop a rapport with working reporters and get his point of view into the news columns of papers that bitterly opposed him. Even more important was his ability to project his personality over the radio. He encouraged his listeners with his confidence and optimism, and he had the uncanny ability to transmit a feeling of personal concern over the air. The people felt that he cared about them and understood their problems; they idolized him all the more for being a sophisticated man of the upper class who did not have to share their cares but chose to do so. He began his first campaign for reelection by calling Americans to a rendezvous with destiny, and the voters responded by giving him one of the greatest landslide victories in U.S. history.

PARTIES, COALITIONS, AND DILEMMAS
OF THE AMERICAN SYSTEM

In 1936 Roosevelt won 60.7 percent of the popular vote, and carried all but two states. The Democrats scored overwhelmingly against the Republicans in the congressional elections, controlling the Senate 76–16 and the House of Representatives 331–89. In addition, there was a small corps of independent and progressive Republican congressmen who had supported most of the New Deal. The President and his program seemed to have won an unprecedented mandate. Yet almost immediately Roosevelt encountered difficulty. By 1939, the New Deal was history; an era of sweeping and apparently popular reform had come to a halt, supplanted by an era of political stalemate that would endure for a quarter-century. This sudden and apparently paradoxical shift, overwhelming a President of Roosevelt's skill and popularity, could have occurred in few countries other than the United States. The nature of Roosevelt's support and the surprising emergence of an effective opposition to him both merit close observation; they define a political structure that was to endure for a generation and illustrate the myriad difficulties of American national political leadership, especially if oriented toward change.

When Roosevelt took office as President, the Democratic party was still the nation's minority party; that is, under normal conditions a decided majority of the people thought of themselves as Republicans. Such had been the case since the 1890s when another serious depression had discredited the conservative Democratic President, Grover Cleveland. Since the days of McKinley, the Republicans had customarily won presidential elections by comfortable margins. The victories of Woodrow Wilson in 1912 and 1916 had stemmed from bitter divisions within the GOP on the issues of progressive reform and wartime neutrality; in both years, Wilson received less than 50 percent of the popular vote. During the 1920s, the Republicans appeared stronger than ever; the Democrats, terribly divided, seemed hardly a serious opposition. The best showing by a Democratic presidential candidate during the decade came in 1928 when Alfred E. Smith lost to Herbert Hoover by 6 million votes, got only about 41 percent of the ballots, and carried only eight states. As political historians never tire of pointing out, Smith did lay the basis for an important realignment by attracting the votes of millions of urban immigrants who previously had been politically apathetic or inclined to support Republican presidential nominees. But this important shift held no promise of permanence; the immigrant groups voted for the Irish-American, Catholic New Yorker who had risen from the slums because he personified their way of life and their aspirations. The election gave no reason to believe that they would support any other Democratic candidate.

By the same token, Roosevelt's landslide in 1932 did not guarantee a permanent political regrouping. It was primarily a vote *against* Hoover; indeed, FDR had carefully refrained from giving the electorate a solid program to vote *for*. In his first term, then, Roosevelt enjoyed an environment that was favorable for political realignment, but still faced the task of rebuilding a party system through programs that would arouse a sense of positive party loyalty among groups that had not previously felt an identification with the Democrats.

His first tactic, necessary and useful at the low point of the depression, was to distribute favors and benefits to virtually every social group, submerge class divisions, and work for a sense of national unity. This effort at what a later generation would call "consensus politics" was a short-range success, but it could endure only so long as the depression seemed to threaten the existence of American society; it was an unrealistic basis for party realignment. As the sense of crisis eased, business leaders and the wealthy, aroused as much by their loss of status and popular reverence as by any restrictions the New Deal had placed on them, began to mount a vociferous and frequently irrational attack against Roosevelt and his programs. In mid-1935 the President responded by endorsing the Wagner Act (which originally had been introduced without his support), higher income taxes directed at the wealthy, tighter regulation of the banking community, and legislation to break up monopolistic utility empires. With these steps, Roosevelt undertook in earnest an effort to make the Democratic party into a coalition of the nonrich and the nonbusiness groups.

The election of 1936 demonstrated his success. Roosevelt based his massive victory on the votes of the urban working classes (including ethnic-religious minorities, white Anglo-Saxon Protestants, and Negroes), the farmers, and middle-class citizens who had been helped in one way or another by the New Deal. He had the support of progressive Republicans, independent reformers, labor unions, northern city bosses, and southern Bourbons. This coalition was as unstable as it was impressive; it included cultural and political antagonisms that could not peacefully coexist; some of its elements, moreover—the farmers and portions of the middle class —were essentially swing voters whose commitment to Roosevelt was extremely tentative. The election of 1936 marked the emergence of the Democrats as a majority party but not by the overwhelming margin that the Roosevelt victory suggested. The groups most firmly brought into the party were the urban working classes, racially and religiously diverse but with a common economic stake in the New Deal, and with them the labor unions. The independent liberals, small in number but influential as intellectuals and planners, found in Roosevelt the leadership they craved; they would remain within the party after his death. The city bosses accepted him as a leader who could deal with them, rouse their constituencies, and provide attractive coattails for their candidates. These groups were the core of what some analysts have called the Democratic presidential party, a formidable coalition which could swamp any challenge to Roosevelt's hold on the Presidency. In the American system of government, however, victory in a presidential election does not necessarily provide a key to legislative success.

Roosevelt's difficulties began in early 1937 when he attempted to secure congressional approval for a bill to enlarge a Supreme Court that had already declared some of his most important legislation unconstitutional and seemed likely to strike down such vital measures as the Wagner and Social Security Acts. His effort to control the Court put him squarely against the constitutionally hallowed system of separation of powers; it was a poor position from which to rally support. The Court-packing fight showed that even a President who had been able to muster enormous popular support could not be assured control of the Judiciary. It also demonstrated that Roosevelt could not even count on the congressional majorities he had carried into office with him. After prolonged debate in which the opposition was led by maverick Democrats, the Senate (with its 76–16 Democratic majority) shelved the proposal. The Court itself was sufficiently intimidated to reverse the thrust of its decisions completely and bring its thinking into line with the New Deal, but the administration defeat on the bill lay the groundwork for Roosevelt's future relations with Congress. In the process of gaining dominance over one rival branch of the federal government, Roosevelt had lost his grip on the other.

But how, one must ask, could the Democratic senators possibly oppose him just a few months after the 1936 election? In part, they could do so because the Court-packing scheme was not an especially popular proposal; to many it seemed anticonstitutional. But there was a more fundamental reason. They could oppose Roosevelt because American federalism provided the organizational basis for the American party system. Although Roosevelt was the leader of the Democratic party, he could not discipline or affect the careers of most of his Democratic opponents. They had their own organizations in their home states, generally well removed from presidential control. In 1938, Roosevelt tried to regain command of the party by intervening in primary elections in an attempt to "purge" several conservative Democrats. The President was unable to sway their constituencies, and the effort was an ignominious failure.

The failure of the Court-packing plan and the purge signaled the beginning of an era of independence for many congressmen who had been privately disturbed by the directions in which the New Deal was moving. The result was the formation in Congress of an informal but effective "conservative coalition" which included most of the Republicans and a large number of Democrats. The conservative Democrats were preponderantly from the South and generally represented rural and small-town areas; usually, they enjoyed "safe" constituencies. They formed the backbone of a Democratic "congressional party" beyond presidential control. After the Republicans scored substantial gains in the congressional elections of 1938, the conservative coalition was in effective command of Congress, able to block new domestic reform programs, although unable to reverse those already enacted. The political pattern that had been established would prevail for the next twenty-five years.

Some reaction against Roosevelt in 1937 and 1938 was probably inevitable. The Court-packing plan and the recession cut into his appeal and undermined his prestige. The militance of labor, as exemplified in the sit-down strikes, alienated many of the nonworking-class people who had voted for him in 1936. Some historians have argued that both the Court-packing episode and the purge were badly handled, that Roosevelt through a better job of managing them could have avoided at least the worst which occurred. Yet in the main the New Deal was not brought to a halt by crises of policy or failures of technique; Roosevelt was the victim of some of the most revered American institutions.

Most Americans consider their Constitution as a guarantor of liberty and rightly so, but few realize that its framers conceived of liberty in terms of limited government and checks against unfettered majority rule. The creation of a federal system, dividing power between state and national governments and the separation of powers among independent branches of the national government, each with checks on the other, were deliberate efforts to contain government and to prevent any single "faction" or interest, even if it could secure the support of a majority, from working its will to the detriment of other interests.

The framers of the Constitution did not foresee the rise of political parties, but the formation of parties along federal lines fit their grand design perfectly. In a nonfederal nation such as Great Britain, political parties are run by powerful national organizations, frequently able to ruin the career of a legislator reckless enough to break with the party leadership. Roosevelt and the Presidents who followed him faced the hopeless task of trying to dominate many state parties; they had neither the time nor the resources to devote to such a struggle. Roosevelt did attempt to expand his party by attracting progressive Republicans to it, but even pro-New Deal state organizations were generally not prepared to welcome GOP politicians.

Party and legislative leadership are among the most important duties that Americans expect their Presidents to carry out. Yet few—including historians and political scientists—understand the constitutional difficul-ties that prevent effective, long-term execution of these responsibilities and tie major domestic reforms to episodes of crisis. The most remarkable political fact of the 1930s was that the New Deal lasted so long and accomplished so much.

THE WORLD SCENE: TIGERS AT THE GATE

During the 1930s, in large part because of the pressures of the worldwide depression, the semblance of world order that had been thrown up after World War I unraveled at a frightening rate. In 1931 the Japanese seized the rich Chinese industrial province of Manchuria and converted it into the puppet state of Manchukuo. In 1937 they undertook a war against China proper, slaughtering civilians with wanton ferocity and displaying an attitude toward Westerners which reawakened fears of the yellow peril. In the Soviet Union, the communist dictator Josef Stalin presided over nightmarish purges which liquidated literally hundreds of thousands of his suspected opponents. In 1935 the Italian dictator Benito Mussolini pursued his dreams of empire by using poison gas and air power against primitively armed Ethiopians. In Germany, Adolf Hitler's Nazi government organized book burnings and anti-Jewish pogroms, proclaimed the goal of a thousand-year Reich, and quickly established itself as the most dangerous threat to peace in Europe.

Contemptuously withdrawing from the League of Nations, the Nazis flagrantly violated the Treaty of Versailles by openly engaging in a large military buildup, by sending their armies to occupy the demilitarized Rhineland region of Germany, and by annexing Austria. Then Hitler demanded the German-speaking Sudeten portion of Czechoslovakia and obtained complete capitulation from Britain and France at the Munich conference in September 1938. In the spring of 1939 he incorporated the rest of Czechoslovakia into his empire. In the meantime, he and Mussolini had extended massive assistance to the Spanish fascist rebels led by Generalissimo Francisco Franco. The Loyalist government could count on assistance from only the Soviet Union; by the spring of 1939 it was forced to surrender. The establishment of Franco as dictator of Spain symbolized the strength of European fascism; it also highlighted the weakness of the European democracies, which had backed away from one confrontation after another. In 1935 and 1936 the democratic nations of Western Europe could have dealt with the fascists from a position of moral and military superiority; by 1939, appeasement had frayed their moral position and had allowed the Germans to achieve military strength.

After the subjugation of Czechoslovakia, Hitler turned his ambitions toward Poland. Britain and France pledged to defend Poland if it were attacked; but Hitler, perhaps believing they would retreat again, did not take their promise seriously. His real obstacle was the Soviet Union, which throughout the 1930s had been the most bitter enemy of Nazism and which had designs of its own on Poland and Eastern Europe. On August 24, 1939, the world received the stunning news that the Nazis and the Soviets had signed a nonaggression pact. Only the German and Russian governments knew of the secret protocol for the division of Poland, but all perceptive observers realized that a general war was imminent.

THE AMERICAN RESPONSE:
HISTORICAL MYTHS, ISOLATIONIST TRADITION,
AND CONCEPTIONS OF SELF-INTEREST

Most Americans felt no immediate involvement in the world turmoil, other than a fervent desire to remain disengaged from it. There was, to be sure, an abundance of moral indignation against the totalitarians and their aggressions, but this indignation was tempered by a firm conviction that the United States should resolutely avoid entanglement in the crises of Europe and Asia. Underlying this conviction and providing firm support for it was a blend of political-economic circumstance, deeply felt historical mythology and tradition, and dimly perceived conceptions of national self-interest.

The most obvious and immediate factor behind the American attitude of noninvolvement was the Great Depression. The depression had set off a worldwide surge of economic nationalism with most major countries throwing up trade barriers and manipulating currencies in vain efforts to save themselves at the expense of their neighbors. The United States had led the way in 1930 with the passage of the prohibitive Hawley-Smoot Tariff, which simply encouraged a retaliation that wiped out much of America's foreign markets. The Roosevelt administration tried to revive foreign trade with a program of reciprocal trade agreements, but one of FDR's first acts was to torpedo a conference that was trying to achieve international monetary stabilization. Convinced that the essential causes of the U.S. depression were internal, the New Deal devoted only peripheral attention to international economics.

The depression also brought to a climax a problem that had plagued the European economy since World War I—the war debts. Germany, forced to the wall economically, was unable to pay her obligations to the European Allies. The Allies, in turn, were unable to meet their payments to the United States. Only Finland continued to liquidate its rather small debt on schedule. The debt defaults, if economically unavoidable, aroused angry emotions in the United States. The ordinary American did not understand the complexities of international finance; he might grasp the difficulty an individual could have during the depression but not a nation. The Roosevelt administration made no effort to educate the public; it was too busy with other matters. In 1934 Congress legislated public wrath into law with the Johnson Act, which forbade American citizens or firms from lending money to or buying the securities of foreign governments in default to the United States. The administration objected to the bill but made no real effort to fight it. The defaulting nations responded by ending token payments they had been making and by heaping angry ridicule on "Uncle Shylock."

The war-debt controversy represented only one aspect of the manner in which World War I had inflicted scars upon American foreign policy. In 1917 and 1918 the American government under the moralistic leadership of Woodrow Wilson had represented the war, not as a necessary struggle to prevent a potentially hostile Germany from gaining control of the Atlantic Ocean, but as a crusade that would make the world safe for democracy. The Wilsonian myth brought most Americans behind the war effort and indeed contributed to the development of an orgy of patriotic millennialism. When the results of the war did not fulfill the expectations Wilson had fostered, most Americans were disillusioned and eager to return to a traditional isolationism.

If Americans had rejected the Wilsonian myth, they increasingly accepted another one—the myth that an innocent United States had been lured to war by a villainous entente of munitions makers, bankers, and British propagandists, that American troops had been sacrificed for the private gain of plutocrats and the selfish interests of the European Allies. In 1934 and 1935, a Senate committee headed by Senator Gerald Nye of North Dakota investigated the munitions trade and provided a highly publicized, if extremely superficial, documentation for what might be called the conspiracy myth of the war. At a somewhat more sophisticated level, revisionist historians, including Walter Millis and Charles A. Beard, took up the same line. During the 1930s, it became part of the conventional wisdom of both the intellectuals and ordinary Americans.

The conspiracy argument could win wide acceptance because of the great disillusionment with Wilsonianism, because indictments of capitalists fit the mood of the depression, and most fundamentally, because it stemmed naturally from one of the oldest and most deeply held American traditions: isolationism. From the beginnings of their history, Americans had believed they were a people apart who had escaped from the tyranny and corruption of Europe and had created a uniquely free and innocent society which served as a model for the rest of the world. The preservation of this freedom and innocence, so this myth ran, rested on America's success in remaining disentangled from the woes of Europe. Reality had rarely interfered with the isolationist mythology. From the defeat of Napoleon in 1815 until World War I, the United States had securely pursued its internal development, protected from potential aggressors by the benign dominance of the British navy over the Atlantic Ocean. World War I had sent America back into Europe, but the unhappy results of that venture served merely to confirm all the fears of traditional isolationism.

Only a clear perception that the country was in peril of foreign aggression could override a mythology so deeply imbedded in the American mind. Few Americans organized their thoughts on overseas happenings in sophisticated terms of national self-interest; as in all societies, such intellectual patterns were the rather exclusive possession of statesmen, diplomats, and academic theorists. Most Americans, however, were pragmatists in the crude sense of that term; if they sensed that the survival of their nation was in danger, they would ignore tradition. During the 1930s, for some very good reasons, they felt no such perceptions.

Americans had never believed that their vital interests were involved on the mainland of Asia. They had pursued missionary activities and struggled to develop markets there, but only a tiny minority had ever entertained the idea that these efforts merited armed support. The American public detested the aggressions in Manchuria and China; many people even participated in economic boycotts of Japanese products. But there was no appreciable sentiment for American military involvement. Americans experienced the same indignation when the Italians attacked Ethiopia, but of course it was utterly impossible to find a vital U.S. interest in Ethiopia. It was equally impossible to depict the posturing Mussolini and his regime as a threat to the United States.

Nazi Germany was a different and more serious matter, but Hitler's proclaimed ambitions involved Central and Eastern Europe. The führer, moreover, donned the cloak of self-determination, arguing that he desired only to bring all the German people into his Reich. Not until 1939 did he annex the non-German areas of Czechoslovakia. Even then, his threat to the Western democracies was indirect and hinged on their pledge to defend Poland.

Finally, Britain and France themselves contributed greatly to American apathy. As long as they felt that their security was not endangered by the Nazis and that it was possible to appease Hitler, Americans, separated from the European continent by three thousand miles of ocean, could hardly feel that the Reich represented mortal peril. If British Prime Minister Neville Chamberlain could declare in a broadcast to his people that the English knew little of Czechoslovakia and had no stake in its fate, how could Americans feel that their security was threatened? One of the by-products of appeasement was the confirmation it gave to American complacency.

There was an argument advanced by a small band of collective-security advocates and by a number of antifascist intellectuals that the Japanese militarists, the Italian Fascists, and the German Nazis taken together represented a critical long-range threat to the United States, that their glorification of conquest necessarily led to one aggression after another and, sooner or later, to conflict with America. According to this line of reasoning, it was imperative for the antimilitarist powers to stop the aggressors as soon as possible, even if this meant risking a small war to avoid a big one. There was much to be said for the collective-security thesis, but it was concerned with a potential rather than an immediate danger. Most Americans were convinced that their country was secure and that isolationism was still the best method of preserving their national identity.

THE POLITICS OF NEUTRALITY

President Roosevelt was intellectually and emotionally committed to U.S. international leadership; privately, he was in general agreement with the advocates of collective security. Roosevelt had been deeply influenced as a young man by the strategic writings of Alfred Thayer Mahan, the great exponent of naval power, by the robust internationalism of Theodore Roosevelt, and by Woodrow Wilson's dream of a peace-securing world order. For most of the 1930s, however, personal conviction ran second to political expediency (or, as Roosevelt saw it, political necessity). Roosevelt had renounced his advocacy of the League of Nations in order to obtain nomination in 1932, and until at least 1938 his primary concern was the construction of support for the domestic New Deal.

Many supporters of the New Deal were among the strongest opponents of international entanglement. Gerald Nye, for example, had won election to the Senate as a spokesman for the debt-ridden farmers of North Dakota; the Senate opponents of collective security included such militant progressives as Robert La Follette, Jr., George W. Norris, Burton K. Wheeler, Henrik Shipstead, William Borah, and Hiram Johnson. The President also had to work to avoid the defection of voting groups that he was trying to weld into his electoral coalition. He seems to have adopted a hands-off attitude toward the Spanish Civil War because so many Catholic groups and spokesmen supported Franco as the savior of the Spanish church. Mussolini enjoyed such a substantial degree of support among Italian-Americans that New York Mayor Fiorello La Guardia, who privately detested Il Duce, carefully refrained from attacking him.

Roosevelt had received a demonstration of isolationist strength in 1935 when he had sought American entry into the World Court. U.S. participation would have had virtually no effect upon American foreign policy. Nor was it a partisan issue; Presidents Coolidge and Hoover had also proposed it. Joining the Court, however, would have been a symbolic expression of international entanglement. Isolationist forces raised such an outcry that twenty Democratic senators deserted the President, and the Court protocols fell seven short of the required two-thirds majority.

Subsequently, with the Ethiopian crisis developing, the Congress virtually forced the administration to accept the Neutrality Act of 1935. The law stipulated that in the event of foreign war, American firms could not sell arms to any belligerent and American vessels could not carry arms to a belligerent; it also empowered the President, at his discretion, to warn Americans traveling on ships registered to belligerents that they did so at their own risk. Roosevelt had hoped for authority to discriminate against aggressor nations, but congressional and public opinion compelled him to accept the bill. In February 1936 the Neutrality Act was extended with a new provision prohibiting most types of loans to belligerent nations.

Nevertheless, Roosevelt made a cautious effort to handicap Mussolini. He rigidly enforced the Neutrality Act in the Italo-Ethiopian war, realizing that its provisions would hamper the Italians far more than the Ethiopians. The administration even attempted to establish a "moral embargo" on the sale of strategic raw materials. The ploy was a failure, in large part because the European democracies were anxious to appease Mussolini. The administration gained nothing and had to defend itself against the protests of Italian-American leaders and isolationists. After this, Roosevelt gave up. When the Spanish conflict began, he actually took the initiative in requesting that the Neutrality Act be extended to civil wars. Mindful of the political dynamite involved, Roosevelt even fought a resolution to allow the shipment of arms to the Spanish Loyalists; its sponsor, ironically, was Senator Nye, who was disturbed by the fascist victories.

In the spring of 1937 Congress passed the most sweeping Neutrality Act yet. It continued the mandatory embargo on the sale of arms or the extension of loans to belligerents and also compelled the President to prohibit travel on belligerent ships. In addition, it gave the President discretionary authority to place all trade with belligerents under a "cash-and-carry" formula—the warring nations would have to pay cash in the United States for the goods they bought and arrange for shipment on non-American vessels. This last provision, as Robert A. Divine has commented, reflected a widespread desire to escape from the world politically while remaining in it economically. It also was based squarely upon the experience of the maritime controversies which had preceded American entry into World War I and was hardly a realistic answer to the very different international challenges of the 1930s.

In October 1937 Roosevelt delivered a major speech in which he warned of the need to "quarantine the aggressor." Shaken by the unfavorable public response (which he probably exaggerated), the President quickly retreated from any implication of collective security. On December 12, 1937, Japanese warplanes sank the U.S. gunboat *Panay* as it was anchored in the Yangtse River. The administration responded with belligerent rhetoric against Japan, but the Japanese government quickly issued an apology and paid an indemnity. It also became apparent that the Congress was unwilling to entertain the thought of military action.

The *Panay* incident led many congressmen to sign a petition to discharge the Ludlow Resolution from the House Judiciary Committee. The resolution, a proposed constitutional amendment sponsored by Representative Louis Ludlow, a Democrat from Indiana, provided that, except in the event of invasion, the United States could engage in war only after a majority of the people had voted to do so in a national referendum. The resolution had, of course, no chance of actually becoming a part of the Constitution; that would have required a two-thirds majority vote in both houses of Congress and ratification by three-fourths of the states. A simple majority of the House had, however, signed a petition to bring it to the floor, and if they voted in favor of it, they would seriously embarrass the President. After the application of great pressure, the administration was able to deny the Ludlow Resolution its majority; the final vote, taken in January 1938, was 188 for, 209 against.

After this narrow escape, Roosevelt made no further gestures toward entanglement in Europe and Asia, although he advocated increased military spending. In the fall of 1938 he even hailed the Munich agreement. Not until after the German seizure of Czechoslovakia did he openly work for an amendment to the Neutrality Act which would repeal the mandatory arms embargo and give the President authority to authorize sales to the victims of aggression. He failed in the House of Representatives by two votes and could not even get the Senate Foreign Relations Committee to report neutrality revision to the floor. As late as July 18, Senator Borah was declaring that there was no immediate danger of war. The Congress and probably a majority of the American people were still convinced that they could escape the travail of Europe.

TWO

Toward the Inescapable:
The Pull of War

1939–41

1939

SEPTEMBER	German-Soviet conquest of Poland; U.S. declaration of neutrality; moral embargo on sale of strategic raw materials to Japan
OCTOBER	USSR attacks Finland
NOVEMBER	Third Neutrality Act
DECEMBER	Moral embargo on sale of scarce metals to Japan

1940

APRIL	German invasion of Denmark and Norway
MAY	German invasion of the Netherlands, Belgium, and France
JUNE	France surrenders; USSR annexes Estonia, Latvia, Lithuania, Northern Bukovina, and Bessarabia; Congress passes Smith Act; Roosevelt requests large defense program
JULY	U.S. trade restrictions against Japan include embargo on high-quality scrap metal and aviation gasoline
SEPTEMBER	Destroyer Deal with Great Britain; passage of Selective Service Act; Japan occupies northern Indo-China; U.S. retaliates with total embargo on scrap metal; Japan joins the Axis
NOVEMBER	Roosevelt defeats Willkie in presidential election

27

1941

JANUARY	Roosevelt commits United States to the Four Freedoms
MARCH	Lend-Lease Act
APRIL	Germany invades Yugoslavia and Greece; United States occupies Greenland and extends naval "patrols" to near Iceland; Japan concludes nonagression treaty with USSR
MAY	Roosevelt proclaims unlimited national emergency
JUNE	German sub sinks the *Robin Moor;* Germany invades the USSR
JULY	United States occupies Iceland; Japan occupies southern Indo-China
AUGUST	United States, Great Britain, and the Dutch East Indies embargo sale of oil to Japan; Roosevelt and Churchill issue Atlantic Charter after meeting at Argentia; Congress extends Selective Service by one vote
SEPTEMBER	United States begins aid to USSR; German sub attacks the U.S.S. *Greer*
OCTOBER	German subs hit the U.S.S. *Kearney* and sink the U.S.S. *Reuben James*
NOVEMBER	Congress authorizes arming of merchant ships and allows their use in trade with belligerents; United States–Japanese negotiations deadlock
DECEMBER	Japan attacks Pearl Harbor; Congress votes declaration of war against Japan; Germany and Italy declare war on United States

"Stalin and I are the only ones that see the future," Adolf Hitler told his generals on August 22, 1939. The two bitter enemies had submerged their mutual hatred and were in the final stages of negotiating a secret division of Eastern Europe. On August 24, they announced a nonaggression pact. On September 1, the Germans sent their dive bombers and armored divisions across the Polish border. Great Britain and France, although helpless to give the Poles any real assistance, fulfilled their promise to fight. World War II had begun with the Western European democracies weak and isolated against the surface unity of the totalitarian nations.

The conquest of Poland took only a month, the Germans annexing the western half, the Russians absorbing the eastern remainder. Re-created as an independent nation only twenty years earlier, Poland no longer existed. On the Western front, British, French, and Belgian forces dug in, waiting behind supposedly impregnable defenses for the Nazi onslaught. The Germans, however, decided to wait for the spring, and bored journalists began to write of the lull that followed as the phony war. Hitler's new ally, seeking to recover old areas of Imperial Russia, moved at once. The Soviet Union demanded territorial concessions from Finland and engaged its small neighbor in a war that aroused worldwide indignation. At first, the USSR suffered embarrassing reverses, but soon the Finns were overwhelmed. In March 1940 they surrendered and gave in to the Russian demands. In June the Soviet Union annexed the Rumanian provinces of Bessarabia and Northern Bukovina and absorbed the tiny independent Baltic republics of Lithuania, Latvia, and Estonia.

In April 1940 the Nazis began their own offensive. German troops occupied Denmark and invaded Norway; the Danes were in no position to fight, and meaningful Norwegian resistance crumbled in a few weeks. On May 10, Hitler began what he hoped would be the decisive thrust of the war. Nazi armored forces with devastating air support moved into Belgium, tore through the Allied lines, and converted the war into a rout. The Belgians surrendered on May 28, but somehow during the next week the British managed to evacuate a third of a million troops from the port of Dunkirk. On June 4, the German armies rolled into France sweeping the opposition before them. Five days later, the government evacuated Paris and declared it an open city. Mussolini launched his own attack in the south. By mid-June, the French were suing for peace. The entire continent was at the mercy of totalitarians.

Only the British were left, their army defeated, most of its equipment left behind in Belgium; English forces in other parts of the world were stretched so thin that they could not prevent the Italian occupation of British Somaliland in Africa. Buoyed by the courage and spirit of their new prime minister, Winston Churchill, the British held on, desperately maintaining control of the Mediterranean-Suez lifeline to the Far East. By late summer, however, they were taking a terrible pounding from German bombers, and their very survival hinged on the skill and daring of about a thousand fighter pilots.

THE AMERICAN RESPONSE

President Roosevelt expressed the contradictory impulses of most Americans. The nation wanted to prevent a Nazi victory and at the same time avoid involvement in the war. Roosevelt's policies and rhetoric at times took on an almost schizophrenic character as they faithfully reflected these irreconcilable desires.

Officially, during the early months of the war, the President pursued a policy of rather strict neutrality. The government banned American vessels from war zones in the North Atlantic, the North Sea, and the Baltic. The United States took the lead in promoting an inter-American conference at Panama City which proclaimed a neutral zone running from the Canadian border to the tip of Argentina and extending 300 miles into the Atlantic Ocean. Yet the President also asserted that he could require neutrality in deed only, not in sentiment; he made no effort to conceal his personal hatred and contempt for Nazism. Most Americans agreed. A Gallup poll revealed that 84 percent of the people hoped for an Allied victory; 14 percent expressed no opinion; only 2 percent were willing to declare that they wanted a Nazi triumph. At the same time, there was practically no sentiment for American entry into the war; some observers even thought they detected popular undercurrents of fear that emotions might lead the United States into an unnecessary conflict. Until the spring of 1940, the war was a remote happening to most people, an apparent stalemate which presented no significant threat to the United States. Whatever the sympathies of the population, the national mood was still isolationist and willing to tolerate only the most cautious assistance to the Allies.

Roosevelt sensed these limits and moved as far as he felt he could. Calling Congress into special session, he again asked for repeal of the arms embargo and extension of the cash-and-carry formula to munitions. The President's proposal would simply allow the Allies to buy weapons in the United States and carry them away on Allied vessels; it prohibited loans and the use of American shipping. All the same, the isolationists—both liberal and conservative—bitterly fought the request, and assailed it as a step toward war. The administration, on the other hand, presented it as a way of keeping the United States out of the fighting and referred to it as a neutrality bill. The measure did not involve a drastic departure from existing policy and was in line with popular sentiment; thus the opposition was lost. After extended debate, the Neutrality Act of 1939 passed the Senate, 63–30, and the House, 243–181. Roosevelt signed it into law on November 4, 1939. Many Americans, possibly even the President himself, believed that they had tipped the balance in favor of the Allies while preserving peace for themselves.

The German victories in May and June 1940 came as a wholly unexpected shock and threw the nation into a fit of near-hysteria. For the first time, many Americans realized that only Great Britain and its Atlantic fleet stood between them and a potentially hostile outside world. Vigilante groups formed to fight off fifth columnists or invading troops. Congress passed and Roosevelt signed the Smith Act, providing for the fingerprinting and registration of aliens and outlawing subversive activities, such as conspiracy to advocate the violent overthrow of the government. For a brief time, when it appeared that the Germans might sweep across the English Channel, the panic was frighteningly widespread.

At the beginning of the year, Roosevelt had not dared to ask for a defense appropriation of more than $1.8 billion, and congressional leaders had planned to cut back on the request. Now the President called for vast new expenditures, and Congress complied with remarkable dispatch. Acutely aware that the nation would have been almost helpless had it faced the Nazi armies, the people and their representatives clamored for defense at any price. By September, Congress had enlarged the military budget beyond even Roosevelt's recommendations to the then-staggering total of $10.5 billion, and everyone realized that this action was but the first step in an ever-spiraling defense program.

Speaking at Charlottesville, Virginia, on June 10, Roosevelt caustically denounced Mussolini's attack on France as a stab in the back; more importantly, he committed himself to a policy of lending all possible aid to Britain. Subsequently, he ordered the War and Navy departments to "scrape the bottom of the barrel" in order to make vast amounts of war material available for sale to England. Against the advice of many of his military experts, Roosevelt had decided to gamble on the staying power of the British. In the meantime, he named two prominent Republicans to the Cabinet—Frank Knox, the party's vice-presidential candidate of 1936, as secretary of the navy; and Henry L. Stimson, who had served with distinction in the cabinets of Taft and Hoover, as secretary of war. With the establishment of a nonpartisan "unity" cabinet on the eve of a presidential campaign, Roosevelt had consolidated his support and had underscored the gravity of the international crisis.

The President also began to gear the economy for war. Shortly after the collapse of France, Roosevelt called for production of 50,000 warplanes a year and established a National Defense Advisory Commission (NDAC). A headless board composed of representatives from industry, labor, agriculture, and the public, the NDAC attempted to coordinate defense production. Its authority was vague and its success limited, but it was the beginning of an increasingly complex mobilization effort. In January 1941 the White House established the Office of Production Management (OPM), under the joint leadership of General Motors industrialist William Knudsen and labor leader Sidney Hillman. In August 1941 the President set up a Supply, Priorities, and Allocations Board (SPAB) to facilitate the direction of raw materials into defense plants. Other agencies also appeared, including an Office of Price Administration (OPA), which attempted to block unjustified price increases, and a National Defense Mediation Board, charged with the job of settling major strikes.

The mobilization campaign was a terribly uneven mixture of failure and triumph. The pretense that the country was still at peace inhibited it. The President's refusal to appoint a single head or "czar" with authority over the entire effort, along with his addiction to fuzzy mandates and overlapping jurisdictions, led to confusion and inefficiency. Yet the industrial mobilization agencies still had more authority to manage the economy than the New Deal had possessed during the depression. Hampered by strikes and by the reluctance of many industrialists to convert existing facilities to defense purposes, the administration nevertheless slowly turned the national economy toward a war basis.

By mid-1940, the earlier hope of a detached neutrality was gone, and most Americans realized that the war was uncomfortably close. The evolution of radio journalism emphasized the point; that fall, Edward R. Murrow began a series of live broadcasts of the blitz of London, bringing the thud of bombs and the snap of antiaircraft guns into every living room. As the war became more immediate, a process of polarization began between groups which rather openly referred to themselves as "isolationists" and "interventionists." The ensuing debate partook of the bitterness which had once characterized controversies over the New Deal and demonstrated that foreign policy issues were partially reshaping political lines in the United States.

The isolationist movement, centered after the fall of 1940 in the America First Committee, was a heterogeneous blend of ethnic groups, radicals, pacifists, midwestern and western politicians, and far right-wingers. German- and Italian-Americans generally were tolerant of the Axis and loath to go to war against their old homelands; many Irish-Americans still hated Great Britain for its centuries-long oppression. The Socialist party of America, led by Norman Thomas, steadfastly opposed involvement in what happened to be a capitalist conflict. For a time, the communists were among the most vociferous advocates of isolationism. Probably a majority of Protestant clergymen were determined to adhere resolutely to Christian pacifism. Independent progressives from beyond the Appalachians—Burton K. Wheeler of Montana, the La Follette brothers of Wisconsin, and several others—fought involvement in the same way Robert La Follette, Sr., and his followers had opposed participation in World War I. Midwestern conservatives, including the prominent Republican Senators Robert A. Taft and Arthur H. Vandenberg, were isolationist, partly out of hatred and distrust of Roosevelt and the New Deal, partly in response to the geographical location and ethnic makeup of their constituencies. On the fringes of the America First movement, but ever more prominent, was a band of self-styled Fascists and pro-Nazis.

Increasingly, the most important spokesman of the isolationists was the one American figure with a charismatic appeal which rivaled that of FDR—Charles A. Lindbergh. The gallant Lone Eagle who had flown the Atlantic, Lindbergh seemed to represent some of the best and deepest American values. As a distraught father whose child had fallen victim to a ruthless kidnapper in 1932, he had become almost a national martyr. But there was a side to his life that went beyond popular sentimentalism. His father had represented an isolationist agrarian radicalism as a Minnesota congressman and political leader. His wife, Anne Morrow Lindbergh, had written that Nazi totalitarianism was the wave of the future. Lindbergh himself had accepted a decoration from the Nazi government; he was convinced that the German air force was invincible and that Germany would overwhelm the decadent and flabby Western European democracies. In one declaration after another, he asserted that the United States should abandon any hope of saving England, arm only for self-defense, and prepare for an era of friendly coexistence with the Third Reich.

Racial theories found their way into his articles and speeches. He argued for Aryan unity and declared that the real enemies of America were the Slavs and the Japanese. In the fall of 1941 he overreached himself by asserting that the American Jewish community was trying to push the country into a senseless war. The remark drew condemnation even from the isolationist publisher William Randolph Hearst, seriously damaged Lindbergh's standing with the public, and disrupted the isolationist movement. Lindbergh was a man of great physical courage and genuine patriotism (with no publicity whatever, he voluntarily flew combat missions in the Pacific at the age of forty-two), but he had demonstrated a political provincialism and naiveté which was unfortunately all too typical of American isolationism during the 1940–41 crisis. Events doubtless would have destroyed the movement, but its fall came all the easier from its failure to construct a compelling moral vision to justify its doctrine of disengagement from Europe.

The "interventionists," centered in the Committee to Defend America by Aiding the Allies, were almost as mixed a group, numbering in their ranks conservative businessmen, ardent New Dealers, prominent intellectuals, ethnic groups who hated Hitler, and, after June 1941, the Communist party. The head of the Committee to Defend America was the progressive Kansas editor William Allen White, but the strength of the interventionist movement was in the Northeast and the South. A large number of conservative Republicans, following the diplomatic tradition of Theodore Roosevelt, advocated a tough anti-Nazi policy. Perhaps their most important representatives were Stimson, who had served TR loyally, and Knox, whose manhood had begun with his service in the Rough Riders. Southern Democrats, many of whom had opposed the New Deal, were, as so often in American history, exponents of an aggressive foreign policy. Most liberal intellectuals, repelled by Nazi barbarism, found themselves driven to the conclusion that no sacrifice was too great to stop the Fascist advance. Jews and Poles, horrified by the persecution and slaughter of their European cousins, naturally tended to support almost any measure against Hitler.

The interventionists had to move cautiously. Most of them realized that, whatever the dangers of the war situation, outright advocacy of U.S. military involvement in Europe remained unacceptable to most Americans. A small group of northeastern journalists, intellectuals, and businessmen urged immediate entry into the conflict, but most of the leaders of the Committee to Defend America understood that such stands were counterproductive. Some in fact were not certain themselves whether they favored total participation in the fighting. The Committee thus limited itself to support of such halfway measures as the Destroyer Deal, the military draft, and Lend-Lease. The influential Republicans affiliated with it served an important function in curbing the most extreme partisan impulses of the GOP leadership.

To combat the deeply rooted isolationist tradition, the interventionists produced not only arguments of national self-interest and survival but also a sense of moral urgency. They deeply believed that Nazism was an unspeakable evil which America had to exterminate not simply for its own safety but for the good of mankind. They appealed to the American impulse, as ancient as the Puritans, to save the Old World from its sin and decay. This moral idealism combined with the factor of national danger to give the interventionists a forceful appeal.

A majority of the American people were neither diehard isolationists nor outright interventionists. They hated Nazism and perceived at least dimly the German threat to America, but as late as the fall of 1941 opinion polls revealed that only about 25 percent felt that the United States should take the initiative in going to war. At the same time, from mid-1940 on, well over 50 percent favored extensive aid to England even at the risk of war. Most Americans were anticipating the worst but still desperately hoping to avoid total participation in the European conflict. It was within this framework of self-contradictory and indeed self-deceptive attitudes that Franklin D. Roosevelt had to formulate a foreign policy and maneuver to maintain his political power.

FOREIGN POLICY AND THE PITFALLS
OF PARTISANSHIP: THE THIRD-TERM CAMPAIGN

Perhaps Roosevelt would have retired had the international crisis not developed. Throughout 1939 and early 1940, he remained silent about his political plans, and it is possible that he was uncertain until the German armies swept into France. Yet Roosevelt's silence itself made a third-term effort nearly inevitable; as long as the President refused to remove himself from contention, no other New Deal Democrat could put together an effective preconvention campaign—and FDR was unwilling to countenance the nomination of a conservative. It was clear also that Roosevelt was the only Democrat who could go into the presidential campaign as a solid favorite. Throughout early 1940, one liberal Democrat after another urged him to run, and party sentiment for another term grew apace.

When the Democratic convention met at Chicago in mid-July even the President's closest advisers were unable to speak with certainty about his intentions. In fact, Roosevelt was prepared to run, but he was determined to assert his mastery over party conservatives by forcing a draft. On the second evening of the proceedings, Senator Alben Barkley read a message from the President to the anxious delegates:

> The President has never had, and has not today, any desire or purpose to continue in the office of President, to be a candidate for that office, or to be nominated by the Convention for that office.
> He wishes in all earnestness and sincerity to make it clear that all the delegates to this Convention are free to vote for any candidate.

There was a moment of stunned, uncertain silence. Then the loudspeakers began to blare: "WE WANT ROOSEVELT. . . . EVERYBODY WANTS ROOSEVELT. . . . THE WORLD WANTS ROOSEVELT." (The speaker, journalists later discovered, was Chicago Boss Kelly's commissioner of sewers.) The inevitable demonstration began, haltingly at first, then became a wild, surging mass of delegates and spectators winding through the convention hall. The next day, some 90 percent of the delegates voted to nominate Roosevelt for a third term. The President then insisted upon the designation of Secretary of Agriculture Henry A. Wallace, a dedicated liberal and militant antifascist, as his running mate. The convention nearly rebelled, for Wallace had a public reputation as a dreamy mystic, was a former Republican, and was notoriously inept in his relationship with professional politicians. For a few hours, it appeared that the harassed delegates might defy their leader and name Speaker of the House William Bankhead. Roosevelt resorted to the ultimate weapon—he threatened to reject the nomination. (One of his emissaries, James F. Byrnes, rushed from one state delegation to another asking, "For God's sake, do you want a President or a Vice-President?") The President had his way, but only at the cost of much bitterness. Wallace was unable even to make an acceptance speech to the angry delegates.

The Republicans in the meantime had nominated a formidable ticket. The Nazi victory in France had wrecked the candidacies of the two leading contenders, Ohio Senator Robert A. Taft and the young gang-busting New York district attorney Thomas E. Dewey. Taft, a conservative isolationist with an austere personality, seemed all too clearly out of touch with the urgencies of the day. Dewey had captured the imagination of a considerable segment of the public with his relentless prosecution of organized crime, but as the Nazis marched into Paris, his youth and vigor, once so appealing, metamorphosed into inexperience and immaturity. After six ballots, the convention turned to an exciting dark horse, Wendell L. Willkie of Indiana. The vice-presidential candidate was Republican Senate leader Charles L. McNary of Oregon, a progressive isolationist.

Willkie, a former Democrat, had achieved prominence during the 1930s as a utilities executive who had led the opposition to the Tennessee Valley Authority. He was an advocate of rapid rearmament and aid to the Allies. A corporate lawyer and businessman of talent and sophistication, he maintained headquarters just off Wall Street. Yet he possessed and carefully cultivated a rustic Hoosier charm, which manifested itself in his country-style haircuts, his baggy suits, and his frank, candid manner. He was the most magnetic and progressive presidential candidate the Republicans had fielded since Theodore Roosevelt.

The Willkie nomination was a victory for a growing group within the Republican party—composed of eastern politicians, international bankers, corporate executives with a somewhat broader vision than many of their fellows, and influential publishers. Rich in money and organizational talent, skilled in media manipulation, moderate in domestic affairs, interventionist in foreign policy, these were the men who would turn to Dewey in 1944 and 1948, and to Eisenhower in 1952 and 1956.

The presidential conventions were hardly over before the country faced two momentous issues which demonstrated how strong the pull of war had become. The first of these involved a request by Prime Minister Churchill for the transfer of fifty "overage" American destroyers to the hard-pressed British fleet. The English had lost nearly half their Channel destroyer force, but although their need was desperate, it would be difficult to hand over the vessels. Fearing charges that he had stripped the nation's sea defenses, aware that Congress might not approve a transfer treaty, Roosevelt delayed for eight weeks, searching for a sure, safe method of giving the destroyers to Britain, allowing the White Committee to build up public sentiment for the transaction. On September 3, 1940, after receiving assurances that Wendell Willkie would not oppose the deal, Roosevelt and Churchill announced an "executive agreement" (as opposed to a treaty, which would have required ratification by two-thirds of the Senate); the United States turned over the destroyers and received in return long-term leases for the use of strategically placed British naval bases from Newfoundland to British Guiana. Able to present the Destroyer Deal to the people as a sharp bargain which strengthened national defense, Roosevelt won wide support. Yet by past standards of international law and practice the transaction was a profoundly unneutral act. Henceforth, Churchill told the House of Commons, the United States and Britain would be "somewhat mixed up together."

The other issue was the push for a military draft. Peacetime conscription was unprecedented in American history and widely considered undemocratic. At first, Roosevelt and even Army Chief of Staff General George Marshall refused to commit themselves. A draft bill received its initial impetus from a group of interventionists outside the administration, mostly moderate northeastern Republicans; within the administration, Secretary of War Stimson pushed it most ardently. Despite the vociferous opposition of isolationists and even some troubled advocates of aid to the British, opinion polls indicated that the public was slowly moving toward the draft. With England still apparently in danger of being overrun, there seemed to be no alternative. In late June, Senator Edward Burke, a conservative Nebraska Democrat, and Representative James Wadsworth, a New York Republican, introduced a selective service bill; Willkie supported it. In August, Roosevelt and Marshall firmly came out for the measure, and in mid-September, it passed Congress. The Burke-Wadsworth Act committed the nation to a military buildup on a scale never before approached in peacetime. Selective service was a drastic step toward war, and the national acquiescence in it was a remarkable demonstration of the way in which the country, without yet admitting it, was reconciling itself to the irrepressible conflict.

The Destroyer Deal and the draft were daring gambles for a Chief Executive about to undertake a presidential campaign. Democracy and the American party system, whatever their ultimate virtues, discourage controversial moves at a time of electoral decision making. Roosevelt had left himself open, and his losing opponent could not resist the impulse to attack. Willkie was in fundamental agreement with the President, but his campaign sputtered badly. The Republican candidate had at first attempted to lambast Roosevelt for moving too slowly to strengthen the nation's defenses; by the fall of 1940, however, defense production was beginning in earnest, and the President underscored the fact by making one "inspection trip" after another. Willkie quite legitimately condemned the administration's failure, after years of effort, to end mass unemployment; but defense jobs were beginning to open up, and the large majority of workers seemed to revere Roosevelt beyond rational appeal. The charge that a third term was somehow un-American apparently stirred few voters.

There was only one tactic left. Willkie foreshadowed his new direction in early September when he approved the Destroyer Deal, but denounced Roosevelt's method of handling it as "the most dictatorial and arbitrary act of any President in the history of the United States." By the end of the month, Willkie was asserting that Roosevelt was trying to maneuver the country into war and establish himself as a dictator. The charges were pure demagoguery, but the Republican candidate began to gain in the public-opinion polls. With Willkie's wild lunges apparently effective, Democratic political leaders were nearly hysterical, and Roosevelt, who had attempted to remain "above" the political debate, began to campaign in earnest on October 23. The President delivered a series of speeches, but he could not avoid the emotion-laden issue his opponent had unleashed. Deluged with pleas from frightened Democratic politicos, Roosevelt delivered the impossible assurance in Boston, the citadel of Irish-American isolationism: "I have said this before, but I shall say it again and again and again: Your boys are not going to be sent into any foreign wars." The almost irresistible forces of partisanship had brought the campaign to a very low ending.

A few days later, Roosevelt carried the election by a substantial but not overwhelming margin of 27 million to 22 million. The President's support declined among almost all voting groups from the monumental proportions of 1936, but his losses were most serious in rural areas (farm prices had slipped badly after 1937) and among ethnic groups which hoped to stay out of the war—German-Americans, Italian-Americans, and Irish-Americans. Jews, Polish-Americans, and even New England Yankees, on the other hand, supported FDR more strongly than ever. If the war was reshaping the Roosevelt coalition a bit, the President's hard core of support remained intact. His victory rested upon overwhelming support in the working-class and lower-middle-class areas of the large cities. The New Deal might be over, but the political-economic divisions it had engendered were on the whole more rigid than ever. The war would change American life in many ways, but subsequent elections would show that the Roosevelt coalition, for all its instability and tendency to splinter, possessed a remarkable durability.

LEND-LEASE:
TOWARD FULL BELLIGERENCY

By December 1940, the British dollar reserves were approaching bottom. Unless the Roosevelt administration could secure a new definition of neutrality, England, still compelled to pay cash for its military equipment, would be able to count on little more than American sympathy. The logical solution would have been a request for legislation to permit loans to the British. But the loan issue carried a great emotional impact; Roosevelt searched for a way to sidestep the often bitter legacies of World War I.

By mid-December, the President had formulated his approach, and he employed a smooth little parable to explain it at one of his press conferences: Suppose that your neighbor's house were on fire, and suppose that you had a length of garden hose which would help put out the fire. You wouldn't charge him for it. You would lend it to him in the expectation that he would return it after the fire was out or replace it if it were damaged. As Roosevelt freely admitted to the reporters who were clustered around his desk, he was trying to "get rid of the silly, foolish old dollar sign."

Two weeks later, he laid out his plans in a nationally broadcast "fireside chat." He was talking, he told the American people, about national security, not about war; his purpose was to avoid war. American civilization had never since Jamestown and Plymouth Rock been in such danger; the United States had to set itself against the Nazi objective of world domination. Isolation would mean national suicide. There were risks in any course, but the best hope of avoiding the dispatch of American troops overseas was a policy of all-out military aid to Great Britain. America had to become "the great arsenal of democracy." Even as he moved the country into greater involvement, Roosevelt persisted in telling the American people what they wanted to hear—that he was going to keep them out of war.

In his annual message to Congress, January 7, 1941, the President went beyond considerations of security. He attempted to give his policies a moral dimension by appealing to the American sense of mission. U.S. foreign policy, he declared, sought not simply to protect the nation from foreign conquest but to export liberty, equal opportunity, prosperity, and security to every corner of the earth. The United States stood for Four Freedoms:

The first is freedom of speech and expression—everywhere in the world.

The second is freedom of every person to worship God in his own way—everywhere in the world.

The third is freedom from want—which, translated into world terms, means economic understandings which will secure to every nation a healthy peacetime life for its inhabitants—everywhere in the world.

The fourth is freedom from fear—which, translated into world terms, means a worldwide reduction of armaments to such a point and in such a thorough fashion that no nation will be in a position to commit an act of physical aggression against any neighbor— anywhere in the world.

On January 10, 1941, the administration introduced in Congress the Lend-Lease bill, giving the President almost unlimited power to lend or lease military equipment to any country whose defense he considered vital to the security of the United States. Isolationists reacted with charges that the proposal would lead the country into war and dictatorship. Montana Democrat Burton K. Wheeler compared Lend-Lease to the New Deal agricultural program—"it will plow under every fourth American boy." The leading isolationist newspaper, the Chicago *Tribune,* warned its readers: "This is a bill for the destruction of the American Republic."

The administration, however, had done a superb job of selling Lend-Lease to the public and mobilizing its forces. Roosevelt and his cabinet members were less than candid about the implications of the measures, especially when they dodged charges that it would inevitably lead to U.S. naval protection for British convoys, but most of the public seemed to prefer to evade the issue also. In early 1941, opinion polls showed that 60 to 70 percent of the people endorsed the proposition that it was more important to help England than to stay out of the war. Inspirationally introduced as House Resolution 1776, the Lend-Lease bill moved easily through Congress. The vocal but outnumbered opposition took its worst blow when Wendell Willkie, who had just returned from a trip to England, endorsed the bill in testimony before the Senate Foreign Relations Committee. When Senator Nye questioned the former Republican candidate about his charges a few months before that Roosevelt was leading the country to war, Willkie summoned all the naive Hoosier charm he could muster: "It was a bit of campaign oratory. I am very glad you read my speeches, because the President said he did not."

Roosevelt signed the Lend-Lease Act into law on March 11, 1941, and promptly requested an appropriation of $7 billion to implement it. He had the money in two weeks. If there had been any doubt about the nation's commitment to England, Lend-Lease surely dispelled it. The American involvement had passed farther beyond the boundaries of traditional neutrality and it could only increase in the long months that lay ahead.

Even as Lend-Lease was going through Congress, U.S. and British military officials were holding secret staff talks in Washington. By March 27, 1941, they had reached agreement on a basic plan of strategy, code named ABC-1. The most important accord was that if the United States went to war against both Germany and Japan, the United States and England would first throw the major portion of their resources into the effort against Hitler. More than eight months before Pearl Harbor, the two countries had arrived at the basic grand strategy of World War II.

Meanwhile, the Germans were undertaking new and powerful aggressive drives of their own. In April 1941 Hitler's troops struck with their usual devastating effectiveness into Yugoslavia, then into Greece, which had just thrown back an Italian invasion. On May 20, in a masterful and audacious stroke, 16,000 German paratroopers descended on the Aegean island of Crete and overwhelmed the British defenders. Hitler had already converted Rumania and Bulgaria into German satellites and had intimidated Turkey into a rigid neutrality. The master of Southeastern Europe, he now began to turn his attention toward his increasingly difficult ally, the USSR. As the German military planners prepared for their greatest campaign yet, the tough Nazi panzer forces in North Africa, under the command of General Erwin Rommel, began a powerful offensive which for the next several months threatened British control of Egypt.

The events in Europe and North Africa placed new demands on the English navy and stretched it thinner than ever at a time when "wolf packs" of U-boats were inflicting heavy losses on British shipping in the North Atlantic and threatening to neutralize the Lend-Lease program. If Roosevelt could not affect events in Europe and North Africa, he could move, albeit cautiously, in the Atlantic; there he could utilize two of the oldest and most deeply held American diplomatic traditions—opposition to foreign incursions into the Western Hemisphere and commitment to freedom of the seas. He allowed damaged British ships to dock in the United States for repairs, and transferred ten Coast Guard cutters to the English navy. On April 9, he announced an agreement with exiled Danish authorities, providing for U.S. bases in Greenland and placing the island under American protection.

The President decided that outright destroyer escorts for British convoys would be too risky both politically and militarily. (Many congressmen were opposed; moreover, the policy would involve a reduction of the Pacific fleet.) But, on April 24, the administration announced that the U.S. Navy would extend its "patrol" operations to 25 degrees west longtitude (a short distance from the western tip of Iceland). In reality, these patrols were scouting expeditions designed to alert British convoy escort vessels to the presence of German submarines. The American patrols were not to engage Nazi submarines, but their search-and-inform mission was only a half-step short of combat and practically guaranteed an incident.

With the battle of the Atlantic still in doubt, Roosevelt attempted to establish a deeper sense of national crisis. On May 27, he delivered a major speech which assailed the Nazis in stronger terms than ever as an immediate menace to American life, asserted his determination to get Lend-Lease supplies through the submarine gantlet, and proclaimed an unlimited national emergency. Still cautious, however, he took no major new actions in the Atlantic, not even after the nation learned on June 11 that a German submarine in the South Atlantic had sunk an American freighter, the *Robin Moor,* some three weeks earlier. It was not until the beginning of July that U.S. forces occupied Iceland and thereby extended the orbit of American naval power a bit farther east. At first the administration announced that it would allow British ships to join American convoys to Iceland, but Roosevelt, fearing the political repercussions, soon reversed himself. Throughout the summer, the American navy continued its ambiguous patrol policy with Roosevelt perhaps waiting for the incident that would allow him to take one more very big step.

Fortunately for the Western powers, relations between Germany and the Soviet Union had deteriorated beyond repair. The alliance between the two totalitarian nations had been an arrangement of convenience almost certain to fail because of fundamental conflicts in national expansionist ambitions. Demanding control of Bulgaria and the Turkish straits, the Soviets were working for hegemony in the Balkans and the Middle East. Hitler, on the other hand, planned not simply for German domination of these areas but ultimately for Nazi rule in the Ukraine. Angered by the demands of the USSR, the führer stepped up his timetable. In December 1940 he ordered his generals to begin planning for an invasion of Russia. By the spring of 1941, Josef Stalin expected the worst and was making conciliatory gestures in the hope of holding off an attack until the Red Army might be prepared to push back a German offensive.

On June 22, 1941, the Germans struck. Stalin, who apparently believed that he had bought time, was practically paralyzed by the shock of Hitler's duplicity. By early July, however, the Soviet dictator had assumed personal command of his armed forces and was exhorting his people to fight to the death, not for communism, but for Mother Russia. The Russian armies did in fact resist desperately, but the seemingly invincible Nazi troops rolled them back and drove toward Moscow.

In England, Winston Churchill, long a vehement foe of Bolshevism, quickly moved to establish an alliance with the USSR. "Any man or state who fights on against Nazidom will have our aid," declared the English leader. Churchill's policy was natural and noncontroversial in a country fighting with its back to the wall. Roosevelt understood that aid to the Soviet Union was in the interest of both England and the United States, but he respected the strength of American anticommunism. In addition, U.S. military experts were practically unanimous in their belief that the Russians would succumb to the German advance and that the United States should devote all its energies to the battle of the Atlantic. The administration thus moved with caution and imprecision, but always in the direction of assisting the Soviet Union. Roosevelt announced that the United States would give aid to the USSR and refused to invoke the Neutrality Act, thereby permitting American ships to carry supplies to the beleaguered nation. At the end of July, the President sent his closest lieutenant, Harry Hopkins, to Moscow to confer with Stalin and make an estimate of Russia's capabilities and aid requirements. Hopkins returned to Washington with an optimistic report which greatly strengthened Roosevelt's determination to assist the Soviet resistance.

In mid-September, with the Soviet dollar balances exhausted, the United States extended a credit of $100 million. (The arrangement was technically legal because the Neutrality Act had not been applied.) Roosevelt attempted to placate the Catholic church and other anticommunist groups. In October, Congress rejected an amendment to the second Lend-Lease appropriation excluding the USSR from the program. The administration thereupon quickly negotiated the first Lend-Lease agreement with the Russians, thus clearing the way for massive, continuing U.S. assistance. On November 6, the administration announced the accord to the public. After months of delay, Roosevelt had decided that it was safe to admit the Soviet Union to full partnership in the anti-Nazi effort.

There could be no doubt after the summer of 1941 that an anti-Nazi partnership existed. In August, Roosevelt and Churchill dramatized the Anglo-American entente by meeting for the first time at Argentia, Newfoundland, and issuing a *joint declaration of war aims*. The declaration, the Atlantic Charter, had no more binding authority or official status than a press release. It avoided specifics, and the cynical might well dismiss it as a collection of Wilsonian platitudes. To many, however, it was an important and inspiring statement of Western liberal democratic values. It rejected territorial aggrandizement and the use of force as an instrument of national policy; affirmed the principles of self-determination and freedom of the seas; advocated equal access "to the trade and to the raw materials of the world"; proclaimed the objective of freedom from fear and want; promised efforts to secure "improved labor standards, economic advancement, and social security." Designed to counter Nazi ideology, the Atlantic Charter joined the Four Freedoms in Roosevelt's attempt to make the American liberal reform tradition, from Wilsonian progressivism to the New Deal, a major part of the rationale for the steadily growing U.S. role in the war.

Isolationists vehemently condemned the Roosevelt-Churchill meeting, but most of the public reacted with varying degrees of acceptance or enthusiasm. Collaboration with Britain had come to seem so natural and necessary that only a small minority protested the flagrant abandonment of neutrality implicit in the conference. Yet the nation still had a deeply divided and confused mind. On August 12, the last day of the Argentia meeting, the House of Representatives voted on a bill to extend the active duty of military draftees by six months. Rejection would have crippled the army, and the administration threw all its resources behind the measure. The final vote was 203–202 with Speaker Sam Rayburn casting the deciding ballot. The victory, such as it was, demonstrated the necessity of diplomatic caution.

On September 4, 1941, the German navy finally gave Roosevelt the incident for which he had been waiting. An American destroyer, the *Greer,* operating 175 miles southwest of Iceland, tracked a German submarine for some three hours and relayed the U-boat's position to a British patrol plane, which dropped four depth charges. Finally, the German vessel fired two torpedoes at the *Greer;* both missed, and the destroyer responded with equally ineffective depth charges. Roosevelt depicted the incident as an unprovoked Nazi aggression. In a national radio address, the President condemned the attack on the *Greer* as "piracy legally and morally." Henceforth, he warned, German and Italian warships would enter the Western Atlantic at their own risk. Comparing Hitler to a rattlesnake, he declared that the United States would no longer wait for the führer to strike. Like other Presidents, he would defend the freedom of the seas. The American navy, moreover, would begin a policy of protecting *all* merchant ships in the Western Atlantic. Although he did not use the term, Roosevelt had initiated a "shoot-on-sight" policy; moreover, he finally had committed the American navy to escort British convoys as far as Iceland. The United States was in an undeclared naval war with Germany. Yet the public supported the President, according to the opinion surveys, by a ratio of at least two to one. Most Americans believed he was defending American rights; in addition, they clung to the self-deceptive belief that this latest military escalation would keep them out of the war.

The Germans attempted to avoid further episodes for over a month, but new naval skirmishes were inevitable. Meanwhile, Roosevelt asked Congress to authorize the arming of American merchant ships. On October 16, the American destroyer *Kearney* took a torpedo in a night engagement with a German submarine; 11 American sailors were killed.

In a fighting speech, Roosevelt asserted that American merchant ships had to be "free to carry our American goods into the harbors of our friends." On October 30, the U.S. destroyer *Reuben James* went under with the loss of 115 lives. In mid-November, Congress authorized the arming of merchant vessels and removed restrictions upon their intercourse with belligerent nations. Lend-Lease already had circumvented the "cash" clauses of the Neutrality Act of 1939; now Congress had repudiated the "carry" provision. The United States had returned to its traditional claim of freedom of the seas, but the congressional margin was close. The administration had moved into a limited conflict with Nazi Germany, but it was clear that even the U-boat torpedoes could not push Congress or the public to the ultimate move. Still desperately hoping to avoid all-out involvement, the nation would not support a declaration of war.

THE FAR EAST:
THE CHALLENGE OF THE RISING SUN

Events in the Atlantic and Europe had overshadowed Japanese aggressions, but by the fall of 1941, Japanese-American relations were vying with the Atlantic for public attention. Step by step, with each move following logically from the interplay of Japanese ambitions with U.S. perceptions of self-interest and international morality, the two nations had lost control of events. Each government, feeling unable to retreat, could only proceed to more extreme positions. By December 1941, leaders of both sides knew that war was inevitable; neither side wanted to fight, but neither was prepared to pull back.

The American feeling against Japan's aggression in China had many roots—the traditional missionary protective attitude toward the Chinese; vague racial fears of the Yellow Peril; the arrogant Japanese abuse of American citizens in the areas they conquered; and a general hatred of authoritarian militarism, Japanese as well as German. Given the equally strong American desire to avoid an Asian war, the Roosevelt administration could do little for the hard-pressed Chinese government of Chiang Kai-shek. The President did authorize several sizable loans and a few shipments of military hardware, but the assistance was barely enough to stave off a complete collapse. By mid-1939, the Japanese had subjugated much of the rich coastal area of China and most of the major cities. Chiang's regime, driven to Chunking in the southern interior, nevertheless continued to resist; and the invaders, for all their military superiority, found themselves unable to bring the war to a conclusion.

One form of indirect assistance to China had gathered widespread support in the United States—the embargo. A cutoff of trade with Japan, especially in war matériel, seemed a relatively painless way of striking a blow at an international bully and helping the underdog. Most Americans were well aware that their commerce in such commodities as oil and scrap iron was providing support for a war effort they detested. In August 1937 the Washington *Post* headed a grim picture story on the Chinese conflict as follows: "JAPANESE RAIN DEATH WITH ONE-TIME JUNK. GUNS, BOMBS AND BATTLESHIPS, ALL MADE FROM OLD METAL, SHIPPED ACROSS PACIFIC IN GROWING AMOUNTS." No less a figure than Henry L. Stimson, even then perhaps the most respected statesman of the Republican party, led the increasingly vocal demand for a suspension of trade with Japan.

On July 26, 1939, with pressure mounting in Congress, the United States gave Japan the required six-months' notice for termination of the commercial treaty between the two countries. Henceforth, U.S.–Japanese trade would be subject to the discretion of the President and the Congress. On September 26, a few weeks after the German invasion of Poland, the administration called for a voluntary "moral embargo" on certain raw materials, including rubber, tin, and quinine, which the United States needed for its own strategic stockpiles. The action was so reasonable and innocuous that the Japanese did not protest. On December 2, the government took a slightly more serious step by extending the moral embargo to metals used in airplane production and banning technical advice for the refining of aviation gasoline. The Japanese delivered a protest, but the policy was hardly a body blow. Japan could still buy its essential war needs in the United States—aviation gasoline, scrap iron, and most fundamental, oil.

The limited American moves stemmed from the fact that the embargo was not the simple, easy way of dealing with the aggressor which popular sentiment believed it to be. U.S. officials were well aware that it could be a road to a Pacific war for which the country was woefully unprepared. If Japan were deprived of the right to buy vital supplies in the United States, it might strike elsewhere for them—into the Dutch East Indies (now Indonesia) or Malaya or the Philippines. Recklessly applied, an embargo could lead to a bigger war and embroil the United States with an enemy not nearly as dangerous to American interests as Germany. Yet to refrain from restrictions would be to encourage an aggressive power which might be a long-range threat to the United States. The dilemma was well-nigh insoluble, and it only worsened as the war progressed.

The aggression in China strained U.S.–Japanese relations, but the crisis which led to war began to take shape only after the Nazi victories of May and June 1940. With France and the Netherlands defeated, with Great Britain in a desperate situation, Southeast Asia and the East Indies were vulnerable as never before to Japanese power and increasingly attractive to a government whose military effort in China had passed the point of productive return. As Japan began to take advantage of this situation, it unavoidably linked itself to the European fascist threat to Western democracy and appeared even more menacing than before. Diplomatic difficulties which involved little more than a nebulous American sympathy for the Chinese and wrath over depredations against American businessmen could be managed probably without serious danger of war. The growing perception among both policy makers and the general public that Japan had become part of a worldwide assault upon libertarian democracy provided a basis for diplomatic escalations which would lead to Pearl Harbor.

Shortly after the fall of France, Japan began to pressure the new quasi-independent French government headquartered at Vichy. The Vichy government quickly acquiesced to a demand for the closing of the border between China and French Indo-China, thereby cutting off some 100,000 tons of war supplies in transit to the Chinese government. Next, Japan pressed Vichy for agreement to Japanese occupation of Northern Indo-China (now North Vietnam) and for return of the provinces of Laos and Cambodia to their former sovereign, Thailand. Tokyo also undertook a campaign to secure major economic concessions from the Dutch East Indies, whose colonial government remained independent of Nazi domination. Few doubted that the ultimate objective was to bring the Dutch possession under Japanese suzerainty. Japanese leaders had long talked of establishing a "Greater Asia Co-Prosperity Sphere" in which their nation would play the guiding role; many policy makers and opinion shapers regarded this ambition as a virtual manifest destiny, and the European war seemed to represent an unparalleled opportunity for its realization.

The American response was increasingly tougher. In June 1940 Congress had given the President authority to limit or prohibit the export of any equipment or supplies useful to the national defense. On July 2, the administration restricted trade in military hardware, key raw materials, airplane parts, optical instruments, and metalworking machinery; the order inconvenienced Japan but was not a crucial setback. On July 26, the U.S. government struck a harder blow. In retaliation against the Japanese demand to occupy Northern Indo-China, President Roosevelt proclaimed an embargo upon top-quality scrap iron and steel and upon high-grade petroleum, including aviation gasoline. Tokyo protested strongly, but the restrictions still were not critical; Japan had the facilities, for example, to convert low-octane gasoline to aviation use. The American action failed to deter the Japanese government's push toward the south.

On September 19, the Japanese occupied Northern Indo-China. The

Imperial Government claimed that its move was incidental to the war against China, but most American policy makers believed that Japan had taken the first step in a drive to subjugate Southeast Asia. Washington responded with an escalation of its own. On September 25, the United States made a substantial loan to China and the next day announced a total embargo on the shipment of scrap iron and steel to Japan. The latest order forced the Japanese to divert a substantial segment of their economic resources to the enlargement of their steel industry, but it was not a serious setback to their military power. Still outwardly unimpressed, Tokyo came back with another diplomatic escalation.

On September 27, Japan, Germany, and Italy announced the conclusion of a treaty which formally linked the three powers for the first time. The document recognized German-Italian hegemony in Europe and Japanese dominance in East Asia. The most important provision stated that the signers would come to each other's defense if one were attacked by a power, other than the Soviet Union, not yet involved in either the European or Asian war. The specific exclusion of the USSR meant that the new Axis alliance was necessarily directed against the only other major power not at war, the United States.

If the new Axis allies had hoped to intimidate the United States, they soon discovered that they had failed badly. The American reaction from the highest levels of government to the general public was one of anger and toughness. The Japanese association with Nazi Germany appeared to indicate a worldwide totalitarian attempt to encircle the United States and perhaps eventually attempt the conquest of the Western Hemisphere. One of the most cautious of American diplomats, Ambassador to Japan Joseph Grew, told his superiors in Washington that the Asian and European crises had become one, that Japan was supporting Hitler's bid for world domination and had become "part and parcel of that system which, if allowed to develop unchecked, will assuredly destroy everything that America stands for." The Princeton Public Opinion Research Project reported that 88 percent of the people supported the scrap-iron embargo and that 57 percent were willing to risk war to prevent Japan from becoming more powerful. Other opinion surveys demonstrated that the Roosevelt administration could count on ample public support for any economic move against Japan; indeed, the administration's persistent refusal to embargo oil seems to have run counter to majority sentiment.

In January 1941 the United States tightened the restrictions on raw material exports, including brass and copper, and in the months that followed added one item after another to the embargo list. Nevertheless, the Roosevelt administration refrained from the ultimate sanction—oil. In November 1940 the Dutch East Indies had approved a six-month contract for the shipment of limited amounts of oil and aviation gasoline to Japan, but the empire depended mainly upon the United States for its oil. The American government refrained from an oil embargo out of the knowledge that Tokyo might be driven to new conquests to meet its needs. So long as Japan made no further moves south, America would supply her with oil, preferring to keep her as a reluctant and ungrateful dependent rather than fight her or acquiesce in new aggressions.

Nevertheless, with the embargo on other items tightening, the two nations already had reached a danger point. In April 1941 Japan secured its northern flank by concluding a nonaggression treaty with the Soviet Union. In the past, the two powers had fought periodic skirmishes along the Manchurian border; now they began an era of uneasy peace. In Washington, the Japanese ambassador, Admiral Kichisaburo Nomura, undertook protracted discussions with Secretary of State Cordell Hull in an attempt to reach a settlement. The Japanese offered to forgo aggression to the south and to remain neutral in the event of war between the United States and Germany. In turn, the United States was to restore normal trade, assist Japan in securing vital raw materials from the Indies, attempt to arrange a Sino-Japanese peace settlement on terms satisfactory to Japan, and, if the effort failed, end all support of China. The Japanese were offering to give up—or postpone—their ambitions for a Greater East Asian Co-Prosperity Sphere, but acceptance of their proposal would have given them a considerable victory. Probably no American government could have agreed to such terms; the Roosevelt administration found them unacceptable morally, politically, and strategically. By July, it was clear that the Hull-Nomura talks had reached an impasse, and Japan was ready to begin another round of military and diplomatic escalation.

On July 21, the Vichy French government acceded to an ultimatum from Tokyo and permitted Japan to occupy Southern Indo-China. Buoyed by the early Nazi victories in the Soviet Union, freed from any immediate danger of military conflict with Russia, the Japanese could extend their push to the south. The protocol that they forced upon the French gave them eight airfields in the area and naval bases at Camranh Bay and Saigon; it placed no limit on the number of troops they could move into the region. The latest advance secured a better location from which to attack the remaining supply routes into China, but its major strategic significance had nothing to do with the Chinese campaign. Japan was in its best position yet to menace Malaya, the Dutch Indies, and the Philippines; the occupation of Southern Indo-China was a prelude to further penetration, diplomatic or military, of the wealthy areas of Southeast Asia and the South Pacific.

Washington reacted with its last economic card. On July 26, the

Roosevelt administration issued an order "freezing" all Japanese funds and assets in the United States (i.e., requiring a government license for any transaction involving them). On August 1, the President imposed a total embargo upon several important commodities, including petroleum products that could be refined into aviation gasoline. In practice, moreover, it quickly became apparent that the United States would not license the export of oil. The governments of Britain and the Dutch East Indies imposed similar restrictions. Thus, Japan faced a worldwide embargo on the one item that it had to obtain from foreign powers. The effect was that of an ultimatum. The Imperial Government would have to retreat or push forward; to stand still would be to invite the destruction of the Japanese economy and the empire's military machine. "From now on the oil gauge and the clock stood side by side," Herbert Feis has written. "Each fall in the level brought the hour of decision closer."

In the fall of 1941 the Japanese government, under intense pressure from military leaders, made a final effort to achieve the empire's objectives of diplomacy; the cabinet had already decided that if diplomacy failed, Japan would go to war. The premier, Prince Fumimaro Konoye, was firmly behind the objective of expansion, but he hoped to avoid a conflict with the United States. In desperation, he even proposed what a later generation would call a summit meeting with Roosevelt; the American government, unable to see how a personal conference could break the deadlock, rightly rejected the offer. On November 20, Japan made a final proposal. Most of the points in the offer were similar to those of the preceding spring, but Tokyo did pledge an immediate withdrawal from Southern Indo-China and an evacuation of the northern region upon the conclusion of a satisfactory peace with China. In return, the United States was to cease its support of China, facilitate Japanese economic penetration into the Indies, and restore normal commercial relations, including the shipment of oil. The Indo-China provision represented a small concession, but the American government found the proposal as unacceptable as the earlier one. On November 26, the Roosevelt adminstration rejected the Japanese proposition and advanced terms that were tougher than any it had yet put forward. The United States would revert to normal commercial relations only if Japan withdrew entirely from both Indo-China and China itself! The Japanese, in short, were to surrender the prizes of ten years of bloody, expensive conquest and turn the clock back to 1931. This impossible counter-demand accurately reflected the way in which the relatively narrow gulf of early 1940 had become utterly unbridgeable by the end of 1941.

All indications are that a strong majority of the public supported the ever-toughening administration position, although few realized that war was imminent. The American and Allied leaders had no illusions; as Secretary of War Stimson put it, all that the United States could do was to make it clear that Japan fired the first shot. There still remained the question of how Japan would proceed—against the Philippines or only against the more valuable British and Dutch possessions? And if they chose the latter course, would Congress vote for a declaration of war? On December 4, Roosevelt secretly promised Churchill that the United States would lend armed assistance if the Japanese confined their attack to Malaya and the Indies; whether he could have delivered on such a pledge is surely debatable. When it came, however, the Japanese thrust possessed no ambiguity.

Shortly after dawn on Sunday, December 7, 1941, Japanese fighter planes from a carrier-based task force stunned the nation with a devastating and brilliantly executed surprise attack upon the Pacific fleet and supporting military installations at Pearl Harbor, Hawaii. Totally unprepared, the Americans were unable to muster an effective defense. Only a few U.S. planes were able to get into the air; about half were destroyed on the ground. Fortunately, the U.S. carrier force was out of the harbor on maneuvers, but the Japanese were able to destroy or disable eight major battleships and several support vessels. Over 2,300 of the defenders were killed and almost 1,200 wounded. Japan launched simultaneous attacks throughout the South Pacific; with the American fleet badly crippled, they could advance almost at will.

On December 8, Roosevelt requested a declaration of war against Japan. Congress might have been reluctant to vote for war against Germany and Italy, but Japan's Axis allies took the initiative in placing themselves against the United States. At last, America was totally committed to the war it had so fervently hoped to avoid.

ROOSEVELT AND THE COMING OF THE WAR: PROBLEMS OF PRESIDENTIAL LEADERSHIP

Many Americans, hitherto secure in their feelings of racial and military superiority over the Japanese, found the Pearl Harbor disaster incomprehensible. Hence, bitter and frustrated isolationists were able to gain an audience when they charged that Roosevelt, determined to enter the war at any cost, had facilitated the Japanese victory by suppressing intercepted intelligence data which could have prepared the military base for the attack. The accusation was incredible and baseless. A Japanese attack would have meant war whether or not Pearl Harbor repulsed it, and even Roosevelt's most violent detractors must find it hard to believe that he would have wanted to enter the fighting with a stunning defeat.

Pearl Harbor was a result of bureaucratic inertia and the unavoidable difficulties of gathering and analyzing military intelligence. The United States had broken the major Japanese diplomatic codes, but no intercepted messages referred in plain language to an attack on Hawaii. American intelligence, as Roberta Wohlstetter has brilliantly demonstrated, received many "signals" that convincingly pointed to Japanese action in other areas; those that indicated the Pearl Harbor adventure became clear in retrospect but were far from obvious at the time. Communication between Washington and Hawaii was poor and may have indirectly contributed to a false sense of complacency at Pearl Harbor. Security at the base itself was astonishingly lax. Only one radar station, manned by two privates, was functioning as the enemy planes came within range; when the operators reported the unidentified flight to the information center, the only officer there, a young and inexperienced air corps lieutenant, told them to disregard it. No one, either in Washington or Hawaii, believed that the Japanese possessed the audacity—or the ability—to attack Pearl Harbor. As is so often the case in military history, improbability was the essential element of victory.

Another charge against Roosevelt, far more worthy of attention, is the assertion that his foreign policy was designed to provoke a conflict with Japan and thereby provide the United States a "back door" through which to enter the European war. Considered in isolation, the tough American position of the last half of 1941 lends plausibility to this thesis. Yet in December 1941 there was no way of being certain that a Pacific conflict could serve as a back door to the European war; a Congress stung by a Japanese attack might well reject further involvement in Europe and insist upon directing all of America's resources against the immediate aggressor. In fact, there was no way to predict the character of a Pacific war. Most Washington officials seem to have believed that Japan probably would move against only the British and the Dutch. Would Congress declare war in such an eventuality? If not, just how much assistance could the United States give its allies? Perhaps Roosevelt was following a back-door-to-war strategy, but its risks were enormous. It was hardly the sure bet it appeared in retrospect.

How, then, did the United States and Japan come to war in December 1941? The answer seems to be twofold. First, the fighting in Europe led each side to engage in a diplomacy of escalation which was nearly certain to end in war. Nazi victories encouraged the pivotal Asian event of 1941, the Japanese occupation of South Indo-China. Conversely, the ever-growing American commitment to the European Allies extended naturally to the protection of their Asian and Pacific possessions; it seemed logical for the United States to impose an oil embargo after Japan had taken a step that was almost certainly a prelude to new pressures on and perhaps invasion of these European possessions. Second, in a near-classic example of Asian-Occidental misunderstanding, each side, convinced of its superiority and moral purity, failed to comprehend the impulses which drove the other. Each nation came to believe that sooner or later the other would realize it had overextended itself, cut its losses, and retreat—the Japanese even expected America to react in this manner to defeat at Pearl Harbor. The United States was more rigid than Japan by the fall of 1941, but neither country felt a need to make the fundamental concessions that would have been necessary for a durable settlement in the Pacific. It might have been possible to work out a fragile modus vivendi which would have delayed the war; whether such an agreement would have been in the best long-term interest of the United States is a moot point.

A third charge against Roosevelt deserves even more serious consideration than the back-door-to-war thesis. This is the allegation that from the beginning of the war to Pearl Harbor he maneuvered the nation into the war by indirection, that he failed to state his purposes to the people candidly, that his leadership was evasive and dishonest. In the years immediately after World War II, isolationist historians, including the redoubtable Charles A. Beard, claimed that Roosevelt, by practicing duplicity, had led America to war against its will. More recently, prominent interventionist historians, notably Robert A. Divine and James Mac-Gregor Burns, have reversed the Beard argument; agreeing that Roosevelt was lacking in candor, they criticize his leadership as weak and apparently believe that he should have employed Churchillian rhetoric to prepare the country for the irrepressible conflict closing in upon it.

The historian can only conjecture about the manner by which Roosevelt defined his purpose to himself or the way in which his conceptions evolved during the years 1939–41. It seems relatively certain, however, that at some point—probably not until after the fall of France—he came to believe that American participation in the war was inevitable, and for all his caution and backtracking, he directed his policies toward this end. But it is neither historically accurate nor analytically meaningful to explain his evasions, and even dishonesty, as either the techniques of manipulative evil or the unhappy drift of political weakness. Roosevelt was not a diabolical madman bent on war for its own sake, and assuredly he was not a weak political leader.

He was rather a democratic leader very much aware of the limitations imposed upon him by his nation's political system and hallowed traditions. Churchillian rhetoric might be very well for a country already at war, bracing for an expected invasion, experiencing the devastation of nightly Luftwaffe bombing raids. A nation an ocean removed from the conflict, impelled by its entire history to avoid the troubles of Europe, might not be so responsive. America was confused, heedful enough of its national security to take intermittent steps toward war and to hazard certain risks, but not really to make a total, irrevocable commitment. The American people might have responded to an undisguised call for intervention, but it is at least equally possible that the situation and the democratic system required that the popular confusion resolve itself, no matter how slowly. Throughout the years of neutrality, Roosevelt embodied the conflicting national aspirations without being paralyzed by them; within the limits of the contradictory American mood he labored to safeguard his country and its values. A truly weak leader would have left the United States far more exposed to the militarists of Asia and Europe. As it happened, Pearl Harbor, military disaster though it was, removed any element of ambiguity; Americans could unite for the hard fight that lay ahead.

THREE

Total War and the Pursuit of Total Peace

CHRONOLOGY
1942–45

1942

JANUARY	Allies issue United Nations Declaration
FEBRUARY	Singapore surrenders to Japan
MAY	American surrender at Corregidor completes Japanese conquest of Philippines; Battle of the Coral Sea; bombing of Cologne
JUNE	Battle of Midway
AUGUST	U.S. invasion of Guadalcanal
SEPTEMBER	Battle of Stalingrad begins
NOVEMBER	USSR stages victorious counteroffensive at Stalingrad; Allies invade North Africa

1943

JANUARY	Encircled Germans surrender at Stalingrad; Roosevelt and Churchill meet at Casablanca
MARCH	Battle of the Bismarck Sea
MAY	German command in North Africa surrenders
JULY	Allies invade Sicily; Mussolini deposed; Battle of Kursk
SEPTEMBER	Allies invade Italy; Badoglio government surrenders
OCTOBER	Italy declares war on Germany

NOVEMBER	Battles of Tarawa and Makin; Roosevelt and Churchill meet with Chiang Kai-shek in Cairo, with Stalin at Teheran

1944

JANUARY	Allies land at Anzio
FEBRUARY	Battles of Kwajalein and Eniwetok
JUNE	Liberation of Rome; invasion of Normandy; Battle of the Philippine Sea
JULY	United States victorious in Saipan; German conspirators attempt to assassinate Hitler; Polish partisans stage uprising in Warsaw; USSR establishes puppet Polish government at Lublin
AUGUST	United States victorious on Guam and Tinian; Allies liberate Paris; Rumania surrenders to USSR; Dumbarton Oaks Conference begins
SEPTEMBER	Allied offensive repulsed at Arnhem; Bulgaria surrenders to USSR
OCTOBER	American invasion of the Philippines and Battle of Leyte Gulf; Polish partisans surrender to Germans in Warsaw; Hungary surrenders to USSR; liberation of Belgrade; Churchill-Stalin agreement on Eastern Europe
DECEMBER	Germans begin Ardennes offensive (Battle of the Bulge)

1945

JANUARY	USSR captures Warsaw
FEBRUARY	Yalta Conference; bombing of Dresden
MARCH	Allies capture bridge at Remagen
APRIL	Stalin-Roosevelt disputes over Poland and Italian negotiations; death of Roosevelt

After Pearl Harbor, the American nation was nearly unanimous in its commitment to absolute victory over the powers that were making war upon it. Given the menacing, frightful character of the Nazi and the Japanese militarists, the resolution was a sound one. To most Americans, however, total victory meant more than the total defeat of the enemy. It implied the elimination of the old, amoral system of power politics which had dominated international relations since the beginning of recorded history. It meant the imposition of an era of total peace based upon the acceptance of liberal-democratic ideals throughout the world.

From the earliest settlements of the seventeenth century, Americans have possessed a universalistic impulse to spread their values over the globe. Detesting militarism, they have insisted that their wars have the compelling justifications of defending the country against an evil aggressor and extending national ideals. The evil of the enemy and the moral prospect of extending liberal democracy both discourage compromise; wars must end in total victory, albeit a victory achieved as quickly and cleanly as possible. The national attitude toward World War II exemplified these traditions. Americans who had come to maturity during the depression liked to believe themselves more hard-boiled than the preceding generation, but like their fathers of the World War I era, they waged World War II as a crusade to transcend the follies of past history and establish a utopian world.

Such objectives sprang so naturally from America's political culture that President Roosevelt and other U.S. leaders accepted them as a matter of course. With the Four Freedoms and the Atlantic Charter, Roosevelt even before Pearl Harbor had based the American war effort on the ideals of liberal democracy, and he worked diligently for a world organized around these values. Yet he also had to cope with the realities of an international power structure which denied to the United States the omnipotence necessary to remake the world. The President faced a classic dilemma of American diplomacy: he had to work within the institutions of a sinful world even as he attempted to eliminate them. The result was an emphasis on military victory and a strategy of postponement and improvisation on the less tractable political issues. Striving to attain the deeply held objectives of his nation even while making the compromises demanded by the real world, Roosevelt never prepared the country for the probability that its definition of success far outran national capabilities.

CHURCHILL, ROOSEVELT, STALIN, AND THE GRAND ALLIANCE

On January 1, 1942, the White House announced that the United States, Great Britain, the Soviet Union, China, and twenty-two other antifascist nations had adhered to a statement of purposes and principles, the United Nations Declaration. The document asserted that the Allies were joined together in a struggle to vindicate the principles of the Atlantic Charter, that complete victory over the enemy was "essential to defend life, liberty, independence and religious freedom, and to preserve human rights and justice." The UN Declaration lifted the morale of most Americans and perhaps of people in other nations. In the spirit of the Four Freedoms and the Atlantic Charter, it depicted a war in which a solid democratic front determined to uphold the natural rights of man was fighting forces of evil attempting to inflict a new dark age upon the world. The description of fascism was accurate enough, but the United Nations were hardly united in principle and objective.

Despite the sentimental inclusion of China as a member of the "Big Four," the United Nations consisted of three great powers and a host of client states. For all the appearances of unity—and the very real hope of extending the alliance beyond the war—only a common enemy held the Big Three together. During the war, their leaders communicated constantly, endured substantial inconvenience to hold personal meetings with one another, and worked more or less in tandem toward the eradication of their foe; but in the last analysis, each national leader had to strive first of all to advance the interests of his country.

Winston Churchill was a war leader comparable in English history to the elder and younger William Pitt. A descendant of the revered duke of Marlborough, son of a colorful and popular Conservative party leader, Churchill had savored fame since the beginning of the century as a journalist, historian, and politician. Leaving his father's party, he had served in the pre-World War I Liberal reform government of Herbert Asquith, during the war, as first lord of the Admiralty. Rejoining the Conservatives but functioning as an independent, he had been one of the most vocal opponents of appeasement during the 1930s.

When the war he had predicted finally came, he was brought into the cabinet; with the fall of France he succeeded the sick and discredited Neville Chamberlain as prime minister. His eloquent speeches imparted his own fighting spirit to a defeated nation, electrified what remained of the democratic world, and perhaps thereby provided the margin of survival for Western civilization. Sixty-six years old when he assumed control of the British government, Churchill invariably reminded observers of a tough old English bulldog determined to preserve his territory against all comers. On inspection trips, he frequently wore a military jump suit and carried a Sten gun; one found it easy to imagine him standing with the troops against the invader and selling his life dearly.

As long as the war continued, Churchill could count on the confidence of both Roosevelt and the British people; yet neither agreed with his most fundamental beliefs. The American President rather patronizingly called him "the old Tory" and hoped to press him into a liberalization of the British Empire. As soon as the Allies achieved victory in Europe, the voters of England, wanting social reforms far beyond those which Churchill could offer them, would turn to Clement Attlee and the Labour party. A conservative, an imperialist, an implacable foe of world communism, Churchill embodied virtues of the past. His attitudes raised disturbing questions, only partially submerged during the war, about reconciling the empire with the Atlantic Charter and about maintaining an alliance that included the Soviet Union.

Josef Stalin seemed in most respects to be the antithesis of Churchill. An Old Bolshevik, ruthless and authoritarian, Stalin had been in effective control of the Soviet Union for a decade and a half. Regarding those around him with a suspicion that bordered on paranoia, he had consolidated his power with a series of bloody purges comparable to the Terror of the French Revolution but far exceeding it in the number of victims. During the mid-30s, Stalin's regime executed hundreds of thousands of opponents—real, potential, imagined—and imprisoned or disgraced many more; at the end, Stalin was no less an absolute despot than the most bloody of the czars who had preceded him.

Many of his victims were officers of the Red Army, which had not fully recovered by the time of Hitler's invasion. Mindful of this fact, Stalin overcame latent army resentment by fragmenting commands, making himself marshal of the Soviet Union, and assuming personal day-to-day control of the vast Russian military effort. Yet for all his brutality, he was remarkably successful in projecting an image of benign authority not unlike that of the "little fathers" who had ruled Imperial Russia. During the war years, he seemed a peasant uncle organizing the defense of the motherland and puffing at his pipe in a calm, deliberative manner as he pondered the decisions that would determine Russia's fate.

In his diplomatic attitudes and objectives, the Soviet dictator was no less an heir of the czars. While he doubtless viewed the world through the lenses of communism, he was ever willing to abandon Red orthodoxy if he could gain by doing so. He had made an alliance with Hitler, was now happy to have one with the capitalist powers, and would reinforce his demands for Allied support by throwing out hints of a new arrangement with the Nazis. He was motivated not simply by communist ideology or even solely by his paranoia but also by a traditional Russianism which combined suspicion of the West with an expansionist drive toward Eastern Europe, the Middle East, and the Far East.

Stalin participated in the Grand Alliance with no utopian illusions. He needed his new partners and realized that they were in at least equal need of the vast fighting power of the Soviet Union. Convinced that the struggle for power was the invariable rule of international relations, he expected the old tension between Russia and the West to resume at the end of the war, and he intended to have the Soviet Union in a position of strength, not dependent upon the uncertain friendship of Great Britain and the United States. There can be little doubt that he believed his allies were equally concerned with their own interests; he probably quite sincerely interpreted the long delay in establishing a European second front in France as evidence that the United States and Great Britain were trying to bleed the USSR as much as possible.

Stalin's minimal objectives seem to have been the reestablishment of Soviet authority over the old czarist domains he had annexed during the alliance with Hitler (Estonia, Latvia, Lithuania, eastern Poland, and Bessarabia), the establishment of a sphere of influence throughout Eastern Europe to buffer Russia against some future military thrust from the West, and the weakening or fragmentation of Germany. Such aims posed no serious threat to the Western Allies, but they were so profoundly at variance with the Atlantic Charter that the Americans could not even discuss them in a frank and explicit manner, and the British, while willing to engage in a fairly large measure of Realpolitik, could not accept them entirely.

Moreover, beyond Russia's minimum demands there existed a large amount of ambiguity, fostered by the difficulties of negotiating with surly and often hostile Soviet officials, by Western apprehensions about the dynamics of communist expansionism, and by the West's inhibitions about frankly carving the map into spheres of influence. The consequent failure to achieve a concrete agreement about the limits of Russian power or even to establish a genuine climate of trust made it easy, and probably justifiable, to believe that Stalin's definition of security took in all the territory that he could occupy or that communist parties could control. American refusal to engage in power politics was partly to blame for this fear, but Stalin contributed mightily; by basing his policies on the expectation of future hostility between the USSR and the West, he brought forth a self-fulfilling prophecy.

Roosevelt, representing as he did a nation that was in a much more secure position than either the Soviet Union or Great Britain and that had a tradition of moral crusading, could afford to be altruistic. The Atlantic Charter expressed not only American idealism but also the interests of a country with no appreciable political empire and, removed from Europe and Asia by two great oceans, with no need to seek security through spheres of influence on these continents. The charter embodied Roosevelt's deepest impulses, but the President also understood that neither paper agreements nor a toothless international organization could prevent future wars. He hoped for a postwar concert of power built around the United States, Great Britain, the Soviet Union, and China, which he believed had the potential to replace Japan as the dominant nation of the

Far East. Roosevelt allowed the State Department to plan for a new world organization, but he had little faith in such panaceas—or indeed in the department itself.

Like most Americans, the President concentrated on military victory as a first priority to which everything else had to be subordinated. Thus it seemed natural to delay the final consideration of political differences or arguments between America and her allies. Roosevelt realized that victory in itself could not guarantee the concert of power he sought, but he seems to have hoped that progress toward victory would establish a better climate for the development of a postwar concert to secure the peace. From this perspective also, postponement seemed justifiable and even necessary.

In perceiving the need for a concert of power to preserve the peace, Roosevelt demonstrated an understanding of the realities of international politics, but it was easier to grasp the necessity than to implement it. Roosevelt's mind was divided between idealism and realism, but the American people conceived of the war as a struggle for idealistic objectives, in large part because of the President's own rhetoric. Roosevelt's justification of the war—itself an expression of traditional American diplomatic innocence and utopianism—thus went far toward creating a situation in which it was impossible to make the frank and cynical power deals which alone might hold the United Nations together. Roosevelt fell back upon his experience as a domestic politician and based his diplomacy on the assumption that conflicts among the Big Three, like internal political differences, could be settled through mutual compromise and personal understanding. For most of the war, he pictured himself as a mediator between the Old Tory and the Old Bolshevik, attempting to forge personal friendships into a three-power alliance.

Churchill never yielded on the question of the empire, but in fact the British era was over. It was increasingly obvious that England had become a junior partner to the United States; common political and cultural traditions made the prospect tolerable. Stalin, suspicious and implacable, the product of cultural and political traditions diametrically opposed to those of Anglo-America, presented a quite different problem. In personal meetings he was friendly with Roosevelt and may have developed a degree of trust in him, although the evidence is uncertain. Whatever his innermost feelings, the Soviet leader never deviated from his objectives; steadily pursuing his goals of security and expansion, apparently looking ahead to new international struggles, he did nothing to make relations with the West easy. The result was consistent postponement of disputes as Roosevelt continued to put his faith in personal diplomacy.

The structure of the war effort made it even more difficult to solve diplomatic problems. By virtue of geography and economic development, the United States was the chief supplier of war matériel for the Allies, all of whom realized that ultimate victory around the globe depended upon a constant expansion of U.S. industrial output. The needs of industry thus placed important limitations upon American military manpower mobilization, which was necessarily modest compared to that of Britain, Germany, or the Soviet Union. The successful Russian resistance at once increased the demands upon U.S. military production and reduced the numbers needed for the American army. At the beginning of the war, U.S. generals, anticipating a Soviet collapse, projected a combat force of over two hundred divisions. The much different situation which developed after Stalingrad led to a constant scaling-down of land-power estimates. The actual combat strength of the U.S. Army never exceeded ninety divisions, about three-fourths of which fought in the European theater.

The relative U.S. concentration on industrial output grew naturally out of the course of the war and was the most appropriate American role if the conflict were to be won as quickly and economically as possible. Yet the emphasis on technology instead of manpower led to a postwar balance in which the West did not have the power to create a universalistic liberal-democratic world. The United States and Britain did, it is true, achieve the greatest air and naval might in history; but the Soviet Union possessed a ground superiority of at least three to one. The Russians, for all their reliance on U.S. Lend-Lease, would argue that they, not the West, had shed the most blood for the Allied cause. The power configurations which grew out of the war effort dictated that political differences between Russia and the West would have to be compromised on a basis that most Americans would consider immoral and unacceptable—or they would have to be postponed.

TURNING THE TIDE:
PEARL HARBOR TO CASABLANCA

In the months after the issuance of the UN Declaration, the Grand Alliance sustained one defeat after another. The British learned in disbelief that Japan had overwhelmed the supposedly impregnable bastion of Singapore. The United States could only watch helplessly as its troops retreated time and again in the Philippines, finally surrendering their last fortress, Corregidor, on May 6, 1942. By mid-year, the Japanese Empire stretched from the western Aleutian Islands to the Solomons and Gilberts, from Burma throughout Southeast Asia to the Dutch Indies. Australia and India both appeared in peril.

In the Atlantic, German submarines terrorized the entire North American coastline, sinking Allied merchant ships faster than they could be replaced and threatening to sever the vital supply lines between the United States and its European partners. Off the coast of Norway, the convoy route to Murmansk and Archangel in the USSR was almost suicidal during the long daylight hours of the Arctic spring and summer. On one run in late June, the Germans sank 23 of 34 ships; shortly thereafter, the British announced a convoy suspension which lasted for several months. In North Africa, Rommel drove deeply into Egypt to make his most serious threat yet against the Suez Canal. In the USSR, the Nazis ruled the areas they had occupied with a calculated savagery, based on the theory that the Russians were subhuman; German commanders sanctioned mass atrocities against prisoners as a matter of policy. Throughout the summer, the *Wehrmacht* pushed the Soviet armies back and conquered vast areas of southern Russia.

The British and Americans strove to counter the Atlantic submarine menace with advanced radar systems, more destroyers, and increased air patrols; but enemy U-boats continued to exact a fearful toll. The battle of the Atlantic would not be definitively won until the spring of 1943. In the meantime, the Russians, barely hanging on, bitterly protested the cutoff of Lend-Lease convoys and urged the quick establishment of a second front in Europe. President Roosevelt appreciated the Soviet plight and did what he could to sustain the Russian war effort. "I find it difficult," he told General Douglas MacArthur in May 1942, "to get away from the simple fact that the Russian armies are killing more Axis personnel and destroying more Axis matériel than all other twenty-five United Nations put together." The administration assigned the highest priority to Soviet Lend-Lease and developed two new routes—one, available to Soviet shipping only, across the Pacific to Vladivostok; another, through the Persian Gulf and Iran—but both presented formidable transportation difficulties. America provided more than 800,000 tons of supplies to the USSR during 1942, but this total represented only about half of what had been promised.

Americans felt their greatest emotional involvement with the war against Japan, and took heart from the first victories against the empire in mid-1942. From May 4–8 a small U.S. naval force commanded by Rear Admiral Frank Fletcher encountered a comparable Japanese fleet in the Coral Sea off northeastern Australia. The enemy vessels were the vanguard of a planned invasion of southern New Guinea, which, if successful, would have allowed direct strikes against Australia. Fought entirely from aircraft carriers, the Battle of the Coral Sea was the first in the history of naval warfare in which the opposing fleets never came within surface range of each other. The weather was difficult and the reconnaissance on both sides faulty; tactical success was more the product of human error and luck than of skillful planning. Statistically, the outcome was indecisive; the Americans lost more tonnage sunk, including one large aircraft carrier, but destroyed many more enemy planes and inflicted serious damage on two major Japanese carriers. In practical terms, the Coral Sea was an Allied victory, for the Japanese, deprived of an effective air cover, postponed the New Guinea offensive; moreover, the United States could replace its naval losses at a much faster rate than could Japan.

On June 3-6, 1942, the Americans and Japanese fought the decisive naval battle of the Pacific war near Midway Island, the most important U.S. outpost between the Japanese Empire and Hawaii. The imperial armada of more than 160 vessels under Admiral Isoroku Yamamoto faced a U.S. Pacific fleet less than half as large under Admiral Chester Nimitz. Nimitz, however, had the advantage of code intercepts which gave him prior knowledge of the Japanese plan; and his lieutenants, Frank Fletcher and Raymond Spruance, were resourceful commanders in their own right. As at the Coral Sea, the fighting consisted of air attacks on enemy ships. The Japanese lost their four largest aircraft carriers, a heavy cruiser, and 322 planes; another heavy cruiser and two destroyers took severe damage. The Americans lost one carrier, one destroyer, and 147 planes. The U.S. Navy had turned Japan back in the northern and central Pacific.

To the south, the United States began the road back with attacks in the Solomon Islands, the major one at Guadalcanal beginning August 7, 1942. For the next six months, U.S. troops advanced slowly through thick, disease-infested jungles against suicidal Japanese resistance. Willing to die to the last man for the emperor, enemy snipers tied themselves to trees, and machine-gun teams dug into caves from which there could be no retreat. It was a preview of many island engagements to come. Painfully, the Americans pressed forward, proving that they could best even the masters of defensive jungle warfare. At sea, the U.S. naval forces, placed under the command of Vice-Admiral William ("Bull") Halsey in October 1942, fought one engagement after another with a strong Japanese fleet. Each side lost 24 warships, but, given the capacity of American shipyards, the infliction of equal losses would ensure ultimate U.S. victory. On February 6, 1943, the Japanese, having suffered 20,000 casualties, evacuated Guadalcanal.

Despite the early Pacific victories, U.S. leaders adhered steadfastly to the ABC-1 decision * that the Allies should concentrate on the defeat of Germany. With typical American directness and optimism, U.S. military

*See above, p. 41.

planners contemplated a direct strike against Germany and a relatively quick end to the war. "We've got to go to Europe and fight—and we've got to quit wasting resources all over the world," declared the chief of the war-planning staff, Dwight D. Eisenhower. In May 1942 President Roosevelt told the Soviet foreign minister, Vyacheslav Molotov, that his government could count on the establishment of a second front in Europe that year.

Actually, there was no hope of staging a successful invasion of the Continent in 1942; the United States and Britain had neither the trained manpower nor the equipment. The Americans produced a plan, rather misleadingly codenamed SLEDGEHAMMER, for a small, probably sacrificial, attack in France if the Soviet resistance were about to collapse. Thereafter, the Allies would concentrate men, shipping, and supplies in the British Isles for a major assault (ROUNDUP) in the spring of 1943.

The British advanced a counter-strategy, based in part upon sound military principles, in part upon England's own special needs and interests. Great Britain had lost a generation of its finest young men in the bloody, indecisive trench warfare of World War I; a premature invasion of Fortress Europe carried the promise of another terrible slaughter. Moreover, with Rommel on the offensive in North Africa, British control of the Suez Canal and the Mediterranean Sea, already tenuous, was in dire peril; German victories in this sector would effectively cut off England's lines to Asia and the Indian Ocean. Churchill and his generals thus pressed hard for an alternative to SLEDGEHAMMER, although they still professed to endorse ROUNDUP.

The British advocated landings in western North Africa, a much safer scheme. Most American strategists, however, predicted that the African venture (TORCH) would disrupt the military buildup in Great Britain, needlessly disperse resources, and kill ROUNDUP. Their predictions were correct—British planners privately had expected the same outcome. TORCH inevitably paved the way for other diversions and became the first step in a peripheral strategy to clear the Mediterranean before the invasion of Fortress Europe.

The British approach may have been excessively cautious, but American military plans in 1942 verged on the reckless. The SLEDGEHAMMER scheme probably would have ended in disaster. ROUNDUP is harder to judge. The Allies might have successfully executed it in the early fall (but not in the spring) of 1943 *if* they had concentrated all their efforts upon gathering troops and matériel in England and had waged only a holding action on all other fronts. A victorious thrust at Germany at that time probably would have ended the war at an earlier date and left the West in a much stronger position vis-à-vis the Soviet Union. On the other hand, a delay of nearly two years in taking the offensive might have caused serious morale problems in the United States and certainly would have damaged Roosevelt politically. Moreover, it would have entailed a surrender of the military initiative to the enemy, perhaps with serious consequences in the Mediterranean or the Pacific. Roosevelt, eager to commit American troops against the Nazis and to do so in a winning campaign, overruled his generals and opted for TORCH.

On November 8, 1942, 110,000 British and American troops, commanded by Eisenhower, struck at the important French North African ports of Casablanca, Oran, and Algiers. The first problem was to neutralize the Vichy French defenders. Eisenhower secured this objective by negotiating an armistice with Admiral Jean Darlan, the Vichy vice premier, on November 10; the arrangement recognized the former Nazi collaborator as the top French political and military leader in North Africa. In strictly military terms, the "Darlan deal" made sense, but the war supposedly was being fought for democratic political objectives. There was widespread denunciation in the United States and Britain. On December 24, Darlan was assassinated by an antifascist Frenchman, and the Allies, doubtless with some relief, named General Henri Giraud, a staunch anti-Nazi French patriot, to replace him. (Subsequently, a shrewder and more charismatic soldier, General Charles de Gaulle, supplanted Giraud as the leader of the Free French.) The Darlan episode demonstrated the way in which the war forced compromises for which most Americans were unprepared; Roosevelt's later proclamation of the goal of unconditional surrender seems to have been partly motivated by the angry public reaction. At the end of the war, other compromises, not so easily explained on the basis of military necessity, would be even more unacceptable.

The Allies had hardly hit the North African beaches before Hitler was sending reinforcements to Rommel. The wily Desert Fox conducted a tenacious defense; however, he faced not only Anglo-American invaders from the West, but also a British offensive from Egypt led by General Bernard Montgomery. Germany could provide Rommel with only enough help to prolong his resistance; he enjoyed an occasional tactical success but had no hope of ultimate victory. In April, with the German forces driven back into Tunisia, Rommel left Africa, never to return. On May 8, 1943, British General Harold Alexander shattered the last German strong point with a lightning armored attack. Five days later, the German command surrendered a quarter of a million soldiers to the Allies. North Africa had been more difficult than expected, but the outcome was a smashing victory.

Even before the North African invasion, the decisive battle of the war had begun in southern Russia in and around Stalingrad. During the summer of 1942, the Germans had hurled back a Soviet offensive and had undertaken a drive of their own which carried them to the Volga River and the strategically located industrial city named for the Soviet dictator. The Russians had already suffered losses incomprehensible to the American imagination—5 million killed, wounded, or captured by mid-1942—yet their supply of manpower seemed inexhaustible, and they could still throw 4.25 million troops, organized into 280 divisions and 44 armored brigades, against the invader. In addition, bands of guerrillas operated effectively behind the German lines. Hitler's forces numbered more than 3.1 million, and had already incurred at least 1.25 million casualties.

In September, large German and Russian armies began the Battle of Stalingrad; in the weeks that followed, Hitler and Stalin both threw in great numbers of reserves. The fighting was desperate and bloody—block by block, even room by room—with most of the city reduced to rubble and men dying by the thousands every day. "I would not have believed such an inferno could open up on this earth," wrote Soviet General Georgi Zhukov. For weeks the Russians seemed on the verge of defeat, but their constant flow of fresh troops absorbed repeated Nazi assaults and exhausted the attackers. On November 19, Zhukov took the offensive; the Russians smashed a Rumanian army and encircled twenty German divisions. While Nazis vainly undertook relief efforts, the entrapped Germans resisted through much of the harsh Russian winter, butchering their horses for food, existing in the most terrible privation. On January 31, 1943, those who were left surrendered. Of the 280,000 originally surrounded, the Germans had managed to evacuate 42,000 by air; another 147,000 were dead or missing. Of the 91,000 who capitulated, only about 6,000 would ever return to Germany. The Russian casualties were even greater; at Stalingrad the USSR lost more men killed than would the United States during the entire war.

During late 1942, relations between the Soviet Union and the West reached a low point because of the Anglo-American failure to invade Europe or fulfill Lend-Lease agreements. The USSR had carried the brunt of the fighting since June 1941. Even the North African invasion, when it finally came, must have seemed a minor affair to Stalin; after all, the U.S. and British troops there numbered only about one-twentieth of the Soviet forces on the Eastern front. The Russian dictator could assume with some justice that his allies were trying to win the war with Soviet blood and weaken the USSR in the process. (The peripheral strategy did in fact carry such an implication; Roosevelt and Churchill seem never to have realized that their desire to minimize Anglo-American casualties necessarily entailed heavier Russian losses.) Continuing to demand a second front, the Soviet government threw out occasional hints of a separate peace with Germany. For a time, Stalin even allowed the Russian press to denounce the Darlan deal as evidence of Western perfidy, but, perhaps recalling his own alliance with Hitler, he eventually decided that the episode was justifiable. By early 1943, moreover, with the Red Army on the offensive, he could at least console himself with the knowledge that the longer the West delayed its invasion, the greater the territory Russian troops could occupy.

Against this backdrop of victory or impending victory in the Pacific, the Atlantic, North Africa, and Russia, Roosevelt and Churchill met at Casablanca, January 14–24, 1943. (Stalin, pleading the demands placed upon him by his day-to-day management of the Soviet war, declined to attend.) At Casablanca, American military planners came face to face with what they had feared for months—the North African venture had drained so many resources that ROUNDUP was no longer possible. The British, well armed with facts, figures, and arguments, suggested and won a continuation of the peripheral strategy in the form of a strike across the Mediterranean to Sicily. U.S. generals realized there could be no major second front until 1944, but they were determined to brook no further delays.

The decision for Sicily raised the problem of satisfying Stalin, who had told his partners that his own military plans rested upon fulfillment of their ROUNDUP pledge. In truth, there was no practicable way to mollify the Soviet leader, but Great Britain and the United States could at least express joint determination to see the war through. Roosevelt, also concerned with the adverse reaction to the Darlan deal, persuaded Churchill to join in a declaration that the fighting would end only upon the "unconditional surrender" of the Axis. The statement made it clear that the Western powers did not contemplate the total destruction of the people in Axis nations, but many critics later asserted that the unconditional-surrender policy gave such an impression, stiffened resistance, and prolonged the war. In fact, enemy propagandists could have found other bogeys to frighten their populations. If unconditional surrender was a blunder, it was such in a different and profound sense. Even though the tide had turned, the policy indicated that the West, and Roosevelt especially, still concentrated almost solely upon military victory, preferring to ignore or postpone the potentially grave political issues that the members of the Grand Alliance needed to resolve among themselves.

TOWARD TOTAL VICTORY

The decision to postpone a major invasion of Europe until mid-1944 generated irresistible pressure for a Pacific offensive; the European theater simply could not absorb the troops and equipment that the United States was producing. The Pacific operations remained secondary, but they received much greater support than U.S. planners originally had envisioned. By the end of 1943, over 900,000 American ground troops were fighting the Japanese; by October 1944, the number was up to 1.3 million, and victory was in sight. Forces under the command of General Douglas MacArthur in the South Pacific and Admiral Nimitz in the Central Pacific hopped from island to island. By October 1944, both commanders were ready to join in the reconquest of the Philippines.

Having secured Guadalcanal and having established naval and air supremacy after the Battle of the Bismarck Sea (March 1–4, 1943), Mac-Arthur launched successful attacks against strategic points in the central Solomons, especially New Georgia, in the summer of 1943. In November U.S. troops took Bougainville at the northern tip of the archipelago. Wisely bypassing and isolating the formidable Japanese outpost at Rabaul in the Bismarck Islands, MacArthur spent the last half of 1943 and early 1944 clearing northern New Guinea and the offshore islands. He then argued passionately that his next major step should be the liberation of the Philippines rather than the conquest of Taiwan, an objective favored by most naval planners. MacArthur's emotional attachment to the Philippines notwithstanding, his arguments were strategically and politically sound. In July Roosevelt gave him a go-ahead; on October 20, 1944, American troops landed on Leyte.

Nimitz and his admirals in the meantime participated in some of the most savage fighting of the war. In November 1943 they took Makin and Tarawa in the Gilbert Islands. In February 1944 they won naval and air victories in the Marshalls, conquered Kwajalein and Eniwetok, and reduced the Caroline fortresses of Truk and Ponape by bombardment. That summer, they brought the war to the Marianas with the capture of Guam, Tinian, and Saipan. In September they invaded the island of Peleliu in the Western Carolines, just 500 miles from the Philippines. In almost every case the Japanese resisted with incredible determination, digging into emplacements that only flame throwers could penetrate, engaging in hopeless suicide charges, and usually fighting to the death. At Kwajalein, where the ratio of Japanese to American killed ran higher than 22:1, an observer surveying the aftermath found himself overwhelmed by the mingled smells of decaying bodies and burned coconut wood.

By mid-1944, the American navy had established almost total supremacy in the Pacific, the product of near-miraculous war production and superior numbers of trained personnel. On June 19–20, 1944, a Japanese fleet hopelessly outnumbered in almost every category engaged Admiral Spruance off Saipan. In the ensuing Battle of the Philippine Sea, the better-trained American pilots virtually wiped out Japan's naval air power and sunk three carriers. Four months later, October 23–25, 1944, the Japanese made their last great sea effort, the Battle of Leyte Gulf, the largest ocean engagement in history. Splitting their forces, the enemy admirals maneuvered with great skill, but American strength was overwhelming. Barely escaping complete annihilation, the Japanese navy was henceforth impotent against American sea power.

On July 10, 1943, some two months after the German surrender in North Africa, an Anglo-American force invaded Sicily. The battle for the island lasted thirty-nine days with the Germans, who even here bore the brunt of the Axis effort, leading a tough defense which inflicted nearly equal casualties upon the Allies. All the same, the Sicilian campaign destroyed what was left of the Italian will to fight; fifteen days after the invasion, Italian military leaders deposed and imprisoned Mussolini. The new premier, Marshall Pietro Badoglio, and his supporters were themselves leading Fascists, but they knew the direction of the wind; they immediately opened not-so-secret negotiations for surrender. On September 3, British forces took Reggio Calabria at the tip of the Italian peninsula, and Badoglio at once surrendered unconditionally. On September 9, the Allies landed at Salerno. On October 13, the Italian government completed its about-face by declaring war on Germany.

As it developed, the diplomatic-military triumph was singularly hollow. The Germans seized most of Italy and, having rescued Mussolini in a storybook paratrooper raid, established Il Duce as head of a puppet government. The rugged terrain of the peninsula was perfectly suited to defensive warfare, and the Nazis could put up a determined resistance with a minimum number of troops. The Allied advance was slow and extremely painful. An ill-conceived landing behind the German lines at Anzio on January 22, 1944, nearly become another Dunkirk. The Allies would be unable to break through until May and would not enter Rome until June 4, 1944. The Italian campaign tied down only fourteen German divisions, and did so at a very high price.

Beginning in 1942, the British had conducted regular bombing raids against Germany; the largest of these operations, against Cologne in May 1942, involved a thousand bombers. At Casablanca, Roosevelt and Churchill authorized around-the-clock strategic bombing of the Reich. For the next several months, the British by night and the Americans by day rained thousands of tons of bombs upon Germany, devastating industrial facilities, burning out huge areas of cities, and killing civilians in much the same manner that the Luftwaffe had once attempted to destroy London. During this early phase at least, the Germans appear to have been no more subdued by the bombing than had the British; civilian morale remained high, and war production actually increased. Forced to perform their missions without fighter escorts, the U.S. B-17s were terribly vulnerable to the Luftwaffe and to the highly effective German antiaircraft fire. By October, the Americans could no longer sustain their losses; they suspended daytime raids. The first effort to win the war from the air had been a failure.

By early 1944, escort fighters were available, and by the end of February, they had ousted the Luftwaffe from the skies over Europe. For the next several months, the bombing raids hit not only Germany but also France and the Low Countries in preparation for, then in support of, the invasion of the Continent. It was not until September 1944 that the air strategists could concentrate singlemindedly on the destruction of Germany, and there can be little doubt that this final six-month bomber offensive was more effective than the earlier effort. Concentrating on transportation facilities and fuel production, it seriously disrupted both. After the war, the U.S. Strategic Bombing Survey concluded that the bombing alone would have paralyzed German war production by May 1945 and compelled surrender by that summer. The historian who has witnessed the limitations of bombing in subsequent wars may possibly be permitted his doubts. That the raids eventually hurt German production and morale is undeniable; that they could have won the war by themselves is surely questionable. Whatever the value of the bombing, the Allies paid heavily; air casualties over Europe amounted to 40,000 planes and 158,000 men.

According to official figures, the bombing of Germany killed 305,000 persons, wounded 780,000, and destroyed or damaged 5.5 million dwellings. From the beginning, the British, realistic about the impossibility of "pinpoint bombing" and anxious to repay the Germans, had advocated saturation attacks designed to wreck the working-class areas of the cities, kill civilians, and thereby undermine the nation's will to fight. The Americans, farther removed from the grisly experiences of war, attempted to concentrate on military-industrial targets, but the actualities of high-level bombing frequently reduced this objective to a pious hope. By the beginning of 1945, the United States no less than England was engaged in terror bombing. Perhaps the most terrible and senseless of all the raids occurred on February 13–14, 1945, at Dresden, a city jammed with refugees from the Eastern front. British bombers dropped incendiaries, causing massive firestorms which killed tens of thousands of people; the next morning, with smoke still rising 15,000 feet into the air, the Americans hit the city with an equally devastating strike. It was, of course, impossible in 1945 for any Allied civilian or military leader to feel much sympathy for the German people who had supported Hitler and thereby made the war possible; nevertheless, in sanctioning the terror raids, the Anglo-American alliance had adopted the Hitlerian ethic of ruthless slaughter. Total war imposed its own logic upon men and events, driving them in the end all down to the same level.

Throughout 1943 and the first half of 1944, the Red Army pressed forward on the Eastern front where, as always, most of the fighting was taking place. By mid-1943, all manner of American supplies were pouring into the USSR through Murmansk and Iran. The Soviet forces not only outnumbered the Germans by about 5.7 million to 3 million; for the first time, they were better equipped. In the summer of 1943 Hitler ordered one last offensive against the Soviet tide; from July 5–12 Soviet and Nazi armor fought the largest tank battle in military history near the city of Kursk. At the end, General Zhukov's forces had destroyed a crack panzer army. From this point on, the Germans faced only perpetual retreat; forced to begin a buildup against the anticipated Anglo-American invasion in the West, they could not even fully replace the casualties that the Russians were inflicting. By the end of 1943, the Russians had advanced 50 miles to the west of Kiev; by mid-1944, they had cleared almost all of the prewar USSR. By then, the fight for Mother Russia was over, the quest for a sphere of influence begun.

Near the end of 1943, President Roosevelt left the United States for conferences at Cairo with Churchill and Chiang Kai-shek, November 23–27, and at Teheran with Churchill and Stalin, November 27–December 2. In retrospect, the Cairo meeting is significant as an indicator of the hollowness of China's claim to great-power status. Roosevelt was happy, even eager, to place Chiang in the spotlight of a Big Three meeting, but, as throughout the war, the President could do little more. Consistently, the United States dealt the Chinese theater the lowest priority. There were good reasons for doing so: Chiang's government was corrupt and incompetent, his armies poorly trained and badly led; U.S. financial aid had a way of disappearing into private bank accounts; strategically, China's fate was least important to the United States. At Cairo, Roosevelt promised support for a major Chinese–British–U.S. campaign in the Bay of Bengal and Burma, but European needs soon forced him to withdraw the pledge. The conference issued a public declaration promising independence for Korea and the restoration of Manchuria, Taiwan, and the Pescadores to China, but the statesmen could not eradicate the serious weaknesses of the Chinese government. For the remainder of the war, Chiang could offer only a desultory resistance to Japan, but probably even massive infusions of U.S. aid would have failed to resuscitate his feeble regime. Roosevelt had attempted for a time to make China a great power by proclamation; toward the end of the war, he realized that his effort had failed, but he could produce no more promising formula.

At Teheran, Roosevelt, Churchill, and Stalin, meeting together for the first time, discussed a wide range of military and political problems. The Soviet dictator, unimpressed by the Western operations in Italy, was determined to get a firm commitment for the invasion of France. Churchill, on the other hand, hoped to avoid a rigid obligation; he argued that an invasion of the island of Rhodes would render the Nazi position in the Eastern Mediterranean untenable, would force Turkey to enter the war, and would not unduly postpone the French invasion (now code named OVERLORD). Roosevelt, to the dismay of his military advisers, had shown interest in this latest extension of the British peripheral strategy. However, his primary concern was the establishment of a cordial understanding with Stalin; he hoped that Teheran would establish a basis for Soviet participation in the Pacific war and for a peaceful postwar relationship. For this objective, the President was willing, even eager, to ingratiate himself with Stalin by disagreeing with Churchill. Roosevelt virtually compelled the British to acquiesce in the scheduling of OVERLORD for May 1944 and in the prompt designation of a supreme commander for the invasion. (A few days after the conference, the President selected Eisenhower.) Stalin promised that Russia would declare war on Japan shortly after the defeat of Germany.

The political talks ranged over many topics and produced concrete solutions for none. The Big Three agreed in vague principle that the Polish boundaries should be moved to the west in order to allow the USSR to retain all or most of the Polish territory annexed in 1939 and that the Baltic states should remain a part of the Soviet Union. Roosevelt, however, pleaded political difficulties with ethnic voting blocs in the United States, and no specific agreements were concluded. All concurred in general that Germany should be disarmed and dismembered after the war, but there were great differences in detail between Churchill's relatively mild proposals and the drastic measures that Stalin and Roosevelt seemed to favor. Roosevelt also discussed his hopes that the French colonies, especially Indo-China, would be given their independence and in private conversations with Stalin talked of the need to loosen the British Empire; surprisingly, the Soviet dictator was not overly receptive and even suggested that the British might appropriately enlarge their holdings at the expense of pro-Axis Spain. Roosevelt and Stalin tentatively explored freer

Soviet access to the Turkish straits and concessions to the USSR in the Far East. Finally, the President brought up his idea of a postwar international organization to be structured around the Big Four, who would act as the policemen of the world (a concept somewhat at odds with the ideas of Secretary of State Cordell Hull, who envisioned a more democratic world assembly). Stalin seemed rather receptive, subject to the proviso that each great power would be dominant in its own area of special interest. Roosevelt responded that the American people would not tolerate the postwar establishment of large units of American troops in Europe. The Soviet ruler was apparently surprised and reassured that the West would accept his bid for regional hegemony.

The Teheran Conference had great military significance, but it failed to produce a single important solid political accord. To Roosevelt, who wanted to postpone such difficult and dangerous questions until after the 1944 election and until military victory was closer, the results were more than acceptable. He considered the meeting a highly successful exploratory operation and felt that he had won Stalin's confidence. The U.S. public reaction to the conference was equally ebullient. Teheran was an exciting symbol of Allied unity and determination, apparently promising a new world after victory. "United in war, united in peace—the United Nations!" exulted the Chicago *Daily News.* Yet behind the symbol there was only the wistful and insubstantial myth that a united military effort would create a united peace effort, that personal friendships could somehow transcend conflicts of national interests and values.

After Teheran, the planning for OVERLORD proceeded rapidly. The American generals, finally given their head by Roosevelt, resolutely turned back British proposals for new Mediterranean projects, aside from the Anzio landing, which they came to regret bitterly. At the Algiers military planning conference in January 1944, Churchill made one last pitch for his Rhodes project. General Marshall, whose public behavior usually was in the strictest gentlemanly decorum, exploded: "No American is going to land on that goddam island!" The British subsequently proposed an invasion of the Balkans at Trieste as an accompaniment to OVERLORD, arguing that the plan carried the political dividend of a substantial Western military presence in Central Europe at the war's end. The American military leaders distrusted the difficult Balkan terrain and refused to consider political questions. Their goal was to end the war as quickly as possible, and the best method of doing so appeared to be to protect the southern flank of OVERLORD with an invasion of southern France. Eisenhower insisted upon the operation, code named ANVIL, and set it to occur as soon as possible after OVERLORD. On D-Day, June 6, 1944, a mighty Anglo-American force hit the coast of Normandy. Within twenty-four hours, the Allies had put 156,000 men on five separate beach areas. After all the long months of planning and delay, the second front had become a reality.

TRIUMPH AND TRAGEDY

The German resistance was determined, but the Allies held the beaches and pressed slowly forward, sustained and strengthened by a great flow of men and supplies from England. By June 12, there were 326,000 American and British troops in Normandy; in five more days, the total was 587,000. By June 26, as U.S. forces captured the important port of Cherbourg, the millionth Allied soldier came ashore; by September 5, the number would reach 2 million. On July 1, one Nazi counterattack after another having been repulsed, the talented German general Gerd von Rundstedt could only reply in despair when the Berlin High Command asked for advice on a next move: "Make peace you fools. What else can you do?" Hitler instantly demoted him. Two weeks later, U.S. planes strafed Rommel's staff car, and the ensuing crash seriously injured the general. On July 20, a strange combination of German idealists and old-line militarists narrowly failed in an attempt to assassinate Hitler. The führer barbarically exterminated all those suspected of participation in the plot. Rommel was forced to commit suicide, but Hitler thought better of revealing his complicity and the nature of his death to the German public. On July 26, the Allies broke out of the Normandy perimeter. On August 15, seven Free French and three American divisions landed in southern France. Four days later, French partisans rose up against the Nazi occupiers of Paris. By August 26, De Gaulle was leading a victory march down the Champs Elysées.

At this point, the German army was in more disarray than its fairly orderly retreat indicated; a swift, hard thrust into the Reich probably would have compelled surrender before the end of 1944. Unfortunately, General Eisenhower's intelligence did not enjoy the sources available to future historians. The western German fortifications—the Siegfried line —appeared formidable, and Allied planners did not comprehend the totality of the enemy collapse. Consequently, Eisenhower failed to heed his most brilliant and daring commander, General George Patton, who requested logistical priority (i.e., a preponderance of available gasoline and other supplies) for a direct strike against the Siegfried line. Eisenhower instead gave priority to the British general Montgomery for a drive into Belgium and the Netherlands with the ultimate objective of flanking the German defenses from the north. Montgomery quickly liberated Belgium and the southern Netherlands, but the Germans inflicted a serious defeat upon British paratroopers at Arnhem on the Rhine River. Thereupon, Eisenhower reverted to the strategy of a slow if steady broad frontal advance. By the end of September, the Germans had regrouped and strengthened their defenses. By mid-December, they were ready to stage one last desperate offensive.

On December 16, 1944, Hitler threw the last of his reserves—a quarter of a million men—against the Allied positions in the Ardennes Forest of southeastern Belgium. The attack had the advantage of near-total surprise and of bad weather, which grounded Allied aircraft for several days. Within a week and a half, the Germans had totally surrounded an American airborne division at Bastogne and had driven a bulge of 50 miles into the Allied lines. On Christmas Day, the Allies stopped the German advance; the next day, General Patton broke through to Bastogne. By then, the weather was clear for air-support operations. On January 13, 1945, Hitler acquiesced to his generals and ordered a retreat. At the end of the month, the bulge was flattened, and the Allies were ready to begin a general advance into Germany. By the first week in March, the Nazis were retiring for a last stand on the east side of the Rhine. On March 7, American troops, through a stroke of luck, captured a still-intact bridge at Remagen, poured troops across it, and thoroughly disrupted enemy defense plans. By the end of the month, the Allies had thrown up temporary bridges all along the length of the river and had effected a general crossing. Hitler issued insane orders for counteroffensives, but his troops were beaten. On April 23, General Patton's Third Army, having cut a swath through southern Germany, reached the Czechoslovakian border. Two days later at Torgau on the Elbe River, U.S. and Soviet soldiers embraced and celebrated the impending end of the war.

The news from the Eastern front throughout the last half of 1944 and early 1945 was even worse for Germany than that from the West. The Americans and British advanced in spurts and were stalled before the Rhine for several months; the Russian armies had become an irresistible tide steadily pressing upon the Reich and its satellites. For the United States and Britain, the Eastern developments both heralded certain victory and foreshadowed future discords.

By the end of July 1944, Soviet troops had reached the Vistula River and the outskirts of Warsaw. On August 1, Polish partisans inside the city began a rebellion against the Germans. The Warsaw uprising brought all the latent divisions within the anti-Nazi coalition to the surface. The partisans were loyal to the Polish government-in-exile, the remnants of the prewar regime based in London and recognized by the United States and England; the London Poles were bitterly hostile to the Russians, who had participated in the obliteration of their country in 1939 and had, it was discovered in 1943, massacred some 10,000 captured Polish army officers in the Katyn Forest. As the Soviet army advanced into Poland, partisan units which cooperated with it found themselves being disarmed and deprived of their officers. On July 24, the Russians established their own puppet government at Lublin. It was imperative for the Poles to establish themselves as masters of their own capital and thereby give the London government some prestige and bargaining power. If the Warsaw uprising was primarily against the Nazis, its leaders and many of its participants conceived of it as also an assertion of independence from the Soviet Union.

The Russians fully understood the implications. Determined to retain the old czarist territories that they had taken from Poland in 1939 and equally bent upon dominating postwar Poland because of its strategic importance as a buffer between Germany and the USSR, they were no more willing to compromise than were the London Poles. In addition, the Soviet army had moved so rapidly that by the time it reached the Vistula it was experiencing real difficulties of supply and reinforcement. The battle for Warsaw provided the Russians with a dual opportunity for a military respite and the elimination of a political enemy. The partisans, ill armed though they were, gained control of most of the city, but they could not hold it unless the Soviet Union kept up the pressure on the Germans. The Russians did not; through August and into September they kept hands off the Warsaw fighting. While the Nazis, using brigades of German convicts and Russian turncoats, crushed the insurgents with appalling savagery, the USSR refused even to grant landing privileges to British and American planes which attempted to drop some supplies to the partisans. The Soviet Union waited until mid-September before sending one of its pro-communist Polish units against the city; the Germans, having used the interval to shore up their defenses, repulsed the attack. At the end of September, the insurgents surrendered. Hitler ordered Warsaw leveled to the ground, and not until January 1945 did the Red Army finally march through the ruins of the city.

Anxious to establish hegemony in the Balkans, the Russians advanced much more rapidly in the south. On August 23, Rumania surrendered; two weeks later, Bulgaria. In October the Russians joined with the procommunist Yugoslav partisans of Marshal Josef Tito in liberating Belgrade. In the same month Hungary surrendered, although the tenacious Germans managed to hold Budapest until February 1945. By early 1945, most of Eastern Europe was under firm Soviet control, and the diplomatic problems of total victory were beginning to become as clear as the advantages.

No Allied statesman was more concerned than Churchill. The British prime minister especially hoped to maintain some influence for the London Poles, and he was determined to establish English dominance in Greece, thus securing the eastern Mediterranean. He was, however, enough of a realist to understand that the Soviet Union would not abandon territory for which it had spent so many lives. Meeting in Moscow with Stalin in October 1944, the British leader proposed an understanding on Eastern Europe: Russia would have predominance in Rumania and Bulgaria, Great Britain in Greece; there would be a 50–50 division of influence in Yugoslavia and Hungary. Stalin quickly agreed. A few months later, the Russian dictator made no protest when the British suppressed procommunist forces in Greece.

The Polish question was not so easily settled. The London Poles demanded the virtual restoration of their 1939 eastern frontiers, refused to be mollified by the offer of substantial German territory, and held out for a dominant voice in any postwar government. Such hopeless demands only undercut Churchill's efforts at a decent compromise, and Stalin contemptuously disregarded the exiles. The most difficult of all the Eastern European issues continued to be a subject for postponement.

The United States refused to associate itself in any way with the Churchill-Stalin agreement. To American policy makers, the sphere-of-inflence concept contradicted the ideals for which the war was being fought, and to Roosevelt himself it was political dynamite. The President respected the power of Eastern European voting blocs, and he had committed the United States to a war waged for the idealistic values of the Atlantic Charter and the Four Freedoms. Publicly, he could not agree to any division of Eastern Europe; privately, he apparently felt Soviet domination of the region was inevitable and sought only a façade which would make the prospect tolerable to U.S. idealists. His central goal remained preservation of the Big Three alliance, and if he would not openly recognize a Russian sphere of influence, neither would he risk a diplomatic break with Stalin. He faced a profound and insoluble dilemma: his internal roles as inspirational war leader and chief of the Democratic party conflicted with his self-assigned external role as the balance wheel of the antifascist alliance. Unable to resolve the dilemma, the President resorted to personal diplomacy and calculated ambiguity.

From February 4–11, 1945, the Big Three leaders met at Yalta in the Soviet Crimea to lay plans for the final defeat of the Axis and the organization of the postwar world. Roosevelt faced the personal task of reconciling his conflicting roles and facilitating American military victory. In Europe, American forces had just resumed their advance into Germany after the Battle of the Bulge. In the Pacific, U.S. troops were still advancing upon Manila, and the fight for Iwo Jima was about to begin. To the military planners the atomic bomb was but the dream of theorists, and the war against Japan was expected to last through most of 1946. Therefore, one of the President's most important objectives was to cement Soviet cooperation in the Pacific war. Here as elsewhere he placed a quick military victory above political considerations. Stalin's price for fighting Japan was high: the return of territories lost in the Russo-Japanese War of 1904–5 (Southern Sakhalin and the Kurile Islands), preservation of the autonomy of Outer Mongolia, and extensive rights in Manchuria including control of the important railways, dominance in the commercial port of Darien, and the establishment of Port Arthur as a Russian naval base. Here as in so many instances Stalin was reverting to the imperial ambitions of the czars. In a secret agreement, more at the expense of China than Japan, Roosevelt acquiesced; in August, after weeks of bargaining, Chiang Kai-shek's government, pleased at least to have Russian recognition, accepted a Sino-Soviet treaty embodying the accord.

The conference also discussed a new international organization, the outlines for which had been drawn up at the Dumbarton Oaks meeting, August–October 1944. The USSR, sensitive to the numerical superiority of the nations amenable to U.S. or British influence, insisted upon full membership and voting rights in the body's General Assembly for each of the sixteen Soviet republics. Churchill and Roosevelt persuaded Stalin to settle for three votes—for the USSR as a whole and for the Ukraine and White Russia. With apparent magnanimity, the Soviet ruler even agreed to support membership for two American states. (The United States never attempted to gain the additional votes.) After considerable debate, Stalin, who had wanted an absolute veto, accepted the principle of free discussion in the organization's Security Council; all agreed that the great powers should be able to veto substantive decisions. These questions resolved, the Big Three called for a conference at San Francisco near the end of April to establish the international body.

The embryonic United Nations preempted much of the time and attention of the Yalta Conference. It had become a symbol of U.S. idealism, and many Americans regarded it as a panacea which would prevent new wars. Roosevelt seems to have hoped that at some future date the new world council could function with strength and effectiveness, but he knew that for the years immediately ahead international peace would depend upon Big Three unity. Thus, in the short run, Soviet adherence to the UN organization was vitally important as a symbol of the continuing Grand Alliance. The American eagerness to secure Russian cooperation enhanced Stalin's already substantial bargaining power. By placing so much hope in a postwar UN, Roosevelt was engaging in yet another form of postponement.

As at Teheran, the Big Three agreed in principle upon the dismemberment of Germany but could not resolve differences in detail. They ratified plans for supposedly temporary zones of occupation and for an Allied military government, but not for a permanent settlement. The question of reparations was even more difficult. A few months before, Roosevelt had been receptive to a plan, proposed by Secretary of the Treasury Henry Morgenthau, for the destruction of German industrial capacity. When news of the idea leaked to the public, however, the reaction was strongly negative. In addition, economists warned that the Morgenthau plan would plunge Europe into chaos and force the United States to support the German people. By the time of Yalta, the President was wary of any excessive economic drain upon Germany. The Russians, while also cool to the Morgenthau Plan, demanded huge reparations. The Allies could agree only upon the establishment of a commission to investigate the problem and arrive at a final sum.

The most difficult matter of all was Eastern Europe, especially Poland, where the Russian army—and the Lublin government—had established mastery despite the protests of the British and the London Poles. Stalin made it clear that the USSR had a vital interest in the erection of a "friendly" Polish regime, that hence there was little room for compromise. The Big Three reached a vague agreement to reorganize the Polish government and hold free elections, but its lack of specifics would permit the Russians to do about what they wanted. There was little debate about redrawing the country's eastern boundary along the lines of the 1939 partition, which had after all been the frontier originally set by the Versailles conference in 1919. Historically and culturally, the Russian claim to what had been eastern Poland was strong. The new western boundary provoked more controversy. The Soviet Union proposed to give Poland large chunks of German territory all the way to the Oder and Neisse rivers. Neither Roosevelt nor Churchill was prepared to endorse such a large cession, and there was no final decision. Nevertheless, Soviet occupiers would in fact expel Germans from this region and turn it over to Poland. One result was the creation of a built-in conflict between Germany and Poland, making the Poles dependent upon the USSR. In all, Soviet statecraft scored a substantial triumph.

For the rest of the Continent, the conference promulgated a Declaration on Liberated Europe. The document pledged the establishment of order, the formation of representative interim governments, and the holding of free elections in the liberated nations. Any actions taken under it, however, depended upon the unanimous consent of the Big Three, and the declaration created no machinery for the execution of its professed goals. In effect, the Declaration on Liberated Europe was a device to conceal the Big Three's failure to reach concrete agreements on Eastern

Europe, a mask of idealism behind which lay the realities of power in the emerging postwar world. As on so many other occasions, the Allies chose postponement and ambiguity as the alternative to open disunity.

In later years, Roosevelt's political opponents would depict Yalta as a callous sellout of China and Eastern Europe, although they never would be very successful in explaining how the President might have protected these areas. It is fairer and more accurate to consider Yalta the last gasp of a diplomatic alliance that had almost, but not quite, outlived its usefulness. Roosevelt's mistakes were not in the agreements he made, all of them much in line with the broad interests of the United States, but in his failure to achieve a definite understanding with Stalin and in the attitudes he continued to encourage after Yalta. The American public received a picture of the meeting as a triumph of Allied unity, the basis for a new era of peace resting upon the accord of the Big Three and the rule of law through the United Nations. Roosevelt himself, perpetual optimist that he was, apparently believed that he had established the personal relationship with Stalin necessary to resolve the difficulties that lay ahead.

The Yalta agreements soon began to unravel. The secret deal to give the USSR three votes in the world organization became public and embarrassed the administration. More importantly, the reorganization of the Polish government stalled completely, and the Russians delayed the elections they had promised. Soviet authorities ruthlessly suppressed the Polish underground. Roosevelt, who may have genuinely hoped to salvage some independence for Poland, joined Churchill in vigorous but unavailing protests. On April 6, the London Poles announced that the USSR had arrested several partisan leaders after inviting them to Moscow for a conference. The Russians, for their part, interpreted negotiations underway for a German surrender in Italy as a prelude to a separate peace between Germany and the West. On April 3, an indignant Stalin cabled Roosevelt: "At the present moment the Germans on the Western Front in fact have ceased to wage war against England and the United States. At the same time, the Germans continue the war with Russia." The next day, the President replied: "Frankly, I cannot avoid a feeling of bitter resentment toward your informers . . . for such vile misrepresentations."

By then, Roosevelt was giving some thought to economic pressures as a means of making the USSR more cooperative. He stalled Russian requests to negotiate a loan and decided to place Soviet Lend-Lease on an ad hoc basis rather than negotiate the standard fixed annual commitment. But he seems never to have wavered in his belief that the alliance could be held together. In a cable to Churchill on April 11, he remarked that problems with the Soviet Union arose almost every day; most of them had a way of straightening out. Roosevelt had seen the nation through its worst economic depression and through the most terrible war of human history. He felt that he understood Stalin and could make the compromises necessary to win the peace on a day-to-day, problem-to-problem basis. However, he was very ill; for more than a year, he had been under the care of a heart specialist. The long journey to Yalta imposed a strain from which he never fully recovered. In the weeks after his return to the United States, he was unable to regain his old energy. His physical appearance frequently betrayed exhaustion, and even his fabulous oratorical powers waned. On April 12, 1945, during a working vacation at Warm Springs, Georgia, Roosevelt died of a cerebral hemorrhage, leaving to his successor only a legacy of goodwill and diplomatic improvisation with which to face the problems of peace.

It is easier to criticize Roosevelt's diplomacy than to suggest viable alternatives. At no time did the President possess the military power to compel Russian adherence to the Atlantic Charter. A cutoff of economic and military aid to the Soviet Union might well have left the Germans with the ability to inflict hundreds of thousands of additional casualties upon the Western democracies, a prospect intolerable to Roosevelt, Churchill, and the nations they led. Stalin might have been receptive to a frank agreement on spheres of influence, such as the limited one he negotiated with Churchill, but the popular idealism behind the Western war effort made such accords morally impossible and politically untenable— most probably in England as well as the United States. Any division of the map with Stalin would have needed to be strictly secret and informal with all the fragility that such conditions imply. Roosevelt thus was caught in a situation which permitted neither the fulfillment of the millennial expectations he had helped arouse nor the creation of a concert of power openly based upon realpolitik. The President in fact had little more than his personal charm and powers of persuasion with which to create Big Three unity. If he were naive, it was less in using these methods than in assuming in common with most Americans that Big Three unity was possible and that the war could usher in a period of lasting peace.

Americans, so prone to anticipate a new era, would soon discover that the apparent total success of the war brought only another round of international crises. Total war had delivered neither total peace nor total security, and the nation was unprepared for a halfway victory. Even during the worst days of the cold war which followed, the country was much safer (at least in conventional terms) than, say, in mid-1940 after the fall of France. Most Americans, however, rejected such relative modes of thought, and many made Roosevelt a scapegoat for the failure to achieve the millennium which he had indeed encouraged them to expect.

Yet the President, whatever his rhetorical excesses, whatever his shortcomings as a diplomat, had only met the demands of a political culture which required the promise of utopia as the price of waging war and sought to impose its values on the rest of the world, even on the totalitarian ally whose contributions represented the margin of victory. Roosevelt's concept of foreign relations was more sophisticated than that of most of his countrymen; but faced with the imperatives of managing and winning a war, he had no opportunity to reeducate them. He himself was torn between America's universalistic idealism and a more realistic understanding of world politics. Functioning within the limitations the American tradition imposed upon him, he managed to engineer the defeat of Hitlerism and Japanese militarism. However, he could not create the brave new world—the escape from history—for which America hoped. This failure, if such it can be called, was less a demonstration of personal naiveté than of the inadequacy of the American approach to war and diplomacy.

FOUR

Organizing for Victory

1941–45

1941

JUNE Fair Employment Practices Committee established

1942

JANUARY War Production Board established

FEBRUARY Civilian auto production ended; internment of Japanese-Americans ordered

JULY National War Labor Board adopts the "Little Steel formula"

AUGUST "Manhattan Engineering District" established

OCTOBER Office of Economic Stabilization created

NOVEMBER Republicans make heavy gains in congressional elections

DECEMBER War Food Administration established

1943

APRIL President Roosevelt orders Office of Price Administration to "hold the line" against inflation; intermittent coal strikes begin; WPA abolished

MAY Office of War Mobilization established

JUNE Smith-Connally Act; Detroit race riot; Jones-Wallace dispute

JULY CIO Political Action Committee established

1944

JANUARY   President Roosevelt advocates an Economic Bill of Rights

JUNE   GI Bill of Rights

NOVEMBER   Roosevelt and Truman defeat Dewey and Bricker

1945

JANUARY   Roosevelt dismisses Jesse Jones as secretary of commerce, names Henry Wallace as his successor

APRIL   FDR dies at Warm Springs, Georgia

Dr. New Deal was retired for the duration, declared President Roosevelt; the old practitioner had been replaced by Dr. Win-the-War. The remark was not an entirely accurate description of wartime life and politics, but it conveyed the manner in which total war was forcing a near-total organization of American society. Twentieth-century global war with its dependence upon technology and its voracious supply requirements placed demands upon all Americans and compelled the mobilization of the civilian population. In the United States the pattern of organization was multidimensional and riddled with surface contradictions: in some respects, it reinforced the status quo, in others, it promoted important social-economic reforms; it entailed repression of some groups, concessions to others; it both submerged and enhanced the New Deal tradition. Underneath all the conflicting tendencies there might exist the purpose of bringing America behind the war, but organization could not be turned off once the conflict ended. It imposed great strains upon the nation, but it also opened new vistas. It brought America out of the tight, constricted world of the depression into the contemporary era.

THE ORGANIZED SOCIETY

Children collected scrap paper in return for play military insignia and saved their pennies to buy $25 war bonds at school. Adults turned in old overshoes and hot-water bottles to rubber-salvage drives and saved used tin cans for scrap-metal collections. Familes dug up their back yards and planted victory gardens. Housewives, constantly reminded that a pound of kitchen fats contained enough glycerin for fifty 30-caliber bullets, turned in jars of fat to their local butcher in exchange for extra meat ration points. Millions of women rolled bandages for the Red Cross or served as nurses' aides. Twelve million people volunteered for civil defense work. In some small way, almost every American was a part of the war effort.

A prime imperative of organization, however, was to pick those who would actually have to do the fighting. With selective service already in operation, it was necessary only to legislate "duration" terms for draftees and establish tight deferment rules. The administration of the draft by 6,500 local boards across the country inevitably led to some differences in criteria, but the demands of the military were so great and the escape hatches so few that inequities were minimal. A man between the ages of eighteen and thirty-eight could anticipate induction unless he possessed a serious mental or physical disability, was a vital agricultural laborer, a defense-plant worker, or a father. Until the practice was terminated in December 1942, many boards found themselves forced to go beyond the age of thirty-eight. By 1943, pre-Pearl Harbor fathers were being called up. Even many technicians and government officials who would have been more valuable in civilian life got induction notices. Over a four-year period, the draft sucked in almost 10 million men; 5 million others volunteered.

It was almost equally important to mobilize labor for the factories which were producing war matériel not only for the American military forces but for the Allies as well. In 1942 the President established a War Manpower Commission (WMC), headed by the former governor of Indiana, Paul McNutt. The WMC attempted to channel workers into defense industries, but its authority was limited. It performed a useful function by surveying the labor market and pinpointing shortages. In January 1944 Roosevelt proposed a national service act which would have authorized the compulsory assignment of workers to defense industries. That December, as American troops retreated before the Nazi offensive in the Ardennes forest, the "labor draft" passed the House of Representatives. Fortunately, cooler heads prevailed in the Senate; at the end of January 1945, with the Allies again on the offensive, the bill was given a decent burial.

As it was, available labor naturally gravitated to the defense plants, which paid higher wages and enjoyed the raw-materials priorities which provided insurance against unemployment. (During 1942, as many civilian industries phased out, a large number of workers suffered "priorities unemployment," an experience sure to direct their job-seeking toward war industry.) The essential problem was not to redeploy the labor force but to enlarge it.

Between the spring of 1940 and the summer of 1943, 4.4 million women became salaried workers, about 3 million more than would have done so under normal peacetime conditions. Patriotically romanticized as "Rosie the Riveter," the female factory worker performed hard industrial labor despite the responsibilities of home and family, despite the prevalence of salary discrimination. Although women were disproportionately hard-hit by the layoffs that accompanied the end of the war, about two-thirds of them either held on to their jobs or found new ones. The net gain in working women during the years 1940–45 was almost as great as during the period 1900–1940.

Industry drew on other groups previously excluded from full participation in the economy. Weak enforcement of child-labor laws allowed about 3 million young people, many of them high school dropouts, to find employment. A million retirees went back to work. A Maine shipyard with a contract for wooden minesweepers actively recruited elderly artisans with long-forgotten skills. Negroes and other minorities moved into jobs that previously had been untouchable. The handicapped often did important work—some aircraft plants used blind employees to sort out usable rivets from floor sweepings. Workers of all sorts gravitated to the defense factories, and they frequently worked a 50- to 60-hour week. Mass unemployment became simply a bad memory (or future nightmare). In 1940, with the depression just beginning to ebb, the average national unemployment rate had been 14.6 percent; by 1944, it was 1.2 percent.

Intellectuals turned their talents toward the war. Scholars prepared analyses of all sorts for government bureaus. Writers and artists worked with such agencies as the Office of War Information (OWI) to maximize popular support for the conflict. Universities, which had lost practically their entire male enrollment, combined patriotism with economic necessity by undertaking educational training programs for the armed forces. The most spectacular example of intellectual mobilization was provided by the Office of Scientific Research and Development (OSRD). Headed by the eminent physicist Vannevar Bush, the OSRD recruited scientists for a wide variety of projects. Some of the OSRD developments, including the bazooka and the proximity fuse, were strictly military in application, but many others, including antibiotic research, blood plasma, radar, and DDT, had important postwar civilian uses.

In mid-1942, the Army Corps of Engineers in cooperation with the OSRD created the phantom Manhattan Engineering District, which served as a cover for atomic research. During the next three years, the Congress appropriated $2 billion for the mysterious Manhattan project without ever knowing the nature of its work. In massive facilities at Oak Ridge, Tennessee, Hanford, Washington, and Los Alamos, New Mexico, Allied scientists, many of them refugees from fascism, worked to beat the Nazis in developing the weapon that surely would win the war.

Industry in the meantime completed the conversion to a war basis. On February 10, 1942, the last new civilian automobile for the duration rolled off a Ford assembly line. The cutoff of car production was only the most dramatic example of the abandonment of business as usual. Most electrical appliances fell under a similar ban, and the government imposed strict limits on the manufacture of almost any civilian product that required essential materials—even the razor-blade companies were limited to 1940 production levels. For many small businesses, conversion to war needs was a necessity of survival. A firm that had turned out floor waxers bored gear housings for antitank guns; another concern switched from orange-juice squeezers to bullet molds. Those companies that played the game well prospered as never before; one small producer of auto springs and bumpers increased its profits manyfold by becoming a prime contractor for armor plating. Grumman Aircraft, which had done a relatively modest $19 million worth of business in 1940, increased its gross to $390 million by 1943.

The war did more than promote the rise of well-managed new corporations; its demands upon science, technology, and industry created new institutional arrangements. The increasing complexity of weapons made a large, highly trained professional military force necessary even in peacetime, dictated constant research and development carried out by a large permanent defense industry, and required men who could move with ease between the executive suites of the corporations and the world of the professional soldier. In brief, the war simply through the logic of its own needs was bringing forth the set of relationships that a later generation would call the military-industrial complex.

The government stimulated defense industry with low-interest loans; gave extremely generous tax credits for plant expansion; and in some cases built new facilities, handing them over to business at low rentals with options to buy at bargain prices. Such policies mitigated the superficially stiff excess-profits tax; moreover, after the war, industries would be allowed to reclaim as much of their excess-profits-tax payments as necessary to cover reconversion losses—a policy that did much to assure a postwar economic boom. The standard defense contract guaranteed payment on the basis of actual cost plus a fixed percentage profit. At its best, the cost-plus system freed management from the specter of bankruptcy and underwrote the production of good items in the largest possible amounts with the smallest possible delay. At its worst, it encouraged a disregard for quality control and turned out matériel that was a menace to the troops who used it.

The shipbuilder Henry J. Kaiser exemplified both the advantages and shortcomings of cost-plus. He employed an expensive and influential Washington lobbyist to get a federal loan, violated priority orders to obtain steel, paid extravagant wages to untrained workers, and by 1943 was launching one Liberty-class merchant ship every twelve days. (Government designers originally had assumed construction periods of six months per ship.) Barely seaworthy, the vessels were an outrage to conventional maritime standards, but, given the submarine crisis of 1942–43, the Allied need was quantity, whatever the cost. Kaiser produced the ships and became a popular hero.

The vast shift to war production was not smooth. Companies might convert and secure defense contracts only to find that they could not get materials. Steel, aluminum, and other essential metals were extremely scarce. Rubber was in such short supply that the government rationed gasoline mainly to prevent people from wearing out their automobile tires. The railroads faced a serious shortage of freight cars. A depression psychology had led most basic industries to resist expansion until the war boom was well underway, and by 1941 such growth requirements as the construction of new steel and aluminum plants, the creation of a synthetic rubber industry, or the building of large numbers of freight cars posed difficult problems, for it was necessary to balance off these long-range needs against the short-run demands of the Allied armed forces.

Before Pearl Harbor, the Supply, Priorities and Allocations Board (SPAB) had attempted to channel available resources into the optimum mix of defense-related industries, but the SPAB had enjoyed only indifferent success. In January 1942 Roosevelt created a new War Production Board (WPB) under Donald Nelson, a Sears, Roebuck official who had been executive director of the SPAB. The WPB fell short of being a superagency with power over the entire war effort; its authority did not extend to manpower, labor relations, prices, agricultural production, transportation, petroleum, or rubber. Nevertheless, it did have extensive power to establish priorities, allocate supplies, fix production quotas, and establish manufacturing schedules. As it developed, the WPB was no more capable than its predecessor of rationalizing the industrial war effort. Staffed heavily by corporation executives who accepted token federal stipends of a dollar a year while retaining their regular salaries, the board was unable to discipline big business and drew heavy criticism for ignoring most of the small firms that sought defense contracts. By the fall, the priorities-allocation system was a shambles; shortages and bottlenecks threatened to strangle defense production.

In October 1942 Roosevelt named Supreme Court Justice James F. Byrnes to the newly created post of director of the Office of Economic Stabilization (OES) with jurisdiction over the WPB and all other special war agencies. A South Carolina moderate who had been a influential senator, a skilled mediator, a talented administrator, Byrnes had the confidence of both President and Congress and the prestige of an office in the White House itself. He quickly forced the adoption of a new priorities-allocations method, the Controlled Materials Plan (CMP), devised by the prominent financier Ferdinand Eberstadt. The CMP fell short of perfection, but it did much to establish industrial order. War production in 1943 was twice that of 1942.

Increasingly preoccupied with price-wage disputes, Byrnes persuaded Roosevelt in May 1943 to convert the OES to an agency primarily concerned with such matters and to appoint Fred M. Vinson, a widely respected federal judge and former congressman, to head it. Byrnes himself became director of another new agency, the Office of War Mobilization (OWM),* from which he could resume his original mission of overseeing the entire domestic war effort. Popularly and accurately styled an "assistant president" in charge of the home front, Byrnes was eminently successful in coordinating the bureaucratic melange over which he assumed jurisdiction. With America's industrial superiority solidly established, military victory was almost inevitable.

WORKERS, FARMERS, INFLATION

The war put an end to hard times. With labor—almost any sort of labor—in great demand, men and women swarmed from the farms and small towns to the shipyards and factories of the coasts and the industrial Midwest. The population of California, 6.9 million in 1940, increased by 2 million during the war years. In the same period Mobile County, Alabama, grew by 64.7 percent; the Hampton Roads, Virginia, area by 44.7 percent; the Charleston, South Carolina, area by 38.1 percent; the Portland-Vancouver area of Oregon and Washington by 31.8 percent; and the Puget Sound, Washington, area by 20 percent. The Detroit—Willow Run area of Michigan experienced an influx of 200,000 people. The atmosphere in such locations was reminiscent of a frontier boom town. Workers might eat in expensive restaurants or splurge on "the works" at the barber shop (or the beauty parlor), then go home to a shabby trailer, a shack

---

* In early 1945 the agency became the Office of War Mobilization and Reconversion (OWMR). Under Byrnes's successors, Fred Vinson and John W. Snyder, it played an important role in the conversion of the economy to a peacetime basis.

reminiscent of the depression Hoovervilles, or a bed rented for an eight-hour shift. An elderly resident of San Diego, marveling at the cafés, theaters, and dance halls which stayed open 24 hours a day, compared the scene to the Klondike in 1898. Deprived of such essentials as decent housing or red meat by shortages, war workers spent their paychecks on the few small luxuries available.

Even some of the most basic needs went unmet. Local real-estate interests and the priorities system discouraged decent government-built housing; during the war, the federal government built 832,000 units, most of them shoddy and temporary, and private companies constructed another million, but the effort left at least 2 million people scrounging for almost any kind of shelter. School systems were overwhelmed by large numbers of new pupils. Day-care facilities for small children of war workers and recreational programs for older ones were rare; juvenile delinquency rose alarmingly. The Lanham Act, which was supposed to provide assistance for housing and community facilities, was inadequately funded and weakly administered. The American worker had more money in his pockets than ever before, but to a remarkable extent the feverish prosperity of the war either perpetuated old problems or replaced them with new ones.

During 1942, sharply rising prices jeopardized such economic gains as the average laborer had achieved. Moreover, the vast streams of new workers pouring into the defense plants presented dangers as well as opportunities for the industrial unions which had emerged during the depression and were by no means generally accepted as a permanent fixture of the American economy. Immediately after Pearl Harbor, Roosevelt obtained a no-strike pledge from the major labor leaders, but it was apparent to all that promises, no matter how well intentioned, might not be able to stand up under the pressure of the real problems that labor faced. The National Defense Mediation Board, established in March 1941 to settle major labor disputes, had enjoyed little success. Roosevelt replaced it with a National War Labor Board (NWLB), a tripartite body representing labor, management, and "the public"; the NWLB was actually similar in composition to its discredited predecessor, but the coming of war gave it greater legal and moral authority. It assumed the jurisdiction over collective bargaining which in normal times would have been exercised by the secretary of labor and the National Labor Relations Board.

The NWLB met the problem of whether or not new workers would be unionized by establishing a "maintenance of membership" policy, a compromise between management's insistence upon an open shop (union membership strictly voluntary) and labor's demand for a union shop (membership required after a probationary period on the job). Maintenance of membership required union members to retain their status for the duration of the war and allowed new workers to join if they wished; in many plants, the NWLB authorized the deduction of dues from payroll checks. In practice, the new policy benefited labor. It recognized the unions, assured them a stable constituency, and gave them a license to augment their ranks. In 1940, American unions had 8.75 million members; by 1945, the number was 14.32 million. The war institutionalized one of the most fundamental New Deal reforms.

The National War Labor Board temporarily met the problem of rising prices in mid-1942 by authorizing 15 percent wage increases for workers, first in Little Steel, then in other major industries. Thereafter, government stabilization policy prohibited further wage increases, although the NWLB did allow the extension of certain fringe benefits and approved piece-rate salary schedules for a few plants. The administration determination to hold the line on wages made a strong price-control program absolutely necessary.

As it was, federal wage policy caused some hardship and even more discontent. Working time lost because of strikes was extremely small—an estimated 1/9 of 1 percent—but during 1943 an atmosphere of crisis hung over the labor front with one relatively brief work stoppage after another—rubber, plastics, railroads, coal—requiring presidential intervention and back-to-work orders. The coal miners, who had not had a raise since 1941, were caught in a genuinely serious food-price squeeze; led by the pugnacious John L. Lewis, they struck intermittently through the summer and fall of 1943. At one point, with some steel plants forced to shut down for lack of fuel, Roosevelt even authorized the Selective Service System to draft striking miners between the ages of thirty-eight and forty-five. The final settlement included the Little Steel formula for hourly wages plus substantial fringe benefits; a new method of computing work time gave the average miner a much larger paycheck.

Work stoppages may have done little harm to the war effort, but they seriously damaged labor's standing with the public. In mid-1943, a coalition of Republicans and southern Democrats secured congressional passage of the War Labor Disputes Act, sponsored by Representative Howard Smith of Virginia and Senator Tom Connally of Texas. The Smith-Connally Act mandated a thirty-day "cooling-off period" and a secret election before a union could strike against a defense industry; it contained mechanisms for presidential seizure of a struck plant and gave the Chief Executive authority to order the workers back on the job; it provided criminal penalties for the advocacy of illegal work stoppages. Another provision, which revealed the strong antiunion sentiments of its sponsors, prohibited labor-union contributions to political campaigns. The bill contained little workable authority that Roosevelt did not already have, and it attempted to cripple his most durable source of political support—the labor movement. The President vetoed the legislation, but Congress quickly overrode his disapproval. The episode was largely symbolic in importance; the Smith-Connally Act would hamper labor neither economically nor politically.

The war brought the same combination of organization and a somewhat unsatisfactory prosperity to the farms as to other segments of American society. The conflict created a demand for every ounce of food and fiber available. With shortages beginning to appear critical in December 1942, President Roosevelt established a War Food Administration (WFA), which was headed for most of the war by Federal Judge Marvin Jones of Texas, a popular former chairman of the House Agriculture Committee. The WFA set production goals, granted subsidies to encourage important crops, and served as an advocate of the farmer's manpower and equipment needs; but its authority was limited by the counterclaims of other civilian agencies and the military. Nevertheless, agricultural production increased by almost 14 percent and did so with rural population declining at a rate of 900,000 a year. As production shot toward the top of the economic chart, prices rose apace; the average parity ratio, only 81 in 1940, reached a high of 113 in 1943. Yet the new prosperity, the greatest since 1919, only increased the alienation between Roosevelt and rural America.

Farmers faced serious practical difficulties. Between the draft and the lure of defense plants, labor was scarce, even with the generous deferment policies for agricultural workers. New equipment was almost impossible to find, and spare parts were difficult to obtain. Secretary of Agriculture Claude Wickard, visiting the family farm in Indiana, found his fences in disarray and his machinery standing idle for want of repair. Tens of thousands of other farmers encountered similar frustrations even as the government was constantly exhorting them to expand production.

The issue that angered farmers more than any other was the government price-stabilization effort. Farm spokesmen asserted that their constituents were as entitled to cost-plus as industry or that the Little Steel formula should be applied to crop prices. The administration, however, increasingly dependent upon labor support and dominated by urban economic viewpoints, considered farm prices to be a prime cause of inflation; in 1941 Roosevelt actually hoped to hold the price level below 100 percent of parity. The powerful farm bloc in Congress forced through legislation providing for ceilings only after prices had hit 110 percent. Most farm leaders, however, were well aware that unrestrained prices would surge far above 110 percent and were convinced that the parity formula failed to allow for the higher cost of farm labor; as for federal subsidies given in lieu of higher prices, they involved a degree of government supervision which the president of the National Grange denounced as "socialism." More prone to feel ill treated than prosperous, resentful of price controls after two decades of depression, the American farmer during World War II became progressively estranged from an administration that had saved him from disaster a few years before.

In many ways the pressures of inflation created more difficult problems for Roosevelt than had the worst days of the depression. People who had experienced years of hardship wanted freedom to enjoy the fruits of prosperity. During the mid-1930s, the New Deal could command wide support by distributing favors to virtually all groups that pressed their needs upon the government. The war administration, on the other hand, faced an almost precisely opposite task, that of holding back civilian claims while channeling men, money, and resources into the military effort; it attempted to do the job by using New Deal-style big-government techniques and consequently identified the New Deal with many of the home-front irritations which accompanied total war.

Economic stabilization was absolutely necessary if the war was to be prosecuted successfully. A runaway inflation would ultimately demoralize most of the civilian population, destroy wage controls, and throw the economy into chaos. Since facilities and materials were insufficient for the production of enough consumer goods to meet demand levels, the government had to resort to methods that would cause almost everyone to feel pinched by federal policy. One technique, the soundest and surest as a matter of economic principle, would have been to pay for the war through a combination of high taxes and compulsory individual investment in government war bonds, but such draconian policies could muster little political support, even among the fiscal conservatives in Congress.

Income taxes were increased steeply, and payroll withholding was introduced to facilitate collection and cut purchasing power. Corporate levies on both ordinary profits and "excess profits" were also pushed up. Special federal excise taxes were placed on many items considered nonessential. Nevertheless, tax revenues paid for only about 40 percent of the cost of the war. In January 1943 Roosevelt requested increases amounting to $16 billion a year; after a delay of thirteen months, Congress voted a $2.2 billion hike. When the President sharply vetoed the bill, Senator Alben Barkley of Kentucky, usually a loyal administration man, resigned his post as Senate majority leader in protest; an angry Congress quickly overrode the veto, and the Senate Democrats unanimously reelected Barkley as their chief. Roosevelt capitulated as gracefully as possible.

Voluntary war-bond purchases were heavy but could not take up the considerable slack left by the inadequate tax program.

The failure to achieve a tax-savings policy that could abate inflationary pressures left only the devices of price control and rationing. The Office of Price Administration (OPA) had been established in 1941, but its limited mandate made strong price controls impossible. The consumer price index, which had averaged 59.9 in 1940, was up to 69.7 in 1942 and 74.0 in 1943. Until the fall of 1942, the OPA could not touch farm prices and had only uncertain jurisdiction over others. That September, Roosevelt demanded strong price-stabilization powers from Congress and threatened to act under his authority as Commander in Chief if legislation were not forthcoming. Grudgingly, Congress gave him the power he wanted.

Subsequently, the price-stabilization effort tightened up considerably. Byrnes, then Vinson, in the OES gave the OPA strong support. At the end of 1942, in an attempt to placate Congress, Roosevelt replaced the OPA's first director, Leon Henderson, a blunt New Deal economist, with Prentiss Brown, a former senator from Michigan. In April 1943 Roosevelt directed Byrnes and Brown to "hold the line" at all costs; when Brown proved too amenable to congressional pleas for exemptions, Roosevelt dismissed him that September in favor of Chester Bowles, a liberal-minded New York advertising executive. Bowles undertook a successful public-relations campaign which identified price controls with patriotism and won him a large following among labor and consumers. From the hold-the-line order until the end of the war, prices advanced only 3.2 percent.

Rationing reinforced price controls and provided a reasonably fair method of distributing the inadequate civilian goods available. The OPA set up local ration boards in every county in the United States and distributed books of ration coupons to every man, woman, and child in the country. The ration allotments involved no drastic reduction in the American standard of living (the average Englishman had only about two-thirds of the American ration), but, especially in regions that had experienced heavy industrial growth, ration books frequently were mere hunting licenses for commodities that could not be found. A flourishing black market developed in beef and poultry as well as luxury items such as liquor; the OPA handed out warnings to approximately 20 percent of all the businesses in the nation. Yet the price-control effort worked fairly well; a Gallup poll found only 25 percent of its respondents willing to condone even occasional black-market patronage. The shortages that developed—in meat, sugar, coffee, butter, canned goods, shoes, fuel—were usually temporary and a relatively small price to pay for a stabilization that was the prerequisite of victory.

The OPA won a measure of popularity among urban consumers, but farmers and businessmen heartily disliked it. Heavily staffed by liberal economists and lawyers, it was one of the havens to which New Dealers retreated during the war. To conservatives, its complex and voluminous regulations (the wholesale beef code ran 40,000 words with minute specifications for meat cutting) and apparent delight in red tape, its reliance upon personnel who allegedly had never met a payroll, all represented a natural outgrowth of the New Deal goal of bureaucraticizing American life. The controversy over the agency provided a rough key to the nature of liberalism and conservatism in wartime America.

REPRESSION AND REVOLUTION: CIVIL LIBERTIES AND CIVIL RIGHTS

The Roosevelt administration hoped to avoid a replay of the repressive hysteria that had accompanied World War I. Attorney General Francis Biddle was a devoted believer in individual liberty; and Roosevelt himself, if more prone to see the need for exceptions, understood the need to maintain standards of freedom in wartime. Yet the organization necessary to fight the war seemed to call for something other than ordinary peacetime standards of liberty. The government had to restrict important military and diplomatic information; it had to explain the objectives of the war to the people and mobilize them behind it; it had to place restraints of some sort upon individuals who posed a threat to the war effort. Few would disagree with these general principles, and, given the pressures of total war, the administration applied them with intelligence and moderation—with one exception, an exception so glaring that it canceled out all the accomplishments, underscored the fragility of American democracy, and revealed to the world a pervasive racism that was hardly compatible with the ideals for which the war was being fought.

In December 1941 the government established the Office of Censorship, headed by Byron Price, a top Associated Press official. In June 1942 Roosevelt created the Office of War Information (OWI) to coordinate all government information programs and undertake campaigns which would explain the war at home and abroad; its head, Elmer Davis, was one of the most respected radio news commentators in the nation. Davis and Price understood and sympathized with the legitimate needs of journalists, but the military frequently made final decisions about what could be printed. During the first year of the war, the army and navy did everything possible to conceal losses; casualty lists were not released until late 1942 and photos of American war dead not cleared until 1943. As the war progressed, however, restrictions gradually were lifted; without the pressures of the civilian agencies the news blackout would have been much more complete than it was.

The OWI's Domestic Bureau used advertising campaigns, pamphlets, radio programs, and films to promote patriotic effort at home, explain the rationale for the war, and sell the Allied powers to the people. It even exercised a loose supervision over the Hollywood film studios, advising against scripts that depicted lack of unity on the home front, contained themes of racial inferiority, or slurred any Allied people or leaders. One directive urged each producer to ask himself: "Will this film help win the war?" The Overseas Bureau attempted to win support among foreigners by stressing the democratic idealism of the war.

All these activities involved little coercion. Press censorship was voluntary, and on occasion editors overrode government objections to stories that did not seem to endanger national security. The radio stations and networks were not obliged to run OWI material, although there was a relatively small danger that a particularly uncooperative station could have its federal license lifted. The movie studios were somewhat more vulnerable since the Office of Censorship could and occasionally did deny export licenses to objectionable films; the filmmakers in addition were dependent upon government priorities. In fact, however, the Domestic Bureau of OWI was so politically weak that it could barely survive the war. In mid-1943, Congress, fearing that the Domestic Bureau might become a propaganda agency for the Roosevelt administration, drastically slashed its budget; the film-supervision program was discontinued. The situation was far from that of World War I when a movie producer had been given a ten-year prison sentence for a film that depicted British soldiers as villains during the American Revolution. The government used the media extensively to organize the civilian population but managed to do so in ways compatible with the ideals for which the nation was fighting.

Nor did the administration engage in wholesale repression of individuals opposed to the war. Attorney General Biddle, using a prominent Catholic layman as an intermediary, persuaded the church hierarchy to silence the right-wing priest Father Charles Coughlin. At Roosevelt's insistence, Biddle obtained sedition indictments against twenty-six proto-fascists who had engaged in constant criticism of the war. Their trial developed into a circus with the defendants and their lawyers engaging in every conceivable means of obstruction and delay. In November 1944, with the seemingly endless proceedings hardly half completed, the judge died; when the war ended several months later, the government dropped the case. Even these prosecutions were probably unwise, but at least they were undertaken against a group that had the appearance of a fifth column. Biddle steadfastly refused to move against less virulent critics of the war.

The administration, however, destroyed what might have been a remarkable civil liberties record by evacuating 110,000 Japanese-Americans from the West Coast. Never in the history of the republic had so large a group of free citizens been systematically deprived of their fundamental liberties by the government, and never had wholesale repression been less necessary. The West Coast had a long tradition of anti-Japanese sentiment, based on race and economic rivalry. The attack on Pearl Harbor created a hysterical demand for removal, encouraged by self-seeking politicians and white farmers who wanted to take over Japanese lands. Even fundamentally decent men such as California Attorney General Earl Warren and Governor Culbert Olson took up the cry. The head of the Western Defense Command, General John DeWitt, a comic-opera figure who had shaken up California with spurious air-raid alerts, joined in the clamor and convinced his superiors that the security of the coast depended upon the removal of the Japanese. In February 1942 Roosevelt authorized the evacuation.

Forced to sell their land, shops, homes, furniture at bargain prices, the Japanese-Americans were allowed to take only what they could carry with them. For the next three years, most of the evacuees lived in miserable "relocation camps" thrown up in some of the most forbidding areas of the United States. About 34,000 agreed to resettle in the Midwest or East; 17,600 joined the army and compiled an enviable combat record. The rest remained behind barbed wire until 1945; eventually, about 90,000 returned to the West Coast. A generation later, the Japanese-Americans had not only recouped their losses, they had become one of the most prosperous and secure minority groups in the country.

Perhaps the most appalling thing about the evacuation was the failure of responsible liberal and moderate opinion to fight it. Biddle quietly opposed it, but he failed to speak out forcefully. Most Americans swallowed their doubts and accepted the decision as an act of military necessity, however regrettable; yet in fact there was no compelling evidence of military necessity. No verifiable act of sabotage was committed by Japanese-Americans. Hawaii, where their numbers were twice as large, was simply placed under martial law with no special restriction upon citizens of Japanese descent. Behind the evacuation was the clear, if unspoken, assumption that, as a matter of race, the Japanese-Americans were less trustworthy than Caucasians with ethnic ties to the Axis. Such steps were never contemplated for German- or Italian-Americans, and only a relative handful of white enemy aliens were interned. Japanese propagandists, who depicted their country's mission as the liberation of the yellow races, could observe with essential accuracy that the United States was following a wartime policy of white supremacy.

While the Japanese-Americans suffered needless and shameful oppression, the fate of the Negro was more mixed. Blacks continued to experience the humiliations of a racism to which most whites subscribed in varying degrees, but the war and the pressures of organization enhanced their bargaining power, opened up new opportunities, and ignited a revolution which could not be stopped.

The most conspicuous example of continuing discrimination was in the armed forces, which segregated Negroes into separate units and assigned them to menial tasks. At the beginning of the war, the navy accepted blacks only as stewards or messboys; the army air corps refused to train them as pilots or technicians, arguing openly that the Negro did not have the intelligence for such jobs. Military leaders were convinced that blacks lacked the courage to be successful in combat. Only a few persons argued that black failures in combat might be a result of the low morale which developed naturally from segregation and the contemptuous attitudes behind it. The navy and air force instituted some minor experimental reforms, but the overall pattern remained the same. As long as the generals insisted that integration would seriously damage the war effort, civilian leaders were not willing to challenge them—indeed, most seem to have agreed. In the military fight to preserve democracy, the Negro remained a second-class citizen.

While military necessity became the rationale for preserving the status quo in the armed services, it led to profound changes in civilian life. The manpower demands of the defense factories and the increasing political leverage of blacks within the Democratic party created a situation of upward mobility for Negro civilians. The first indication of the new state of affairs came in 1941. With Negroes experiencing widespread discrimination in defense industry, A. Philip Randolph, president of the Brotherhood of Sleeping Car Porters, and other black leaders urged the administration to establish machinery to give Negroes equal opportunity in the defense plants. When Roosevelt declined to act, they established the March on Washington Movement, which planned a mass demonstration of 50,000 Negroes in the capital. In June 1941, shortly before the march was to occur, the President acceded to the black demands and established a Fair Employment Practices Committee (FEPC) to facilitate minority job opportunities in war-related industries.

As a creation of the President rather than Congress, the FEPC had only limited authority; a determined employer could defy it with impunity. It was, however, a valuable educational agency, and the very fact that non-discrimination was official federal policy made life easier for those industries willing to hire from minority groups. The need for production alone would have opened up many new opportunities for Negroes, and the efforts of the FEPC unquestionably broadened those opportunities. The war compelled the organization of blacks into the civilian effort; the most feasible method was reform rather than repression.

But the FEPC by no means resolved Negro grievances. Most blacks were well aware that the American treatment of minorities did not square with the eloquent liberalism of the Four Freedoms; the continued practice of white supremacy in most areas of American life while the country was fighting against a master-race ideology could only arouse demands for equality. The movement of tens of thousands of Negroes into the industrial cities from the rural South created explosive new social pressures. The result was the emergence of a new militance.

Randolph expressed the new attitude when he declared in organizing the March on Washington Movement that "only power can affect the enforcement and adoption of a given policy," and "power is the active principle of only the organized masses, the masses united for a definite purpose." The National Association for the Advancement of Colored People (NAACP) increased its membership from 50,000 in 1940 to 450,000 in 1946; in the spring of 1942 one of its top officials, Roy Wilkins, remarked that no Negro leader with a constituency dared ask for unconditional support of the war. The major black newspapers were so strong in their condemnation of military segregation that commanders barred them from many installations unil the War Department stopped the practice in 1943. In 1942, a small Chicago-based organization, the Congress of Racial Equality (CORE), forecast the future of the civil rights movement by beginning a campaign of sit-ins against segregated restaurants and places of amusement.

In the military forces, racial brawls, sometimes full-scale riots, occurred frequently, although the government managed to suppress the news of most incidents. White officers who led segregated units into combat suffered unusually high casualties, perhaps not always from enemy bullets. Among civilians in the crowded cities, tensions were also high. In 1943 major race riots broke out in Mobile, Beaumont, Detroit, and Harlem, featuring all the themes that would be so familiar to a later generation: conflict between blacks and working-class whites, black accusations of police brutality, the looting and destruction of stores owned by white merchants, the large-scale involvement of teen-agers on both sides, the use of federal troops to halt the violence.

Roosevelt, fearing that he had gone as far as possible with the FEPC, concerned primarily with the prosecution of the war, rejected the urgings of advisers who wanted him to appoint a special presidential committee on civil rights, but he seems to have been prepared to push for racial reform at the end of the war. If so, he had correctly gauged the dynamism of a movement that would not shut itself off.

POLITICS IS NOT ADJOURNED

Ideally, a nation engaged in a war for its very existence closes ranks in a vast patriotic effort and submerges domestic controversy. In Great Britain the two major parties took advantage of the flexibility of parliamentary government and an unwritten constitution by forming a unity cabinet and postponing national elections until the end of the European fighting. American institutions were not so malleable. By mandating a national election campaign every other year, the Constitution encouraged partisanship. The separation of powers between the executive and legislative branches made the formation of a genuine unity government much more difficult than in England, where the party chiefs were at once the legislative leaders and the ministers of the cabinet. The war itself, although it touched the life of almost every American, was too far away to produce the desperate sense of urgency which might have overcome these constitutional barriers. The nation might achieve a certain degree of unity behind the war effort, but at bottom the American system did not permit the adjournment of politics.

The process of organization caused social disruptions which in the short run cut into the strength of the Roosevelt administration. There was no easy and popular way to manage inflation, fairly distribute scarce civilian goods, or deal with the demands of blacks who wanted democracy for themselves as well as the rest of the world. By causing a vast relocation of workers and drawing so many young men into the armed forces, the war made it difficult for many of Roosevelt's strongest supporters to vote. Roosevelt himself had to assume the role of Commander in Chief, deemphasize his identity as party leader, and forgo his depression-era appeals. Yet while the President talked about retiring Dr. New Deal, the war only submerged old issues. To many, wartime prosperity seemed abnormal and transitory, a resumption of the depression after the war probable. Given such expectations, the New Deal and the controversies connected with it could not remain far below the surface of American politics.

The logic of organizing for victory nevertheless imposed a certain specious unity and seemed to give Dr. Win-the-War the dominant position of which Roosevelt had spoken. Businessmen held more levers of power in Washington than at any time since the Hoover administration. They not only ran the War Production Board; they found key permanent niches in the Washington bureaucracy. The Wall Street banker James V. Forrestal was secretary of the navy at the end of the war; two equally prominent Wall Street figures, Robert Patterson and John J. McCloy, held important positions in the Department of War, and in September 1945 Patterson would succeed Stimson as secretary. Edward R. Stettinius, Jr., the chairman of the board of U.S. Steel, moved from the War Production Board to the Department of State, becoming secretary at the end of 1944. Most of the top business figures in wartime Washington were extremely able and some were rather liberal-minded, but their very presence demonstrated an important departure from the revivalistic antibusiness atmosphere of the New Deal at its zenith.

The congressional elections of 1942 forced the New Deal further on the defensive. An unusually low voter turnout, attributable in large part to wartime dislocations, hurt the Democrats badly. The Republicans gained 47 seats in the House (a turnover of only 5 more would have given them a majority) and 10 in the Senate. The GOP congressional delegation, with only a few exceptions, was strongly conservative. In combination, the Republicans and right-wing Democrats could easily control Congress. The coalition moved against labor with the passage of the Smith-Connally Act. It undertook an offensive against the government agencies identified with the New Deal, abolishing the Works Progress Administration and the National Youth Administration, although the latter was engaged in training young people for defense industries. The appropriation for the Farm Security Administration was so low that the FSA survived in name only and under less aggressive leadership. (In 1946 the FSA was replaced with the Farmers Home Administration, which was empowered to make loans to small farmers and rural communities but was not a rural antipoverty agency.) Conservatives blocked funds for the National Resources Planning Board, a haven for New Dealers seeking to draw blueprints for the postwar era. In 1944 Congress did pass the GI Bill of Rights, an impressive package of educational and loan benefits for returning veterans. Nevertheless, fearing that servicemen would vote heavily for the President in the fall election, it rejected efforts to set up federal standards for absentee voting by men in uniform.

More unable than ever to command majorities on domestic issues, Roosevelt sought to placate the legislative branch with a series of key appointments: Byrnes to OES, then OWM; Vinson to OES; Jones to WFA; and, briefly, Brown to OPA. All were men with friends, experience, and respect on Capitol Hill; all presumably could protect the interests of their agencies better than the President could. During his last years in office, Roosevelt was acutely aware of the need to have men who could deal with Congress, to facilitate not only the prosecution of the war but the organization of the postwar world as well.

The President also faced the problem of a badly divided party. The southern conservatives were strong in Congress because of their tacit alliance with the Republicans; in presidential elections, however, the states they represented were less important than those inhabited by the blocs that made up the urban-labor-liberal wing of the party. During the war, Vice-President Henry Wallace emerged as the leading spokesman of these reform-oriented groups. Seeking to identify the war effort with democratic idealism, he argued that the ultimate purpose of the conflict was to produce a "century of the common man" and bring about a "people's revolution." His domestic pronouncements were strongly prolabor and pro-civil rights; he was a vociferous advocate of postwar economic planning to maintain prosperity. Wallace's ideas alone would have made him anathema to conservative Democrats, but his austere personality and inability to get along with most professional politicians compounded his difficulties. He won the distrust not only of the southern conservatives but also of the northern bosses who would have swallowed his ideology.

The Democratic split came to the surface when Wallace, acting in his capacity as chairman of the Board of Economic Warfare (BEW), attacked the secretary of commerce and federal loan administrator, Jesse Jones. The BEW had been created to procure vital raw materials from foreign countries; staffed heavily with New Deal liberals, it sought to fuel the war effort with little regard for expense and frequently accepted higher costs to ensure decent living standards for the foreign workers involved in its projects. Jones, who had long held down the right wing of the Roosevelt administration and had great influence among conservative congressmen, was appalled at BEW procedures and objectives. He delayed the financing of one BEW contract after another. In mid-1943, Wallace shocked Washington by charging that Jones was undermining the war effort; Jones's countercharges were equally bitter. Roosevelt, unwilling to tolerate open bickering at a crucial point in the war, relieved both men of their economic warfare responsibilities. Privately, he seems to have agreed with Wallace, but he was also upset at his vice-president's impetuousness and thereafter convinced that Wallace's political skills were not commensurate with his responsibilities.

While the Democrats were hacking away at one another, the Republicans were dropping their 1940 campaign leader and achieving a substantial degree of unity. From his support of the Lend-Lease bill on, Wendell Willkie had become increasingly identified with the administration's handling of the war effort, even acting as FDR's representative on trips abroad, and he had taken an increasingly moderate stance toward the New Deal-type reforms. His criticisms of Roosevelt, such as they were, appeared to be delivered from a liberal perspective rather than one of

Republican conservatism; the rhetoric of his best-selling book *One World* (1943) seemed remarkably similar to that of Henry Wallace. He refused to play the role of partisan leader, and by 1944, he was alienated from the conservative Republican rank and file and most of the party leadership. He abandoned his candidacy for renomination after running a poor fourth in the Wisconsin presidential primary.

The Republican presidential nomination went to Governor Thomas E. Dewey of New York. Dewey had none of Willkie's personal charisma, but he and the people around him were superb organizers. By the standards of the day, he was a moderate Republican who attacked the New Deal while accepting its essentials and stood for American assumption of international responsibility. His nomination was a victory for the northeastern Republican establishment, but he was acceptable to the more conservative and isolationist midwestern Republicans, one of whom, Governor John W. Bricker of Ohio, served as his running mate.

There was of course no question that with the war still on Roosevelt would be the Democratic nominee. Months before the Democratic convention, the President began to address himself to two problems—the need to chart a course for postwar America and the necessity of unifying his party. In his January 1944 State of the Union message to Congress, Roosevelt advocated an "Economic Bill of Rights" which would guarantee every American the right to decent employment, housing, living standards, education, medical care, and security. The President spoke only in general terms, but he made it clear that he intended to call Dr. New Deal out of retirement once the war was over.

In a series of private meetings with party leaders, most of them representing the northern machines, the President agreed to drop Vice-President Wallace from the ticket. Wallace's successor had to be a person who could appeal to all segments of the party; this requirement at once eliminated Supreme Court Justice William O. Douglas, whom Roosevelt favored, and Office of War Mobilization director Byrnes, the choice of most southerners. Instead, the President and the party chieftains agreed upon Senator Harry S Truman of Missouri, who had won prominence by conducting highly effective and responsible investigations of defense spending, was liked in every faction of the party, and had influence in Congress. Operating with his customary indirection, Roosevelt never squarely communicated his decision to Wallace but instead sent the vice-president on a mission to China during the weeks before the convention. Returning to the United States, Wallace mounted a last-minute drive for renomination and nearly succeeded; Truman was not chosen until the third ballot. Shortly afterward, Roosevelt, in a move which exemplified both his penchant for balancing forces and his genuine fondness for Wallace, secretly offered the vice-president his choice after the election of any cabinet department other than State; Wallace chose Commerce.

In the meantime, the President had secretly explored the possibility of a party realignment with Willkie, hoping to bring the former Republican leader and his liberal following into the Democratic party and possibly oust the southern conservatives or at least reduce their power. (In Texas, right-wing forces had gained control of the party and had almost succeeded in placing independent, anti-Roosevelt electors on the Democratic ballot.) Roosevelt was almost certainly sincere; he long had sought to bring liberal independents into the Democratic party. Willkie, however, hung back from any commitments, preferring to wait until after the election and perhaps run for mayor of New York in 1945. In September he suffered the first in a series of heart attacks; on October 8, Willkie, only fifty-two years old, died, and the hope of realignment went with him.

The presidential campaign did not revolve around sharp ideological differences. Dewey denounced the New Deal for extravagance, excessive bureaucracy, and failure to solve the unemployment problem, but announced that he would preserve all its important programs. His most telling issue was the assertion that the administration was old, tired, and incapable of managing the war firmly, for such charges stirred widespread concern about the President's physical condition. Roosevelt's health was in fact quite shaky; he appeared haggard in news photos and some of his radio speeches were weak and ineffective. At least twice that summer he suffered severe chest pains, once in the midst of an important address.

As the campaign progressed, the President began to bounce back. In late September, he delivered a nationally broadcast speech which was a masterpiece of political sarcasm, ending in mock resentment at alleged Republican attacks upon his pet dog. In New York, then in Philadelphia, he rode in an open car for hours through cold, drenching rain. Speaking to a massive crowd in Chicago, he began to fill in the Economic Bill of Rights, pledging support for full employment legislation ("sixty million jobs"), a permanent FEPC, regional development authorities, and federal subsidies for housing, transportation, health facilities. Temporarily at least, he had regained his old vitality; he was still America's champion campaigner.

Roosevelt benefited enormously from a new political organization. The CIO Political Action Committee (PAC) under the leadership of Sidney Hillman brought labor into politics on a stronger basis than ever. Formed as a response to the Smith-Connally Act's ban on union *donations* to campaigns, the PAC functioned as an independent force. In many large cities, it supplanted decaying Democratic machines and did invaluable work in registering workers and low-income voters. The PAC horrified many conservatives, who depicted it as a vehicle of proletarian radicalism and exaggerated Hillman's considerable influence with Roosevelt. (The most famous charge was the assertion that Roosevelt had told party leaders who wanted Byrnes for vice-president to "clear it with Sidney" and that Hillman alone had vetoed the choice.) The PAC contributed mightily to the Roosevelt campaign, and its exhibition of power doubtless convinced the President that his revival of the New Deal had been a correct course.

On election day, Roosevelt won by a comfortable margin with 25 million votes (53.6 percent) to Dewey's 22 million (46 percent). The Democrats lost a seat in the Senate but gained 20 seats in the House. The congressional result was hardly enough to destroy the grip of the conservative coalition; Roosevelt's victory had produced no opening to the left.

The President began his fourth term by keeping his promise to Wallace. He dismissed Jesse Jones and appointed the former vice-president to replace him. The move reopened all the wounds that had been patched over during the campaign. Wallace was narrowly confirmed by the Senate only after the powerful Federal Loan Administration, subsequently placed under Fred Vinson, was separated from the Department of Commerce. Roosevelt encountered more difficulty when he tried to appoint the militant southern liberal Aubrey Williams to head the Rural Electrification Administration; the nomination was soon hopelessly stalled in the Senate.

This pattern of appointments and congressional response forecast immense difficulties for any move to the left. On the April afternoon that Roosevelt died, the revival of the New Deal faced a bleak future.

By any reasonable standard, Roosevelt had functioned effectively as a war leader. He tooled a rusty American industrial machine to full production, organized the nation to keep it going, stabilized the economy, and secured from the people the degree of sacrifice necessary to feed the war effort. Considering the fact that America was not beleaguered in the same fashion as Britain or Russia, all this was a considerable achievement. Yet the process of organization led also to a trampling of individual rights, in the case of the Japanese-Americans, unprecedented in American history. It brought forth forces that could be managed during the war but would be more difficult to contain in peacetime—the widespread demands for full employment, the attendant inflationary pressures which threatened to wreck the economy, the surging drive for racial equality. At his death Roosevelt had not developed the political means to deal with these forces—it is indeed uncertain that the American system was capable of producing them.

FIVE

The Ashes of Victory: The Cold War

CHRONOLOGY

1945–51

1945

APRIL
Battle for Okinawa begins; Harry S Truman inaugurated as Roosevelt's successor; United Nations Conference begins in San Francisco

MAY
Germany surrenders; Harry Hopkins confers with Stalin

JUNE
U.S. forces secure Okinawa

JULY
First atomic bomb exploded at Alamagordo; Potsdam Conference begins; Senate ratifies UN Charter

AUGUST
Atomic bombs dropped on Hiroshima and Nagasaki; USSR declares war on Japan; Japan surrenders; Lend-Lease terminated

SEPTEMBER
London Conference

DECEMBER
Pro-Soviet government established in northern Iran; Moscow Conference

1946

FEBRUARY
Acheson-Lilienthal report on international control of atomic energy; Kennan analysis of Soviet foreign policy

MARCH
Churchill's "Iron Curtain" speech

107

MAY	Soviet troops withdraw from northern Iran; German reparations agreement collapses
JUNE	Baruch Plan for international control of atomic energy presented to UN
SEPTEMBER	Byrnes's speech at Stuttgart; Wallace's Madison Square Garden speech and dismissal from the cabinet

1947

JANUARY	General Marshall, recalled from unsuccessful mission to China, becomes secretary of state
MARCH	Truman Doctrine proclaimed
MAY	Congress approves aid to Greece and Turkey; communist coup in Hungary
JUNE	Marshall proposes European recovery program
JULY	USSR rejects Marshall Plan
SEPTEMBER	Cominform established; General Wedemeyer recommends increased aid to Chinese Nationalists

1948

FEBRUARY	Communist coup in Czechoslovakia
APRIL	Communists lose Italian elections
JUNE	Berlin blockade begins

1949

JANUARY	Truman announces Point Four program
MAY	Berlin blockade lifted
JULY	Senate ratifies North Atlantic Treaty
AUGUST	Chinese Nationalists abandon the mainland
SEPTEMBER	USSR tests its first atomic bomb

1950

JANUARY	Truman orders development of hydrogen bomb
JUNE	Invasion of South Korea
SEPTEMBER	UN troops land at Inchon
OCTOBER	Truman-MacArthur conference
NOVEMBER	Chinese Communists enter Korean war and drive UN forces back into the South

1951

JANUARY	Communists capture Seoul
MARCH	UN retakes Seoul; MacArthur issues ultimatum to China
APRIL	Truman dismisses MacArthur
APRIL–OCTOBER	Battle lines stabilize in vicinity of the 38th parallel
JULY	Truce negotiations begin

From July 17 to August 1, 1945, the leaders of the United States, Great Britain, and the Soviet Union met at Potsdam, Germany. The code name of the gathering—TERMINAL—was appropriate; the heads of the three great powers would not face one another across the conference table again for a decade. With Nazi Germany crushed and Japan facing defeat, the need for an alliance was disappearing. War made cooperation the price of survival; peace removed old dangers and presented opportunities for expansion and aggrandizement. Victory meant power vacuums in Europe and Asia, the division of spoils, the organization of a different world order. Russia and the West, with different ideologies, economic systems, and perceptions of self-interest, could hardly maintain unity in such a situation. The job of statesmen on all sides was to keep the coming conflict limited.

BETWEEN TWO WORLDS: POTSDAM AND HIROSHIMA

The new American President, Harry S Truman, had been chosen for the vice-presidency in 1944 because of his friendships throughout his party and his influence in the Senate. His only experience overseas had been as an artillery officer in France during World War I; his interest in foreign policy was largely limited to enthusiastic support of an international organization. Roosevelt had used him as an emissary to Congress on domestic political matters and had never bothered to keep him briefed on international developments. When Truman assumed office on the evening of April 12, 1945, he faced a massive cram effort just to develop a grasp of past policy, and during his first weeks in office events occurred with bewildering rapidity. In the Pacific the Americans had secured the key island of Iwo Jima and were in a desperate struggle for Okinawa. In Europe the Allied armies were sweeping through Germany. The conference to establish the United Nations began in San Francisco on April 25. On April 30, as the Red Army fought its way into Berlin, Hitler committed suicide; on May 7, his successors signed the instrument of unconditional surrender.

Truman could not rely upon his secretary of state, for FDR had picked Edward R. Stettinius, Jr., more for his skill as a spokesman than his acumen as a diplomat. During most of his brief tenure, Stettinius was at the United Nations conference in San Francisco, and the experienced careerist Joseph Grew managed the State Department. Truman quickly decided to replace Stettinius with James F. Byrnes and made the appointment official with the conclusion of the San Francisco conference in July. At that time, federal law placed the secretary of state next in line for the Presidency; it appeared fitting that the office should go to an individual of Byrnes' accomplishments. Yet he had little more experience than Truman in diplomacy; and his skills, like the President's, were those of the domestic political wheeler-dealer rather than the diplomat. His conviction that he rather than Truman should have been Roosevelt's successor led him to act with an independence which hardly contributed to a smoothly functioning foreign policy and eventually alienated the President.

Like many Americans, Truman vaguely but firmly believed that the United States had a divinely ordained mission of world leadership, tended to personalize complex diplomatic problems, and took a moralistic-legalistic attitude toward international issues. At first, insecure in his role as a diplomatic leader, he attempted to mask his uncertainty with displays of blunt decisiveness. The most immediate problem he faced was the disrepair into which Soviet-American relations had fallen. Having been left no clear guidelines by Roosevelt, Truman followed his impulses and took a rigid view of the Yalta agreements, probably believing that he was adhering to Roosevelt's intentions. Several of his closest diplomatic advisers—Grew, Byrnes, the President's Chief of Staff Admiral William D. Leahy, Secretary of the Navy James V. Forrestal, and Ambassador to the USSR W. Averell Harriman—all favored a policy of firmness toward the Russians. Just eleven days after assuming office, Truman sternly lectured Soviet Foreign Minister Molotov on the need for a representative government in Poland. At the conclusion of the European war, he signed an order immediately halting European Lend-Lease shipments to the USSR (which was still neutral in the Pacific).

Yet, whatever his instincts, the President also had a sense of balance and restraint, and he possessed no intention of breaking up the alliance. He quickly modified the Lend-Lease order, carefully considered the ad-

vice of Joseph Davies and Harry Hopkins, both of whom urged conciliation toward the USSR, and refused to meet separately with Churchill
before Potsdam, fearing that Stalin would feel that the Atlantic democracies were "ganging up" on him. In May, alarmed by the deterioration of
Soviet-American relations, he dispatched Hopkins to meet with Stalin.
The two men worked out an agreement in which the United States accepted the Lublin government in Poland and Russia went along with the
American-supported provisions for the UN. A diplomatic victory for the
USSR, the Hopkins-Stalin talks revealed that Truman's main purpose was
the preservation of the alliance. He had attempted firmness in the belief
that it was the best way to deal with the Russians, but he was unwilling to
risk a break which might lead to Soviet withdrawal from the United
Nations or refusal to cooperate in the war against Japan. His personal
attitudes fluctuated between detestation of the communist dictatorship
and the conviction that East and West must cooperate to secure the peace.
For the time being, however, the maintenance of unity was the central
purpose which united his surface contradictions.

As the European fighting drew to a close, Americans at Okinawa
engaged in one of the most desperate battles of the war. Outnumbered
three to one, Japanese troops fought for more than two months with their
usual tenacity; only 7,000 of the 90,000 defenders were ever taken prisoner. Waves of kamikaze planes hurled themselves suicidally at the
Allied fleet offshore, sinking 21 ships and damaging 66. When enemy
resistance finally collapsed on June 21, 1945, the American forces had
suffered 45,000 casualties.

By then, Japan was experiencing the worst bomber raids of the war.
In March the Twenty-first Bomber Command, headed by General Curtis
LeMay, began a campaign of systematic incendiary raids against enemy
cities. New B-29 bombers, faster and more heavily armed than the B-17s
and B-24s which had been used in Europe, overwhelmed the weak Japanese air-defense system and inflicted devastation from one end of the
country to the other. On the evening of March 9, 334 B-29s attacked Tokyo
and set off a conflagration that destroyed 267,000 buildings, killed almost
84,000 people and wounded about half as many. By the end of September,
LeMay estimated, there would be no targets left; the Japanese nation—or
what remained of it—would be compelled to surrender.

By July, however, the Manhattan Project scientists had finally readied
an atomic bomb for testing. Near Alamogordo, New Mexico, in an
isolated area of the desert called Jornada del Muerte (Journey of Death),
technicians suspended the new weapon from a hundred-foot tower. Just
before dawn on July 16, J. Robert Oppenheimer and the other scientists
who had devoted years to the project assembled at a control shack almost

two miles away. The blast with its blinding light, its awesome and beautiful fireball, its stunning shock wave, exceeded their expectations. A few laughed, a few cried, most were silent. Oppenheimer himself recalled a line from Hindu scripture: "Now I am become death, destroyer of worlds."

The news reached President Truman at Potsdam on the first day of the Big Three meeting. In a move symbolic of the artificiality of the Grand Alliance, the Americans informed Churchill * at once but said nothing to Stalin for several days. At the conclusion of a formal session on July 24, Truman told Stalin as casually as possible only that the United States had developed "a new weapon of unusual destructive force." The Russian dictator, who probably knew of the atomic project through his espionage apparatus, displayed little interest and expressed the hope that America would make good use of the device.

Truman and the American negotiators tended to be firmer in their rhetoric than Roosevelt, but the Potsdam Conference nevertheless was relatively friendly. The Russians confirmed that they would enter the Pacific war about ninety days after the defeat of Germany, but on the substantive issues growing out of victory in Europe, the meeting reflected emerging East-West divisions. The Big Three reached no final agreements about such vital questions as the western Polish boundary, the governments of Eastern Europe (and, by implication, the extent of Western political-economic influence there), the political future of Germany, the amount of German reparations, the Soviet request for a share of the Axis colonies, and the Russian demand for freer naval access to the Mediterranean through the Turkish Straits. Truman and Byrnes still hoped to preserve the alliance—Truman in fact seems to have been optimistic when he left Potsdam—although they no longer felt that they needed Soviet participation in the fight against Japan. In effect, they were continuing Roosevelt's policy of postponement, and as always, the USSR, possessing as it did the power to organize the areas under its military control, was amenable.

By the time Truman returned to the United States, the Senate had ratified the charter of the United Nations by a vote of 89–2. The administration considered the approval a great victory for international responsibility, and many Americans hoped for a new era of world cooperation. In fact, the new organization could not impose international harmony. It could discuss diplomatic disputes, but the decisions of its Security Council were subject to a veto by any of the five major powers (the United States, the USSR, Britain, France, and China). It could

* Near the end of the conference, Clement Attlee, whose Labour party had won the British elections, succeeded Churchill as prime minister.

request, but not levy, military forces or financial support. It provided a new and at times useful diplomatic forum, and its social-economic organizations undertook many worthwhile projects. But, strictly limited by national sovereignty, it could not create a world order; it was based upon the false assumption that the Grand Alliance had already done so.

At the conclusion of the Potsdam Conference, the United States and Britain issued an ultimatum to Japan; it did not specifically mention the atomic bomb but threatened total destruction if the enemy refused to surrender unconditionally. The Japanese government, divided between civilians who knew the war was lost and military leaders who wanted to fight on, rejected the demand, the premier using the unfortunate phrase "treat with silent contempt." Actually, Japanese diplomats in Switzerland and Moscow were putting out peace feelers for a negotiated surrender which would preserve the status and authority of the emperor. The Russians, anxious to enter the war at the right moment, did nothing. Most Americans, including many leading policy makers, were convinced that the emperor was a war criminal; others more correctly perceived that as a theoretically divine and absolute monarch he was an important symbol to the Japanese military caste. Sentiment in the United States was in any event overwhelmingly in favor of unconditional surrender. Any clear deviation would have been almost impossible politically and would have caused diplomatic difficulties with the Soviet Union.

On August 6, an atomic bomb leveled the city of Hiroshima, killing at least 70,000 people and injuring an equal number. On August 8, the Soviet Union declared war against Japan and invaded Manchuria. The next day, with Japanese military leaders still opposed to unconditional surrender, a second bomb destroyed Nagasaki. On August 10, the Japanese offered to surrender with the provision that the Allies agree to preserve the status of the emperor. The U.S. response promised only that the people of Japan would ultimately have the right to choose their form of government; thus, even if the emperor were retained, he would be a democratically selected monarch rather than a divinity. The administration withheld shipment of a third atomic bomb to the Pacific but ordered conventional raids continued with the usual intensity. On August 14, at the request of the civilian politicians, the emperor dictated capitulation and recorded a speech of surrender. Even then, fanatical young army officers made a last attempt to continue the war by invading the imperial palace, assassinating the commander of the guard, and searching vainly for the recording. On August 15 a stunned Japanese population listened to the voice of its chief of state for the first time and learned of its defeat.

As Americans from Los Angeles to New York engaged in riotous celebrations, sober men realized that the atomic bomb had opened a new and frightening era in human history. The employment of the bomb against civilians made it seem particularly hideous; even some military leaders, including General Eisenhower, were convinced that its use was immoral. Truman and the leading figures of his administration, however, had no hesitation; they considered the bomb the one instrument that would stop the fighting as quickly as possible.

In retrospect, they seem to have been correct. It probably would have been politically and diplomatically impossible to modify the unconditional-surrender doctrine enough to satisfy the Japanese military leaders. Some scientists recommended a demonstration at a deserted site, but there is little evidence that this alone would have led to surrender. The only sure alternative to the use of the bomb was a continuation of LeMay's fire-bombing raids in conjunction with a starvation naval blockade; it would have caused the deaths of more Japanese than did the two atomic bombs and, more important to Truman and other American leaders, would have meant several thousand additional American casualties. Most military leaders, moreover, assumed that without the bomb an actual land invasion would be required; this assumption, fallacious though it may have been, was another powerful motivation for dropping the weapon.

Some revisionist historians have argued that, since the war could have been ended without the bomb and probably without an actual invasion of the home islands, it was dropped primarily as a demonstration of American power to the Soviet Union and was actually the first blast of the cold war. Expressing deep moral revulsion against both the use of the bomb and the cold war, this interpretation is a convenient vehicle for young radicals who want to demonstrate the depravity of their elders; it is based, however, more on indignation than substance.

Truman and Byrnes unquestionably believed that the bomb would enhance American bargaining power vis-à-vis the USSR, and they understood that one important dividend of a quick victory would be the minimization of any Soviet claim to joint control over postwar Japan. No solid evidence exists, however, to show that these were controlling considerations in the decision to use the bomb. The cold-war mood was barely beginning to emerge after Potsdam; the mood of wrath against Japan was overwhelming. The assumption that the bomb would be used as soon as it was ready had been implicit in the entire Manhattan Project, and, after three and a half brutalizing years of total war against a tenacious enemy, generally considered racially inferior, it would have been extremely difficult to justify a failure to use the new weapon to either Congress or the American people. Truman's decision was actually a nondecision; the President made no attempt to reverse strong impulses and refrained from interfering with machinery which went into motion of its own accord.

THE EMERGENCE OF THE COLD WAR

By bringing the war to an end, the atomic bomb eliminated the need for a Grand Alliance. The very process of administering victory brought Soviet-American tensions to the forefront of world diplomacy. Problems developed in areas as far-flung as the war itself—Eastern Europe, Germany, the Middle East, the Far East—and the American atomic monopoly added a stark and dangerous dimension to an increasingly difficult situation.

Obsessed with the danger of future attacks from Germany or some other Western nation, the Soviet leaders moved to establish an Eastern European sphere of influence. In Poland and Rumania, they crudely and brutally imposed pro-Russian regimes. In Yugoslavia and Albania, they consolidated relations with communist governments which had emerged from wartime partisan movements. In Bulgaria and Hungary, they moved to establish Russian dominance behind a noncommunist façade. In Finland and Czechoslovakia, they tolerated genuinely independent leaders who promised to subordinate their foreign policies to those of Moscow.

Here and elsewhere, Stalin was practicing a traditional Russian expansionism reinforced by the communist assumption of capitalist hostility. His determination to inflict Soviet dominance on Eastern Europe personally offended American officials on the Allied control commissions and contradicted the principles for which the United States had fought World War II. American leaders, moreover, had to deal with ethnic voting groups which might respond to Republican denunciations of a sellout of Eastern Europe. There was also an ultimate consideration: If Russia was breaking the Yalta agreements to establish hegemony over one part of the continent, was it not possible, even probable, that her ambitions extended farther?

In Germany, the disagreement over political organization and reparations quickly became apparent. The Russians systematically expelled Germans from the region east of the Oder-Neisse line and turned the area over to Poland, thus unilaterally establishing a new western Polish boundary and creating a serious economic problem for the food-poor western zones, which absorbed most of the displaced Germans. In the zone they reserved for Soviet control, they set up a communist-dominated government. The Western occupiers floundered, unable to agree upon a common political-economic policy. The United States remained determined to avoid situations that would compel America to support the Germans financially and increasingly feared that the Russians would attempt to export communism into the disorganized Western areas.

The Middle East, important strategically as the land mass that unites Europe, Asia, and Africa, and important economically as the prime source of oil for Western Europe, had been under French and British domination between the wars, but long had been a goal of Russian imperial ambitions. In the immediate postwar period, Soviet diplomats focused upon two objectives—some form of sovereign or semisovereign control over the Turkish Straits in order to give the Russian navy guaranteed access from the Black Sea to the Mediterranean; and the establishment of a sphere of influence in northern Iran, which the USSR had occupied during the war. As it turned out, the West could cope with these challenges. It would take the establishment of the State of Israel to give the Soviet Union a good opportunity to penetrate the Arab world.

Less pressing difficulties developed with the conclusion of the Far Eastern war. In addition to the concessions handed over by the Yalta agreement, the Soviet Union demanded a significant role in the administration of occupied Japan. In Manchuria the Russians began to dismantle and remove Japanese industrial plants without waiting for a reparations settlement and without regard for the claims of China. The Korean peninsula, occupied above the 38th parallel by the USSR, below it by the Americans, remained divided in the absence of an agreement on unification.

Over all the emerging East-West tensions hung the grim specter of the atomic bomb. With public pressures forcing a rapid demobilization of U.S. military forces, the bomb may have been instrumental in discouraging any Soviet adventurism beyond Eastern Europe, but it hardly gave the United States omnipotence. At best, the bomb served as a balance to the still-considerable Russian ground power (according to a conservative estimate the USSR retained sixty well-trained divisions). Truman and Byrnes soon realized that their new weapon was as much a diplomatic problem as a military advantage. By the fall of 1945, they saw that possession of the bomb could do little to secure their objectives in Eastern Europe and that the Soviet Union would eventually (estimates ran from four to twenty years) be able to manufacture the device. The bomb had ended the war, but in the postwar world it only promoted distrust and instability.

At an extraordinary cabinet meeting on September 21, 1945, the retiring secretary of war, Henry L. Stimson, proposed that the United States make a direct approach to the Soviet Union for cooperative scientific development of the peaceful uses of atomic energy. The bomb itself, he believed, should be placed under United Nations control, but he hoped that limited cooperation with the Russians would win their trust and preserve the wartime alliance. The reactions of the other cabinet members were almost evenly divided. After some deliberation, the President decided against the Stimson proposal, but the fact that the question was even discussed indicated that the Truman administration was not yet frozen into a hard-line anti-Soviet policy.

Truman soon became convinced that international control of atomic energy was a necessity. He appointed a committee headed by Under-secretary of State Dean Acheson and David Lilienthal, head of the Tennessee Valley Authority, to prepare a plan. Completed in the spring of 1946, the Acheson-Lilienthal report advocated the establishment of a United Nations authority with a monopoly over the employment of atomic power for military purposes and a general supervisory jurisdiction over all uses of atomic energy. Essentially a renunciation of American military superiority over the USSR, the report demonstrated that many American leaders were still not reconciled to a cold war with Russia.

Nevertheless, a cold war was beginning to take shape. From the fall of 1945 into the spring of 1947, a series of great-power conferences at the foreign-minister level grappled with the whole range of East-West issues, for the most part unsuccessfully. The first of these meetings, held at London in September 1945, resolved nothing and degenerated into a name-calling contest. For a time, it appeared that Soviet-American relations had reached an impasse.

Byrnes, however, was determined to achieve some sort of an agreement, apparently believing that public opinion demanded it. He took the initiative in requesting another conference, which assembled in Moscow in December 1945. Byrnes agreed to recognize the pro-Soviet governments in Rumania and Bulgaria. The Russians dropped demands for a meaningful role in the occupation of Japan, accepted the principle of UN control of atomic energy, and agreed to a general peace conference for the summer of 1946. The main substantive result of the conference was tacit acquiescence by both sides in the hegemony that each possessed in the areas its armies occupied.

Truman reacted with anger to the Moscow accords and the independence with which Byrnes had negotiated them. The President resented the emerging pattern of Soviet domination in Eastern Europe as a violation of the Yalta agreements and an affront to democratic principles. The conference, moreover, had failed to halt the steady increase of Soviet pressure upon Turkey or arrange a Russian military withdrawal from northern Iran, where a pro-USSR secessionist state had been formed. The two leading Senate spokesmen on foreign relations—Democrat Tom Connally of Texas and Republican Arthur H. Vandenberg of Michigan—shared Truman's wrath, and their support was vital to the functioning of American diplomacy. Vandenberg, the chief of the substantial Republican internationalist bloc, was an especially important figure. The administration wooed him to the point of discouraging a serious challenge to his reelection; if he could not himself make policy, he would wield an implicit veto. Hostile toward communism and attentive to his large Polish-American constituency, he strongly reinforced administration tendencies toward a "hard line."

On February 2, 1946, George F. Kennan, the counselor of the U.S. embassy in Moscow and the foremost American diplomatic expert on Russia, sent the Department of State an analysis of Soviet intentions. Kennan argued that the USSR possessed both a historical and an ideological hostility to the Western world and was seeking to extend its power into any area where the West would yield. Concessions would accomplish nothing—in fact, the Kremlin leaders depended upon the existence of a hostile outside world in order to justify their autocratic rule; the only way to deal with the Soviet Union was to contain it within its sphere by a firm but constructive diplomacy. Distributed throughout official Washington, the communication provided an intellectual basis for a policy change that already had been developing. The administration would soon bring Kennan back to the United States to speak throughout the country and play a key role in developing a new Russian policy.

On February 28, Secretary Byrnes abandoned his former conciliatory approach and delivered a speech which contained his strongest attack yet against Soviet foreign policy. On March 5, Winston Churchill captured the attention of the Western world with an important anti-Soviet address at Westminster College in Fulton, Missouri. With President Truman sitting on the platform in obvious approval, Churchill asserted that the Soviet Union had lowered an "iron curtain" across Europe. The former prime minister virtually advocated an Anglo-American alliance based on the atomic bomb to block Russian expansion.

A few weeks before the Byrnes and Churchill speeches, the Russians had begun an ideological offensive of their own. In a ceremonial election speech on February 9, Stalin predicted the collapse of capitalism, forecast a probable reversion to the chaos of the 1930s, and called upon the Russian people to prepare for the sacrifices necessary to maintain the economic and military power of the Soviet state. Subsequently he characterized the Churchill speech as a neo-fascist incitement to war. The Russian regime purged itself of individuals and ideas friendly to the West and proclaimed the inevitable communization of Europe.

Against this background, the Iranian crisis reached a peak, with the USSR augmenting its military forces in the northern secessionist area, and the United States responding with stiff demands for immediate withdrawal. On March 24, the Russians gave in; by mid-May, the Soviet troops were gone. The Iranian army restored the authority of the central government, and the Iranian parliament rejected a proposed Russian oil concession. The confrontation demonstrated that the USSR had imperial ambitions, but it also showed that the Soviet rulers were more interested in consolidating their power in Central and Eastern Europe than in pursuing Middle Eastern oil. In addition, it persuaded U.S. leaders of the wisdom of a tough policy.

Thereafter, Soviet-American relations broke down on other fronts. Protracted discussion on a U.S. loan to Russia collapsed. The Russians refused to join the World Bank or the International Monetary Fund. They rejected a proposed American treaty which provided machinery to guarantee German disarmament for twenty-five years and looked toward the reunification of the country. The USSR in fact was unwilling to risk loss of control over the segment of Germany it dominated. On May 3, 1946, the shaky German reparations agreement collapsed as the American commander in Germany, General Lucius D. Clay, retaliated against the Soviet zone's economic separatism by halting reparations deliveries from the American sector. In August the United States dispatched a show of naval strength to the eastern Mediterranean to encourge Turkish resistance against Soviet pressure. Meanwhile, from April on into October, a Big Four foreign-ministers' meeting, then a twenty-one-nation peace conference, assembled in Paris to draft final peace treaties for Italy, Bulgaria, Rumania, Hungary, and Finland. A seemingly interminable wrangle, the gatherings further sharpened East-West differences. Completion of the treaties required another meeting in New York that November and December; their paper guarantees of civil liberties in no way affected the continuing reality of Soviet dominance in Eastern Europe.

Nevertheless, the United States went ahead with the proposal for international control of atomic energy. In June 1946 Bernard Baruch, acting as a special representative to the United Nations, presented a somewhat stiffer version of the Acheson-Lilienthal report, the major difference being that the new Baruch Plan contained an unequivocal elimination of the UN Security Council veto in any vote pertaining to atomic matters. The debate that followed demonstrated the depth of East-West misunderstanding. It is doubtful that Congress or the American people would have sanctioned any agreement that lacked ironclad guarantees against cheating. On the other hand, the Russians probably quite sincerely interpreted the effort to eliminate the veto as an attempt to parlay the Western majority in the United Nations into a permanent anticommunist atomic monopoly. The deteriorating international situation left little room for agreement on the trickiest and deadliest issue that had grown out of the war. By the end of the year, the Baruch Plan was dead.

On September 6, 1946, Secretary Byrnes went from Paris to speak at Stuttgart, Germany. Essentially a bid for German support against Russia, the Stuttgart speech reassured its listeners that America was permanently involved in Europe, an indirect way of promising that the United States would not lapse into isolationism and leave Germany to the communists. Byrnes called for the political and economic unification of Germany under a demilitarized and democratic government, the subsequent reduction of occupation forces, and possible shifts in the Oder-Neisse Polish boundary in favor of Germany. With the Stuttgart speech, Byrnes had, as Joseph Davies put it, crossed the Rubicon. By appealing to the Germans, he indicated that American policy makers had come to perceive that they were locked in a long-term struggle with Russia for the control of Europe and that Germany was the key to the outcome. The United States and Britain, meanwhile, began negotiations for an economic merger of their own zones.

Much of the American public, however, was still unprepared for a long cold war; a few dissenters remained within the administration. Just six days after the Stuttgart address, Secretary of Commerce Wallace publicly advocated frank U.S. recognition of a Soviet sphere of political influence in Eastern Europe and an end to the "get-tough" approach. Wallace long had argued to Truman that Soviet-American friendship could be achieved by a formula which included concession of Eastern Europe, a U.S. loan for Russian reconstruction, minor changes in the Baruch Plan, and the establishment of close trade relations. He passed lightly over such problems as China, from which he hoped to exclude the USSR; Germany; and the Middle East. It is doubtful, in fact, that the Russians would have accepted his program in its entirety.

Wallace's speech, moderate though it was, amounted to a strong criticism of the Truman-Byrnes policy of 1946. Truman, who respected Wallace's liberal political following, was prepared to patch over their differences; but Byrnes, communicating from the Paris Conference with the strong support of Vandenberg and Connally, demanded Wallace's resignation and threatened his own. On September 20, Truman fired Wallace and replaced him with the firm anticommunist, W. Averell Harriman. The period of debate within the administration was over. Henceforth, the American government was committed to a cold war with its former Soviet ally.

WHY THE COLD WAR?

How had it happened? Critics of the American role in the cold war, then and since, have offered two explanations: (1) the cold war developed because Truman, Byrnes, and Forrestal and other American leaders were too narrow-minded, in some versions too evil, to understand the USSR's legitimate needs and continue the Roosevelt policy of friendship and cooperation; (2) American capitalism, constantly in need of foreign markets and investment outlets, required a U.S. attempt to make the world over in the American economic image to the exclusion of a separate Soviet orbit. These two lines of interpretation are not necessarily mutually exclusive—both, for example, depict American diplomacy as negative and counterrevolutionary—and some historians blend them together. Nevertheless, the differences are important and striking. The first argument is essentially the product of an idealistic liberalism and non-Marxist radicalism frustrated by the failure of World War II to secure an era of genuine peace; the second, actually the most radical, expresses an analysis of capitalism most prominently, although by no means exclusively, associated with Marxian theory.

The idealist interpretation is strongest in its insistence that the United States failed to appreciate the Soviet obsession with security, but, in the manner of absolutisms, it goes beyond this valid point to an overarching interpretation which outstrips the historical evidence and is characterized by a moral confusion hardly appropriate to the work of moralists. The assertion that Truman and those around him reversed a well-defined Roosevelt policy of collaboration with the USSR ignores both the fluidity of Roosevelt's own approach to policy making and the inconsistency about Russia apparent in Truman's own mind during 1945. The thesis that the use of the atomic bomb was directed primarily against the Russians is based on a web of circumstantial evidence that lacks historical credibility. The emphasis on the disputes over Eastern Europe tends to obscure the fact that the United States took definite action against communist expansion only when American policy makers began to fear that it would move *beyond* Eastern Europe; for all the indignation the American leaders felt, they never seriously attempted to roll back the Soviets, only to prevent the further extension of their power. Truman and other U.S. leaders may have entertained exaggerated apprehensions about Russian ambitions and certainly they engaged in hyperbolic rhetoric for congressional and public consumption, but who can say that in the chaotic situation of postwar Europe such fears were baseless?

Finally, idealist revisionism tends to undermine its own moral credibility by engaging in a double standard of international conduct. It is one thing for a hardened realpolitiker to argue that the United States should not have interfered with the Soviet establishment of a sphere of influence around the Russian borders; it is quite another thing for idealistic moralists to depict the USSR as an injured giant seeking only to protect itself against a hostile America and to play down the fact that the

Russian mode of protection involved the imposition of a brutal totalitarianism upon tens of millions of people. Moral absolutists should feel especially obliged to write history from a consistent frame of reference.

The economic interpretation is in many respects more challenging, proceeding as it does from a more coherent and fundamentally radical vision of human society than that of the idealists. Certainly, the economic revisionists have succeeded in demonstrating that U.S. policy makers sought to structure the postwar world around a liberal capitalism characterized by the revival of international trade and that the makers of American diplomacy sought maximum advantage for the United States in the process. Such disclosures are less than startling. Surely, one expects the representatives of a powerful and victorious nation to assume the superiority of their way of life; and it is hardly surprising that negotiators for any society attempt to secure the greatest possible benefit for their country. Within certain broad and ill-defined limits, moreover, nations unquestionably have a legitimate right to pursue their economic self-interest.

The economic revisionists, however, seem to assume that capitalism is inherently exploitative, and hence any advocacy of its interests becomes illegitimate. By stressing the alleged inexorable pressures upon capitalism to expand for its own survival, they conveniently bypass the major reason for the U.S. insistence upon revived trade—the general consensus that World War II had developed from the economic nationalism of the 1920s and '30s and that expanding international trade could stimulate worldwide economic development and create the general prosperity which alone could establish the basis for peace and stability. By treating these liberal capitalist assumptions as a façade for aggrandizement, the revisionists escape the necessity of examining their merits. In addition, it becomes easy to ignore or explain away the fact that American policy makers really believed that their economic policies would benefit the entire world.

Perhaps an even greater weakness of the economic revisionists is their tendency to ignore or arbitrarily assign secondary status to noneconomic factors. The fuss over Eastern Europe in 1945–46 may have involved an attempt by American capitalism to integrate the entire continental economic unit into its system, but it seems probable that principles, along with domestic political pressures from Eastern European ethnic groups, were more important. The revisionists deserve credit for reminding traditional historians of the important economic dimensions of diplomacy, but their single-cause view of history fails to enhance our understanding of the cold war.

A more satisfactory thesis is the argument that the cold war developed naturally out of the way in which World War II destroyed the old balance of power in Europe and Asia. With Germany and Japan reduced to impotence, with Britain and France unable to continue as imperial powers, vast areas of the globe had become power vacuums into which some organizing force had to flow. The need to rearrange the power balance inevitably led to some rivalry for territory and influence, but it might have been managed with less disastrous results if the United States and the Soviet Union had possessed some common outlook which could have served as a basis for trust.

Instead, the Russians approached the postwar world with a frame of reference shaped by a centuries-old quest for security and empire, a traditional distrust of foreigners, a communist ideology that assumed capitalist hostility and anticipated the eventual victory of the proletariat throughout the world, and the outlook of a leader pathologically suspicious of every nation or individual he was unable to dominate. The USSR had its national priorities, but its adoption of communism as a state religion made its ultimate goal appear to be world domination. The behavior of Stalin and Molotov in the fluid postwar situation made it difficult, if not impossible, for the West to separate immediate Russian objectives from long-range ambitions; one may wonder indeed if the Kremlin could always do so. At the least, there was no reason for the West to assume that the Soviet Union would foreswear the expansion of communism beyond Eastern Europe if the opportunity beckoned.

The Americans, on the other hand, regarded the postwar world from a frame of reference made up of centuries of free security and a crusading democratic moralism. Unable to grasp the way in which invaders had ravaged the Russian state for over a millennium, they never realized the extent to which any Russian regime would have been obsessed with security. Having made liberal democracy into a state religion, having justified World War II as an effort to rid the world of totalitarian inhumanity, they found Soviet despotism hard to suffer and its extension intolerable. They could not accept in principle the Russian establishment of dominance in Eastern Europe, although Soviet might forced them to accept it in fact. Thus, they fell back on rhetorical protest.

Nevertheless, in the absence of any alternatives, the United States would have learned to live with the Soviet subjugation of Eastern Europe. The cold war may have begun to take shape in 1945–46, but it became the dominant factor of world diplomacy because of communist pressures and apparent Russian designs on areas beyond the power of Soviet armies. By early 1947, these pressures were pushing Eastern Europe into the background and calling forth an American response that went beyond rhetorical protest.

CONTAINMENT IN EUROPE

By 1947, the focus of Soviet-American tensions had shifted beyond the unchallenged sphere of Soviet dominance. Greece, existing as it did on the edge of the Russian orbit, and occupying a strategic position in the Eastern Mediterranean, was in an area at once vital to Western interests and vulnerable to Soviet expansion. The small nation seemed particularly ripe for a communist revolution. Ravaged by the Nazis, still in a state of economic collapse, ruled by a corrupt and reactionary government, Greece was in turmoil. A powerful insurgent guerrilla movement enjoyed a substantial popular following and only British military support kept the Athens regime in power.

Since the guerrillas were communist-dominated, Western diplomats assumed that they were directed from Moscow and that their efforts were part of the Soviet design for expansion. Actually, it appears that Stalin had scant hope for a successful takeover of Greece and gave the insurgents little direct encouragement or aid. He did not interfere, however, with the communist governments of Bulgaria, Yugoslavia, and Albania, all of which provided the Greek Communists with arms and supplies in return for promises of territorial concessions. Had the Greek rebels been successful, Moscow undoubtedly would have moved to establish control over them.

The West thus faced a situation that would throw it on the defensive time and again in the decades to come. It had to support a repressive and incompetent government against an uprising motivated by legitimate grievances. To let the rulers in Athens fall would be to give the USSR a foothold in the Mediterranean, thereby endangering the Western position in Turkey and the rest of the Middle East and giving encouragement to the growing communist movements of Western Europe. Also as in subsequent instances, the United States found itself forced to handle the difficulties arising from the collapsing imperialisms of its allies. By early 1947, Great Britain was near bankruptcy; on February 21, Britain formally notified the United States that it could no longer continue assistance to the Greek regime it had established.

The swift and decisive character of the American response revealed the way in which cold-war attitudes had come to permeate administration thinking. American diplomatic and military officials from the President down were all convinced that Greece and the Mediterranean area had to be protected, primarily because of the strategic importance of the region. The administration consensus, however, did not yet extend to the Congress or the general public. Truman and his advisers faced a serious task of salesmanship, made all the more difficult by the fact that economy-minded Republicans had won control of Congress in the 1946 elections.

In General George Marshall, whom Truman had named secretary of state that January, the adminstration had a chief diplomat of great stature and prestige, but at a confidential meeting even Marshall seemed unable to convince Senator Vandenberg and other key congressmen. Undersecretary of State Dean Acheson, who would succeed Marshall in 1949, won the support of the legislators by depicting the Greek situation not in terms of the balance of power but as a critical episode in a new struggle of communist totalitarianism against democracy with American security and freedom hanging in the balance. Vandenberg and the others agreed to support aid to Greece and a smaller program for Turkey, but they warned that the request would have to be presented to Congress and the people in the same apocalyptic terms. Just as before World War II, Congress and the public were not prepared to respond to a foreign policy problem unless it could be presented as a crisis.

On March 12, 1947, President Truman appeared before Congress to ask for $350 million for aid to Greece and $50 million for Turkey. He described the situation much as Vandenberg had advised and declared:

> I believe that it must be the policy of the United States to support free peoples who are resisting attempted subjugation by armed minorities or by outside pressures.
> I believe that we must assist free people to work out their own destinies in their own ways.
> I believe that our help should be primarily through economic and financial aid which is essential to economic stability and orderly political processes.

This declaration—the "Truman Doctrine"—seemed to give an open-ended commitment to any government having difficulty with communism. In fact, however, neither Truman nor his advisers approached American foreign policy with such a sense of mission. They felt a need to impress Congress and the people with universalistic rhetoric, but they were determined to consider each case on its merits and, above all, to avoid dangerous military involvements. Neither Truman nor Acheson would feel impelled to apply the Truman Doctrine to China, for example; nevertheless, they had established a rhetorical precedent that would make it more difficult in the future to follow a cautious and rational foreign policy.

The Greek-Turkish aid bill passed the Senate on April 22 by a vote of 67–23 and cleared the House on May 8, 287–107. In both cases, the majorities were bipartisan; Truman had skillfully welded together a Republican-Democratic coalition that would support one program after another to contain communism in Europe. The opposition came from both the left and right of the political spectrum, but neither the conservative isolationists who opposed any European entanglements nor those on the left who followed Wallace in refusing to accept Soviet-American hostility were able to offer coherent alternatives to the cold war. The best critique of the Truman Doctrine was put forth by liberals and moderates who agreed with the general objective of containing communism but argued that aid to unpopular right-wing governments was self-defeating and that only a thorough plan of economic reconstruction for Europe could stop the spread of communism.

The administration in fact agreed and envisioned the Greek-Turkish appropriation only as a stopgap. As late as the spring of 1947, the European economy was in a shambles. For all its trained manpower and great industrial potential, the Continent had failed to recover from the devastation of the war and seemed incapable of doing so on its own. Great Britain had been paralyzed by severe cold and blizzards during the previous winter. France had attained only 50 percent of its prewar industrial production. Germany remained prostrate, its people existing on food rations barely sufficient to sustain life. Everywhere the working classes and large portions of the middle class faced unemployment and grim deprivation. The large, well-organized Communist parties of France and Italy, following the new tough Russian line, began a drive for power which included parliamentary disruptions, civil disturbances, and crippling strikes. Returning from Europe at the end of April, a shaken General Marshall ordered Kennan to assemble a staff of experts and formulate within two weeks the outline of a program for European recovery.

On June 5, in a highly publicized address at Harvard University, Marshall called upon the nations of Europe, including the Soviet Union and its satellites, to prepare a cooperative plan for economic rehabilitation. Each nation would be expected to contribute as much of its own resources as possible to the common effort, and the United States would give whatever additional aid was necessary. Despite the inclusion of Russia in the offer, the Marshall Plan was primarily a device to contain Soviet expansionism. American policy makers also realized that in the long run a revived Europe would provide important market and investment outlets for the United States, but they knew that for the short run large-scale aid would increase already severe postwar inflationary strains upon the American economy. They accepted these strains as part of the price of containment.

The offer to include Russia was a gamble, taken because the

administration did not want to bear responsibility for having solidified the already emerging division of Europe. If the USSR were to accept, the cost requirements of the program would rise drastically, and Congress might reject it. But Russian participation would also force the USSR to make substantial raw materials contributions and reveal unprecedented amounts of information about its economy; the Americans believed that Soviet society was too closed for such developments. When the Western European nations rapidly arranged a planning conference, which met in Paris, the Eastern bloc sent delegations, but in a matter of days, it became apparent that there was no room for agreement. Molotov withdrew denouncing the Marshall Plan as further evidence of Western malignancy. In the minds of most Westerners, the Russians had assumed responsibility for the division of Europe.

The Paris walkout was only the most symbolic of a series of events. Throughout 1947, the USSR pursued a vituperative propaganda campaign against the United States, encouraged every conceivable species of communist obstructionism in Western Europe, and ruthlessly consolidated its hold upon Eastern Europe. On May 30, six days before Marshall's Harvard speech, communists in Budapest seized control of the Hungarian government in a coup d'etat. From Poland to Albania, communist regimes backed by Soviet military power drove independent politicians from public life, purged themselves of pro-Western or nationalist elements, and assumed the starkest characteristics of Stalinist totalitarianism. In September the Russians set up the Communist Information Bureau (Cominform) to coordinate Communist parties around the world and facilitate the subordination of international communism to the interests of Moscow.

In February 1948 communists seized power in Czechoslovakia; shortly thereafter, Foreign Minister Jan Masaryk, son of the founder of the republic and a figure beloved in the West, died in a mysterious fall from a window of his apartment, possibly a suicide, probably the victim of an assassination. The Czech tragedy was a traumatic event throughout the Atlantic community. The Russians had brutally crushed the one genuine democracy of Eastern Europe and had done so with no regard for the fact that the noncommunist Czech leaders had complied fully with Moscow's dictates. The experience of Prague seemed to show that there could be no middle ground.

In a sense, the events from the Hungarian coup to the Czech takeover amounted to an admission of weakness by a Russian government which feared any manifestations of independence within its sphere of influence. Yet the USSR's tactics, if not countered in Western Europe, could also extend Soviet power to the English Channel. At the end of 1947, Truman obtained congressional assent to an emergency European aid program. By the spring of 1948, Marshall Plan appropriations and the reinstitution of the military draft were moving through Congress with powerful bipartisan support. Communist setbacks in the Italian elections demonstrated a reaction against the disruptive methods that Moscow had ordered and forecast the politics of the future in those areas of the Continent beyond the reach of Soviet troops.

The division of Europe into opposing blocs and the imperative of economic recovery led irresistibly to the unification of the noncommunist zones of Germany. By the spring of 1948, the United States, Britain, and France had merged their areas of occupation into an economic unit, had carried through vital currency reforms, and were planning the establishment of a West German state. A Europe that was to be economically—and militarily—strong against Russia would have to contain a healthy, resurgent West Germany; otherwise all of Germany might eventually be brought into the Soviet orbit, thereby ensuring the eventual triumph of communism in Europe. Such were the stakes involved in the Berlin blockade.

On June 24, 1948, the Russians cut off all surface traffic to the Western-held zones of Berlin. The Soviet objective was clearly to force a withdrawal from the old capital, undermine confidence in the United States and her allies, and thus prevent the establishment of West Germany. Neither the USSR, which was still without atomic weapons, nor the United States, whose army was paper-thin, were willing to start a full-scale war over the issue. As the Soviet challenge was limited, the American response was cautious, albeit dramatic and daring. The West decided to undertake the difficult job of supplying West Berlin via an airlift. For 324 days, transport planes, limited to the three air corridors and airports granted to the Western Allies at the end of World War II, flew every conceivable provision into Berlin. By the spring of 1949, a cargo flight was landing every three minutes, and the West Berlin standard of living was higher than before the blockade. In May 1949 the Russians lifted the barriers, having gained nothing other than a face-saving and unproductive foreign ministers' conference on a German peace treaty. Two days after the end of the blockade, a semisovereign West German government was proclaimed; in the fall, the USSR established an East German republic. The formal division of Europe was completed with the line which split East from West running through the middle of the old wartime enemy.

Even with the Marshall Plan taking hold, even with the successful defiance of the Berlin blockade, Western Europe felt insecure against the apparently aggressive USSR. After the U.S. presidential election in November 1948, the Truman administration negotiated America's first long-term European alliance since the eighteenth century, the North Atlantic Treaty. The signatories—the United States, Canada, Iceland, Great Britain, Norway, Denmark, the Netherlands, Belgium, Luxembourg, France, Portugal, and Italy *—pledged to defend each other against aggression and established a North Atlantic Treaty Organization (NATO) to prepare plans for the common defense and command the armed forces committed to the alliance. Despite its repudiation of a hallowed tradition against peacetime "entangling alliances," the treaty cleared the Senate, 82–13, in July 1949. In a decade, the United States had moved from a position of determined disengagement to one of nearly total commitment.

The Greek-Turkish program, the Marshall Plan, and NATO were the most important features of a containment effort that managed to keep the Russians within their postwar military sphere. In 1948 the Greek insurgency began to decline, as much because Marshall Tito had broken with Stalin and closed the Yugoslav borders to the Moscow-oriented Greek rebels as because of American aid. By 1950, the European economy had surpassed prewar production figures and was about to begin a period of rapid growth. Recovery did not automatically resolve the genuine grievances of the French and Italian working classes, who continued to vote communist in large numbers, but it at least averted the chaos which probably would have made it impossible for them to exercise their franchise.

The security provided by NATO was more psychological than real—in an attempt to free money for domestic programs, Truman drastically cut defense expenditures at the very time he was requesting Senate approval of the historic new alliance system. In September 1949 the USSR made its first successful test of an atomic bomb, thereby eliminating the West's most important military edge. In early 1950, Truman responded by ordering development of a hydrogen bomb. He and his national security advisers also decided that it would be necessary to undertake a substantial enlargement of conventional military forces; the Korean war would force rapid implementation of this policy.

European containment thus was not an unalloyed success, but it was a substantial victory for the United States and, on the whole, enormously constructive and beneficial for the entire Atlantic community. Western Europe, with its cultural ties to America, its fear of Russia, and its highly developed economic potential, had provided the best possible testing ground for the effort to block communist expansion. The situation in the Far East was much different.

---

* Greece and Turkey were added in 1952, West Germany in 1955.

ASIA AND THE DIPLOMACY OF MISCALCULATION

A relatively inexpensive program of economic development could block communism in Europe because Europe already possessed a highly advanced economy which required only a strong shot in the arm. The Asian societies by and large were feudal and agrarian, their ruling classes reactionary and exploitative in a manner reminiscent of the ancien régime before the French Revolution, their masses illiterate and unskilled. Contrary to the Marxist dogma that communism could only follow the ultimate stages of capitalist development, Asia in fact presented more possibilities for revolution than Europe.

A Marshall Plan-type American response was not feasible because Asia was unprepared to make use of such aid. Moreover, American policy makers constantly and quite rightly based all their calculations on the assumption of a European priority—that is, they considered Europe more important to American security than Asia and sent most of the limited resources available to them across the Atlantic rather than the Pacific. It was not until 1949 that the Truman administration announced an economic effort for the underdeveloped areas of the world (the Point Four program); while responsible for many worthwhile individual projects, it was slow to take shape, ill funded, and piecemeal in conception—in each instance the reverse of the Marshall Plan.

No nation exemplified the obdurate problems of Asia so graphically as China, and the U.S. approach to China clearly revealed the deep-rooted American difficulties in coming to grips with the culture and politics of the Orient. Americans in general and the Protestant middle class in particular had long felt a missionary impulse toward the Chinese. During World War II, the United States had attempted to build China into a great power, had insisted upon regarding her as one of the "Big Four," and had obtained a permanent seat in the United Nations Security Council for her. These actions represented an effort to fill the Asian power vacuum which would result from the defeat of Japan, but they also proceeded from a genuine desire to bestow the blessings of American life and Western liberalism upon the Chinese.

Most Americans, including those responsible for foreign policy, failed to understand the extent to which such traditions as individual liberty, the legitimacy of political opposition, and democratic rule were alien to a culture in which rulers claimed the "Mandate of Heaven," mercilessly exterminated their opponents, and expected the masses to accept their edicts without question. Chiang Kai-shek's Nationalist government, dependent upon American aid for its survival, paid lip service to Western ideals; actually Chiang was a dictator, a weak and unsuccessful one.

By the end of the war, Nationalist China was in an advanced stage of disintegration, its armies shot through with corrupt and incompetent leadership, its economy ravaged by a feverish inflation which forestalled economic recovery, encouraged government officials to engage in graft, and demoralized the population. Chiang and his ministers were unable and unwilling to institute the drastic reforms that the situation demanded, indeed, they had a financial if not a political interest in perpetuating the status quo. Nevertheless, in what must rank as one of the greatest public-relations feats in the history of diplomacy, Chinese propagandists sold Chiang to the American people as an inspirational democratic leader striving to fulfill the aspirations of his struggling, downtrodden people.

The U.S. failure to understand the nature of Chiang's major opposition was almost as great. In 1945 the Chinese Communists under Mao Tse-tung controlled a large area of northern China and governed about a quarter of the nation's people. Remarkably in view of later developments, most Americans did not consider the communists a menace to U.S. interests or even a totalitarian force. The war and the Soviet alliance had made communism in general appear benign enough, and the Red Chinese, realizing the importance of popular support, ran their territory in a fairly democratic manner.

Until he gained ultimate victory, Mao was prepared to tolerate a political opposition and capitalist enterprise; his government was more honest, efficient, and interested in the welfare of the people than Chiang's. Perhaps he felt it necessary for China to pass through a bourgeois-liberal stage before it could begin the dictatorship of the proletariat. Stalin and Molotov for their part solemnly, and perhaps sincerely, assured Western diplomats that the Chinese Communists were not real communists at all. Americans, conservative as well as liberal, who visited the Maoist regions of China assumed that the communists were at most radical agrarian reformers. Contrary to a later right-wing mythology, this designation was not a plot of a few procommunist diplomats; it was a description of what was actually happening, if unfortunately not an accurate prediction of the future.

By the end of World War II, the Communists and Nationalists had been sporadically fighting each other for eighteen years; each side was committed to the other's total destruction. Washington, however, assumed that they viewed each other with the same tolerance as American political parties and could be brought together in a coalition government. During

1946, General Marshall spent much of his time in China trying to arrange a settlement to the civil war; by the end of the year, it was obvious to all that an agreement was impossible. Thereafter, the Truman administration moved toward disengagement and threw Chiang only enough aid to satisfy Republican critics in Congress.

Nevertheless, the Nationalist army outnumbered the Communist forces by more than two to one and enjoyed a far greater superiority in firepower. It suffered one reverse after another, not for lack of American aid, but because of miserable generalship and a corruption so pervasive that many officers pocketed the money with which they were supposed to supply their troops and sold weapons to the enemy. In 1947 the administration sent General Albert Wedemeyer, who had been the chief American military official in China at the end of the war, to survey the situation. Wedemeyer's report to the President fully exposed the failures of the Nationalist government and outlined the need for drastic reforms. But the general was also determined to stop communism in Asia; he recommended greater aid to Chiang, including the dispatch of military advisers to train the Chinese army.

The administration, however, had already decided to concentrate on Europe where the chances of success were greater than in the morass of Asia. To the historian who has witnessed the experience of Vietnam, Truman's decision may seem wise and obvious, but it disturbed many conservative Republicans who were opposed to the Marshall Plan and to involvement in Europe. Led by Senator Robert A. Taft, this group wanted to economize and avoid European entanglements, yet engage in an all-out fight against communism and save the Asian masses from its horrors. Accepting the basic impulses of the cold war, but appalled by the means required to wage it, the New Isolationists, as their critics called them, condemned the Truman administration's European programs and oscillated between advocating total withdrawal from Asia and total involvement there. Such attitudes led quite logically to a flight from foreign reality and a search for internal scapegoats (a cheap and politically rewarding method of expressing anticommunist impulses) which would culminate in the witchhunts led by Senator Joseph R. McCarthy.

Secretary of State Acheson and State Department China experts had assumed that Mao was an independent national leader not under Stalin's thumb and that tension was certain to develop between Russia and China with their different cultures and 4,000 miles of oft-disputed boundary. In 1949 the Truman administration awaited the final collapse of Chiang's government with the intention of establishing as decent a relationship as possible with the new Communist rulers and encouraging Mao to engage in an Asian version of Titoism. As a long-range prediction, the State

Department assumption was valid; for the short run, however, Mao apparently feared the United States more than Russia. On July 1, 1949, he explicitly rejected the idea of neutrality in the cold war and aggressively proclaimed his alignment with the Soviet bloc. Thereafter, as the Communists extended their area of control, they engaged in a calculated, violent, and abusive anti-Americanism which wrecked U.S. hopes for amicable relations.

Nevertheless, Chiang Kai-shek hardly presented a viable alternative to fall back upon. In the fall, the defeated Nationalists fled to the offshore island of Formosa (Taiwan), and the State Department, in a belated effort to secure public support, issued a 1,000-page "white paper" condemning their misrule. The China white paper also condemned Mao's decision to side with the Russians, and the Truman administration did in fact perceive the new Chinese government as a potential expansionist threat which had to be contained. At the beginning of 1950, the U.S. government ended a long period of neutrality in the Indo-China war between the French and the insurgents led by Ho Chi Minh; fearing that Ho was under the influence of the Soviets or Chinese, the United States recognized the French-dominated regime of the Emperor Bao Dai and began to send it military aid. Yet, at the same time, America took no steps to defend Formosa and awaited Chiang's final defeat in the hope that it would soon be possible to do business with the Chinese Communists.

The administration's Far Eastern plans received a bad jolt on June 25, 1950, when the communist North Korean army launched an attack upon South Korea. Divided between East and West since 1945, the Korean peninsula had been a forgotten area of the cold war. The Russians had established a communist government north of the 38th parallel under Kim Il Sung. The United States had arranged UN-supervised elections for the South; the winner, Syngman Rhee, was a venerable old advocate of Korean independence. A conservative who conducted himself in as dictatorial a manner as the South Korean constitution permitted, Rhee nevertheless had one characteristic in common with his communist counterpart Kim. Both men were fanatical nationalists determined to unify their nation.

The attack, probably planned by Kim and approved by Stalin, presented the United States with a situation for which it was wholly unprepared. The United States had given only limited aid to the South Korean army out of a fear that Rhee with a first-class military force would attack the North. Rhee had not wanted American troops on his soil, and the military cutbacks of 1949 would have made a meaningful presence impossible anyway. U.S. military and diplomatic planners had assumed that any communist attack would be of global dimensions, in which case

Korea could not be defended. In January 1950 Secretary Acheson had delivered a speech which seemed to exclude Korea from the U.S. Pacific defense perimeter, although he did not foreclose military support through the UN. Thus, it is extremely likely that Kim and Stalin expected the United States to allow them to overwhelm the weak South Korean defenders. If so, they were guilty of a miscalculation as great as those America had made in Asia.

Truman and his advisers quickly decided to resist. With memories of pre-World War II appeasement indelibly written into their international outlook, they were convinced that acquiescence in Korea would destroy American credibility, discredit the United Nations, and encourage new, more serious communist aggressions. Within a matter of days, the President had ordered American troops to Korea on his own initiative* and had obtained a United Nations Security Council mandate for a "police action" against the invaders. Some fifty nations eventually contributed small forces. (The Russians were boycotting Security Council meetings in protest against the failure to hand over Nationalist China's seat to the Communist Chinese and thus were not present to cast a veto.) In a related move, designed to stabilize the Far Eastern situation, the President ordered the U.S. Seventh Fleet to patrol the waters between Formosa and Red China with the objective of preventing any offensive action by either Chiang or Mao. Truman's decision to repel aggression and to do so under the aegis of the United Nations won strong support from most Americans. Neither the American people nor their leaders, however, had fully succeeded in defining their objectives. This fuzziness of goals would soon make them the prisoner of events.

During the early weeks of the war, the South Koreans and the poorly trained U.S. occupation forces flown in from Japan could not resist the well-prepared communist attack. Quickly driven into a small defensive perimeter around Pusan at the southeastern corner of the peninsula, they barely escaped being thrown into the sea. The UN commander, General Douglas MacArthur, conceived a brilliant and daring plan for taking the offensive. On September 15, UN forces executed an almost impossible amphibious landing at Inchon midway up the west coast of Korea far behind enemy lines; those in the southwest began an offensive out of the Pusan perimeter. In a matter of days, the North Korean army was routed; of the 400,000 men the enemy had sent south, some 75 percent were killed,

---

* Truman never requested a congressional endorsement of any sort for the dispatch of U.S. troops to Korea. In later years, critics argued that he could have escaped the subsequent attacks of his Republican opponents had he forced through a resolution of support at the beginning when there was wide approval of his action. The failure of Lyndon B. Johnson's effort, fifteen years later, to use the Gulf of Tonkin Resolution as a barrier against congressional criticism of the Vietnam war casts serious doubt upon this argument.

wounded, or captured; many of the rest, however, were able to form small guerrilla bands and harass the UN army from the rear.

The sudden victory, far more complete than Washington had expected, was one of the greatest in American military history. It also compelled the Truman administration to define its objectives more precisely, convinced MacArthur that he was invincible, and so overawed civilian and military leaders in Washington that they surrendered their independent judgment to the increasingly megalomaniacal Far Eastern commander. With total victory apparently in sight, the President and his advisers succumbed to the temptation of attempting to conquer all of Korea and unite it under a freely chosen government. They allowed MacArthur to advance north of the 38th parallel freely as long as the Chinese or the Russians refrained from intervention and made no announcement of intended entry; the provinces adjacent to the USSR and Manchuria were to be occupied only by Korean troops; in the event of intervention, MacArthur was to assume the defensive and await instructions from Washington.

The general's orders were carefully drawn because China openly and through diplomatic channels had been threatening to enter the war if UN troops proceeded to its borders. Manchurian industry received much of its power from facilities across the Yalu River in North Korea. The Chinese may have genuinely feared MacArthur's intentions, and certainly were determined to secure some sort of buffer zone between themselves and any Western military presence. Washington did not fully perceive the depth of the Chinese resolve to prevent the destruction of the North Korean state, but at least it was apprehensive and sent MacArthur orders which, had they stood, probably would have prevented a disaster. On October 15, President Truman met with MacArthur on Wake Island. The general, supremely confident, assured him that the war was nearly over and that if the Chinese were foolish enough to intervene, the UN forces would slaughter them. Like everyone else, Truman appears to have been overwhelmed by MacArthur's apparent mastery of the situation.

On October 19, American forces captured the North Korean capital, Pyongyang. Five days later, MacArthur disregarded the restrictions on the forward movement of non-Korean troops and ordered a general advance to the Yalu River with as much speed as possible. On October 27, Chinese forces that had crossed into North Korea began a limited offensive, inflicting heavy casualties upon a Korean regiment and a detachment of the American Eighth Army. On November 6, MacArthur warned his superiors in Washington that he faced a new and fresh army which threatened the destruction of his command. Whether to further augment their forces or await a Western diplomatic approach, the Chinese made no effort to follow up their initial victories; instead, they broke off all significant contact. Washington, for its part, failed completely to probe for a diplomatic settlement. MacArthur quickly regained his confidence and, asserting that the Oriental mind would give way before a decisive display of force, planned a new offensive. The civilian and military leaders in Washington, still paralyzed by the memory of Inchon, acquiesced. On November 24, MacArthur announced an offensive that would end the war, unify Korea, and allow American soldiers to be home for Christmas.

The result was a debacle. The Chinese had quietly amassed a three-to-one numerical superiority and had a better command of the terrain. Their counterattack rolled the UN troops back into South Korea; for a time MacArthur, sliding back into deep pessimism, feared it would be necessary to evacuate the peninsula. By the end of January 1951, however, the Chinese had been contained. Under the skillful and inspirational command of General Matthew B. Ridgway, the Eighth Army resumed the offensive. By the end of March, the UN forces had driven back to the region of the 38th parallel; the line of battle would remain in this general area for the duration of the Korean war.

Chastened by the Chinese intervention, the Truman administration reverted to the apparent initial objective of simply expelling the aggressor from South Korea. Fearing that an overcommitment to Asia might encourage a Soviet attack in Europe, Washington decided to devote most of its resources to a rearmament program which would make NATO into an effective military deterrent. Ridgway and MacArthur were told that they could not be given the reinforcements necessary for a drive to the Yalu.

Ridgway accepted the limitations, but MacArthur reacted in the manner of a gambler attempting to recover his losses by raising the stakes. He was well aware that in the United States, to which he had never returned after assuming command of the Philippine army in 1936, he was a living legend and a special hero of the New Isolationists. Since the end of World War II, he had ruled Japan in a manner reminiscent of the great Roman proconsuls. Having lived in Asia for fifteen years, he was convinced that it was more important than Europe. He already had publicly advocated an American commitment to Formosa and had flagrantly disregarded orders. On March 24, he issued on his own authority an ultimatum to China in which he called for immediate surrender and threatened to extend the war to China's "coastal areas and interior bases." The statement wrecked diplomatic efforts for a peace agreement. On April 5, the Republican leader in the House of Representatives made public a letter from MacArthur protesting the restrictions that Washington had placed upon the conduct of the war. The general had delivered a political and constitutional challenge that Truman could not ignore. On April 12, 1951, the President relieved MacArthur of all his commands.

When the general returned to the United States, he received at first a hero's welcome from a population that shared his frustration at the stalemate which had developed in Korea. From San Francisco to New York, he rode in motorcades with local dignitaries, relished the cheers of millions of people, and was deluged with ticker tape and confetti. In an emotional and eloquent speech to Congress, he called for total victory and won a great ovation. His return served as a catharsis for a nation accustomed to *winning* wars. Truman's decision to fight a limited conflict was foreign to the American temperament, all the more so because the enemy represented a hated ideology which most Americans had come to perceive as a mortal threat to their way of life.

The administration arranged a long congressional inquiry into the MacArthur incident, and the emotional binge eventually subsided. Top military leaders, including the Joint Chiefs of Staff, expressed support of Truman. MacArthur's own replies to probing questions about the dangers of widening an Asian war were unconvincing. Few Americans wanted either a bigger conflict or a denuding of U.S. defenses in Europe, and right-wing Republicans who seemed to advocate such courses had no chance of building a majority. Nevertheless, the MacArthur firing and the simultaneous death of Senator Vandenberg gave them an opportunity to harass the administration with strong effect; for if the New Isolationism did not express the reasoned sentiment of most Americans, it was in a position to capitalize upon the deep-rooted frustrations arising from the Korean involvement.

Truce talks were finally begun in July 1951, but would drag on through the remainder of Harry S Truman's Presidency, stalled in large measure by the American refusal to repatriate communist prisoners against their will. Normal diplomatic relations with China had long since become unthinkable. Truman's effort to contain communism, so successful in Europe, was ending in the maddening bog of Asia.

To some extent, the President and his advisers had only themselves to blame. They had failed to anticipate an attack upon South Korea, had erred grievously in trying for total victory, and had too long deferred to MacArthur's egomania. Yet, after the MacArthur dismissal, they had recovered and undertaken the only rational course—that of devoting most of their attention and resources to the greater priority, Europe, while keeping the Korean fighting as limited as possible and attempting to reach an honorable settlement. It was precisely over this policy, however, that the mood of national anger and frustration developed. Just as in World

War II, the American people thought of war as a once-and-for-all fight against a totally evil enemy who could not be allowed to survive. Indeed, the Truman administration had found it necessary to appeal to this concept in order to win support for the Greek-Turkish aid program, the Marshall Plan, and NATO.

All the same, neither Truman nor any of his secretaries of state had thought of themselves as leaders of a crusade. Their decision to opt for the moral victory of simply repelling the aggressors in Korea was the appropriate culmination for a cold-war policy that had sought only to contain the expansion of communism in Europe and the Middle East and had avoided military commitments in China. Truman's inability to duplicate his European successes in Asia stemmed primarily from the far more intractable situation of the Far East. His determination to avoid total war was both strategically and morally sound, but a people whose emotions and experience demand absolute success could not cope with such policies. The President's declining popularity in 1951 and 1952 paved the way for an administration that would promise new departures.

SIX

The Fair Deal

CHRONOLOGY
1945–52

1945

SEPTEMBER   Truman asks Congress for broad reform legislation

1946

FEBRUARY   Employment Act of 1946; resignation of Harold Ickes
MAY   Truman requests power to draft railroad strikers
JUNE   Truman vetoes weak OPA bill
JULY   Truman signs second weak OPA bill
SEPTEMBER   Wallace-Byrnes dispute; Truman dismisses Wallace
OCTOBER   Truman lifts meat controls
NOVEMBER   Republicans sweep congressional elections

1947

MARCH   Truman initiates federal loyalty program
JUNE   Taft-Hartley bill passed over Truman's veto
OCTOBER   Presidential civil rights committee issues its report
DECEMBER   Justice Department files amicus curiae brief in restrictive covenant cases; Henry Wallace declares third-party candidacy for the Presidency

139

1948

FEBRUARY	Truman advocates comprehensive civil rights program
JUNE	Republicans nominate Dewey and Warren
JULY	Presidential executive orders prohibit discrimination in armed forces and U.S. civil service; J. Strom Thurmond nominated as States' Rights candidate for President
AUGUST	Elizabeth Bentley and Whittaker Chambers testify before congressional committees
SEPTEMBER	Truman begins "whistle-stop" campaign
NOVEMBER	Truman defeats Dewey

1949

APRIL	Brannan Plan introduced in Congress
JULY	Housing Act of 1949
AUGUST	Chinese Nationalists abandon the mainland
SEPTEMBER	USSR explodes first atomic bomb
OCTOBER	Communist party leaders convicted of violating Smith Act

1950

JANUARY	Alger Hiss convicted of perjury
FEBRUARY	Senator Joseph R. McCarthy makes initial charges of communist influence in the administration; Julius and Ethel Rosenberg arrested
JUNE	Korean war begins
SEPTEMBER	McCarran Internal Security Act passes over Truman's veto
NOVEMBER	Democratic losses in congressional elections
DECEMBER	Office of Defense Mobilization established as head of full economic-control apparatus

1951

JUNE	Supreme Court affirms conviction of communist leaders; McCarthy attacks General Marshall

1952

APRIL	Attorney General McGrath dismisses Special Prosecutor Morris; Truman fires McGrath; Truman seizes steel industry

JUNE   Supreme Court rules steel seizure unconstitutional
NOVEMBER   Eisenhower defeats Stevenson

Shortly after the campaign of 1944, the vice-president-elect, Harry S Truman, talked with an old friend and political supporter. He spoke of the loneliness of his new position, and the fear with which he faced the future. Roosevelt, he said, wore the pallor of death on his face; it seemed certain that the Presidency would pass to the vice-president before FDR's fourth term was over. The prospect, the friend recalled, seemed to scare the very devil out of Truman. A few months later, the day after he took the oath of office as President, Truman told a group of reporters: "Boys, if you ever pray, pray for me now."

At first fearful of his office, Truman learned to live with the Presidency and discharge its duties with confidence and pride. Presiding over some of the most difficult years of American history, he made epochal decisions with courage and resolution. Yet, although he left a lasting imprint upon American foreign policy, Truman found himself in the same predicament as Roosevelt after 1938 or John F. Kennedy from 1961–63 when it came to domestic change. Some observers, including the political analyst Samuel Lubell, have argued that Truman, for all his advocacy of new reform measures, sought only the stalemate which alone could preserve the uneasy equilibrium of the Democratic party. As a judgment of Truman's intentions, this interpretation is both too harsh and too mechanical; but as a summary of the results of his years in the White House, it is fairly accurate. For reasons beyond Truman's control, these were years of consolidation in which the President could do little more than lay the groundwork for a new era of reform in the hope that some future Chief Executive might initiate it.

HST AND THE CHAOS OF RECONVERSION

Born in 1884, Truman spent most of his early life in Independence, Missouri, then a small-town county seat near Kansas City. His father was an ambitious farmer, livestock dealer, and speculator, his mother a genteel and overprotective woman who encouraged an interest in books and arranged piano lessons for him. An introverted boy, he read avidly and dreamed of being a military leader or great administrator. As a young adult, he initially sought careers other than politics. His myopic eyesight frustrated his hopes of becoming a professional military officer. His dissatisfaction with rural life vitiated his success as manager of the family farm. His investments in various business enterprises were unrewarding; the most disastrous, a partnership in a men's clothing store which failed during the post–World War I recession, left him in debt for twenty years. It was not until 1922, when he was thirty-eight years old, that he decided to go into politics; he quickly realized that he had found his vocation.

Affiliating with the powerful Kansas City machine of Thomas J. Pendergast, he won office as a county administrator. Functioning as leader of the rural wing of the Pendergast machine, he fed patronage to the organization but scrupulously abstained from graft and established a solid record of honesty and efficiency. Like many men who wanted to get ahead in politics, he accepted association with a corrupt machine as part of the price of success, and he gave Pendergast unflagging loyalty and gratitude.

Elected to the Senate in 1934, after winning a close primary marred by voting irregularities on all sides, Truman usually supported the New Deal. Nevertheless, he failed to develop close ties with President Roosevelt, who had little love for Pendergast. Truman's own background, temperament, and shrewdness led him to make friends among the moderates and conservatives in the Senate power structure; he gained the respect of his colleagues by quiet, hard work which won him a reputation as an expert on transportation policy. With the Pendergast machine smashed by 1940, he faced a difficult battle for renomination. In an effort that would foreshadow his 1948 bid, he waged a shoestring campaign, spoke all over the state, won the support of labor unions and Negro leaders, secured the last-minute backing of the Saint Louis machine, and eked out a narrow victory.

Returned to the Senate in the general election, he soon won a national reputation as chairman of a special investigating committee that probed waste and dishonesty in war mobilization. The committee avoided sensationalism, cooperated with the Roosevelt administration, contributed greatly to wartime efficiency, and won nearly universal praise. By 1944, Truman was one of the most powerful Democrats in Washington. As a respected figure with friends and influential supporters in every faction of the party, he was a natural choice for the vice-presidency.

Truman's career paralleled the history of the Democratic party during the first half of the twentieth century. Adding one layer after another to his political identity without repudiating the past, Truman, originally a small-town southern Democrat, became a representative of the aspirations of labor and urban minorities. He moved from a vague Bryanite populism to the urban liberalism of the New Deal. But he was above all a professional politician, devoted to the Democratic party far more than to any group or ideology and seeking to keep it open to all viewpoints.

Where Roosevelt the patrician had won the awe of the common man, Truman attempted to win political support by appearing as the epitome of the common man. In a sense, this effort was an exercise in artificial image building. Truman genuinely believed in the traditional virtues of middle America, but he was also widely read in history and biography, sophisticated in the ways of politics, frequently thoughtful and balanced in his decisions, if not his rhetoric. Although he tolerated the myth that his favorite tune was "The Missouri Waltz," he was actually a lover of classical music. He established a sense of identity with the ordinary citizen and frequently seemed decisive in a feisty, scrappy manner. But he could also appear unable to cope with the enormous problems he faced, too much the machine politician, and too lacking in the dignity expected of a chief of state. His "common man" image probably hurt him as much as it helped him.

In addition to the difficult foreign policy problems which consumed so much of his time, the new President faced the delicate tasks of establishing his own political identity, managing the unresolved issues of the New Deal, and converting the economy from war to peace. This last issue, reconversion, dominated Truman's first year and a half in office. A prosaic, dull-sounding term, it covered a wide range of explosive problems, all of them involving in one way or another people's pocketbooks. The depression years, followed by the priorities of war, had left the nation with a critical shortage of low- and middle-income housing; returning veterans and their families had to double-up with parents or pay exorbitant rents for slum-style hovels. Blacks, hit hard by defense-plant layoffs, desperately needed to maintain the gains they had won during the war. Businessmen demanded an end to controls on prices and the allocation of raw materials. The labor unions pushed for termination of wage ceilings. Consumers increasingly resented shortages. After V-J Day, there was little motivation for continued patriotic sacrifice.

The short-run economic pressures all pointed toward an inflationary boom, which the administration needed to contain. However, many economists believed that the long-run outlook was for a resumption of the depression unless the nation could apply the lessons of the 1930s. Truman thus simultaneously faced the job of preventing inflation and depression, aware that if the first got out of hand, it might well cause the second.

With the end of the war, Truman spelled out a domestic program clearly in the New Deal tradition: broad housing legislation, extension of the Fair Employment Practices Committee on a permanent basis, expanded social security, and a national health insurance system. To meet the danger of depression, he advocated increased unemployment benefits, a higher minimum wage, public works projects, and a law that would commit the government to underwrite national full employment. To control inflation, he recommended the extension of price and rent controls.

Congress was no more amenable than it had been to Roosevelt's suggestions. It approved only a small program of aid to veterans' housing, let the FEPC expire, and killed most of the other proposals. In early 1946, it did finally approve a watered-down version of the full-employment request. The Employment Act of 1946 contained no machinery to assure full employment, although it vaguely proclaimed "maximum employment" to be a national objective. Yet it was one of the most important legislative accomplishments of the postwar era because it established a three-man Council of Economic Advisers responsible directly to the President, charged with providing comprehensive information on the state of the economy and making policy recommendations to him. Predominantly manned by eminent academic economists who represented no special interests and were conversant with the newest trends in economic thought, the council gave the White House a means it never before had possessed for formulating a coherent economic policy.

The administration's most immediate problem in late 1945 and early 1946 was labor-management relations. The major unions demanded wage increases of about 30 percent to make up for lost overtime pay and raises forgone during the war. Truman, though he hoped to keep the lid on prices, was willing to support wage settlements of around 15 percent, but all of Washington's efforts at compromise failed. Strikes developed in one major industry after another, hampering industrial reconversion and aggravating consumer shortages.

In December 1945 Truman requested legislation that would delay work stoppages pending recommendations by government fact-finding committees. Union leaders attacked the idea as antilabor; Congress failed to enact it. In May 1946 two railway unions went on strike although the government had attempted to avoid a walkout by seizing the lines; enraged, the President demanded a law that would allow him to draft the strikers into the army. Fortunately, cooler heads prevailed; the strike was quickly settled, and the bill was buried in a Senate commitee. Throughout 1946, Truman was engaged in a running dispute with the United Mine Workers; near the end of the year, he ordered prosecution of the union for striking in defiance of a government injunction. Such actions undercut his labor support at a time when he was alienating farm and business groups by standing for price controls and New Deal welfarism.

In order to settle strikes in such key industries as auto and steel, the administration had to sanction price increases that would compensate for higher wages. These "bulges" in the price line were the first indication of the collapse of the control effort. By early 1946, many commodities—including razor blades, nylons, choice cuts of meat, automobiles, and premium liquors—were for the most part available only through illegal black-market transactions, and a frustrated consuming public appeared increasingly willing to pay outrageous prices for the small luxuries which had been scarce for so many years.

Through the early months of the year, the adminstration appeared divided and uncertain on price controls. Chester Bowles and the OPA fought for their continuance, but some Truman appointees, including John W. Snyder, head of the Office of War Mobilization and Reconversion, openly favored rapid decontrol. The President tolerated the semi-public dispute. On June 29, 1946, just a day before controls were to expire, Congress passed a bill to continue them, but in a seriously diluted form. Truman responded with a stinging veto which charged that the legislative branch had unleashed a potentially catastrophic inflation; he demanded reconstitution of the OPA with its full wartime authority. For more than three weeks, the nation was without controls, and prices soared upward. Near the end of July, Congress passed another bill fully as weak as the first one; Truman gave in and signed it. Meaningful controls were at an end. Given the widespread desire to return to normal peacetime conditions, it probably would have been impossible to preserve a strong OPA, but almost all sides found something in Truman's role to criticize. He had alienated practically every important group by advocating a tough bill, then finally signing a weak one.

Despite his espousal of a New Deal–type program, the President angered liberals by dropping many figures who had been associated with the Roosevelt era. Many of the New Dealers who left the government did so out of necessity, having been physically or financially exhausted by hard years of federal service. Yet it was indisputable that they felt no close ties to the new President and that he tended to replace them with regular party men more amenable to moderate and conservative Democrats. By the beginning of 1946, only three Roosevelt appointees remained in the cabinet. One of them—Secretary of the Navy James Forrestal—was a conservative. The others—Secretary of the Interior Harold Ickes and Secretary of Commerce Henry Wallace—were to leave under the worst possible conditions for the President.

In February 1946 Ickes, a respected old veteran of progressive battles dating back to the Bull Moose campaign of 1912, resigned in angry protest when Truman attempted to appoint a conservative oilman and close political supporter, Edwin Pauley, as undersecretary of the navy. Ickes charged that Pauley had offered to secure large campaign contributions for the Democrats in 1944 if the Interior Department would be friendlier to oil interests. Pauley denied the allegation, but the Senate refused to confirm him. The Ickes affair marked the first clean break between Truman and the independent progressives who had supported Roosevelt and the New Deal. The firing of Henry Wallace in September accentuated the split. With his strong support from labor, Negroes, and liberal intellectuals, Wallace had become a symbol of the Roosevelt heritage. His ejection from the cabinet seriously divided the Democratic party in the key urban states on the eve of a crucial congressional election campaign.

By the fall of 1946, Truman's stock had declined drastically. He was personally unimpressive and unable to lead the nation in the manner of his charismatic predecessor. Most of his legislative program was buried in congressional committees. He had positively alienated the labor movement and middle-class intellectuals and had left other groups at best apathetic toward him and his party. Both his weakness and the public temper became apparent when livestock producers rebelled against what remained of price controls by refusing to ship their hogs and cattle to market. As meat disappeared from the butcher shops and grocery stores, a national demand for the lifting of controls developed. In mid-October, the President, under great pressure from party leaders, surrendered and removed all controls; it was a humiliating defeat.

Republican candidates, buoyed by the smell of victory, campaigned under such slogans as "Had Enough?" and "To Err Is Truman." The Democratic leaders asked the President to stay out of the campaign and desperately put Roosevelt's old speeches on the radio. In November the Republicans won control of Congress by solid majorities for the first time since the election of 1928. The New Deal, it seemed, was over; the country was returning to normalcy, and Truman's political future was very bleak indeed.

THE EIGHTIETH CONGRESS AND THE ELECTION OF 1948

The Republican leaders of the new Eightieth Congress were conservatives who had bitterly opposed the New Deal. One of their first moves, motivated by the memory of Franklin Roosevelt, was to push through Congress the Twenty-second Amendment to the Constitution; ratified by three-fourths of the states in 1951, it limited future Presidents to two terms. Led by Speaker Joseph Martin in the House and Robert A. Taft in the Senate, the Republican majority was determined not simply to block the reform measures Truman had recommended but also to roll back the New Deal at least a bit. Frequently supported by conservative Democrats, the GOP legislators cut appropriations even for such popular programs as public power and school lunches, prepared tax legislation designed primarily to give relief to the higher brackets, passed laws to reverse Supreme Court decisions which had extended social security coverage, and moved to place restrictions upon the labor movement.

Truman's first reactions were cautious and conciliatory; for a time in early 1947, it appeared that he might opt for moderation. The President's instincts and political sense, however, soon led him toward an aggressive liberalism. With the other party in control of Congress, the public could hardly hold Truman accountable for legislative results. He was free to make any request, no matter how hopeless, and to criticize at will without being accused of a failure of legislative leadership. By mid-year, he was shrewdly depicting himself as a defender of New Deal liberalism against a reactionary Congress. For the next year, he would alternate between sharp vetoes, frequently overridden, and strong calls for progressive reforms, almost invariably ignored. He made no serious attempt at legislative leadership; his objective was to define alternatives as sharply as possible and build a platform for the campaign of 1948.

The turning point came with Truman's veto of the Taft-Hartley bill in June 1947. The legislation, which had swept through Congress with large majorities, reflected wide public indignation against the aggressiveness of the labor movement as well as a conservative impulse to modify one of the most important accomplishments of the New Deal, the National Labor Relations (Wagner) Act. The bill outlawed certain "unfair labor practices"—including refusal to bargain in good faith, the secondary boycott, and the jurisdictional strike. Unions were made liable for breach of contract, and management could petition the National Labor Relations Board for new representational elections whenever employers felt that a union no longer enjoyed majority support. The President could request court injunctions for "cooling-off periods" of up to eighty days in strikes that imperiled the national interest. The bill prohibited the closed shop—the arrangement in which prior possession of a union card was a condition of employment—and its most important provision, Section 14b, permitted the individual states to ban the union shop—the arrangement in which employees were required to join the union after a brief probationary period on the job. Universally condemned by labor leaders as a "slave labor bill," Taft-Hartley was the most important of the Republican attacks against the New Deal legacy. It would have little effect on the established unions, but it did impair efforts to extend organization to new geographical and industrial areas.

Truman responded to the bill with a strongly worded veto message and thereby regained the support of practically every union chief in the country. It mattered little that Congress swiftly overrode the veto or that the administration was unable to muster even a majority of the

Democrats in the House. Truman had emerged as a defender of the ordinary working man and could count upon the invaluable assistance of the unions in the campaign of 1948.

Shortly thereafter, the President was battling with Congress over a whole range of reform issues. He successfully vetoed a tax-reduction bill, observing that it granted savings of less than $30 to individuals earning $2,000 a year while it gave $5,000 in relief to those in the $50,000 bracket. He continued to advocate broad government assistance to low- and middle-income housing. As inflation continued unabated, he urged Congress to authorize the resumption of economic controls, although he and his advisers were privately convinced that it would be impossible to put the lid back on prices. For the record, he called for national medical insurance and federal aid to elementary and secondary education.

The President also took steps to bring Negroes behind him. He was genuinely indignant over incidents of violence in the South against blacks, many of them veterans determined to claim equal rights. He was also aware that Negroes had voted Democratic for little more than a decade and that, despite his support of civil rights as a senator, they felt little personal attachment to him. Truman was too much of a southerner to believe in social integration, but he was an honest advocate of equal opportunity, never realizing the artificiality of the line he drew between the two concepts. In later years he would condemn direct-action tactics such as the sit-ins of the early 1960s; yet his acts as President gave an important impetus to the Negro revolution.

In the fall of 1946 Truman appointed a special presidential committee on civil rights and packed it with noted liberals. In his speeches he made a stronger commitment to civil rights than had any American President before him. In 1947 he authorized the Justice Department to present an amicus curiae (friend of the court) argument to the Supreme Court in the case of *Shelly* v. *Kraemer*. The administration brief gave strong support to Negro plaintiffs who were challenging the legality of restrictive housing covenants. In May 1948 the Court unanimously declared that such agreements were not legally enforceable.

In subsequent cases, all decided in favor of Negro plaintiffs, the Justice Department submitted arguments attacking segregation and discrimination in interstate transportation (*Henderson* v. *US* [1950]) and higher education (*Sweatt* v. *Painter* [1950] and *McLaurin* v. *Oklahoma State Regents* [1950]). In all cases, the administration challenged the established doctrine that minority rights were satisfied by so-called separate but equal accommodations. In December 1952 the government carried its position to a logical conclusion by supporting blacks seeking to desegregate the elementary and secondary schools.

In the fall of 1947, shortly before the first amicus curiae argument, the Civil Rights Committee issued a report advocating a broad civil rights program to attack discrimination and segregation. In February 1948 Truman asked Congress to adopt several of the committee's most important recommendations, including an antilynching bill, a voting-rights act, prohibition of discrimination in interstate transportation, and a permanent FEPC. He thus became the first President since Reconstruction to advocate civil rights legislation designed specifically to assist the black quest for first-class citizenship.

In July 1948, with a presidential campaign approaching and southern conservatives already in revolt, the President issued executive orders establishing policies of nondiscrimination in the federal civil service and the armed forces. The second order met resistance from most military leaders, but by the end of Truman's Presidency the U.S. Army was almost totally integrated. The President's directives led to a quiet but significant revolution which would affect the attitudes of the millions of Americans connected in one way or another with the military.

Truman's election strategy was to reassemble the political coalition that had sustained Roosevelt, and the programs he offered seemed to have the best chance of doing so. All the same, he faced challenges from both the left and right wings of his party. Moreover, his personal stature remained so low that even those who supported his policies questioned his ability to represent them. As late as the spring of 1948, he could not even be certain of nomination, and, if he were chosen by the Democratic convention, his defeat in November seemed a foregone conclusion.

One challenge came from Henry Wallace, who announced at the beginning of the year that he would run for President as a third-party candidate. Throughout 1947, Wallace had denounced administration foreign policy; he drew large crowds on speaking tours and appeared to have retained much of his following among labor, liberals, and Negroes. In February 1948 one of his supporters, Leo Isaacson, won a special congressional election in New York City as a candidate of the American Labor party, an established New York organization which functioned as a branch of Wallace's new Progressive party. The incident, actually a fluke which occurred under special circumstances, convinced impressionable observers that the Democrats were through and that Wallace would poll 5 to 10 million votes.

The President's civil rights program led to a revolt by southern conservatives motivated not simply by racism but also by broad opposition to the administration's liberal social-economic platform. Throughout the spring, some southerners planned for the establishment of another new party while others joined in a movement to deny the President renomination. It became abundantly clear that neither Truman nor any other liberal Democrat could count upon the votes of a solid South.

Convinced that Truman was a certain loser, many Democrats attempted to block his nomination. An implausible coalition of big-city bosses, anti-Wallace liberals, and southern moderates attempted to draft the most popular living American hero, General Dwight D. Eisenhower. The Eisenhower boom was a desperate move by politicians who feared that their party was falling apart and felt that only a charismatic leader could unite it and deliver another victory. That Eisenhower had expressed himself on few, if any, domestic issues was irrelevant; it made him all the more attractive. Presidents are usually able to dictate to their party conventions, but Truman's position was so weak that Eisenhower, if he had given his supporters any encouragement, probably could have been the Democratic candidate in 1948.

With the general refusing to be considered, the convention could only turn to Truman. The vice-presidential nomination went to the popular Kentucky senator Alben Barkley. In a gesture of independence the delegates rejected administration efforts to appease the South with a vacuous civil rights plank. Acting ironically against Truman's wishes, a coalition of urban bosses, labor leaders, and liberals pushed through a point-by-point endorsement of the program the President himself had recommended to Congress in February. Delegates from Mississippi and Alabama walked out of the convention; other southerners stayed to cast a large protest vote for Senator Richard Russell of Georgia. In mid-July, southern conservatives established the States' Rights ("Dixiecrat") party in a ploy designed to divert support from the national Democratic party and throw the presidential election into the House of Representatives. The new party's candidate for President was Governor J. Strom Thurmond of South Carolina.

The Republicans, meanwhile, had turned again to Thomas E. Dewey and had nominated as his running mate the popular liberal governor of California, Earl Warren. Headed by the successful chief executives of the two largest states in the country, the Republican ticket seemed assured of victory over a weak and divided opposition. Seeking above all to avoid mistakes, Dewey pitched his pronouncements to such vague themes as the restoration of national unity and shied away from specific stands on controversial issues.

Dewey's strategy was the textbook approach for a candidate confident of winning, but it played into Truman's hands. In his speech accepting nomination, the President announced that he would call a special session of the Republican Congress to request passage of housing, antiinflation, and other progressive bills. He did so in the expectation, indeed the hope, that Congress would fail to act and thereby give him a powerful campaign issue. The Republicans followed the administration script almost to the letter, and Truman took to the rails in a "whistle stop" tour which featured hard-hitting condemnations of GOP conservatism. Making as many as a dozen informal talks a day, frequently speaking to small audiences from the rear platform of his train, the President both established a rapport with the ordinary American and pounded across the message that the Republicans were planning to dismantle the New Deal. Dewey, unable to disavow the Republican legislative leadership, retreated into lofty platitudes, convinced that he need only ignore Truman to win the Presidency.

As a result, the President was able to appeal effectively to middle- and lower-income citizens who wanted action to halt rising prices and provide adequate housing, to Negroes who responded to his advocacy of civil rights, to union members who believed that the Taft-Hartley Act was the first step in Republican plans to destroy the unions, and to farmers who watched grain prices drop because Congress had failed to appropriate money for new government storage facilities. The campaign that took shape was concerned almost exclusively with domestic issues, a field where the Democrats had a natural majority. Dewey's flat personality and his failure to deliver convincing rebuttals gave Truman far more of an advantage than anyone suspected.

The surprising election results demonstrated the soundness of Truman's strategy. The President polled 24.1 million votes to Dewey's 22.0 million. Thurmond and Wallace each drew less than 1.2 million, although Thurmond carried four southern states and Wallace drew enough normally Democratic votes to throw New York, Michigan, and Maryland to Dewey by narrow margins. Truman came out with 303 electoral votes, 37 more than the bare majority of 266 needed to avoid a decision in the House of Representatives. He had succeeded by drawing together a coalition of the underprivileged who wanted new reforms and the newly emergent middle class whose tenuous status had grown in one way or another out of the work of the New Deal. This coalition would deliver a majority to a Democrat who could convince them that the Republicans planned to return to the 1920s; whether it had laid the basis for an *extension* of the New Deal remained to be seen.

THE FAIR DEAL
AND THE POLITICS OF ANTICOMMUNISM

"Every segment of our population and every individual has a right to expect from our Government a fair deal," declared Truman as he laid a far-ranging legislative agenda before the new, solidly Democratic Congress in January 1949. Truman's Fair Deal was, of course, a direct descendant of the New Deal, but it differed in certain matters of emphasis and technique. Fair Deal economics, most eloquently expressed by Leon Keyserling of the Council of Economic Advisers, rejected the depression psychology which took scarcity for granted; the Fair Deal strove for the expansion of abundance. As early as 1949, Keyserling was arguing that a sustained rate of economic growth could bring the income of every American family above the poverty level.

The administration's farm program, the Brannan Plan, named for Secretary of Agriculture Charles F. Brannan, combined the economics of abundance with a political effort to transform the Democratic party into a farmer-labor coalition that would make the cause of reform invincible. Brannan proposed a departure from the New Deal method of maintaining farm income through crop restrictions, which meant higher prices for consumers. He advocated an end to government rigging of agricultural production and commodity prices; the result would be significantly lower prices for practically every farm product. The government would support farm income through direct payments based upon the size of a farmer's crop but subject to a maximum limit which would force the dissolution of factory-type farms and encourage family-size enterprises.

The administration preached the necessity of urban-rural unity and organized farm-labor conferences in an attempt to manufacture mutual support for such objectives as repeal of the Taft-Hartley Act and passage of the Brannan Plan. The strategy, while superficially attractive, was a failure. Farmers preferred the price-support system with its much smaller degree of government supervision over production, and large operators naturally fought a proposal that would force them into liquidation. Large or small, most farmers possessed an individualistic and entrepreneurial mentality which made them suspicious of labor organizations and inclined them to favor the Taft-Hartley Act. Labor leaders had little understanding of agricultural economics but were wary of what seemed to be a proposal to give farmers a guaranteed annual wage without corresponding benefits for workers. The Brannan Plan failed to overcome one of the most persistent themes of modern American history, the misunderstanding and antagonism between urban and rural cultures.

The President did obtain passage of the Housing Act of 1949, a major piece of legislation, but its provisions for large-scale public housing were neither effectively administered nor adequately financed. He also secured generous enlargement of New Deal programs, including the minimum wage, social security, and public power. On these counts alone, the Eighty-first Congress was the most liberal in a decade. Nevertheless, it rejected not only the Brannan Plan but also the other reform programs primarily identified with Truman—Taft-Hartley repeal, national health insurance, federal aid to education, and civil rights. A brief economic recession halted rising prices and made antiinflation legislation unnecessary.

The results were sparse when measured against expectations, and some disappointed progressives accused Truman of a failure of leadership. In fact, however, any President would have experienced great difficulty in working for passage of such a wide range of controversial legislation, even under the most favorable circumstances. Truman faced a Congress in which Republican and Democratic conservatives still possessed great leverage; the Democratic legislative leadership, especially in the Senate, was to a great extent the tool of party conservatives and moderates and inclined to offer the President little more than token help in any all-out effort for new departures. Nor could Truman claim an overwhelming public mandate. He had received less than 50 percent of the total popular vote in 1948, and public-opinion surveys failed to uncover mass support for his program. It seems likely that most of those who voted for him had done so with the hope of protecting what they already had rather than initiating a new era of reform. Truman was successful in preserving the heritage of the New Deal, but his own Fair Deal proposals amounted to little more than an agenda he would pass on to his Democratic successors.

The public mood and the structure of Congress may have been most significant in frustrating domestic reform, but the cold war was also a powerful factor. It diverted public attention from domestic needs and led Truman to define his priorities in such a manner that the Fair Deal nearly always ran second to the imperatives of foreign policy. The cold war made it all the more difficult for the President to rouse the nation with progressive rhetoric and led him to use whatever leverage he possessed with Congress in working for his foreign policy objectives. Perhaps most importantly, certainly most ironically, the deep ideological overtones of the Soviet-American conflict created a climate of anticommunist hysteria which ricocheted against the very administration that had dedicated itself to containing communism abroad.

America, so overwhelmingly a middle-class, capitalist society, has always been prone to react with terror against any form of radicalism; and American conservative politicians have been quick to accuse their opponents of sympathy with whatever far-left doctrine appears most menacing at a given moment. During such periods of emotionalism, whether against Jacobinism in the 1790s, anarchism in the late nineteenth century, or Bolshevism after World War I, right-wingers have argued that the major threat to American freedom came from within rather than without, that liberals were either too soft on subversives or had come under their influence.

During the 1930s and '40s, the charge that the New Deal and then the Fair Deal were in some manner communistic had become a common feature of conservative rhetoric. By the end of 1949, three factors were converging to give such charges great prominence and a degree of credibility: the desperation of Republican politicians who had seen their party lose a fifth consecutive presidential election, frustration at American reverses in the struggle with communism, and evidence of domestic subversion.

In mid-1945, federal agents had raided the offices of *Amerasia* magazine, a leftish journal of Asian affairs, and had discovered hundreds of classified State Department documents on U.S.–Chinese relations. But the papers were relatively unimportant, and the government found no evidence that any of them had been passed to the Russians. It was a common practice, then as now, for government officials to make classified papers available to favored journalists. The case created a brief sensation, but led only to fines for the magazine's editor and one minor State Department official.

The *Amerasia* episode might have been quickly forgotten if not for subsequent events. In 1946 Canadian authorities uncovered an extensive Soviet espionage apparatus. The Federal Bureau of Investigation privately warned the White House of the need to ferret out similar activities in the United States. The enunciation of the Truman Doctrine in March 1947 crystallized the cold war and contributed to public uneasiness over Red subversion.

Just two weeks after requesting aid for Greece and Turkey, Truman signed an executive order initiating a drastic government loyalty program. It provided for investigations of every federal employee from atomic scientists engaged in supersecret research to janitors in the least strategic of government agencies. If an investigation turned up "reasonable grounds to suspect disloyalty," the employee was subject to dismissal.

Hastily drawn up, involving at least cursory inquiries into the lives of millions of individuals, the loyalty program inevitably committed serious abuses. While it failed to uncover a single verifiable case of espionage or find even one card-carrying communist in the public service, it was responsible for the dismissal of 378 individuals. Frequently, these persons were not permitted to face their accusers or introduce evidence in their behalf; at times, they were not even told the nature of the charges against them. On occasion, they were the victims of investigators with a right-wing police mentality who tended to equate liberal sympathies with adherence to an international communist conspiracy. Justice usually prevailed, but it nevertheless was thwarted enough to make the program one of the most serious blots on the record of the Truman administration. The historian can only guess at the damage it did by way of intimidating policy-making officials in key federal agencies, but there can be little doubt that many fewer than before were willing to hazard the risks of originality or unorthodoxy.

In another questionable move, the administration obtained indictments against the leaders of the U.S. Communist party, charging them under the Smith Act with conspiracy to advocate the violent overthrow of the government. After a turbulent and controversial trial, the communists were convicted. In *Dennis* v. *United States* (1949), the Supreme Court upheld the result, in effect repudiating the principle that individuals or groups were liable to punishment for sedition or subversion only if their activities represented a "clear and present danger" to the republic. Cold war as well as total war placed serious strains upon constitutional guarantees of liberty.

Because of the loyalty program, the Smith Act prosecutions, and the candidacy of Henry Wallace, who was openly supported by the Communist party, Truman did not have to face charges of softness toward the Red threat in the 1948 campaign. After the President's upset victory, however, many GOP politicians, led by the New Isolationists, began to perceive that only the issue of procommunism might return them to power. Events soon gave them an opportunity.

In 1948 two former communists—Whittaker Chambers and Elizabeth Bentley—appeared before congressional committees, admitted that they had engaged in espionage for the Soviet Union, and implicated several prominent figures. Miss Bentley, who had left the party in 1945, leveled accusations against Harry Dexter White, a high official in the Treasury Department during World War II and head of the International Monetary Fund for a year after the war; Lauchlin Currie, who had been a White House assistant to President Roosevelt; and William Remington, an important official in the foreign-trade section of the Department of Commerce. Chambers, who had broken with the party in 1938, charged that Alger Hiss, an important State Department figure from the late 1930s until 1947, had passed documents to him for a two-year period in the 1930s. Chambers and Miss Bentley had made these charges to the FBI, but intensive investigation had failed to verify them. Truman curtly dismissed the allegations as a "red herring" calculated to divert attention from the real issues of the 1948 campaign.

Miss Bentley's charges were in fact never proven. No evidence was ever uncovered against Currie, although his career was seriously damaged. White delivered a strong rebuttal and died of a heart attack shortly afterward. Remington was cleared by the federal loyalty program and successfully sued Miss Bentley for libel. Nevertheless, he was eventually ousted from the Commerce Department and in 1951 was convicted of perjury for having denied that he had been a communist while a college student in the 1930s. In 1954 he was killed by accident while watching a prison-yard fight.

Chambers' charges against Hiss led to one of the most sensational legal battles of American history. After Hiss instituted a libel suit against him, Chambers melodramatically produced microfilmed copies of confidential State Department reports, a few in Hiss's handwriting, the rest almost certainly copied on a typewriter Hiss had once owned. On the basis of this evidence, a federal grand jury voted a perjury indictment against Hiss for having denied espionage activities and past membership in the Communist party. The proceedings which followed created sensational headlines and emotional debates throughout 1949.

Hiss was the very prototype of the northeastern intellectual who had done so much to shape the New Deal. Most liberal Democrats were convinced that he *had* to be innocent, and most conservative Republicans equally certain that he must be guilty. His case developed into a symbolic test of the whole Roosevelt administration. The first trial ended in a hung jury, the second in a conviction. The evidence was tenuous, consisting of little more than Chambers' word that Hiss himself had passed the documents; and in a less explosive atmosphere the outcome might have been different. As it was, the Hiss case provided ammunition for those who charged that America was being betrayed by men in high places.

Accusations of betrayal could find an ever-wider audience in late 1949 and early 1950. The fall of mainland China came as a shock to Americans and outraged even most of the internationalist Republicans who had cooperated with Truman, including Senator Vandenberg. Vandenberg would not have broken with the administration, but his health was failing; increasingly, the major Republican spokesman on foreign policy was Robert A. Taft, the intellectual leader of the New Isolationists.

The equally stunning news of the first Russian A-bomb in September 1949 was followed, shortly after the Hiss conviction in early 1950, by the arrest of a band of atomic spies, including Julius and Ethel Rosenberg. Hiss, once a respected and trusted official, had been found guilty in essence of espionage, if in fact only of perjury. A Justice Department clerk, Judith Coplon, was convicted at about the same time of having passed information to the Russians.* The government now admitted that the Rosenbergs and their confederates had penetrated the heavy curtain of

---

* Miss Coplon's conviction was subsequently reversed because the evidence used against her had been illegally obtained.

secrecy that had surrounded the Manhattan Project. Most Americans probably assumed, quite erroneously, that the Russians could never have developed an atomic bomb otherwise. The situation was ripe for ambitious politicians who hoped to bring down the Truman administration by asserting that there were other spies and traitors within the government and that they could operate only because of official tolerance or softness.

In February 1950 Senator Joseph R. McCarthy, a hitherto obscure first-term Republican senator from Wisconsin, astounded the nation by telling a Republican gathering in Wheeling, West Virginia, that the State Department had 205 card-carrying communists on its payroll. The senator apparently was a bit surprised that his partisan rhetoric won national attention, but he seized the opportunity. For the next four years, he was one of the most powerful forces in American politics. A demagogic propagandist of the first order, McCarthy somehow moved easily and credibly from one preposterous charge to another, always evading demands that he produce tangible proof. Other right-wing demagogues had lacked his audacity and had retreated when unable to prove their accusations. McCarthy employed not only the technique of the "Big Lie"—the charge so astounding that there *had* to be something to it—he used what Richard Rovere has characterized as the "multiple untruth"—a series of allegations so complex and involved that it was impossible to discredit them rapidly. He was a master at the art of producing "documentation" which purported to prove his charges but upon close examination failed to do so. He was equally adept at blurring the vital distinction between left-wing associations or opinions on the one hand and treasonable acts on the other.

He never produced his list of 205 communists, although he reduced the number several times. He unsuccessfully charged Owen Lattimore, a Johns Hopkins professor whom he extravagantly described as the major architect of America's unsuccessful China policy, with being the chief Soviet spy in the United States. He attacked Philip Jessup, a distinguished diplomat, because Jessup had been connected with the institute that sponsored *Amerasia* magazine. When a special Senate committee, headed by Millard Tydings, a conservative Maryland Democrat, found McCarthy's assertions to be unfounded, the Wisconsin Republican helped to defeat Tydings in the 1950 elections by arranging for the circulation of a faked photograph that showed Tydings in intimate conversation with the head of the American Communist party.*

---

* Observers at the time and historians since have noted that Tydings was vulnerable and might well have lost in any case. Whether McCarthy tipped the balance against him can only be a matter of conjecture. It is undeniable, however, that the *appearance* of decisive influence strengthened McCarthy greatly.

McCarthy was able to survive despite his incredible mendacity because the events of 1949 and 1950 shook popular faith in the Truman administration and because many Republican leaders saw him as a tool who could lead the party back to power. A few elder statesmen, including Henry L. Stimson, denounced him, and a half-dozen Republican senators, led by Margaret Chase Smith of Maine, signed a "Declaration of Conscience" repudiating his methods, but McCarthy had the support and encouragement of GOP Senate Leader Wherry and of Taft, who told him: "If one case doesn't work, try another." Most Republican legislators yielded to the impulses to tolerate their Wisconsin colleague.

McCarthyism—journalists had coined the word by mid-1950—was, as Samuel Lubell has written, a "politics of revenge" which appealed especially to groups that had hated the New Deal and resented World War II—the conservative Republicans and the old isolationists. It meshed nicely with the emerging New Isolationism, whose hatred of communism was matched only by its revulsion from the methods required to combat it. Both the New Isolationism and the old demanded a search for internal scapegoats, and McCarthy satisfied this need. The ordinary American, worried over such events as the fall of China, the Soviet A-bomb, the Hiss case, and the espionage arrests, was prepared at least to give McCarthy a hearing.

Some revisionist historians have suggested that in McCarthyism the Truman administration was reaping a whirlwind which it had sown in 1947 by depicting international communism as a mortal enemy and initiating a loyalty program which underscored the danger of internal subversion. The thesis has a certain superficial plausibility; Truman and the cold warriors in his administration doubtless contributed to public concern over communism at home and abroad. But can one assume that there would have been no public worry had the Truman administration chosen to ignore the problems of communism? Only if one assumes that the Soviet Union had no expansionist ambitions whatever and therefore could have been ignored; otherwise, the backlash might have developed more quickly.

KOREA, COMMUNISM, CORRUPTION

By June 1950, McCarthy had kept American politics in a state of turmoil for months. It is doubtful, however, that even so talented a demagogue could have retained his following had it not been for the Korean war. The Korean conflict gave McCarthyism a new lease on life and indeed impelled most legislators to engage in anticommunist demagoguery. Congressmen, led by the Republicans Representative Richard M. Nixon and Senator Karl Mundt, and the conservative Democratic Senator Pat McCarran, stampeded to pass anticommunist legislation. A few honorable exceptions aside, the liberal bloc caved in. In September 1950 Congress passed by overwhelming margins the McCarran Internal Security Act.

The bill required communist organizations to register with the attorney general and disclose full information about their finances. It declared that membership in a communist group was not in itself a crime, but a vague and ill-defined clause outlawed any act that would substantially contribute to the establishment of a totalitarian dictatorship. The State Department could not grant passports to communists. Defense plants could not employ them. A Subversive Activities Control Board was established to investigate suspect organizations and label them subversive. The President might order the summary arrest and internment of individuals suspected of subversive activities during national emergencies. Any alien who had ever been connected with a totalitarian organization was prohibited from entering the United States. (This last provision was liberalized in 1951, critics having pointed out that its main effect would be to discourage communist defectors.)

Truman, although he knew his cause was hopeless, responded with a veto which argued that the bill did practically nothing to discourage espionage or sabotage, sought instead to punish or inhibit free speech and open political activity, and was so vague that it might be used against democratic groups. "In a free country," he declared, "we punish men for the crimes they commit, but never for the opinions they have." The veto was courageous and prophetic. Years later, Supreme Court decisions struck down the registration and passport provisions. (The internment authority was never used; Congress repealed it in the calmer atmosphere of 1971.) The President's objections were quickly overridden in the House, 286–48, and in the Senate, 57–10. The overwhelming numbers indicated that the tide of panic over communism was still rising.

In such an atmosphere, McCarthy and his supporters thrived. The Wisconsin senator was a leading campaigner for the Republicans in the fall congressional elections, freely accusing the Democrats of softness toward communism. Most of the candidates McCarthy denounced lost to conservative Republicans, and many politicians assumed with considerable exaggeration that the Wisconsin senator had played a decisive role. Actually, Democratic losses in the 1950 elections were relatively modest; but most of the losers were liberals vulnerable to McCarthyite accusations. Henceforth, most politicians employed great prudence when dealing with McCarthy.

Truman's decision to fight a limited war in Korea, as demonstrated by his dismissal of General MacArthur, created a vast pool of public frustration in which McCarthy and his followers frolicked. They incessantly denounced Truman and Dean Acheson as procommunist and hurled attacks at officials of the State and Defense Departments almost at random. In June 1951 McCarthy accused General George Marshall, hitherto the most respected and unassailable man in American life, of having participated, knowingly or not, in the communist conspiracy. There was, of course, no truth to McCarthy's charge that Marshall had blood on his hands, but Marshall was never again able to serve as a symbol of national unity. An outraged Truman might make speech after speech denouncing right-wing extremism and upholding civil liberties, but those to whom McCarthy appealed were beyond his reach.

The President only worsened his deteriorating political situation by moving too slowly and uncertainly against instances of corruption in his administration. By 1951, Senate investigators, for the most part Democrats who usually supported Truman, had uncovered examples of influence-peddling involving one or two White House assistants and the chairmen of both the Democratic and Republican parties, tax fixing by certain officials of the Bureau of Internal Revenue, and corruption among tax-enforcement officials for the Justice Department. Truman ignored the accusations for months; he sincerely did not believe charges against his close aides and preferred to handle the rest with quiet dismissals. The "Truman scandals" were hardly among the worst in American history; they did not compare with the big-time corruption of the Harding era and were probably no worse than the finagling that went on during World War II. But they were the worst to come to public attention since the Harding administration, and Truman's refusal to face them permitted his critics to magnify their importance and add a new dimension to their attacks upon the President's credibility.

In early 1952 Truman gave in to public demand and appointed an independent Republican, Newbold Morris, to undertake an investigation of corruption in the government. The project was ill fated from the start. Morris, who had long been active in New York reform causes, was a man of courage and integrity, but he had neither the temperament nor the experience for such a broad yet delicate job. He was further handicapped by being placed under Attorney General J. Howard McGrath, who displayed little zeal for probing his own department. Morris could not even count on the support of the Republicans, many of whom attempted to discredit him out of a fear that he might actually succeed in cleaning up the administration and thus kill the corruption issue.

Their worries were exaggerated. Morris and McGrath soon became embroiled in a bitter dispute. At the end of April, the attorney general fired his new investigator without consulting the President; Truman instantly dismissed McGrath. The President might have recovered from this fiasco by reinstating Morris or replacing McGrath with a man known as a fearless prosecutor. Instead, he picked Federal Judge James McGranery, an old friend unknown to the public, and made no effort to interfere with Morris's return to New York. In the following months, McGranery prosecuted several wrongdoers, but the political damage was beyond repair.

The communism and corruption issues effectively obscured the considerable success the administration enjoyed, after an uncertain start, in managing the economy during the Korean war. Convinced that growth was the best long-run answer to inflation, the administration hoped to enlarge the economy enough to fit a small war into it without serious strain. The process of expansion might generate short-term inflationary pressures, but over the long haul would pay much greater dividends than stifling, rigid controls.

At the beginning of the war, the administration, expecting only a small and brief conflict with North Korea, decided against requesting extensive economic authority. The decision had important diplomatic significance as a signal to the USSR that the United States accepted the Korean conflict as a limited challenge. It was also the beginning of an attempt to produce both guns and butter in abundance through an orderly process of economic growth. During the fall of 1950, prices shot up at the rate of 1 percent a month as consumers who remembered the austerity of World War II engaged in a wave of panic buying; the administration considered this initial inflationary burst unavoidable and expected it to subside as people grasped the limited nature of the war. When Congress, accurately reflecting public concern, voted more extensive control powers than the President wanted, Truman appointed a laissez-faire conservative, Alan Valentine, as director of Economic Stabilization. Valentine made no effort to build a staff or prepare for unexpected emergencies.

Administration plans probably would have worked rather well had it not been for the Chinese intervention of November 1950, which touched off a new wave of scare buying, initiated a significant enlargement of the war, and made it impossible for Truman and his advisers to hope that inflation would take care of itself. The President moved quickly to create a new control structure for the economy. In December 1950 he established the Office of Defense Mobilization (ODM), under Charles E. Wilson, the president of General Electric. The ODM, an agency similar to James Byrnes's World War II Office of War Mobilization, had broad authority to determine priorities and allocate raw materials; it exercised a general supervision over wage-price policy. Eric Johnston, a former industrialist with experience in the World War II bureaucracy, replaced Valentine as director of Economic Stabilization and exercised a loose authority over a Wage Stabilization Board (WSB) composed of representatives from labor, industry, and the public, and the Office of Price Stabilization (OPS) under Michael V. DiSalle, a liberal Democrat who had been mayor of Toledo, Ohio.

By March 1951, the new control apparatus, so similar to that which had been thrown up in the last war, had effectively halted the inflationary spiral. Prices, which had risen 8 percent during the first eight months of the Korean conflict, would increase by only 2.5 percent for the remainder of 1951 and by less than that during all of 1952. The scare buying subsided. Higher taxes, restraints upon consumer credit, and a "tight money" policy initiated by the Federal Reserve System all discouraged excess demand. A policy of tax writeoffs to businesses expanding plant facilities presaged abundant consumer and defense production and thus dampened expectations for long-run inflation.

In early 1952, however, the whole stabilization effort appeared endangered by a labor dispute which demonstrated the tenuousness of Truman's authority and the shadowy nature of the Korean conflict. The United Steelworkers Union and the steel industry had failed to reach agreement on a new contract, their old pact having expired at the end of 1951. Truman ordered the Wage Stabilization Board to recommend a settlement (it did not have authority to compel one), and at his request the workers stayed on the job without a contract for ninety days. In March the WSB recommended moderate increases in wages and fringe benefits, and both Truman and the OPS took the position that steel profits were high enough to permit absorption of the labor concessions without a price increase. The steelworkers promptly accepted the proposal, but the companies insisted upon large price increases. Charles Wilson resigned as director of the ODM when the administration rejected the management position. A strike followed and threatened to cripple defense production.

Truman might have requested a Taft-Hartley injunction to postpone a work stoppage for eighty days, but he felt that the union's voluntary ninety-day continuance prohibited such a course. In early April, after the union had been out for a week, the President condemned management stubbornness, invoked his war powers as Commander in Chief to seize the steel mills, and ordered the workers back on the job. The companies immediately initiated a legal challenge to the seizure, and on June 2, 1952, the Supreme Court in *Youngstown Sheet and Tube Company* v. *Sawyer* ruled in their favor. In the absence of an official state of war and without specific authorization from Congress, the Court declared that the President could not seize private property. A seven-week strike followed, finally ending in a compromise settlement in which the government allowed the steel industry about half the price increases it originally had demanded. The agreement did not, as many observers had feared, set off a new round of inflation; but the episode demonstrated both Truman's political weakness and the difficulties of managing a limited war.

Truman had already announced at the end of March that he would not run for reelection. Exempt from the Twenty-second Amendment, he sincerely believed in the two-term tradition for Presidents; but he could have won only against a very weak opponent. Stalemated at home and abroad, a victim in part of unscrupulous demagoguery but also of his own insensitivity to the public concern over corruption, Truman was at another low point in his career. Seeking only to turn his party leadership and his office over to the best man, he first approached Dwight D. Eisenhower, only to discover that the general had come to consider himself a Republican; then he asked the governor of Illinois, Adlai E. Stevenson.

At first genuinely reluctant to run, Stevenson submitted to a draft as genuine as any in American political history at the Democratic convention, which chose him over Senator Estes Kefauver and W. Averell Harriman. A man of wide experience in several federal positions before he had run for office in Illinois, Stevenson possessed a rare eloquence and thoughtfulness which gave him special appeal to those who worked with words. He brought middle-class intellectuals into politics on a more active and committed basis than ever before. He also sought to disassociate himself from Truman by locating his campaign headquarters in Illinois, appointing a new national Democratic chairman, and even promising to clean up "the mess in Washington." Temperamentally and ideologically, he was a bit more moderate than Truman, and he was never able to establish the President's bond with the ordinary person.

During the fall, Truman campaigned tirelessly, as much to seek vindication for his own record as to elect Stevenson. But the appeal of Eisenhower was overwhelming; he won the election easily. Truman took unprecedented measures to facilitate the transition of the Presidency, although his admiration for the general had failed to survive the campaign. On January 20, 1953, Truman went into an active retirement, perhaps feeling repudiated, surely unaware that most of the public would soon adopt him as a folk hero who apotheosized the common man, but confident that he had served the nation well.

SEVEN

The Ike Age

CHRONOLOGY

1952—60

1952

JULY — Republicans nominate Eisenhower for President
SEPTEMBER — Nixon's "Checkers" speech
NOVEMBER — Eisenhower and Nixon swamp Stevenson and Sparkman

1953

MARCH — C. Wesley Roberts resigns as chairman of the Republican National Committee; Senator McCarthy opposes designation of Charles Bohlen as ambassador to the USSR
MAY — Eisenhower signs offshore oil bill
OCTOBER — Eisenhower names Earl Warren Chief Justice of the United States
NOVEMBER — Truman-Brownell controversy

1954

APRIL — Army-McCarthy hearings begin
MAY — Supreme Court strikes down school segregation; Congress approves Saint Lawrence Seaway
JUNE — Atomic Energy Commission suspends security clearance of J. Robert Oppenheimer
AUGUST — Agriculture Act of 1954 provides for flexible price supports

OCTOBER	Atomic Energy Commission approves Dixon-Yates contract
NOVEMBER	Democrats regain control of Congress
DECEMBER	U.S. Senate censures McCarthy

1955

AUGUST	Secretary of the Air Force Talbott resigns
SEPTEMBER	Eisenhower suffers major heart attack
DECEMBER	Merger of AFL and CIO; Montgomery bus boycott begins

1956

FEBRUARY	Eisenhower reluctantly vetoes natural gas bill
MAY	Agricultural Act of 1956 includes "soil bank" program
JUNE	Eisenhower undergoes surgery for ileitis; Federal Highway Act
NOVEMBER	Eisenhower and Nixon overwhelmingly reelected

1957

SEPTEMBER	Civil Rights Act of 1957; federal troops enforce desegregation at Little Rock
NOVEMBER	Eisenhower suffers mild stroke

1958

SEPTEMBER	National Defense Education Act; resignation of Sherman Adams
NOVEMBER	Democrats sweep congressional elections

1959

JUNE	U.S. Senate rejects appointment of Lewis Strauss as secretary of commerce
SEPTEMBER	Landrum-Griffin Act

1960

APRIL	Civil Rights Act of 1960
AUGUST	Kerr-Mills Act

By 1952, Truman's mistakes and misfortunes had cleared the way for the Republicans to capture the Presidency. The party needed only an attractive candidate, a problem which it solved by choosing the most popular figure in American life; a solid majority of the people loved Dwight D. Eisenhower and had an unshakable faith in him. But if the Ike Age were to be more than an interval between Democratic administrations, the Republicans had to identify themselves with policy positions that embodied the aspirations of the majority, and they had to build a record of achievement that would give the public faith in their ability to manage the nation. Seeking to demonstrate that they had gone beyond the 1930s, they attempted to transform their traditional conservatism into a responsible moderation. In the abstract, the idea of moderation had great popular appeal, but in practice it was unable to capture the response for which the GOP had hoped. By 1960, the Republican party was far weaker than in 1952. The Ike Age had been an interlude rather than a new beginning.

IKE AND THE ELECTION OF 1952

Born in 1890, Dwight D. Eisenhower had spent his early life in Abilene, Kansas, before going to West Point and embarking upon a career as a professional soldier. A steady twenty-five-year climb up the military ladder prepared him for years of supreme success in World War II. Neither a great strategist nor a brilliant tactician, Eisenhower nevertheless possessed qualities vital to the leadership of a vast coalition war effort. A tough, efficient organizer, an excellent diplomat and conciliator, he manipulated prima donna generals, reconciled conflicting national viewpoints, and held the Anglo-American alliance together in relative harmony. Accepting and relishing the nickname Ike, he endeared himself to Western democratic society by assuming the role of a soldier's general who understood the problems of the man in the ranks and sought to identify with him.

After the war, Eisenhower served a term as army chief of staff, then accepted the presidency of Columbia University; in late 1950, President Truman called him to active duty to assume the military command of NATO. His presence at NATO headquarters in Paris seemed to give hope and spirit to Western Europe. "I am glad to learn that Ike's name is the symbol of united effort in Europe," Truman told Averell Harriman in late 1951.

"My faith in him has never wavered nor ever will. He is the man for the job and he has all the dynamic qualities of the true leader." Truman himself in 1945, 1947, and 1951 had offered to support Eisenhower for the Democratic presidential nomination. As he worked to give NATO some semblance of credibility, the general was indeed a towering figure who, the journalist Elmer Davis observed, probably could have been elected president of Europe, had such an office existed.

Eisenhower's appeal was broad and deep, for he combined the aura of military success with expressions of civilian democratic values. The general conveyed a quality of command which dominated his aides; yet he also had a popular touch, evident above all in the broad grin he flashed to crowds. A democratic figure who nevertheless radiated strength and trust, Eisenhower became the hope of those Republicans in quest of an alternative to the dour, conservative Ohio senator Robert A. Taft.

Senator Henry Cabot Lodge, Jr., of Massachusetts and other emissaries representing the northeastern branch of the party made pilgrimages across the Atlantic to induce Eisenhower to resign his NATO command, return to the United States, and campaign for the Republican nomination. Inclined toward the Republican party and hostile to Taft's isolationism, the general was interested, but he also felt a sense of duty to NATO. In early 1952 he wanted to stay at his post, and, still rather naive in the ways of partisan politics, he appears to have entertained the belief that *both* parties might draft him.

The American political system, however, does not give even the most popular heroes such opportunities. In the presidential primaries, Eisenhower scored an impressive victory in New Hampshire, drew over 100,000 write-in votes in Minnesota, and won victories in New Jersey, Massachusetts, and Oregon; but Taft came out on top in Wisconsin, Nebraska, Illinois, Ohio, West Virginia, and South Dakota. When Eisenhower returned to the United States at the beginning of June to campaign actively, he trailed the senator by a hundred delegate votes, and Taft appeared to control the convention machinery. The Eisenhower organization, consisting mainly of the old Dewey forces, undertook a successful, brilliantly managed effort in behalf of "Fair Play" and secured the rejection of contested Taft delegates from Georgia, Louisiana, and Texas; Eisenhower's nomination on the first ballot followed quickly.

The Eisenhower victory was less a triumph of moderation than a demonstration of the Republican longing for victory. The convention and the platform were dominated by the rhetoric of McCarthyism, neo-isolationism, and right-wing conservatism. Eisenhower himself sought to appease the defeated Taft forces by selecting as his running mate Senator Richard M. Nixon of California, known chiefly for his support of Whittaker Chambers against Alger Hiss, his sponsorship of anticommunist sedition legislation, and his use of McCarthyite tactics against liberal Democratic opponents. In September, Eisenhower united the party by meeting with Taft and agreeing to a statement which affirmed their joint dedication to budget cutting and domestic conservatism. Decried by some party moderates as a surrender to the GOP right wing, the statement was more accurately a revelation that Eisenhower was himself a conservative whose major argument with Taft involved foreign policy.

Republican strategists announced that their formula would be $K^1 C^2$—Korea, Communism, Corruption. The frustrations arising from Korea and the entire cold-war stalemate probably were most important to the Republican campaign. During the fall of 1952, the political analyst Samuel Lubell interviewed one voter after another who was in the process of deciding that the prospect of an end to the Korean war under Eisenhower outweighed the danger of depression under a Republican administration. Most observers agree that Eisenhower clinched the election on October 24, when he promised that, if elected, "I shall go to Korea."

The domestic side of the Republican drive was largely a "crusade" against alleged communist influences and corruption in the Truman administration. Prominent Republicans, including the chairman of the national committee, attacked the Democrats as subversive. A week before the election, McCarthy himself went on national television to hurl charges of procommunism at Adlai Stevenson and his advisers. Eisenhower attempted to pitch his appeal on a higher level, but for the sake of unity he swallowed hard and endorsed all Republican candidates, including McCarthy and the lesser McCarthyites. Convinced by jittery counselors that victory might depend upon it, Eisenhower welcomed McCarthy aboard his train and deleted a laudatory reference to General George Marshall from an important Wisconsin speech.

The Republicans were on strong ground in charging that the Truman administration had been too tolerant of corruption, but it appeared momentarily that this aspect of their campaign might backfire when it was discovered that Senator Nixon had been the recipient of a special fund raised by a group of wealthy Californians. Eisenhower nearly asked his running mate to resign from the ticket. Instead, he allowed Nixon to deliver an explanation on television.

Nixon's performance was a near-tearful account of his childhood, war service, and marriage, of the difficulty of maintaining payments on a mortgage and a life insurance policy while providing for his family, and finally of another gift he had received—a pet dog, Checkers, which his daughters loved and which he would never give up. Democrats and political cynics might charge that the "Checkers speech" was a cornball evasion of hard questions, but it touched a nerve in the upwardly mobile

American middle class and produced an outpouring of support which kept Nixon on the ticket. For the moment at least, as Eric Goldman has observed, Nixon had established a sense of identification with the man who had left the depression behind him and was working to secure a degree of affluence for himself and his loved ones.

For all its drama, the affair probably had little effect on the outcome of the election; at best, Nixon's speech forestalled a possible negative impact upon the Eisenhower crusade. By the same token, it seems doubtful that McCarthyism swayed many voters except in its role as one aspect of the larger frustration with Korea and the cold war. Some prominent Democrats against whom McCarthy campaigned were defeated, but their power bases were so weak that they probably would have lost anyway. McCarthy, himself a candidate for reelection, was returned to the Senate by only a modest plurality and ran behind every other Republican on the statewide ballot in Wisconsin.

The outcome stemmed more from foreign policy than from domestic concerns over corruption or communist subversion.* Above all, the election was a vote of personal confidence in Eisenhower. The general polled 55.2 percent of the vote to Stevenson's 44.5 percent and buried his opponent under a 6.6 million plurality. The Republican party, on the other hand, gained control of Congress by only the narrowest of margins, 48–47 in the Senate, and 221–212 in the House. The voters had reconciled their divided impulses by electing Eisenhower to end the war and keep the country at peace while frequently splitting their tickets in the fear that an overwhelmingly Republican government might take the nation into a depression. This pattern would continue throughout the 1950s. Eisenhower's mandate for change was a limited one indeed.

Like many other military figures who had entered political life, Eisenhower hoped to make his office and duties more manageable through the establishment of a staff system with a clear chain of command and reasonably precise delegations of responsibility. His wartime success in handling the greatest coordinated combat effort in human history rather naturally and reasonably led him to consider himself an expert in the science of organization. The Supreme Commander, he believed, should not involve himself in countless tactical decisions, master volumes of typewritten reports, or engage in multitudinous telephone conversations; if he attempted to do so, he would be unable to fulfill his mission of making the ultimate decisions of grand strategy and following through on their implementation at the highest levels. The conception was sound for the leadership of a disciplined, unified military force ready to follow

---

* Many voters complained about inflation to pollsters, but since the consumer price index had leveled off in 1951, it seems likely that this was simply a respectable manner of expressing opposition to the war.

orders without question and attempt the impossible; it was less workable for the control of independent bureaucrats and politicians.

It is questionable that Eisenhower ever fully grasped that most of his important directives as President were not self-executing. The general can reasonably assume that his commands will be obeyed as rapidly and effectively as possible; the President frequently must follow up a directive with pressure and persuasion to secure its acceptance and implementation. On most issues and especially during the first six years of his Presidency, Eisenhower generally refrained from a vigorous follow-up.

In operation, the staff system frequently insulated Eisenhower from important problems. In an effort to achieve the organization Eisenhower demanded, the President's chief of staff, former Governor Sherman Adams of New Hampshire, worked tirelessly, reducing complex issues to one-page summaries and handling many of the political problems that came to the White House. Eisenhower's precarious health—he suffered a serious heart attack in 1955, underwent major abdominal surgery in 1956, and incurred a minor stroke in 1957—probably necessitated arrangements to relieve him of as many burdens as possible. Nevertheless, the command structure frequently deprived the President of information on issues he could not ultimately avoid; as a result, presidential action, when it did come, was even more likely to be uncertain and indecisive.

Of course, it is possible that more was involved than misconceptions about technique. Eisenhower's conception of the Presidency was Whiggish in domestic affairs, although he was an activist in foreign policy matters, which he handled directly with Secretary of State John Foster Dulles. On most domestic issues, he had little more than half-formulated prejudices rather than carefully conceived opinions. In addition, he was never altogether comfortable with the ways of partisan politics. The staff operation thus became a way of evading direct engagement with many political problems and with the messy partisanship which accompanied them, a technique of avoiding decisions on many issues about which Eisenhower was uncertain. Perhaps the design was quasi-intentional; if so, the President had himself formulated a system which served to perpetuate not only his own philosophical confusion but that of the party he hoped to lead out of the political wilderness.

COMMUNISM AND CORRUPTION: THE REPUBLICAN PHASE

One of the arguments in favor of voting for Eisenhower was that only a moderate Republican President could resolve the problems which most exercised the electorate—the Korean war, corruption, and the communist issue. Such a President could negotiate a compromise end to the war without risking vituperative denunciation by the right-wing extremists in his own party. He could sweep out the grafters who had injured the Truman administration and do so with unanimous GOP support. His presence could put an end to the poison of McCarthyism, for even the Wisconsin demogogue would not dare to attack a Republican administration led by a national hero. The argument was persuasive, and in the case of the Korean war perfectly accurate. But governmental corruption did not automatically go out the door with the Democrats, and during Eisenhower's first two years, McCarthyism continued unabated.

Now that the Republicans were in power, the GOP leadership attempted to shelve McCarthy by assigning him the chairmanship of an obscure Senate subcommittee on government operations. But to the dismay of the administration, the senator was soon proclaiming his intention of "helping" Eisenhower clean out the remaining communists in Washington and conduct a tough anti-Soviet foreign policy. He raised a political uproar by challenging the administration's appointment of Charles E. Bohlen as ambassador to the USSR, although Bohlen had been one of the major formulators of the containment policy during the Truman era. Robert A. Taft pushed the nomination through the Senate, but 11 of the 13 "nay" votes were cast by McCarthyite Republicans.

There followed a series of events with overtones both comic and ominous. A right-wing zealot whom McCarthy had employed caused a stir by charging that the Communist party had managed a serious infiltration of the Protestant clergy, but the senator made no attempt to follow through when the public reaction proved adverse. Two other staff members, Roy Cohn and G. David Schine, undertook an investigation of the Voice of America, charging among other things that an engineer who had placed transmitters in allegedly unfavorable positions must be procommunist. The assertion was ridiculous, but the accused individual, apparently fearing that his career had been ruined, killed himself. Then Cohn and Schine toured U.S. information libraries in Europe searching for books by "subversive" authors and inflicting devastating blows upon the morale of State Department and Foreign Service employees.

In early 1954, after Schine had been drafted into the army, McCarthy undertook an investigation of subversion in the military, doing so, some observers asserted, out of anger at his failure to obtain preferential treatment for Schine. Nationally televised, the hearings made a test of strength between McCarthy and his opponents inevitable, but the outcome was by no means certain.

The Gallup poll reported in January 1954 that the senator had reached his high point of popularity with 50 percent of those interviewed expressing a "favorable" opinion of him, 29 percent "unfavorable," 21 percent "no opinion"; the comparable figures in April 1953 had been 19 percent, 22 percent, and 59 percent. Even if one gives a generous discount for sampling errors, it seems clear that McCarthy's prestige had grown enormously during the first year of the Eisenhower administration.

Part of the reason for McCarthy's rise was that, more than ever, the Democrats in Congress were petrified by him. Several senators against whom he had campaigned in 1950 and 1952 had gone under. Who could say that McCarthy's opposition had not been decisive? The Democratic congressional leadership, headed by Sam Rayburn in the House and Lyndon B. Johnson in the Senate, decided that their best course was to lie low and avoid making McCarthy's actions a partisan issue which might unite the Republicans behind him. They were perfectly willing to let McCarthy embarrass the new administration until it would feel forced to do something about him. The strategy was shabbily expedient but made sense in terms of Democratic self-interest. Throughout 1953, the Democrats sniped at McCarthy occasionally but avoided a consistent, all-out assault.

Eisenhower refused to move. Instead, he allowed one concession after another to McCarthy. The State Department installed a McCarthy follower, Scott McLeod, as its chief security officer and reacted to the Cohn-Schine trip to Europe by removing suspect books from its overseas libraries and destroying many of them. Eisenhower delivered a speech warning against "book burning" but did nothing to countermand the policy. The President was the one man in American public life who could have destroyed McCarthy; yet, although he privately loathed the senator, he would not attack him directly. With the Democrats reduced to Fabian tactics and with Eisenhower holding back, McCarthy's public standing could grow as if in a hothouse.

Eisenhower was motivated in large part by his repugnance for McCarthy and the type of dirty politics McCarthy represented. As the President told his intimates, he would not get down into the gutter to brawl with McCarthy; he even convinced himself that he would only give McCarthy additional publicity. Eisenhower's conception of the Presidency as an office of dignified leadership left little room for nasty political infighting, and McCarthy was hardly eager for a direct conflict on a more genteel level. Yet more was involved—the Eisenhower administration was inhibited from moving against McCarthy because during its first two years in office, it also engaged in McCarthyism on a large scale and thereby contributed mightily to the climate that fostered the senator's rapid rise in the polls.

One of the administration's first actions was to revise the federal loyalty program and begin a whole new round of investigations of government personnel. The new standard for dismissal was apparently more tangible than the old: an individual was to be investigated not for abstract loyalty to the United States but only for the probability that his employment might impair the national security. In actual operation, however, the Eisenhower program was more sweeping, and the administration engaged in a numbers game to demonstrate the laxness of its predecessor. It announced that during the first four months of the new program, it had dismissed more than 800 "security risks"—over twice the number fired during the nearly six years of the Truman program—and had accepted the resignations of another 600 who were under suspicion. By the end of 1954, the numbers had reached 3,000 firings and 5,000 resignations. The White House proclaimed the totals with pride. Having done so, how could it argue with McCarthy's assertion that subversives were still hiding in the federal bureaucracy?

In November 1953 Attorney General Herbert Brownell revived the long-forgotten Harry Dexter White controversy and made the incredible charge that Truman had appointed White to the International Monetary Fund despite proof that White was a communist agent. The Republican chairman of the House Commiteee on Un-American Activites issued a subpoena that attempted to compel Truman to testify on the White case. The former President refused to honor the summons—there was no attempt to enforce it—and went on national television to deliver a blunt denial of Brownell's charges.

The most spectacular and probably the most tragic episode was the investigation of J. Robert Oppenheimer, the brilliant physicist who had organized the development of the atomic bomb during World War II. Oppenheimer could be personally abrasive and was politically naive—he had some left-wing friendships—yet no one accused him of having betrayed secret information. After the war, he had served in various important government advisory posts dealing with atomic energy. With the election of Eisenhower, he left the government to become director of the Institute for Advanced Study at Princeton. The Atomic Energy Commission, chaired by the Eisenhower appointee Lewis Strauss, moved to suspend Oppenheimer's security clearance; after long hearings, a special review board upheld the suspension. The Oppenheimer affair outraged and demoralized the intellectual and scientific communities, which believed that the suspension had rested not on security grounds but on personality conflicts and legitimate differences of opinion about the hydrogen bomb (which Oppenheimer had opposed) and about military strategy.

Oppenheimer remained at Princeton, rejecting suggestions from his close friend George F. Kennan that he could easily continue his work abroad—any of the nations of Western Europe would have welcomed him. His case became not only a symbol for the intellectuals but also a matter of conscience for many Democratic politicians who had remained silent. In 1959 a heavily Democratic Senate rejected Strauss's nomination as secretary of commerce. In 1963 an Atomic Energy Commission dominated by Kennedy appointees restored Oppenheimer's security clearance and bestowed its highest honor, the Enrico Fermi Award, upon him. The presentation was made personally, shortly after Kennedy's death, by President Lyndon Johnson.

In a sense, the Eisenhower administration was a victim of the campaign tactics it had condoned in 1952, when Republican campaigners from Nixon on down had charged that the government was filled with subversives. The new security program, the attack on Truman, and the smearing of Oppenheimer all followed naturally. As late as the 1954 congressional campaign, Nixon and other GOP leaders continued to push the Red issue. The result was to give McCarthy a greater degree of credibility than he ever had possessed and to make it all the harder to bring him down. Yet his attacks on the army made it imperative to discredit him.

The televised army-McCarthy hearings hurt the senator by projecting his callousness and arrogance into millions of American homes. By May 1954, his Gallup popularity rating had fallen to 35 percent and would hover at that level for the rest of the year. With behind-the-scenes encouragement from the White House, moderate Republican Senator Ralph Flanders of Vermont introduced resolutions to censure McCarthy and strip him of his committee assignments. The issue was referred to a special committee of three Republican and three Democratic senators, carefully selected for their conservatism and their standing with their peers. After exhaustive hearings, the committee recommended censure against McCarthy for conduct that brought the Senate into disrepute. Four weeks after the November elections, the upper house adopted the recommendation, 67–22, with all the dissents from conservative Republicans.

After that, the communist issue began to lose its power and credibility. The Eisenhower administration soft-pedaled it, and McCarthy himself, though he still retained a loyal hard-core following, became dispirited and ineffective. On May 2, 1957, he died, only forty-seven years old; McCarthyism had expired well before him, a victim of its own excess rather than White House suppression.

Eisenhower was equally ineffective in dealing with the other great domestic issue of 1952: corruption. The Republicans may have thrown the Democratic grafters out of Washington, but abuse of public trust was not a monopoly of either party. The vast post–New Deal bureaucracy contained too many points of access for the hustler after a fast buck, and neither the Democrats nor the Republicans could guarantee 100 percent honesty. All the same, any scandal was certain to embarrass Eisenhower after his campaign as a crusader for good government, and one by one, episodes came to light which rivaled the Truman Presidency's contributions to the annals of crooked politics.

Eisenhower himself set an unfortunate tone for his subordinates by accepting a vast array of gifts from admirers. His private home, a farm near Gettsyburg, Pennsylvania, was almost a collaborative effort on the part of his benefactors, who donated trees, landscaping services, champion livestock, expensive equipment, and antique furnishings. Such gifts were in no sense bribes; the givers were probably unanimous in considering them only expensive tokens of admiration for a national idol, and Eisenhower accepted them in much the same manner as an Oriental potentate receiving tribute from his subjects. His free-and-easy attitude toward the acceptance of favors nevertheless established a bad example for other government officials less able to ignore implications that favors were expected in return.

In March 1953 the newly designated Republican national chairman, C. Wesley Roberts of Kansas, resigned under fire after having been accused of unlawful behavior in a state land transaction. In 1955 Secretary of the Air Force Harold Talbott and Commissioner of Public Buildings Peter Strobel both quit under pressure after it appeared that they had used their public offices, naively or otherwise, to drum up business for private firms in which they retained an interest. In 1956 Edmund Mansure, the head of the General Service Administration, departed after charges of political favoritism and boodling in the award of contracts. In 1957 Robert T. Ross, an assistant secretary of defense, hurriedly left the administration after the discovery that he had facilitated government contracts for companies owned by his wife and brother-in-law. In 1958 two Eisenhower appointees to the Federal Communications Commission resigned after an investigation revealed that they had padded government expense accounts and accepted favors from some of the radio and television stations they were supposed to regulate.

The Dixon-Yates controversy overshadowed all these episodes. Originally an issue with only ideological implications, the Dixon-Yates affair grew out of the administration's determination to stop the growth of Tennessee Valley Authority electrical production. To meet the huge power demands of an Atomic Energy Commission facility at Paducah, Kentucky, the administration authorized the commission to negotiate a contract with a private utility combine headed by Edgar H. Dixon and Eugene A. Yates, although the Dixon-Yates arrangement would have cost the government some $50 million more than expansion of the TVA. Democrats, who characterized the agreement as the first step in a plot to dismantle the agency, were fighting a losing battle until it was discovered that the government consultant who had backed Dixon-Yates over another private competitive bid was connected with the investment firm which was preparing to handle Dixon-Yates securities. The Democrats had a field day with the disclosure, but the administration might have gone ahead with the plan had not the city of Memphis, Tennessee, voted to build a large new power plant which rendered the proposal superfluous. In mid-1955 the federal government canceled the contract; subsequently, in fighting a suit for damages brought by the Dixon-Yates company, the administration itself asserted that the pact had been invalid because of illegal conflicts of interest in its negotiation.

Perhaps the hardest blow of all came in 1958 with the revelation that Eisenhower's own political chief of staff and trusted adviser, Sherman Adams, had accepted generous gifts from Bernard Goldfine, a Boston industrialist, and had interceded for him with federal regulatory agencies. The Democrats made great political capital out of the discovery, and with the congressional elections approaching, Eisenhower reluctantly allowed Adams to be maneuvered into a resignation. The President gave his outgoing chief of staff a silver bowl with an inscription extolling Adams's public service, sense of duty, and patriotism.

The Adams incident was typical of the President's refusal to believe that a member of his government had done anything seriously wrong. The Eisenhower scandals usually were handled with resignations as quiet and circumspect as possible. They produced no outpouring of indignation and few political dividends for the opposition. Critics have charged that most of the press—then overwhelmingly Republican in its management—effectively muffled Eisenhower corruption just as it had magnified Truman corruption. But surely more fundamental was the fact that Eisenhower, the President and the man, continuously enjoyed the confidence and devotion of the public. Corruption had been an important issue against Truman because he was politically weak in many other respects and possessed only a superficial appeal to the American people. Eisenhower, by contrast, remained unassailable, no matter what the mistakes or misdeeds of his subordinates.

THE MOOD OF MODERATION

In its approach to politics and social questions, the Eisenhower administration mirrored and reinforced a mood of moderation that characterized the America of the 1950s. With much fanfare, the President proclaimed the virtues of the middle of the road. The Democratic congressional leadership, dominated by the Texans Rayburn and Johnson, avoided confrontations with the White House. The major figure in Democratic presidential politics, Adlai Stevenson, sought consciously to present himself as a moderate. Liberals tended to assume that economic prosperity had largely solved the "quantitative" problems of the distribution of wealth and talked instead about social programs designed to improve the "quality" of American life.

A many-faceted intellectual movement calling itself the "new conservatism" rose to prominence. Its most durable manifestations could be found in William F. Buckley's *National Review;* established in 1955, the *National Review* militantly reaffirmed traditional Hamiltonian conservatism with a substantial admixture of right-wing Catholicism and Burkean thought. Another variety, more ephemeral but more in keeping with the mood of the Ike Age, was expressed by writers such as Clinton Rossiter and Peter Viereck, who identified "true conservatism" as the measured acceptance of progress and reform in the interest of social stability. Of course, the American tradition of gradualist change within the capitalist system fit such a pattern well. During the 1950s, the Rossiter-Viereck new conservatism had wide appeal to intellectuals conscious as never before of the extraordinary degree of consensus in American politics and of the U.S. role as a bulwark against revolutionary communism. Too shallow to endure over the long run, the equation of almost any nonrevolutionary change with conservatism was for a time fashionable and widely accepted. In the 1960s, under Presidents who would attempt to set a different tone for the nation, the new conservatism would quickly disappear.

Eisenhower and those around him talked of "dynamic conservatism," "modern Republicanism," and "middle of the road" positions. These slogans never received very adequate theoretical development, although Undersecretary of Labor Arthur Larson made a brave attempt in *A Republican Looks at His Party* (1956). Larson defined the "new Republicanism" as a doctrine of "the Authentic American Center" synthesizing traditional beliefs in individualism, local responsibility, and private enterprise with recognition of government responsibility for the promotion of economic prosperity, collective bargaining, and the general welfare. Eisenhower gave the book his personal endorsement.

Whatever the reconciliation of such opposites meant in theory, the practical shape of Modern Republicanism was fairly clear. More a creed imposed by the necessity of gaining and holding political power than a coherent and convincing philosophy, Modern Republicanism attempted to jam the traditional ideals of the GOP into the broad framework of the New Deal. Where Truman had sought to go well beyond the New Deal, Eisenhower was content in the main with the status quo, hoping to take a step back in some areas, ready to move perhaps a half-step ahead in others, but going in either direction with a sense of caution.

His domestic agenda was remarkably similar to that proposed a few years earlier by Senator Taft, with whom he worked closely in the few months before Taft died in mid-1953. It drew complaints from those conservative Republicans who hoped to return to the 1920s and from liberal Democrats who considered the White House programs weak and inadequate. At times, these elements formed a strange coalition which rejected the President's proposals. But Eisenhower could appeal to the loyalty of the Republicans, threaten the Democratic liberals with a veto, and appeal to the moderates of both parties. As often as not, he got what he wanted.

The President was willing to back expansion of social security and unemployment insurance, an increase in the minimum wage, even a small public-housing program. At times, Congress, controlled by the Democrats after 1954, went beyond his requests, but on these issues the President decided that the deviation was tolerable and that acquiescence was the course of political wisdom. By 1956, the minimum wage had been raised from $.75 to $1.00, an additional 11 million people were eligible for the social security program, and Congress had authorized construction of 35,000 units of public housing a year for four years.

The President supported federal assistance to private voluntary medical insurance plans for the needy, but throughout the 1950s most liberal and moderate Democrats favored universal coverage through the social security system, and many conservative Republicans opposed even the slightest federal entry into the health field. During Eisenhower's second term, the debate revolved around medical insurance for the elderly. By the election year of 1960, the administration approach was substantially embodied in a bill sponsored by two southern Democrats, Senator Robert Kerr of Oklahoma and Representative Wilbur Mills of Arkansas. Differing in detail from administration proposals, the Kerr-Mills bill nevertheless preserved the principle of assistance to the needy only and would be financed by matching state and federal appropriations; in effect, it would operate as a welfare program and was similar in design to a plan developed by Taft almost a decade and a half earlier. The alternative, sponsored by Representative Aime Forand of Rhode Island and Senator John F. Kennedy of Massachusetts, consisted of a federal insurance program for the elderly operated as part of the social security system. Debated under campaign pressures, the Kerr-Mills bill breezed through Congress, and Eisenhower signed it. The Kennedy-Forand bill was narrowly defeated; Medicare would continue to be a controversial political issue for the next five years.

Eisenhower advocated small programs of federal aid to education, but he appears to have been even more conservative than Taft on the issue. He did not offer a concrete plan until midway through his first term, gave administration proposals little personal support, and encountered the opposition of most educators, who felt that his recommendations were extremely inadequate. As in the 1940s, aid to education ran afoul of the emotion-packed factors of race and religion. The issue of federal assistance to the schools was controversial enough—opponents argued it entailed federal control of teaching and, hence, the seeds of totalitarianism —and when weighted down with demands for subsidies to parochial schools and termination of racial segregation, aid bills were nearly impossible to get through Congress. In 1960 legislation providing large-scale financing of school construction won majorities in both houses of Congress only to be buried by a parliamentary maneuver after the President led Republican leaders to believe that he might veto it.

The only significant education bill to emerge from the Eisenhower years was the National Defense Education Act (NDEA) of 1958, a product of near-hysteria passed after the Soviet Union had orbited the first space satellite in human history *(Sputnik I)*. The bill provided aid for instruction in the sciences, mathematics, and foreign languages, established sizable loan funds for college students, set up a program of graduate fellowships, and gave assistance to high school counseling programs and vocational instruction. An important piece of legislation, it nevertheless failed to meet the major problems of American education—lack of classroom space and low teacher salaries.

On one other issue, Negro civil rights, Eisenhower's leadership was even more uncertain and inconsistent. The northeastern wing of the Republican party, which had engineered his nomination, had long been friendly toward civil rights measures, but the election of 1952 had revealed possibilities for GOP growth in the South—Eisenhower and Nixon had carried Virginia, Tennessee, Florida, and Texas—which a party of moderation could hardly ignore. In addition, Eisenhower had spent most of his career in the United States Army, which until the late 1940s had been a rigidly segregated institution permeated with assumptions of Negro inferiority; he had been cool toward the beginnings of military integration during the Truman administration. He believed in states' rights and considered racial problems to be social problems which the federal government should approach with caution. The President stopped short of outright opposition to the desegregation movement, but his position was well to the right of Truman's.

Prodded especially by his attorneys general, Herbert Brownell (1953–57) and William Rogers (1957–61), Eisenhower gave some encouragement to civil rights advocates. He allowed the Justice Department to continue the Truman practice of submitting amicus curiae briefs in important judicial cases, completed the process of military integration, and encouraged desegregation in the District of Columbia after the Supreme Court had struck down racial separation there. With some plausibility, he could present himself as sympathetic toward Negro aspirations; in 1956, he scored significant voting gains in black districts.

All the same, Eisenhower was unwilling to give his wholehearted support to the most critical racial issue of his Presidency—school desegregation—and refused to endorse the Supreme Court decision ordering it, although he later claimed that he privately agreed with it. As a believer in limited national government and state autonomy, the President was willing to settle for limited, gradual compliance. Only when faced with an act of blatant defiance would he act; in 1957 he sent federal troops to Little Rock, Arkansas, to enforce a school desegregation order which Governor Orval Faubus had attempted to override. Otherwise, he would remain silent.

He was also reluctant to support civil rights legislation, coming out for a mild voting-rights bill in 1956 only after a remarkable combination of pleas and pressure from Brownell. In 1957 and 1960 he signed civil rights bills aimed primarily at facilitating black suffrage in the South. Shepherded through the Senate by Democratic majority leader Johnson, the legislation was the first of its kind since Reconstruction and had the appearance of a historic breakthrough. However, it was also unworkable and ineffective. The civil rights acts of the 1950s did little to assist the disenfranchised Negro and ignored the problems of school integration, equal employment opportunity, and access to public accommodations. By the end of the decade, blacks could expect little more than "tokenism"—a few students in formerly white schools, some increased recognition, but no fundamental progress. The Eisenhower administration and the Democratic congressional leadership seemed in tacit agreement on the formula.

But new forces were developing. In 1956 a hitherto unknown Negro minister, Martin Luther King, Jr., led a successful mass boycott against segregated buses in Montgomery, Alabama. In 1960 a group of students in Greensboro, North Carolina, engaged in a sit-in action to integrate local lunch counters. Unable to secure justice through traditional channels, American blacks were resorting to new, direct tactics which would serve as the basis for a revolution.

POLITICS, ECONOMICS, AND ELECTIONS

The most important test of the New Republicanism would inevitably be its overall management of the economy. Above all, the GOP had to blot out the public's memory of Herbert Hoover and the Great Depression. Eisenhower and his associates realized that they could not return to a bygone era; yet neither could they entirely escape the rhetoric and assumptions of Republican fundamentalism. Moderation became an effort to split the difference between Coolidge and Keynes, to buffer classical laissez-faire policies with a minimum of New Deal interventionism. The new and still insecure small-propertied middle class which had emerged from the New Deal and World War II could sympathize with such objectives as limiting government spending, stopping inflation, and cutting taxes; and the Republicans had good reason to hope that these goals could bring them to a position of political parity with the Democrats. But this same middle class, precisely because of its newness and insecurity, would experience deep anxiety over any slackening of prosperity. The Republicans could achieve new vigor as a party only if they could keep the economy functioning at full tilt.

Eisenhower did not hesitate to support two measures—the Saint Lawrence Seaway and the interstate highway system—that involved large-scale government interventionism because he felt they had national defense implications as well. Approved in 1954, after twenty years of debate and delay, the Saint Lawrence Seaway Act provided for cooperation with Canada in a project that would give Atlantic oceangoing vessels access to the Great Lakes as far west as Duluth, Minnesota, and contribute greatly to the economic development of the American heartland. The Federal Highway Act of 1956 provided for 42,000 miles of expressways to replace the obsolete and unsafe road system which had been built in the 1920s. In a manner characteristic of the economics it espoused, the administration recommended toll financing, but Congress opted for higher taxes on gasoline, tires, and heavy vehicles. Saint Lawrence Seaway bonds were to be retired from toll revenues. Both spending programs thus were "fiscally responsible."

In general, the Eisenhower administration hoped to reduce the level of federal participation in the economy and cut back on government spending. While liberal Democrats argued that underconsumption was the major threat to the economy, the Eisenhower Republicans saw inflation as the great menace; from their perspective, the Democratic tendency to stimulate consumer consumption by resorting to spending programs or tax cuts amounted to throwing gasoline on a fire. The first objective of Republican economics was to stifle inflation by lowering and balancing the federal budget; the next priority would be to decrease taxes. The assumption was that retrenchment would bring more funds into the private investment flow, which would in turn maintain a healthy economic growth and achieve full employment. In essence, the administration was reaffirming the traditional GOP faith in free enterprise as the foundation of American prosperity. The President and his secretaries of the treasury, George Humphrey (1953–57) and Robert Anderson (1957–61), strove to balance the budget, reduce the federal monolith, and liberate business. They would gamble on that faith, but if the worst seemed in prospect, they would not go the way of Hoover. For the sake of principle and, they were convinced, long-range dividends, they would tolerate dips in the business cycle but not economic disaster.

By almost any standard, the results were disappointing. The federal bureaucracy and federal expenditures increased. Eisenhower could balance only three of his eight budgets and in 1959 presided over the largest peacetime deficit in American history. Economic growth lagged well behind that of the Western European nations. Three separate recessions (1953–54, 1957–58, 1960–61), made unemployment an increasingly serious problem and reduced the tax revenue the government needed to bring the budget into balance. Most embarrassingly, during Eisenhower's second term, inflation set in at a slow but steady rate of about 2.5 percent a year.

The President was not about to precipitate a depression by asking for increased taxes to balance the recession budgets; in fact, he was willing to speed up expenditures already planned and push for low interest rates. But neither would he request the spending programs or tax cuts necessary to boost employment. Even in the spring of 1958, with unemployment peaking at 7.6 percent, the dominant opinion in the White House was that inflation remained the greater danger, and Eisenhower rejected pressures for tax reduction. As recovery set in, the President redoubled his efforts to achieve a balanced budget and thereby contributed to the development of another economic slump.

Of course, the stagnation-cum-inflation economy of the 1950s had sources other than administration policy. The unemployment problem was partly traceable to cuts in defense expenditures and to the ever-increasing use of automated equipment. The inflationary trend appears to have been of the "cost-push" variety possible only in an oligopolistic economic structure—giant labor unions compelled large wage settlements and mammoth corporations pushed up prices to pass the costs along, usually with some additional padding, to the consumer.

Nevertheless, if the Eisenhower administration did not create these problems, it did little to meet them and hardly acknowledged their existence. Having only half escaped from GOP economic fundamentalism, Eisenhower and his advisers could not conceive of fiscal policy as a compensatory mechanism which could maintain growth and reasonably full employment. Their main accomplishment was negative—they avoided a full-scale depression. Republican orators boasted of peace and prosperity, but prosperity became thinner as the Ike Age progressed. The New Republicanism's lackluster economic performance became a serious political liability, not for Eisenhower, but for all those other members of the party who lacked his political invincibility. One of them was Richard M. Nixon.

Agriculture provided Republican political economy with perhaps its most difficult challenge. During the 1952 campaign, Eisenhower had appealed to the farm vote by promising to work for 100 percent of parity "in the marketplace." (His supporters played down the qualifying phrase and contrasted the pledge favorably with Adlai Stevenson's support of 90 percent parity, federally guaranteed.) Actually, both the President and his secretary of agriculture, Ezra Taft Benson, a devout Mormon elder from Utah, were strong opponents of price supports. Practical enough to realize that twenty years of agricultural policy could not be dropped overnight, they sought to reverse its thrust and gradually remove the government from the business of agricultural production and marketing.

The basic device that Eisenhower and Benson favored was abandonment of the rigid 90 percent principle in favor of flexible, sliding-scale supports. Under the sliding-scale concept, the amount of federal support for a commodity would decrease if production increased and would go back up when production declined. The effect would be to encourage farmers to shift their efforts in another direction—either to a different commodity or out of agriculture altogether—but the establishment of minimum support levels would prevent a full-scale agricultural depression. The attempt to combine classical laissez-faire price-production theory with New Deal activism was typical of Eisenhower's middle-of-the-road aspirations.

The new approach was unsuccessful, both economically and politically. The Agricultural Act of 1954 authorized supports as low as 75 percent of parity by the crop year 1956. Subsequent legislation in 1958 provided for a gradual drop to 65 percent. In 1956 the President vetoed a Democratic bill reestablishing rigid 90 percent supports and forced in its stead the passage of a "soil bank" conservation program which made payments to farmers who took their land out of production. The soil bank somewhat mitigated a rural recession which had developed from the 1954 legislation, but the Republicans still were hurt by mounting dissatisfaction and losses in farm areas.

As one would expect, commodity prices, farm income, and rural population all declined throughout the 1950s, but, unexpectedly, surpluses mounted and the cost of the agricultural program increased to record highs, even at the lower support levels. The administration had run up against spectacular advances in agrarian technology which spurred increases in production far outstripping the amount of land being retired; the classical economic postulates which underlay the sliding-scale legislation had failed to anticipate the short-run impact of twentieth-century science.

Under the circumstances, no agricultural program could have been wholly satisfactory. The Democratic alternatives would have been even more expensive, although at least they would have maintained farm income. A reversion to the policies of the Coolidge era would have created intolerable suffering. Yet the Eisenhower attempt to split the difference pleased no one, not even the President and Secretary Benson; certainly, it had little appeal to most farmers, and it became a heavy burden for midwestern GOP politicians.

Eisenhower's labor policies reflected an inclination toward the status quo. Although he was committed to revising the Taft-Hartley Act, he sought a business-labor consensus on proposed changes, thereby precipitating the resignation of his first secretary of labor, Martin Durkin. (The president of the plumbers's union, Durkin was, as liberal Democrats hastened to observe, the only nonmillionaire in the cabinet.) The changes that Eisenhower finally recommended were relatively minor; attracting little support from either unions or business spokesmen, they languished in Congress.

After congressional investigations revealed corruption in some major unions, most notably the Teamsters, the President strongly backed and signed into law the Landrum-Griffin Act of 1959. The new legislation sought to curb labor racketeering; it banned ex-convicts from union office, required fair and secret elections, and established regulations for financial reporting to the government. In addition, it tightened federal restrictions upon secondary boycotts and picketing, in effect, slightly stiffening the Taft-Hartley Act.

In a sense, the limited nature of the Landrum-Griffin Act was a measure of labor's new position. By the 1950s, the unions had won general acceptance and had demonstrated great power. In 1955 the two great rival federations, the AFL and the CIO, effected a merger which gave rise to conservative apprehensions about monolithic labor political clout. The unions themselves grew steadily with total membership peaking at 18.5 million in 1956 and thereafter slowly declining, less from adverse government policies than from a parallel drop in the number of blue-collar workers. On balance Eisenhower's attitudes were a bit antiunion, but his administration did little to alter the basic labor-management relationships that had grown out of the New Deal–Fair Deal era.

Eisenhower's policies, while fairly consistent in their objective of reducing government interference in the economy, meshed more neatly with the interests of big business than with those of labor and agriculture. In selecting his first cabinet, the President surrounded himself with corporation executives and attorneys. Secretary of Defense Charles E. Wilson expressed the outlook of this group when he made an oft-caricatured remark to the effect that the interests of the United States and General Motors were identical. With such attitudes prevalent in the administration, it was hardly surprising that Eisenhower's appointees to the federal regulatory agencies—especially the Federal Communications Commission, the Federal Power Commission, and the Civil Aeronautics Board —tended to conceive their function as one of serving the very businesses they were supposed to police.

In no area was this outlook clearer than in the administration's approach to the powerful energy industries—electricity, oil, and natural gas. The President publicly labeled the Tennessee Valley Authority an example of "creeping socialism," expressed to his cabinet the wish that the government could sell it to private industry, and oversaw drastic cuts in its appropriations from $185 million in 1952 to $12 million by 1960. The Dixon-Yates scandal was an unwelcome by-product of the anti-TVA outlook. The administration also refused to underwrite large-scale public power projects elsewhere, always preferring to encourage private enterprise. The White House secured legislation providing for private operation of atomic power facilities, deleted a provision for federally produced electricity from the Saint Lawrence Seaway bill, and blocked Democratic proposals for a huge hydroelectric project at Hell's Canyon, Idaho.*

In 1953 the President signed legislation—vetoed by Truman in 1946 and 1952—giving the states jurisdiction over immensely valuable offshore oil and gas deposits to a 3-mile limit in the Atlantic and Pacific oceans and, because of special historical circumstances, to a 10½-mile limit in the Gulf of Mexico. Liberal Democrats had long advocated strict federal leasing of these deposits with the revenue to be set aside for aid to education; they

---

* Styles of liberalism change. By the early 1970s, liberal environmentalists were attempting to prevent further development of Hell's Canyon.

denounced the offshore-oil bill as a giveaway to the corporations, which could exert overwhelming power within the individual states.*

In 1956 the President was prepared to sign legislation that would have stripped the Federal Power Commission of control over natural gas prices, but after conservative Republican Senator Francis Case of South Dakota denounced an industry lobbyist who had offered him a bribe, the President changed his mind. When the natural-gas bill passed Congress, he vetoed it but committed himself to similar legislation in the future if passed under "clean" circumstances. As it developed, liberals were able to block another "ripper bill," but the FPC wielded its authority over the gas companies lightly.

The Democrats, for their part, were split over the virtues of moderation. The congressional leaders, Sam Rayburn and Lyndon Johnson, had sought the center as a matter of their own political survival at home, and saw moderation as the formula which could unite the warring northern and southern blocs of the party; morever, their political judgment told them that Eisenhower was invulnerable to militant attacks. Other prominent Democrats, especially those connected with the "presidential" wing of the party, wanted to stake out a militant position well to the left of Eisenhower's "middle of the road." By 1957, Democratic National Chairman Paul Butler had established a Democratic Advisory Council which included such individuals as Harry S Truman, Eleanor Roosevelt, Adlai Stevenson, and Hubert Humphrey. In the House of Representatives, liberal congressmen from the North and West persuaded Rayburn to tolerate the formation of a Democratic Study Group to work for reform programs. These groups spelled out and promoted the alternatives to the New Republicanism which would be enacted during the Kennedy and Johnson administrations.

The electoral history of the 1950s demonstrated the fundamental weakness of the Republicans. Despite Eisenhower's smashing victory in 1952, the GOP had won control of Congress by only 8 votes in the House and 1 in the Senate. In 1954, with the elections being held shortly after the recession had bottomed out, the Democrats came back to power on Capitol Hill, taking the House by 29 votes and the Senate by 1. In 1956, although Eisenhower swept to reelection, the Democrats maintained their grip on the legislative branch, actually increasing their House margin to 33. In 1958 the Democrats took the House 282–154 and the Senate 64–34. With its popular leader constitutionally prohibited from seeking the Presidency again, the Republican party looked to 1960 from its worst congressional defeat since 1936.

*As it developed, the federal government was able to lay claim to vast oil reserves discovered on the continental shelf beyond the 3-mile and 10½-mile limits.

The 1958 debacle underscored the sources of GOP weakness. The party was seriously hurt by the second "Eisenhower recession," this one marked by the persistence of inflation. In several key states Republican organizations committed themselves to "right-to-work" referenda and thereby brought forth a maximum anti-GOP effort from the labor unions. Five years of recession caused the farm-belt revolt to peak—in 1952 the Democrats had won only 3 of the nation's 20 richest farm districts; in 1958 they took 13. Such results seemed to indicate that, while the Republicans had avoided a depression, they had not totally erased the identifying marks which the 1930s had left upon them.

Whether Eisenhower's failure thoroughly to reshape the Republican party was outweighed by other positive achievements remains a matter of perspective. By pre-World War II standards, his administration would have appeared successful, but by the 1950s the American people, although attracted to the idea of moderation, demanded full employment, high economic growth, and, if possible, price stability. Eisenhower prosperity was real enough for many people, but it was inequitably distributed and too uncertain to capture the nation's confidence. By the canons of the liberals, the President failed when he refused to throw his moral authority behind the civil liberties and civil rights revolutions which were gaining momentum during his tenure. They charged that he had delivered American only an era of vacuous blandness. Yet one might argue that blandness was preferable to the hysteria that had dominated American politics in 1952. At least Eisenhower had given the nation a breathing spell—many observers, however, might argue that four years would have been sufficient—and the country could look to the election of 1960 in a rational mood.

EARL WARREN, THE SUPREME COURT, AND THE CONSTITUTIONAL REVOLUTION

One of the most unexpected developments of the Eisenhower era was the transformation of the Supreme Court into an activist institution concerned not with the protection of property rights, as had been the case with an activist judiciary before the New Deal Court-packing controversy, but with the extension of civil rights, civil liberties, and the equalitarian ideal. In the space of a few years, a once remote and conversative institution found itself in the forefront of a drive for change which profoundly affected American life. The new trend would reach its zenith under John F. Kennedy and Lyndon B. Johnson, but Eisenhower initiated it, perhaps unwittingly, in 1953 when he appointed Earl Warren chief justice of the United States.

The most liberal of the national Republican leaders, Warren had been elected governor of California three times; he had based his success upon mass Democratic support and counted among his friends and admirers Harry S Truman. Eisenhower made a conscientious effort to balance his Court appointments between liberals and conversatives, but with Warren's force and charm as a decisive factor the new activism gathered more momentum than the President probably had intended. Kennedy and Johnson would worry less about balance; their appointments would give Warren a decisive majority on most issues.

The Court's fullest consensus was in the area of civil rights. Here, earlier decisions under Roosevelt and Truman had paved the way; by 1952, the Court had outlawed the white primary, restrictive housing covenants, segregation in interstate transportation, and discrimination in higher education. It faced next a group of challenges to segregation in elementary and secondary education, an emotional issue that could affect the lives of millions of people.

The Court had to decide not simply *whether* to strike down segregation in these cases but *how* to do so. The rule established in *Plessy* v. *Ferguson* (1896) was that racial separation was permissible so long as facilities were equal. The amicus curiae briefs presented to the Court under Truman had challenged the "separate but equal" rule, but the Court had continued to follow it and had outlawed specific instances of segregation on the basis of nonequality. So long as the Court held to separate-but-equal, it at least accepted the possibility of segregation; to abandon separate-but-equal would challenge the whole structure and theory of segregation.

The cases, five in all, headed by *Brown* v. *Board of Education of Topeka, Kansas,* were first argued in late 1952 with the Truman administration filing a strong amicus curiae argument in support of the black plaintiffs. Moving with great caution, the Court scheduled a reargument for December 1953, with a new President in the White House and, as it developed, a new chief justice. Eisenhower's Justice Department submitted a milder and more ambiguous brief than had Truman's. Warren, however, was anxious to go beyond his predecessor, Fred Vinson, and override the *Plessy* rule. Warren's skills as an advocate and conciliator were probably decisive in producing a unanimous court. On May 17, 1954, the Supreme Court, speaking with one voice, rejected the separate-but-equal concept and outlawed all school segregation. Since the decision was so momentous, the Court took another year to ponder the problem of implementation and in the spring of 1955, after the Eisenhower administration had submitted another amicus brief calling for gradualism, ordered only "a prompt and reasonable start toward full compliance" and desegregation "with all deliberate speed."

The *Brown* decision, speedily followed by others which applied the same principles to all segregation statutes, was the most important document in American Negro history since the Emancipation Proclamation; yet the "all deliberate speed" formula frustrated its purposes. The gradualists had sought in good faith to accommodate the South, expecting good faith in return. Instead, they had to struggle against "massive resistance," the revival of the long-buried doctrine of "state interposition," attempts to supplant school districts with spurious state-assisted "private" schools, and a few total shutdowns of public education. After striking down all these devices, the Court faced new schemes designed to produce only the barest minimum of integration, including pupil placement tests and "freedom of choice" plans. A decade after the *Brown* decision, not a single school in Mississippi had been integrated and only .004 percent of the Negro students in South Carolina were attending formerly all-white schools; the statistics for the rest of the South were only a bit better—most under 1 percent, Florida and Virginia over 1.5 percent, Tennessee at 2.7 percent, and Texas at 5.5 percent.

Yet the story was not one of unalloyed frustration. The border states, which had required segregation by law in 1954, complied reasonably; this development alone made the *Brown* edict worthwhile. Under strong pressures from the courts and the Kennedy-Johnson administrations, even the Deep South began to crack. By the fall of 1970, an estimated 40 percent of southern black children were in integrated classrooms—a greater percentage than in most northern cities. By then, however, the *Brown* principle could no longer count upon support from the White House; moreover, it had run up against the most difficult obstacle yet, the relationship between residential and educational segregation and the necessity of mass school busing if it were to be overcome.

In the segregation cases, the Court almost invariably was unanimous. Other decisions with libertarian and equalitarian implications were characterized by division and backtracking. Eisenhower's policy of alternating between liberal and conservative appointees could at times transform a four-man minority into a five-man majority. The libertarian-equalitarian bloc would not be dominant until the Kennedy-Johnson era, but its work would begin under Eisenhower.

Aside from racial questions, no area of American political life had been so thoroughly characterized by demagoguery and disregard of individual rights as loyalty and sedition questions. As McCarthyism waned, the Warren Court moved to eliminate its vestiges. In *Pennsylvania* v.

Nelson (1956) and subsequent decisions, it effectively smothered most state sedition laws. As early as 1957, in *Yates* v. *United States,* it began a series of rulings that effectively blocked prosecution of communists or other alleged seditionists under the Smith Act. It struck down one provision of the McCarran Act after another. Other decisions forced procedural safeguards in federal and state loyalty programs and curbed the abuses of such legislative investigating committees as the House Committee on Un-American Activities. The basic assumption behind all these holdings was that political dissent, even in its totalitarian varieties, was a basic constitutional right; the espionage, treason, and other criminal laws were sufficient to deal with any threat to the Republic.

In the cold-war atmosphere of the 1950s and early '60s the loyalty and sedition rulings drew much criticism. By the middle 1960s, however, the Court's critics were beginning to focus upon another area into which it had moved: criminal procedure. *Gideon* v. *Wainwright* (1963) required states to provide legal counsel for indigent defendants. *Escobedo* v. *Illinois* (1964) and *Miranda* v. *Arizona* (1966) held that police must inform arrested individuals of their constitutional right to remain silent and grant them access to an attorney at any pretrial interrogation. Law-enforcement officials across the country condemned the *Escobedo-Miranda* principles as a menace to the public safety. Actually, they and the *Gideon* ruling simply extended to the poor and ignorant the same protections already available to the wealthy; but with crime and disorder increasingly a matter of concern, the Warren Court became a scapegoat.

Engle v. *Vitale* (1962) and other rulings that prohibited prayers, Bible readings, and religious exercises in the public schools were even more unpopular. The vehement reaction against them—Senator Robert Byrd of West Virginia accused the justices of "tampering with America's soul"—demonstrated that vast segments of the American population conceived of America as a Christian nation and believed the nurturing of the religious impulse was an integral part of the teaching of patriotism. In vain, the Court's defenders might argue that religious instruction was primarily a duty of church and family rather than the state. They could even show that the Court had upheld Sunday-closing laws and state aid to parochial schools. The prayer and Bible-reading cases were nevertheless its most widely criticized works, and in many localities school officials disregarded them with impunity.

Far more significant, although less controversial to the ordinary citizen, was the Court's determination to compel principles of equitable representation in the state legislatures and the House of Representatives. As late as the early 1960s, legislative districts in most states were grotesquely malapportioned in a manner that reflected population distributions half a century out of date and threw effective political control to rural politicians, although the large majority of the population lived in the cities and suburbs. Since the state legislatures drew up the districts for the U.S. House of Representatives, the same situation, in a less acute form, carried over to the Congress.

Before the Warren era, the Supreme Court had refused to touch the districting problem, arguing that it was a "political question." In *Baker* v. *Carr* (1962), however, the Court held that the Tennessee apportionment system, unchanged since 1901, was open to judicial review under the Fourteenth Amendment's guarantee of "equal protection of the laws." Vague in substance but sweeping in implications, the *Baker* ruling touched off a vast wave of apportionment suits. In *Wesberry* v. *Sanders* (1964), *Reynolds* v. *Sims* (1964), and several subsequent cases, the Court firmly established that the only standard of apportionment for state legislatures and congressional districts was "one man, one vote." By the end of the decade, it was invalidating even minor deviations from the rule. As inconceivable as it would have seemed at the start of the 1960s, the gerrymanders and rotten boroughs which had characterized almost every state were swept from the political map, replaced by rules of pure majoritarian democracy.

Reformers hailed the apportionment revolution as the beginning of a new era of progress; alarmed and outraged conservatives started a movement for a constitutional amendment which would override the Court. Both sides appear to have miscalculated. The main effect of equitable districting was to increase the political power of the suburbs, whose representatives tended to disregard urban problems about as much as had rural legislators. The apportionment cases had made American government more democratic in the abstract, but, whatever their long-run consequences, they had failed to produce instant change.

Warren's retirement in 1968 marked the end of a constitutional era. President Johnson's failure to obtain confirmation of Abe Fortas, a liberal activist in the Warren mold, as the new chief justice was an indication that the Warren Court had imposed upon American society all the change it could manage. In the main, the post-Warren Court would move toward a conservative passivity, but it was doubtful that the most reactionary collection of justices could undo the work of fifteen years. In 1970, the Court by a 5–4 margin even managed another landmark decision, this one extending to eighteen year olds the right to vote in federal elections. In 1972 it outlawed the death penalty, in most cases, as a "cruel and unusual punishment."

Critics of the Warren revolution included not only conservatives who disagreed with the substance of the Court's decision but many liberal-minded thinkers who argued cogently that the Court had rushed into areas from which it should have remained aloof, had engaged in ill-founded "judicial legislation" on matters which the representative branches of government should have handled, and had placed the judiciary in a vulnerable position. They asserted that the Warren bloc had too frequently departed from well-established precedent and had assumed for the courts a larger burden of the drive for social reform than society would tolerate. Such a critique had great substance, but to Warren and his colleagues other considerations were more compelling. When the chief justice stepped down in 1968, America was a freer and more democratic country than it had been in 1953. Strangely, Warren's leadership of the most radical Supreme Court in American history was the most enduring legacy of Eisenhower moderation.

EIGHT

Caution at the Brink

CHRONOLOGY
1952–60

1952

JULY Republican foreign policy platform advocates
"liberation" of communist-controlled nations

DECEMBER Eisenhower makes secret inspection of Korean front

1953

FEBRUARY Eisenhower announces "unleashing" of Chiang Kai-shek

MARCH Death of Stalin

JUNE Rioting in East Germany

JULY Korean armistice signed

AUGUST Mossadeq overthrown in Iran

1954

MAY Dienbienphu surrenders

JUNE Guatemalan revolution

JULY Indo-China partitioned

AUGUST France rejects European Defense Community

SEPTEMBER Communist China begins shelling Quemoy; SEATO
established

OCTOBER France agrees to Western European Union

DECEMBER U.S.–Nationalist China mutual-defense treaty

1955

JANUARY — Congressional resolution authorizes use of force to defend Formosa and the Pescadores

FEBRUARY — Baghdad Pact

APRIL — Bandung Conference

MAY — Shelling of Quemoy ends

JUNE — Austrian peace treaty

JULY — Geneva summit conference

1956

JULY — United States withdraws aid for Aswan Dam; Egypt nationalizes Suez Canal

OCTOBER — Polish demonstrations; Hungarian revolution; Anglo-French-Israeli invasion of Egypt

1957

MARCH — Congress approves "Eisenhower Doctrine"

OCTOBER — Rapacki advocates nuclear disengagement in central Europe; USSR orbits *Sputnik I*

1958

JUNE — European Common Market established

JULY — Iraqi monarchy overthrown; U.S. troops land in Lebanon

AUGUST — Chinese Communists begin shelling Quemoy and Matsu

OCTOBER — Shelling of Quemoy and Matsu reduced

NOVEMBER — Khrushchev threatens separate peace with East Germany

1959

JANUARY — Castro comes to power in Cuba

MAY — Death of Dulles

SEPTEMBER — Khrushchev visits United States

DECEMBER — Eisenhower visits South Asia, North Africa, and Europe

1960

FEBRUARY — Eisenhower visits Latin America

MAY — U-2 incident; failure of Paris summit conference

JULY   United States suspends Cuban sugar quota
AUGUST   Neutralists overthrow pro-U.S. government in Laos

Eisenhower and his secretary of state, John Foster Dulles, came to power with promises of a new foreign policy which would eliminate the communist menace. Yet whenever their rhetoric threatened to collide with reality they drew back, exercising a caution that placed their actual conduct of diplomacy well within the pattern established by Truman and Acheson. At times, the gap between aspiration and accomplishment could be embarrassing, most notably in the case of the Hungarian revolution, but the national interest was served better by caution than by aggressiveness. The major question about the diplomacy of the Ike Age was whether a continuation of the Truman-Acheson style of anticommunism was the best policy in an era when the nature of the cold war was changing profoundly.

IKE, DULLES, AND THE "NEW LOOK"

Eisenhower's credentials for the conduct of diplomacy were more substantial than those of many politicians. Typically, American Presidents had reached the White House through their skill at building coalitions around domestic concerns, their ability to handle foreign relations being almost irrelevant. Eisenhower, by contrast, knew little of most political questions, although that did not prevent him from forming strong opinions about them; but his experience at the highest levels of military command had put him in touch with the world of diplomacy and had required the tact and shrewdness of a coalition leader.

To his reputation as a military expert and man of decision, the President thus added the reassuring warmth of the conciliator. He had in fact accepted the onset of the cold war reluctantly and he genuinely hoped to moderate Soviet-American hostility. During his administration, most initiatives toward a settlement with the USSR would emanate from the White House rather than the State Department. Eisenhower's definition of conciliation, however, involved style more than substance, demonstrations of goodwill rather than solid agreement. Whatever his initial misgivings, Eisenhower accepted the rhetoric and assumptions of the cold war, and his gestures of conciliation were largely negated by an unwillingness to make the compromises that any genuine modus vivendi would require.

Until weeks before his death in May 1959, Dulles was the chief formulator of foreign policy. His qualifications were impressive, and with some reason, he practically considered the State Department his birthright. His grandfather, John Foster, was Benjamin Harrison's secretary of state; his uncle, Robert Lansing, had held the same post under Woodrow Wilson. Dulles's own diplomatic career had begun in 1907, when at the age of nineteen he had served as his grandfather's secretary at The Hague Peace Conference. Subsequent assignments took him to Latin America in 1917 and to Versailles in 1919. During the 1920s and '30s, he built an eminently successful career in corporation law and international finance. During World War II, he became prominent as one of the leading northeastern internationalist Republicans and almost certainly would have become secretary of state had Dewey been elected President in 1944 or 1948. (As it was, Governor Dewey could only appoint him to fill a brief unexpired term in the U.S. Senate in 1949.) Instead, he became one of the chief symbols of bipartisan anticommunism under the Truman administration, which appointed him to a variety of posts and assigned him the responsibility of negotiating the final peace treaty with Japan in 1950–51.

In 1952 Dulles executed a sudden shift which revealed two apparently contradictory aspects of his personality—a ruthless opportunism and a rigid moralism. Although he had been closely identified with the diplomacy of Truman and Acheson, he now became one of its leading critics. In a widely read magazine article and in the foreign policy section of the Republican platform, he attacked the doctrine of containment as passive and defeatist. He pledged himself and his party to "liberation" of the peoples under communist control. Containment implied accommodation to the status quo with only the hope that Soviet rule might mellow over the decades. American foreign policy had to undertake a more dynamic effort to free the captive peoples of Eastern Europe and China, but not through war. Liberation was to be accomplished by exhortation and moral suasion!

There can be little doubt that Dulles, with his vast experience in cold-war diplomacy, realized that liberation was not a feasible policy. Rather it was a slogan to appeal to the neo-isolationist Republicans and to a public in revolt against the seemingly endless and unwinnable war in Korea. When aimed at the Democrats rather than the communists, liberation was a successful tactic in the frenzied, bitter atmosphere of the 1952 campaign. But how could it be employed without war against a nation armed with atomic weapons and convinced that an Eastern European sphere of dominance was essential to its security?

Dulles displayed the same opportunism in his dealings with the Republican right wing in Congress. Constantly haunted by the way his predecessor, Dean Acheson, had been villified and hamstrung by the

McCarthyites and their fellow travelers, and surely aware that Eisenhower wanted to avoid combat with them, Dulles resorted to appeasement. He appointed a McCarthy follower chief security officer for the State Department, literally gave McCarthy control of the International Information Administration, and acquiesced in a cynical purge of career diplomatic officials who had served in the Truman administration.

For all his concessions to expediency, Dulles possessed—and at times appeared possessed by—a rigid, moralistic anticommunism. Indeed, his conviction that he should lead the free world in a crusade against communism probably provided his own mind with justification for his opportunistic tactics. Eisenhower, although hardly immune from moralistic anticommunism, was inclined to accept the idea of coexistence and seek out ways of reducing Soviet-American tension. Dulles thought in terms of constant and implacable hostility between the two blocs and adopted a Manichaean dualism which portrayed their rivalry as one of absolute good versus absolute evil. Such a viewpoint left little room for permanent coexistence—or for that matter for neutrality—yet coexistence remained a practical necessity which Dulles could not ignore. The secretary enjoyed Eisenhower's admiration and the President gave him wide discretion in the conduct of diplomacy; thus Dulles rather than Eisenhower established the tone of American foreign policy, but he worked under constraints that kept his practice at variance with his philosophy.

Foremost among these was the Republican drive to reduce government spending. Spurred by the Soviet atomic bomb and the Korean conflict, the Truman administration had planned years of increasing defense expenditures; in order to hold the line on the budget, the Eisenhower administration initiated policies of strict economy. The result, which Washington slogan makers called the "New Look," was an emphasis upon U.S. air power and nuclear capability ("more bang for the buck") and a reduction of American ground and sea forces. Henceforth, the United States would expect its overseas allies to develop greater conventional military power.

In theory, the New Look was logical; in practice, it posed new problems for the conduct of diplomacy and created dilemmas which the administration never solved. The concept of American air and naval power working in tandem with foreign armies prepared to fight their own battles on their own ground was appealing, but the ideal was hard to realize. Western European politicians could hardly expect their people to support higher defense budgets against the backdrop of U.S. cuts. Many of the nations of the Middle and Far East lacked the political stability and military traditions necessary to maintain credible deterrent power, no matter how generously the United States might subsidize them.

Therefore, the power behind American diplomacy had to be "more bang," and Dulles proclaimed a policy of "massive retaliation" to replace the Truman-Acheson doctrine of limited war. He underscored the implications in 1956 when he told an interviewer that the United States had gone and would continue to go "to the brink of war" to face down the communist world. Quite literally, he was saying that he was prepared to incinerate the civilized world to meet any military challenge, whatever its size, wherever its location. American liberals and Europeans of most persuasions, aware they would be caught in the middle of the Soviet-American thermonuclear exchange, were horrified. In fact, neither Dulles nor any other U.S. statesman could carry out such apocalyptic threats unless the survival of the nation were at stake; and with every year, brinksmanship and massive retaliation became less believable and more threadbare.

Yet Eisenhower's massive prestige gave his military-diplomatic policies an appearance of substance which they could not have enjoyed under a lesser leader. Eisenhower's reputation was formidable abroad and practically unassailable in America. Even when situations went badly, the President could command overwhelming popular confidence. As the electoral campaign of 1956 drew to a close, the unhindered Soviet quashing of the Hungarian revolt demonstrated the hollowness of liberation, and the concurrent Suez crisis revealed the temporary disintegration of the Atlantic alliance. It mattered little; political analysts were practically unanimous in their belief that Eisenhower actually gained votes from the situation. The popular conviction was that he was uniquely qualified to lead the nation in a time of crisis. To a far greater extent than any other political figure, he could reassure the country that he was doing what was necessary to protect it.

HOLDING THE LINE IN EUROPE AND ASIA

Shortly after the election, Eisenhower made good on his most notable campaign pledge and secretly traveled to Korea. His personal front-line observations produced no new key to victory; rather, they appear to have convinced him that the war was deadlocked and that he had to end it on the basis of the status quo. He pursued this aim with a policy that combined brinksmanship and compromise. Through indirect diplomatic channels, the administration threatened all-our war against China, including the use of nuclear weapons. (Available historical sources do not indicate just how explicitly the warning was conveyed or whether in fact contingency plans for a nuclear offensive had been approved.) At the same time, American diplomats searched for a face-saving solution to the one issue that had stalemated the long truce negotiations—the communist demand for forced repatriation of nearly 50,000 North Korean and Chinese prisoners who had declared their unwillingness to return home. As Washington began this dual strategy, an unexpected event half a world away strengthened its hand immeasurably—in early March 1953 the Kremlin announced the death of Stalin. The Soviet leaders who jockeyed for the succession had little interest in continuing the fighting.

Brinksmanship, compromise, and the death of Stalin combined in unmeasurable proportions to bring a settlement. Even a last-ditch attempt by South Korean President Syngman Rhee to scuttle the negotiations by unilaterally releasing some 25,000 North Korean prisoners failed to halt the coming of peace. On July 27, 1953, after the United States had forced Rhee to adhere to American policy, the communists signed an armistice. The document turned prisoners of war over to an international commission and gave the Chinese a chance to appeal to those who had rejected repatriation. It provided for a halt to the fighting along the battle line, which roughly approximated the old border, and for the maintenance of specified force levels on both sides. No further agreement was ever reached.

A termination of the Korean stalemate was clearly in the best interests of the United States, but the truce hardly squared with the doctrines of liberation and victory over communism. Soon the North Koreans would openly violate the armistice restrictions on military forces. Observing the situation from retirement, Harry S Truman accurately remaked that he would have been politically crucified had he negotiated the agreement. Eisenhower, rising above the principles he had professed, won general acclaim as the bringer of peace.

The Korean truce should have provided an opportunity to normalize relations with Red China, but it did not. The Chinese were partly to blame. Anxious to capture the leadership of the world communist movement, they engaged in a vituperative anti-Western rhetoric which made ordinary diplomatic contacts extremely difficult; life was hard and frequently dangerous for the few capitalist foreigners they admitted within their boundaries.

Still, with war ruled out as an alternative, diplomacy presented the only possibilities for dealing with China. Acting upon the well-established principle that recognition did not imply approval and reasonably assuming that a country so large and potentially powerful could not be ignored, Great Britain and several other Western powers had undertaken diplomatic relations with Mao's government as soon as it had demonstrated its control over the mainland; they had doggedly maintained relations despite calculated provocations and an apparent Chinese disinterest.

The American refusal to recognize China was understandable and in itself not necessarily detrimental to the national interest; one could make an argument for waiting until the Chinese were prepared to conduct diplomacy in accordance with generally accepted standards of civility. It was quite another thing, however, to conduct a campaign of international ostracism which increasingly became an adventure in unreality. Partly as a matter of politics, partly as an expression of moral indignation, the Eisenhower administration seized every occasion to proclaim the illegitimacy of the Maoist regime and sought to isolate it by dissuading as many nations as possible from giving it recognition and by leading a successful drive to keep it out of the United Nations. Refusing to deal with Mao either by war or by diplomacy, the United States was reduced to the pretension that his power was only temporary. In fact, his control over China was greater than that of any previous ruler in its modern history; Washington could hope for his demise but lacked the means to effect it.

Only the existence of Chiang Kai-shek's government on Formosa made such a fantasy possible. Truman and Acheson had given Chiang protection by ordering the U.S. Seventh Fleet to "neutralize" the straits between Formosa and the mainland—a decision somewhat akin, as Louis J. Halle suggests, to neutralizing the struggle between a cat and a mouse —but they kept the Nationalist government at arms' length. Eisenhower and Dulles undertook a strong U.S. commitment to Chiang.

The first indication of the new approach came in February 1953. In his first state of the union message to Congress, Eisenhower characterized the Seventh Fleet interposition as a tactic designed to protect the Red Chinese! Henceforth, he announced, the U.S. Navy would "no longer be employed to shield Communist China." For all the fanfare that accompanied it, the "unleashing" of Chiang brought no diplomatic or military dividends. The Nationalists could do no more than launch an occasional commando raid or sabotage foray against the mainland.

The Chinese Communists instead took the offensive, not against Formosa some 130 miles away, but against several small Nationalist-held islands just a few miles off the Chinese coast. The two most important targets were Quemoy, situated just six miles from the port of Amoy, and Matsu, nine miles from the northern approach to Foochow. In the fall of 1954 they came under fire from Red artillery. Mao, apparently attempting to demonstrate Chiang's military impotence, hoped to score a quick and easy victory.

The United States responded by concluding a mutual-defense treaty with the Nationalists. U.S. forces were committed to the defense of Formosa and the nearby Pescadore Islands, but not Chiang's offshore bases. In an unofficial corollary to the treaty, moreover, the Nationalists promised to refrain from offensive activity against the mainland without

American agreement. By the end of 1954, Eisenhower and Dulles were admitting that the Seventh Fleet could act as a shield only for the Nationalists, and they had effectively released Chiang.

Nevertheless, they had come to believe that Quemoy and Matsu possessed great symbolic importance. 'Thus, while they advised Nationalist evacuation of the Tachen Islands some 200 miles to the north, they put up a show of determination over Quemoy and Matsu. In January 1955 the President asked Congress for prior authorization to defend the islands if he judged an attack upon them to be preliminary to an attack upon Formosa.

Public-opinion samplings revealed wide misgivings about the request, and clearly it made little sense militarily. Eisenhower's justification was political. The shelling of Quemoy and Matsu had begun just weeks after the French defeat in Indo-China; another Western setback, he feared, would undermine the anticommunist cause throughout Southeast Asia. The House of Representatives gave its approval within twenty-four hours, 410–3. A bloc of liberal Democrats, including Hubert Humphrey and John F. Kennedy, in the Senate argued that Quemoy and Matsu were too insignificant and militarily untenable to be assigned such pivotal importance, but they could muster only 13 votes for an amendment that would have emasculated the administration's enabling resolution. On the final vote, the Senate gave the President the authority he wanted, 83–3. Few politicians were prepared to argue openly with Eisenhower's judgment, and the Red Chinese were unwilling to take risks. By May 1955, the Communists had ended the shelling and instituted an informal cease-fire.

In August 1958 the crisis erupted again, and the American response differed only in detail. Eisenhower proclaimed the transcendent importance of Quemoy and Matsu to the cause of anticommunism in Asia, provided naval escorts for Nationalist supply convoys, and gave Chiang's forces howitzers capable of firing nuclear shells. But he also persuaded the generalissimo to reduce the offshore garrisons, thereby demonstrating to the world that no offensive action was planned against the mainland. In October the Red Chinese halted the shelling for three weeks, then announced that artillery would be used against the islands only on odd-numbered days, apparently considering this a face-saving device.

The administration could claim that the gamble of brinksmanship had paid off. The Chinese Communists were doubtless embarrassed by their failure to secure territory only a few miles off their coast. But by restraining Chiang, Eisenhower and Dulles had done more than free Red China from nuisance military raids. They had also signaled that they sought only the status quo and would make no attempt to destroy the Communist government. The victory thus was not clear-cut.

It was at the least an open question whether Quemoy and Matsu were critical enough to justify such dangerous tactics. And it was surely debatable whether the Eisenhower administration had constructed a viable Asian policy by attaching itself so closely to the Chinese Nationalists. It might well have been impossible to reach any sort of modus vivendi with Mao in the 1950s, but by clinging to an untenable status quo, Eisenhower and Dulles were leaving necessary adjustments to some successor administration.

Much the same was true for Europe; for all their rhetoric about a dynamic new policy, the President and his secretary of state wanted simply to preserve the balance of power that existed when they took office. Events soon demonstrated that the doctrine of liberation was as meaningless for Eastern Europe as it had been for China. In the summer of 1953 the East German "dictatorship of the proletariat" faced a genuine proletarian revolution as blue-collar workers in the important industrial cities rioted in protest against their miserable living and working conditions. Three years later, in Hungary, a popular revolution overthrew the communist government and proclaimed a neutralist democracy. In both cases the United States refrained from interference as Soviet armor crushed the uprisings; having done much to kindle the hope of freedom in the Russian satellites, the administration could provide only some pious words of consolation.

It would, of course, have been irresponsible to intervene in either East Germany or Hungary. No compelling national interest was at stake, and so direct a challenge to the USSR's security belt might well have set off a nuclear holocaust. Nevertheless, it also had been terribly irresponsible to dangle the lure of liberation before nations that wanted freedom from Soviet repression and were encouraged by the tide of de-Stalinization. Many of the Hungarian rebels who fled to the West complained bitterly that they had been urged to take up arms by Radio Free Europe, an obstensibly private organization which secretly drew most of its financing from the U.S. Central Intelligence Agency (CIA). As Eisenhower and Dulles used the occasion to condemn Red imperialism, the Hungarian leaders paid the price of death, imprisonment, or exile.

After Hungary, Eastern Europeans realized that they could achieve only whatever small degree of independence they could force on their own, that it would be unrealistic to strive for more than the Polish example of a nationalist-minded communist dictatorship firmly aligned with the Russian security system. The United States for its part belatedly discovered reality and dropped the theme of liberation.

From the beginning, the main Eisenhower-Dulles objectives were the same as those of Truman and Acheson, the establishment of anticommunist unity in Western Europe and the strengthening of NATO; the New Look made such policies all the more necessary. However, a stronger NATO inevitably would mean a rearmed Germany, a prospect that caused understandable apprehension throughout the rest of the Continent. Dulles employed a form of brinksmanship against his own allies by threatening an "agonizing reappraisal" of America's position if the Western European democracies refused to authorize a defense force in which the Germans would participate. In 1954 the main stumbling block, France, first rejected a long-planned European Defense Community, but then under pressure approved a hastily devised substitute proposal for a Western European Union which would include German troops and operate as an arm of NATO. In order to obtain even this result, the administration had to commit a much larger number of U.S. troops to NATO than the New Look contemplated. At last, however, the alliance could put up a show of unified military power.

In the end, the effectiveness of NATO would not be based on conventional military power—the Soviet bloc would inevitably possess vastly superior numbers of troops at the ready—but upon diplomatic unity between the United States and Western Europe. In this respect, NATO was only intermittently effective. The nadir came in 1956 when Britain and France covertly planned to seize the Suez Canal without consulting the United States. The consequent American refusal to support the Anglo-French action once it was underway became very possibly the most embarrassing incident in the history of Western cold-war diplomacy.

Subsequently, the British, under Prime Minister Harold Macmillan, worked to repair relations with the United States and establish a "special relationship" of English-speaking peoples. The French took a different tack. Defeated in Indo-China, bogged down in a debilitating and unpopular war in Algeria, fearful of relinquishing Western European economic and military primacy to West Germany, resentful of the Anglo-American "special relationship," France was unready to assume the role of the dutiful, subordinate ally. After Charles de Gaulle came to power in 1958, the French republic began a process of disengagement from NATO. France refused use of its airfields to U.S. nuclear bombers, developed its own atomic bomb, resisted all plans for supranational military integration, and, as the United States perceived it, behaved as if obsessed with dreams of Napoleonic grandeur. When Eisenhower left office, NATO, a relatively unified alliance in 1952, appeared in serious disarray.

It is doubtful, however, that Eisenhower and Dulles can be assigned much responsibility for this development. The unity of 1952, which Eisenhower himself had done so much to build, had occurred against the backdrop of the Korean war and a genuine fear of Soviet military aggression. By the end of the 1950s, the USSR seemed less menacing, despite its renewal of the Berlin crisis. It is worth noting, moreover, that the French, for all their day-to-day disruptions, stood firmly with the Germans on Berlin. The Western powers would still act in concert if they all perceived a truly serious threat to their existence.

Western Europe in the meantime was making greater progress toward economic cohesion. In 1954 France, Germany, Italy, Belgium, the Netherlands, and Luxembourg joined to establish a European Coal and Steel Community as the first step toward the establishment of an integrated economy. A European Atomic Energy Commission (EURATOM) followed in 1957. In 1958 the same countries, with U.S. encouragement, established a Common Market. The objective was the submersion of national economies into a vast and powerful supranational unit which would lay the basis for a United States of Europe.

America supported the Common Market. In some areas, it might compete with U.S. industry, but the Republican administration, no less than the Democratic ones that had preceded it, shared the belief that free trade and economic development carried benefits for all concerned. Moreover, an economically stronger Europe would be able to assume a greater share of its defense. Whatever short-range problems it might present, the Common Market appeared to be one of the most hopeful developments of the 1950s.

There remained only the perennial and perhaps insoluble problems of Germany and Berlin. Germany was the pivot upon which the future of Europe would turn; its economic and military power held out the promise of continental dominance for whichever bloc controlled it, but German strength also posed a danger that other European nations, communist and noncommunist alike, could not ignore. West Germany, under its first postwar chancellor, Konrad Adenauer, had followed a policy of integration with its former North Atlantic enemies; the East German government was probably the most subservient regime in the Soviet bloc. By any objective standard, West Germany was a free and prosperous nation, East Germany a gray Stalinist despotism still trying to climb out of the rubble of World War II. The West Germans wanted unification and, if possible, a return to prewar boundaries—they did not recognize the Oder-Neisse Polish border. They were also strongly anti-Russian and anticommunist.

Under the circumstances, the USSR could hope for little more than continuation of the East-West division of Germany; moreover, it might legitimately fear a rearmed West Germany which could at some date be strong enough to attempt reunification by force. Nevertheless, at intervals during the 1950s, Russia held out the possibility of German reunification if the country were disarmed and neutral. The offers were always tentative and vague. One variant proposed an East-West confederation with each side to have equal representation. Another appeared to require the nationalization of West German industry.

The Western governments treated such overtures as diplomatic ploys designed to hamper German rearmament and never attempted to engage in the long negotiations which would have been needed to explore them. Any genuine unification plan would have to be based on free elections and mutual military withdrawals, and no disinterested observer could imagine that the German Communists would have any chance under such an arrangement. The neutralism of a reunified Germany would inevitably lean toward the West, and even with goodwill on both sides rearmament could not be postponed forever. The vision of a united Germany even made many Westerners uneasy. In 1955 the Russians agreed to an Austrian peace treaty which united and neutralized that small nation, but Germany presented prospects that were far more difficult to handle. Both sides in the cold war were happy enough to settle for the status quo.

The one festering sore left in Europe was West Berlin, which constituted an increasingly serious threat to the existence of East Germany. Access between the communist and noncommunist zones of Berlin was unrestricted; potential defectors from anywhere in the East German republic needed only to get to Berlin and to be willing to leave their possessions behind them. West Berlin was a magnet for the dissatisfied who wanted to share in the freedom and prosperity of the other Germany. From 1949 to 1958, nearly 2.2 million East Germans, almost one-eighth of the 1949 population, moved to the West; a disproportionate number of them were professionals, technicians, and skilled workers.

On every other European issue, the primary drives of Russia and the West had converged toward consolidation of preexisting arrangements; but Berlin was bleeding East Germany to death and doing it in the most embarrassing way one could imagine. At the end of 1958, the USSR announced that within six months it would conclude a separate peace with East Germany, the most important effect of which would be the termination of occupation rights in Berlin. The Russians and East Germans seemed determined to drive the West out. The most serious cold-war crisis of the Eisenhower Presidency had begun.

THE THIRD WORLD AND THE GLOBALIZATION
OF THE COLD WAR

In 1955 the representatives of twenty-nine Asian and African nations met at Bandung, Indonesia, and adopted resolutions that denounced imperialism and affirmed the right of self-determination for all peoples. The event attracted great attention, not so much for its substance as for its symbolism. The governments at the conference had all gained their independence within the past decade; with the notable exception of Red China, most were aligned with neither side in the cold war. Bandung marked the emergence of the Third World as an international force.

In the broadest sense, the Third World consisted of all the underdeveloped nations populated by nonwhites bitterly resentful of economic and political colonialism, usually committed to neither the USSR nor the United States. Encompassing Latin America as well as most of Asia and Africa, the Third World contained most of the earth's people and a sizable portion of its most valuable natural resources. In varying degrees, its nations suffered from neo-feudal social systems characterized by mass poverty and a perpetual Malthusian crisis in which population threatened to outstrip food supply. Yet the twentieth-century revolution in communications had made its peoples aware of better alternatives, and the decay of old spiritual and political restraints cleared the way for them to demand alleviation of their misery. Leaders of the Third World, having cast off outside control, had also to deal with a revolution of rising expectations at home.

The situation appeared to present both the United States and Russia with vast opportunities. The historian, writing with the benefit of hindsight and some detachment, may argue that the liabilities and dangers outweighed any possible gains, but the framework of U.S.–Soviet rivalry practically mandated a competition for power and influence among the underdeveloped nations. As the old points of confrontation were being stabilized, the emergence of the Third World opened up new ones all over the planet. The multiplication of areas of conflict in itself created the possibility that the cold war might go out of control. It entangled the United States and the Soviet Union in many volatile local and regional rivalries and left them open to manipulation by politicians who milked both sides for assistance and maintained their power by externalizing domestic problems, that is, by deliberately pursuing rivalries with neighboring states instead of concentrating on nearly insurmountable internal problems.

The globalization of the cold war created especially difficult situations for the West. The imperialism which the Third World had cast off was Western, usually British or French. The native ruling elites in many underdeveloped nations were notoriously linked with the former imperialist rulers; in those countries where the old elites had been overthrown, the new leaders were likely to be anti-Western in one form or another. The American experience of democratic national development and capitalistic economic growth contained few usable examples for nations that had vast social divisions, mass poverty, and no democratic traditions. The Soviet experience of revolution, authoritarian rule, and state planning was more relevant; the USSR, moreover, could score some cheap points by giving rhetorical and moral support—but little actual aid—to "wars of liberation." Only a few "new nations," most notably India, could successfully draw upon such Western practices as English democratic socialism, and even in these instances the veneer of democracy was thin indeed. Third World statesmen might engage in self-righteous denunciations of imperialism and present themselves as arbiters of international morality—Western liberals frequently encouraged them to do so—but of necessity most were dictators and not infrequently small-scale imperialists themselves.

Any American effort to deal with the Third World thus faced formidable obstacles; even an administration that acted with great skill and tact would face countless frustrations. Eisenhower and Dulles too frequently displayed a rigidity that practically guaranteed reverses in situations other than those where the United States and its allies could command overwhelming power. Dulles's declaration in an important 1956 speech that neutralism was in most instances immoral could hardly win friends and influence people in nations which considered nonalignment an intelligent and virtuous national policy, nor was it likely to be persuasive, coming as it did from the representative of a nation which itself had made a virtue of neutrality before World War II. Dulles and Eisenhower attempted to deal with the Third World with carrot-and-stick tactics ranging from personal bribery and economic aid to subversion and military power. Holding the line here, however, proved to be a much harder task than in Europe or North Asia.

Of all the Third World crises Eisenhower faced when he took office, none was more critical and intractable than the one in Indo-China. Since the end of World War II, a determined insurgent movement, the Viet Minh under the leadership of Ho Chi Minh, had been fighting one of the epochal anticolonial revolutions of the twentieth century against France. Before 1950, America had steered clear of the trouble and had advised Paris to work for a compromise settlement with Ho. Then China fell to the communists, and Mao Tse-tung rocked the Truman administration by proclaiming his alignment with Moscow. So long as U.S. policy makers accepted the thesis that Oriental Communism was independent and indigenous, the prospect of victory by Mao or Ho was tolerable. But Mao seemed to have disproven the thesis, and suddenly it became natural to view Ho as part of what seemed after all a monolithic communist world. In the spring of 1950 the United States began to extend military aid to the French effort in Indo-China. After the beginning of the Korean war,

Washington greatly increased its assistance and actually steeled itself for military intervention should the Chinese move into the conflict.

As it developed, there was no need for the Chinese to participate, and we now know that Ho would have welcomed them only as a last resort. (Later events would demonstrate that the initial Truman-Acheson impression of Asian Communism as separatist and independent was substantially more correct than the post-1949 view of it as a component of an international monolith.) The French and their puppets had little popular support, while Ho was a revered national leader, not just a communist functionary. He and his lieutenants won the support of most of the population and conducted an increasingly effective "people's war" against the foreign imperialists; the French sank deeper into a quagmire.

By early 1954, the French, besieged at Dienbienphu, were in desperate trouble; only massive American intervention could avoid defeat. Pledged as he was to roll back communism on the one hand and avoid Korean-style wars on the other, Eisenhower faced a dilemma. The New Look defense posture practically foreclosed the use of ground troops—General Matthew Ridgway, closing out his military career as army chief of staff, opposed such an involvement, warning that it would be more costly and difficult than the Korean enterprise. Nevertheless, Admiral Arthur Radford, chairman of the Joint Chiefs of Staff, advocated one or two heavy bombing raids, possibly employing tactical nuclear weapons, to relieve Dienbienphu. Secretary Dulles and Vice-President Nixon delivered speeches hinting at American intervention. Eisenhower himself warned that Indo-China was only the first in a row of dominoes which threatened to topple in rapid succession, that victory for communism there might lead to its spread throughout Southeast Asia.

All the same, compelling factors held the administration back. Eisenhower's own military judgment was against intervention. He was privately appalled by the blundering French strategy and must have wondered whether any aid to an army with such incompetent leadership was worthwhile. In addition, he doubted that nonnuclear air strikes could seriously hurt the communists, and the use of atomic weapons, probably diplomatically impossible anyway, carried the serious danger of obliterating Dienbienphu as well as its attackers. The British were adamantly opposed to any widening of the Indo-China crisis and so were the Democratic leaders in Congress. Under the circumstances, the administration could do little more than undermine its credibility. On May 6, 1954, Dienbienphu fell, and, though the French still had the power to fight for Indo-China, they no longer had the will. On June 18, a new government, headed by Pierre Mendès-France, came to power, pledged to negotiate a truce within five weeks.

Subsequently, a conference which had convened at Geneva shortly before the French defeat arrived at a settlement. Indo-China would be partitioned into the neutralist kingdoms of Laos and Cambodia and the republic of Vietnam. Vietnam in turn would be temporarily split at the 17th parallel pending national elections in 1956; Ho's Vietminh would establish a government in the north, and the Western-supported group under Ngo Dinh Diem would administer the South.

The Geneva accords gave the West as good a deal as it could expect, and France was glad to accept them; the United States, however, never reconciled itself to the agreements. At Geneva, Dulles ostentatiously refused to shake hands with the Red Chinese premier, Chou En-lai, whom he seemed to regard as the embodiment of evil; the United States disassociated itself from the final document. Thereafter, the American government sought to transform South Vietnam into a bastion of anticommunism. Having decided against military intervention, Eisenhower now sanctioned a political involvement which might someday have to be supported by armed force; his judgment as a general proved sounder than his foresight as a diplomat.

With American backing, President Diem canceled the scheduled 1956 national elections. (All of Washington, from Eisenhower down, was aware that Ho would have won an overwhelming victory.) The United States extended heavy military and technical assistance, sending a former army chief of staff, General J. Lawton Collins, to act as Diem's military adviser and setting up what amounted to a shadow bureaucracy to guide the Vietnamese administrators. In turn, Ho's supporters, now called the Viet Cong, began a new insurgency, and, with Diem becoming increasingly repressive and unpopular, they gained support. Year by year, the Vietnam situation became more precarious.

The United States also moved to extend its influence into Laos, formerly the northwestern province of Indo-China. The tiny country was landlocked, possessed only 3 million inhabitants, and was so isolated from the outside world that Eisenhower himself later admitted Washington had only the vaguest grasp of the political situation there. Nevertheless, he came to consider Laos as vital as South Vietnam and sanctioned a large American assistance program in which the U.S. Central Intelligence Agency (CIA) * was heavily involved. Through a series of interventions in Laotian politics in 1958 and 1959, the CIA managed to dump the neutralist government and install a pro-Western regime, thereby incurring the hos-

---

* The CIA had been established during the Truman administration. Its functions at first appear to have been primarily espionage and information gathering. Under Allen Dulles, the secretary of state's brother, it moved rapidly during the Eisenhower years into a wide variety of "counter-subversion" activities and frequently failed to do an adequate job of concealing them.

tility of the strong communist force, the Pathet Lao, and the wrath of the neutralists, who had managed to retain considerable influence in the Laotian army.

In August 1960 neutralist army officers staged a coup d'etat in an attempt to establish a nonaligned civilian government. Eisenhower, refusing to distinguish between the neutralists and the communists, authorized aid to the pro-Western attempt to reverse the coup. The result was to drive the neutralists and communists together, and start a vest-pocket civil war. As Eisenhower's administration entered its final months, the pro-Western military situation deteriorated, and the President gave serious consideration to unilateral armed intervention. On his last day in office, the old general met with his young successor and warned him that if Laos fell, all of Southeast Aisa probably would follow, that hence it probably would be necessary to fight a limited war there.

Meanwhile, a few months after the Geneva agreements the United States had thrown up an anticommunist alliance, the Southeast Asia Treaty Organization (SEATO), consisting of the United States, Great Britain, France, Australia, New Zealand, the Philippines, Pakistan, and Thailand, which rapidly became an important U.S. base area on the Southeast Asian mainland. The signatories agreed to oppose communist expansionism and specifically included Indo-China as part of their area of concern, although none of the Indo-Chinese states were parties to the agreement.

SEATO was the first of a series of military alliances designed to contain the communist thrust into the Third World. Consistent with the New Look defense policy, these pacts contemplated effective local ground forces. The practice unfortunately rarely approached the concept. SEATO was a paper tiger never able to play a meaningful role in Indo-China or anywhere else. In this and other regions of the Third World, many important nations refused to consider communism a serious threat to their interests and resented Dulles's effort to bipolarize the world. Burma, India, and Indonesia all remained aloof, and America's standing was hardly improved when in 1958, the CIA was discovered to be involved in a blundering attempt to overthrow Indonesia's President Sukarno. SEATO and the other regional defense pacts were probably counterproductive, for they conveyed an illusion of security at variance with reality.

The Middle East presented an equally unpromising and even more complicated prospect. Here also, the tide was running in favor of revolutionary, anti-Western nationalism, and the traditional ruling classes in most countries were fatally compromised by an affiliation with colonialism. In addition, the area, vital to the West because of its strategic location and its oil fields, had long ranked second only to Slavic Europe as an objective of Russian imperialism, czarist and Soviet alike. Here, the clash of interest between the USSR and the West was basic and long standing, and Western influence was waning.

The existence of the State of Israel immeasurably increased the opportunities for Russian penetration. The terrible fate of European Jewry during World War II had given unstoppable impetus to the movement for the establishment of a Jewish state in Palestine, an objective which incurred almost fanatical nationalist-religious opposition from the Arabs. In the years immediately after the war, Jewish refugees clamored for the right to emigrate to Palestine and establish a national identity. Western diplomats realized that Zionism could only damage the interests of their countries and attempted to frustrate it, but to sizable segments of the public, morality dictated a place of refuge for the Jews. Palestine from 1945 to 1949 was one of those instances in which self-interest and idealism clearly conflicted and seemed irreconcilable. The Palestinian Jews themselves ultimately settled the issue by mustering the military power to carve out the State of Israel and beat back the Arab armies. An armistice in 1949 ended the first Arab-Israeli war, but the Arab states still refused to acknowledge Israel as a legitimate nation and continued to conduct sporadic raids into it.

Although Israel received little tangible help from the West in its formative years, it was nevertheless in many ways an outpost of Western civilization and technology, sustained by moral, financial, and political support from the United States and other Western nations. Hence, it was easy for Arab leaders to denounce Israel as the last manifestation of Western imperialism. Indeed, anti-Zionism served as a convenient distraction from the failure of Arab governments to reverse the trend of ever-declining standards of living for their masses. It was equally easy for the Soviet leaders to join in—Russia after all had a tradition of anti-Semitism which went back well before the Bolshevik revolution. On the other hand, no important Western democratic politician was prepared, either morally or in terms of his own future, to advocate the eradication of Israel. The USSR could never hope to dominate the Middle East as it dominated Eastern Europe, but the combination of revolutionary nationalism and anti-Zionism gave it plenty of opportunities to wield influence and inflict damage upon Western interests.

As Eisenhower and Dulles saw it, American diplomacy in the Middle East had two major tasks: the construction of a military alliance to contain the Soviet thrust and the establishment of a good relationship with the charismatic leader of Arab nationalism, President Gamal Abdel Nasser of Egypt. The first objective was based on a mistaken perception of the Russian threat—there was little danger that the USSR would attempt a military invasion of the Middle East, but great danger that it would achieve an ideological identification with radical Arab nationalism. The second objective was realistic but so erratically handled as to wreck American prestige in Egypt rather than to enhance it. Western power and influence in the Arab world was certain to decline, no matter what tactics the United States employed, but a more informed diplomacy might have made the descent less precipitous.

In erecting a military alliance the administration could count on two nations of the Islamic world that were not embroiled in the Arab-Israeli conflict, Turkey and Iran. Having been subjected to centuries of Russian pressure, the Turks felt that their national survival rested upon ties to the West. Iran became a dependable ally after a CIA-managed coup overthrew its nationalist-neutralist prime minister, Mohammed Mossadeq, and restored the authority of the shah. (The Truman administration had found Mossadeq erratic and exasperating but had some sympathy for his grievances against the British and had sought to mediate Anglo-Iranian disputes; the Eisenhower administration was quickly convinced that Massadeq was a tool of the communists.) Among the Arab states, the republic of Lebanon and the monarchies of Iraq, Jordan, and Saudi Arabia were most pro-Western.

Out of this material, the United States engineered the establishment of a Middle Eastern Treaty Organization, frequently called the Baghdad Pact. Concluded in 1955, the pact was an alliance between Great Britain, Turkey, Iraq, Iran, and Pakistan; the United States avoided formal membership but was the moving force behind the treaty. To Eisenhower and Dulles, the Baghdad Pact was a barrier against communist expansion, but to Arab nationalists the alliance was a despised reassertion of Western imperialism. Able to muster little military power, the Baghdad Pact was, like SEATO, a paper organization.

Under the best of circumstances, Nasser would have been hard to manage. Ambitious, shrewd, and charismatic, he pursued policies designed to establish him as the leader of the Arab world: the achievement of total national independence through the expulsion of the remaining British troops stationed at Suez, a buildup of Egyptian military power to destroy Israel, and a plan of economic development through the construction of a huge dam across the Nile at Aswan.

The United States could not look with favor on Nasser's anti-Israel policy, but it realistically supported his demand for the ouster of British forces. The effort to expel the British had begun under the old monarchy, and the thrust of Arab nationalism was so strong as to make a British withdrawal practically mandatory. At U.S. insistence, the English agreed to a treaty, signed in October 1954; it provided for an evacuation subject to the British right to return if an outside power attacked the Middle East.

Eisenhower and Dulles also decided to extend economic aid. In December 1955, Great Britain and the United States offered to give substantial economic aid in the building of the Aswan Dam. The proposal was so generous that Iran and Turkey grumbled about the West's relative ingratitude toward its friends. Still Nasser engaged in long negotiations for a better deal; as he did so, Egypt recognized Red China, drew closer to the USSR, and intimated that the Russians were prepared to help.

Nasser was not simply trying to parlay the cold war into a maximum payoff; he sought military aid also for his aggressive foreign policy. In September 1955 he had negotiated a large arms agreement with Czechoslovakia, pledging the Egyptian cotton crop as collateral for payment. In the ensuing months it became clear that Nasser wanted economic development financing from the West while using a substantial portion of his own country's resources to buy arms from the Soviet bloc. The design of combining external adventurism with massive internal projects was economically unsound for Egypt; for the leaders of the United States and Great Britain, it was diplomatically and politically embarrassing.

Nevertheless, the United States handled the problem crudely and ineptly. In July 1956, with Egypt apparently anxious to seize the assistance offer, Dulles abruptly withdrew it. The Aswan project was unpopular in Congress and bad election-year politics; moreover, the administration was increasingly convinced that it was not economically viable. But Eisenhower and Dulles also hoped to strike blows at both Nasser and the USSR. Believing that Moscow could not put up the financing required for Aswan, they intended to expose Russian weakness. By pulling the rug from under the Egyptian president, they expected to teach him a moral lesson about the pitfalls of duplicity and perhaps even force him out of office. The decision may have strengthened Eisenhower's already impregnable political position a bit, if only in the short run, but every other premise behind it proved mistaken.

Nasser's response was daring, but it should have been predictable. In a matter of days, he seized the Suez Canal from the Anglo-French company that had operated it since its construction. Henceforth, Nasser announced, the canal would be operated by Egypt, and the tolls would help pay for Aswan.

The British, who felt that Suez was absolutely critical to their national interests, and the French, long outraged by Nasser's support of the Algerian rebels, immediately began to plan military intervention, only to be restrained by the United States. Eisenhower and Dulles, following international law and traditional American policy, recognized the right of expropriation, providing that Egypt made fair compensation and kept the canal open to all nations. Hence, they advocated negotiations. The USSR for its part encouraged Nasser to remain intransigent. An international conference, held in London, accomplished little, and in private talks Nasser displayed an unwillingness to compromise. By mid-October, Eisenhower and Dulles began to sense a breakdown of trust and communication with their Atlantic allies. Simultaneously, the Arab-Israeli confrontation reached a crisis stage with Egypt, Syria, and Jordan signing a military alliance and Israel responding with a general mobilization.

On October 29, in the midst of the Hungarian revolution, Israel, Britain, and France began a military scenario that they had carefully concealed from the United States. Israeli forces, using ironically the blitzkrieg tactics the Germans had employed at the beginning of World War II, launched a devastating attack which quickly routed the Egyptians. As the Israeli army drove toward the Suez Canal, England and France issued an "impartial ultimatum" to both sides demanding the demilitarization of the canal zone. Israel at once complied, but the Egyptians refused. Thereupon, Britain and France launched their own attack against Egypt and proceeded to retake the canal. The Soviet Union, after it had suppressed the Hungarians, entered the scene with blustery threats of atomic intervention in behalf of Egypt.

In the circumstances, the American attitude was decisive. The administration refused to support Britain and France and instead forced a settlement which resulted in the withdrawal of foreign troops; in return, Egypt agreed to open the canal to all nations (except Israel!), allow Israeli shipping passage through the Gulf of Aqaba into the Red Sea, and accept a United Nations peacekeeping force which would attempt to prevent the border raids that had led to Israeli belligerence. Strangely, the nation that had hoped to humiliate Nasser a few months before now saved him from the consequences of a total military defeat.

The Suez fiasco amounted to a serious setback for the West. Israel scored some modest gains, but England and France had been seriously embarrassed, and the Atlantic alliance appeared in tatters. Britain moved to repair relations with the United States, but France was increasingly inclined toward separatism. Nor did the United States profit from having pulled Nasser out of the fire. The Arab world was inclined to remember Dulles's withdrawal of the Aswan offer and to give the USSR's threats credit for forcing the Anglo-French withdrawal. The Russians moved to consolidate their influence by extending financing and technical assistance for the Aswan Dam. In the wake of Suez, America's position in the Middle East declined apace with that of other Western nations; the Soviet standing was higher than ever; and Nasser remained free to pursue his aggressive foreign policy.

Having rebuffed the British-French attempt to establish a sphere of influence at Suez by force, the United States now paradoxically moved to define the Middle East as an American sphere of influence and to back up the claim with military power. In January 1957 Eisenhower went before Congress and asserted that the Middle East was vital to American security. He requested a broad enabling resolution—which journalists predictably tagged the Eisenhower Doctrine—allowing him to initiate military or economic programs in the area and use U.S. armed forces if necessary to repel communist aggression. Not surprisingly in view of the events of 1956, there was more congressional debate and opposition than over the Quemoy-Matsu resolution, but in two months the President had his authorization by votes of 355–61 in the House and 72–19 in the Senate.

The immediate objective of the Eisenhower Doctrine was to give support to the pro-Western governments of Iraq, Jordan, and Lebanon. Hardly six weeks after congressional passage of the doctrine, Eisenhower dispatched the U.S. Sixth Fleet from its French bases to the eastern Mediterranean in a display of strength designed to bolster the government of the young Jordanian king, Hussein. The real test, however, came in July 1958, when Western influence was on the verge of total expulsion from the Arab world.

In Iraq, anti-Western nationalists overthrew the monarchy and slaughtered the royal family. The coup was quickly executed and, for all practical purposes, irreversible. The problem was to preserve the Western position in Lebanon and Jordan. Hussein promptly requested armed assistance from the British. Lebanon was on the brink of civil war, more because of conflicting internal political ambitions than because of grand ideological considerations. Nevertheless, the insurgents were receiving help from Egypt and Syria, which had joined in a political confederation. Responding to a request from President Camille Chamoun, the United States landed 14,000 troops on the Lebanese beaches; Great Britain sent a smaller force to Jordan. Neither intervention met resistance. The Lebanese conflict was settled on a basis acceptable to all, but the new government was more neutralist than the old. Hussein faced no overt challenge. Three months later, the Western soldiers were on their way home.

It is hard to say whether the landings accomplished much. Most Arabs probably considered them about as imperialist as the Suez invasion, and the USSR capitalized on this sentiment by threatening the "aggressors" with nuclear devastation. Eisenhower, on the other hand, was convinced that Lebanon and Jordan had been "saved" from pro-Nasser or procommunist rulers. Perhaps he was right, but the generally negative Arab reaction practically foreclosed future interventions. Unable to change the situation in Iraq, the administration could do little more than extend recognition after satisfying itself that the new military rulers were not taking orders from Moscow. The Baghdad Pact had to be reorganized as the Central Treaty Organization (CENTO), headquartered at Ankara, Turkey, a capital presumably safe from anti-Western revolutions; without Iraq, it was more impotent than before.

Of course, no communist tide swept over the Middle East. Eisenhower and his supporters might attribute this good fortune to the demonstration of Western resolve in Lebanon and Jordan, but it is more likely that the United States simply had exaggerated the danger. It was necessary to worry about and work against the growth of Soviet influence in the region, but by misunderstanding the challenge, American policy makers had accomplished little. The fate of the Baghdad Pact demonstrated that the communist threat, such as it was, consisted of ideological subversion rather than the possibility of outright military aggression from the USSR; paper alliances could do nothing to prevent internal ferment.

At the same time, the administration exaggerated the possibility of a Red Middle East. If successful, ideological subversion could give the Soviet Union enhanced influence; but only large numbers of combat-ready Russian troops could transform an Arab state into a Soviet satellite. The most "procommunist" governments of the Middle East—Egypt, Syria, and after mid-1958, Iraq—were happy to accept rubles, military hardware, and technicians from the USSR, but they wanted no Soviet divisions, and they kept their internal Communist parties under tight control. The administration's hostility toward neutralism led it to blur the distinctions between communism and radical Arab nationalism; hence, figures such as Nasser and the lesser-known neutralist-nationalists of the Arab world could appear much more menacing to Western interests than they actually were.

It is fair to say in defense of Eisenhower and Dulles that even the most adroit diplomacy would surely have failed to check the erosion of Western influence in the region. The history of the area guaranteed that its nationalism would have an anti-Western tinge, and the elemental passions which stirred its politics and diplomacy were not susceptible to rational management. The United States could have achieved an identification with Nasser and his counterparts only if it had been willing to extend a blank check for grandiose development projects and commit itself to the destruction of Israel.

Still, the critic may regret that the Eisenhower administration did not pursue more informed and consistent policies, which could have minimized the loss of U.S. prestige. And he may especially regret that after eight years as President, Eisenhower felt impelled to describe the Middle East with a word that is usually reserved for the mysteries of the Orient—"inscrutable."

With the possible exception of Black Africa, the least-noticed portion of the Third World for most of the Eisenhower Presidency was, strangely enough, the area which the United States had historically claimed as a special sphere of influence, Latin America. The major hemispheric event of Eisenhower's first term was the CIA-arranged overthrow of a Popular Front government in Guatemala, although it was at the least debatable that any real danger of Soviet domination existed. (The Guatemalan regime appears to have been social reformist, demagogic, and authoritarian—a combination not unknown in Latin America—and it did have some communist officials, but the evidence suggests that it was far from communist-controlled at the time of its ouster.) The Guatemalan episode was symbolic of a failure to understand that the forces of Third World revolutionary nationalism were strong in the southern part of the Western Hemisphere and that they were coupled not with simply a general resentment of Western colonialism but with a very specific and long-standing hatred of Yankee imperialism. Not until 1958, after Vice-President Nixon faced violent mass demonstrations on a Latin American visit, did the United States initiate important economic-aid programs. One may wonder whether this new concern would have long survived the memory of the anti-Nixon mobs had it not been for the rise of Fidel Castro.

Castro became the ruler of Cuba in January 1959, the leader of a popular peasant-based movement which overthrew the tottering, corrupt dictatorship of Fulgencio Batista. At first, he was widely hailed in both the United States and Cuba as a great mass leader who would bring democracy and social justice to his island. The hopes were only partially fulfilled. The revolution began reform programs which brought much-needed benefits to the impoverished masses, but which also threatened large segments of the middle class with economic liquidation. Refusing to hold the free elections he had promised, Castro instituted a regime with many of the trappings of totalitarianism—circus trials, public executions, suppression of all opposition, and a purging of potential rivals from the revolutionary movement. By the end of his first year in power, Castro had become heavily dependent upon the communists, once a small part of his movement but always the most organized segment of it, and his marathon speeches were increasingly devoted to anti-U.S. harangues.

The administration's initial attitude was wary but stopped short of outright hostility. Eisenhower was repelled by Castro's actions almost from the beginning, and refused to see the Cuban dictator when he came to the United States on a speaking trip in April 1959. Vice-President Nixon, however, spent three hours with Castro and concluded that he was "either incredibly naive about Communism or under Communist discipline." On the other hand, the State Department sent a sympathetic ambassador to Havana and expressed willingness to open negotiations on an economic aid program. All the evidence indicates that, had he desired it, Castro could have established a working relationship with the United States without compromising either his social revolution or his own power. The Eisenhower administration would work with dictators and was at the least prepared to tolerate internal radicalism; it was alienated by Castro's pro-Sovietism.

By mid-1960, the administration was preparing to overthrow Castro. Washington suspended U.S. purchases of Cuban sugar, an economic blow which Castro partially countered by arranging a sugar deal with Russia. In the meantime, the CIA had begun to organize Cuban exiles for an invasion of the island, training them in Guatemala and assuming that what had taken place there in 1954 could be repeated in Cuba. Hoping to prove that its opposition was not only to communist penetration, the administration undertook a diplomatic offensive against the hated right-wing dictator of the Dominican Republic, General Rafael Trujillo, and the CIA gave help and encouragement to his opponents. The State Department redoubled its advocacy of progressive reform for the hemisphere, and Eisenhower got a half-billion-dollar Latin American aid appropriation from Congress.

In Latin America as in other areas of the Third World, Eisenhower faced a difficult situation, the nature of which he and many of his aides only half perceived. The emphasis on social reform and the new economic assistance programs were constructive and worthwhile, although the policy would take many years to produce dividends even if it were successful. On the other hand, the notion that Castro could be toppled by a revolt made in the United States woefully underestimated the strength and popular support which the Cuban revolution retained even after it had become odious in Washington. The Eisenhower approach contained an impossible internal contradiction: it advocated social revolution even as it secretly planned to destroy the hemisphere's most important social revolutionary. Conveniently, it would be left to Eisenhower's successor to demonstrate the bankruptcy of such a program.

THAWING AND REFREEZING THE COLD WAR

As the Eisenhower Presidency began, the West faced a reasonably united and implacable communist world and was fighting the Korean war. With much reason, most Americans assumed the perpetual hostility of the communist world and anticipated a long period of tension highlighted by displays of naked power. Against this pattern of expectations, hard-line anticommunism made sense, and even the desperate cry of liberation carried a certain emotional logic. Yet Eisenhower and Dulles had hardly assumed control of American foreign policy before the communist world changed drastically in an unexpected manner which demanded a more flexible diplomacy.

The death of Stalin created a situation at once less harsh and more uncertain. No successor could establish the same iron grip upon the Soviet state. Henceforth, Russian leaders would have to calculate their moves, internal and external, with the realization that they were dependent upon the support of a majority—not of the people as a whole, of course, or of the general membership of the Communist party, but at least of the communist elite, who in turn possessed a degree of responsiveness to the attitudes of the party members and the needs of the masses. For the average Russian, the transformation meant a marked softening of the harsh despotism that Stalin had practiced and a somewhat greater emphasis on the production of consumer goods. For the foreign diplomat, the new order presented both possibilities of accommodation and the erratic behavior which stems naturally from internal instability.

Stalin's ultimate successor, Nikita Khrushchev, added to the problem of unpredictability. Emerging in 1954 as the dominant figure in the complex struggle for political supremacy, Khrushchev combined a shrewd toughness with a mercurial personality. His foreign policy zigged and zagged, partly because he alternatively responded to pressures from Soviet "hawks" and "doves," partly because the logic of the cold war made any attempt at détente extremely difficult. A performer who relished his prominence on the world stage, he moved easily between the persona of the jovial Red Santa Claus and the role of the wild, angry Russian bear. He might in one month talk exuberantly of friendship and coexistence only in the next to threaten the West with nuclear destruction in words far more intemperate than any ever employed by Stalin. He hardly had consolidated his power before the Soviet bloc established its own military organization, the Warsaw Pact, as a counterweight to NATO; yet this mildly threatening gesture was more than balanced by the decisions to end the occupation of Austria, engage in diplomatic relations with West Germany, and push for the first summit conference since Potsdam.

Such an antagonist required a more flexible and sophisticated approach than Dullesian anticommunism, but by 1954 the cold war had reduced American diplomacy to a series of reflexes. Every Russian overture was automatically a snare, every threat a true indication of the everlasting hostility of a united international communist movement. Prominent Democrats, including Dean Acheson, subscribed to this analysis about as fully as the Republicans, whatever their differences with the GOP on tactics. The pattern of cold-war thinking could not be easily reversed, especially in the face of a Soviet diplomacy which oscillated between rapprochement and bluster.

Largely at the insistence of Britain and France, Eisenhower agreed to meet with Khrushchev and other top Soviet leaders at Geneva in July 1955, but he and Dulles expected little to come from the conference and discouraged the secrecy essential to hard diplomatic bargaining. To counter the charge that the administration rejected communist disarmament proposals without offering constructive alernatives, the President advocated an "open skies" disarmament plan which would be policed by air reconnaissance inspections. The Russians rejected the idea, no doubt because it would deliver the United States greatly increased information about Soviet military capabilities while giving the USSR little intelligence not available from other sources. Geneva produced a surface atmosphere of goodwill, which for a time made the cold war seem less menacing. The failure to go beyond the façade of goodwill to hard agreement, however, indicated that at bottom mistrust and hostility were dominant on both sides.

After Geneva, in early 1956 the Soviet Union suggested a twenty-year friendship treaty with the United States, possibly as a propaganda stunt but also possibly as the first step in a détente with the West. In retrospect, one can see the early signs of Soviet-Chinese rivalry beginning to appear, and it is not inconceivable that the Russians hoped to lessen tensions with the West. But if such was the Soviet intention, the maneuver was uncharacteristically subtle; an American administration deeply committed to cold-war attitudes and perceiving only international communist unity would not explore oblique offers. Washington might have been well advised to probe Soviet intentions; instead, it demanded a settlement of practically every outstanding cold-war issue as evidence of Russian sincerity. The dialogue came to a halt in the barrage of insults and threats which accompanied the Suez and Hungarian crises.

Then the possibility of détente rose again. In the fall of 1957 Adam Rapacki, the Polish foreign minister, advocated the establishment of a nonnuclear zone comprising Czechoslovakia, Poland, and the two Germanys. The Rapacki Plan was doubtless made in Moscow, and in early 1958 the Russians endorsed an "amended version" which held out in addition the promise of a reduction in conventional military forces. In the meantime, no less a diplomat than George F. Kennan, who had left government service in 1953, delivered an influential series of lectures calling for military disengagement in Central Europe. The Kennan lectures, motivated primarily by a revulsion against the ever-escalating nuclear arms race, were highly controversial and in some particulars militarily unrealistic, but Kennan's passionate hope of preventing an atomic holocaust had great appeal. The Rapacki Plan, put forth as NATO was preparing to deploy nuclear weapons in Germany, indicated that the

USSR understood the strength of this sentiment and, possibly, even shared it.

The U.S. reaction was by now predictable. The Eisenhower administration simply refused to accept the possibility that the Soviet Union might be serious, that in addition to its problems with China (which still were unrecognized), the USSR might be willing to tolerate a degree of international control in the satellites to forestall a nuclear-armed West Germany. The gut reaction in Washington was to consider the Rapacki Plan part of a grand design to emasculate NATO, and, instead of exploring Russian seriousness, the Western responses again argued the need to include the whole range of fundamental cold-war contentions in any agreement. At mid-year, the proposal was submerged in the new wave of Soviet threats which accompanied the Lebanese landings.

In the meantime, the Russians had scored an important psychological victory by orbiting *Sputnik I* in the fall of 1957. The achievement gave new prestige to Soviet science and left the appearance that the USSR held a significant lead over the United States in missile technology. With the manned bomber obviously entering the twilight of its brief existence as the most fearsome weapon of war, the possibility of Russian superiority in rocket development was cause for grave concern. How could "massive retaliation" possess even a shred of credibility if the other side had superiority in the means to deliver nuclear weapons?

In the winter of 1957–58, a confidential government study (the Gaither report) and a prestigious private analysis (the Rockefeller report) both advocated substantial increases in the defense budget and a buildup of conventional military forces. The administration channeled more funds into missile research and development, but, confident that America still had the power to retaliate in strength, Eisenhower refused to embark upon a crash defense program. Throughout the remainder of his years in office, independent military analysts—and Democratic politicians—talked ominously of a "missile gap," and embarrassingly visible failures of rocket tests at Cape Canaveral, Florida, provided impressionistic confirmation for the fears of U.S. impotence.

Actually, the Russians had not converted what proved to be a temporary lead in missile development into military superiority or even parity, but they cultivated the illusion well and drew strength from it. As early as the Suez crisis, Khrushchev had brandished atomic-tipped rockets against Britain and France, although he had done so only after the situation was nearly resolved. By the Lebanese intervention, he was making threats of nuclear devastation with abandon.

Having failed to make any progress with gestures at disengagement and apparently strong enough to be belligerent, the Soviet Union initiated the second Berlin crisis at the end of 1958. Khrushchev's clearest objective was to cut off the exodus from East Germany, but he may also have hoped to gain a peace treaty that would secure the Rapacki objective of de-nuclearizing West Germany. At the same time, he suspended Soviet nuclear testing and proclaimed the need to keep atomic weapons out of the Far East (i.e., China and Japan). Moreover, while threatening a situation that could erupt into World War III, he pressed for an invitation to visit the United States.

Dulles, by now a dying man, was willing to negotiate minor changes in the status of Berlin, but he would not accept proposals to make it a "free city" or fundamentally alter Western occupation rights. The American position, quite flexible for the secretary, did little to ease the crisis. Pursuing a strategy of belligerent pronouncement, the Russian premier orchestrated a crisis climate while avoiding any precise commitment to action. In exchange for a foreign ministers' conference in the spring of 1959, he withdrew an initial six-month ultimatum, and when the gathering failed to produce an agreement, he accepted an invitation to meet personally with Eisenhower and tour the United States; the President in turn was to make a similar visit to the USSR in 1960. In something of a carnival atmosphere, the Soviet dictator spent ten days in September 1959 traveling from Manhattan skyscrapers to Iowa cornfields to Hollywood film studios. His conferences with Eisenhower were amiable, and upon his departure the Berlin crisis seemed remote and unreal. The President was to return the visit in mid-1960 after a major East-West summit conference in Paris.

Eisenhower, having taken over much of the responsibility for foreign policy, engaged in ambitious personal diplomacy himself. In December 1959 he embarked upon a trip that carried him to eleven nations in South Asia, North Africa, and Europe. In February 1960 he visited Argentina, Brazil, Chile, and Uruguay. Cheering throngs provided abundant evidence of the President's personal popularity and demonstrated that the United States could still draw on a reservoir of goodwill around the world. But tourism could be at most an adjunct to diplomacy, and critics charged with some cogency that the trips concealed an essential aimlessness of policy. The foreign masses, moreover, could be as fickle with Eisenhower as with other leaders. In mid-1960, after the collapse of the Paris summit, angry mobs of radical students rioted for days and forced the cancellation of a presidential visit to Japan.

It is hard to imagine what the Paris conference might have accomplished—Berlin presented practically no room for maneuver—but events destroyed whatever hope of success existed. On May 5, 1960, just days before Eisenhower's scheduled departure for the summit, the USSR announced that it had shot down an American U-2 reconnaissance plane engaging in aerial espionage deep within Russian territory.

The historian must wonder about the timing of this incident. The U-2, capable of functioning at altitudes believed to be beyond the reach of Soviet antiaircraft missiles, had been photographing Russian military installations for four years, and the Russians had long been aware of its existence. Was it possible that the Soviet Union had just developed a weapon capable of downing it? Did the Soviet military "hard-liners" hoping to wreck the summit meeting wait for the most embarrassing opportunity? Did Khrushchev himself order the downing of the U-2 as a means of avoiding an unfruitful conference or perhaps simply as a device that would put the Americans on the defensive?

Khrushchev acted as if he expected the Paris conference to be held. Producing the captured pilot, Francis Gary Powers, and his photographic equipment, the Russians quickly destroyed the U.S. story that the U-2 was a lost "weather plane," but the premier also expressed confidence that Eisenhower had known nothing of the flights. There the matter could have rested with some American embarrassment, but no real harm—after all, the United States had in the past seized Soviet spies without seriously disrupting great power diplomacy (one of them, Colonel Rudolf Abel, would be traded back to the USSR for U-2 pilot Powers during the Kennedy administration). It was left to Eisenhower to elevate the incident to one of the central events of his Presidency.

Incredibly, he assumed full responsibility for the spy incursions, told the world they were morally justified, and intimated they might be continued. After such a performance, negotiation was impossible. Eisenhower would fly to Paris only to find Khrushchev behaving in the angriest and most boorish manner he could muster. The presidential trip to Russia was canceled. In the fall the Soviet dictator again came to the United States, this time not to see the President but to do everything possible to disrupt the United Nations General Assembly session and create an impression of Soviet belligerence.

The cold war had reached its most frigid point since the death of Stalin.

Why had Eisenhower's diplomacy ended so badly? In part, no doubt, the answer was a failure of technique. The handling of the U-2 affair had been unimaginably horrendous; a more intelligent management could surely have prevented the precipitate deterioration of Soviet-American relations which occurred in mid-1960. But the U-2 incident reflected a fundamental assumption of the Ike Age, the belief that the Russo-American conflict was basic and irreconciliable. Hence, it was necessary to authorize a risky spy flight within weeks of a summit conference and permissible to justify the mission as an act of morality. Given the prevalence of such attitudes in Washington, encouraged to be sure by Moscow's erratic behavior, the cold war could only work itself out.

Eisenhower and his foreign policy advisers were prone to think in grand ideological terms rather than to consider the cold war as a number of separate clashes of interest, some of which might be negotiated on a one-by-one basis; Khrushchev and those around him, whatever their motivations, declined to engage in the frank, consistent overtures which might have altered the shape of U.S. policy. With ideological hostility enduring even after most of the basic post–World War II points of conflict had reached a de facto settlement, the cold war took on a cyclical nature of crisis followed by accommodation followed by crisis, and so on.

When Eisenhower left office, leading analysts of contemporary affairs were in substantial agreement that his foreign policy was a failure and that the nation was caught in a dangerous, potentially catastrophic drift. A decade later, however, many observers, having witnessed the horror of Vietnam, were inclined to praise Ike with a certain nostalgia as a leader who had held the reins on the military and had avoided needless wars. Such revisionism is superficially appealing, but it comes apart if one examines the Eisenhower legacy more closely.

Eisenhower and Dulles sought only to perpetuate, not to settle, the cold war, even while cutting back on the means required to wage it. The administration viewed the Third World through the distorted lenses of ideological anticommunism. It approached China with unremitting hostility and risked nuclear war over a group of worthless islands. It systematically sabotaged the Geneva accords of 1954, and by its actions in Laos and South Vietnam nurtured the seeds of a new war. It planned the use of military force against Cuba, conveniently scheduled for early 1961.

In truth, Eisenhower could boast of few positive accomplishments, and he gave no signs of understanding the changing nature of Soviet-American rivalry. At bottom, his reputation rested upon his ability to juggle and postpone difficult problems rather than confront them. It would be unreasonable to expect from him or any other statesman a satisfactory solution to all or most of the cold-war problems he encountered, but it seems fair to observe that his method of dealing with them amounted to preparing a series of time bombs for his successor.

NINE

Cultural Revolutions

CHRONOLOGY

1949–73

1949	*Death of a Salesman* by Arthur Miller
1950	*The Lonely Crowd* by David Riesman
1951	*The Caine Mutiny* by Herman Wouk
1952	*American Capitalism* by John Kenneth Galbraith; Batton, Barton, Durstine & Osborne handle Republican presidential campaign
1954	*Playboy* magazine established; Supreme Court school desegregation decision
1955	*The Man in the Gray Flannel Suit* by Sloan Wilson
1956	*The Organization Man* by William H. Whyte; *The Power Elite* by C. Wright Mills; success of Montgomery bus boycott
1957	Establishment of Southern Christian Leadership Conference
1958	*The Affluent Society* by John Kenneth Galbraith
1959	Grove Press publishes unexpurgated American edition of *Lady Chatterley's Lover*
1960	*Growing Up Absurd* by Paul Goodman; sit-in movement begins in Greensboro, North Carolina; establishment of Student Non-violent Coordinating Committee
1962	Establishment of Students for a Democratic Society as an independent organization—issuance of Port Huron Statement; *The Other America* by Michael Harrington
1964	SNCC Mississippi summer registration project; Berkeley Free Speech Movement; Martin Luther King awarded Nobel Peace Prize
1965	Watts race riot

225

1967   Detroit and Newark race riots; *Bonnie and Clyde*

1968   *Hair* begins New York run; Living Theater performs *Paradise Now; The Graduate;* assassination of Martin Luther King

1969   *I Am Curious (Yellow); True Grit; The Wild Bunch; The Selling of the President* by Joe McGinniss; *them* by Joyce Carol Oates; Woodstock music festival; Berkeley "people's park" disorders

1970   *The Greening of America* by Charles Reich; *Joe;* University of Wisconsin bombing

1971   Television debut of "All in the Family"

1972   *A Clockwork Orange;* establishment of *Ms.* magazine; *Deep Throat*

1973   *Last Tango in Paris;* Supreme Court rules in favor of "community standards" for censorship

1975   Federal aid averts New York City bankruptcy

Although Americans had lived in dread of a return to hard times after World War II, the dominant fact of postwar life for most was prosperity and affluence. Over a quarter-century, the nation slowly forgot the depression and began to take economic well-being for granted. The new prosperity represented a culmination of the development of the U.S. economy into a postindustrial phase oriented toward the production of consumer goods and services, allowing and indeed requiring more leisure time than had previously been available. The onset of this change, surely one of the most far-reaching in American history, called forth life styles and protest movements which by the 1970s occupied the forefront of American life and politics.

GROWTH AND AFFLUENCE

Despite occasional recessions, despite an inflation that almost always creeped and too frequently galloped, the economy performed in a manner which would have been considered an unmitigated success in 1939. It grew constantly, fell usually only two or three percentage points short of full employment,* and provided Americans at almost every social level with a steadily rising standard of living. The gross national product and disposable per capita income, both measured in constant dollar values, had

---

* Most economists agree that an economy has reached "full employment" when the unemployment rate is close to 3 percent. Recently, economists associated with Republican administrations have argued in favor of a 4 to 5 percent standard.

more than doubled by 1970. The new prosperity did not include everyone, but affluence was probably more widely distributed than ever before in American history. The fact that many economists, social critics, and political leaders demanded an even stronger and more equitable performance constituted testimony that a revolution of rising expectation existed at home as well as abroad.

Perhaps no group experienced so dramatic an increase in economic security and well-being as the organized blue-collar workers. It became a common joke—common because it had a ring of truth—that electricians and plumbers were unavailable because they were on nearly perpetual vacations in the Bahamas or at Sun Valley or some other resort once frequented only by the upper crust. Truck drivers frequently earned more than college professors, and the president of the United Steel Workers seriously argued that the men in the mills needed periodic paid "sabbaticals." In 1971 a team of sociologists investigating working-class consumption patterns found that color television sets were so widely owned that they were no longer a status symbol; staying ahead of the blue-collar Joneses required the purchase of a camper trailer. In such a society, status distinctions were less a matter of income than of life styles.

For the average middle-class American, whether he wore a blue or a white collar, the new affluence entailed a remarkable degree of comfort. During the 1950s and '60s, the American way of life increasingly came to be symbolized by the suburban condition: the three-bedroom split-level house in a too hastily developed neighborhood; a plethora of gadgets and conveniences; the rounds of life negotiated in automobiles, probably two to a family, one of them likely to be equipped with air conditioning. Middle-class existence might have its special tensions and anxieties, such as the constant push to acquire new possessions and the spiritual malaise frequently associated with materialism, but it also had a luxury beyond the reach of even the depression-era man who held a steady job.

One of the most visible products of affluence was a rapid growth in foreign and domestic travel. European tourism became an increasingly middle-class industry with a bewildering array of special air fares and package plans designed for a mass market. The untutored camera-carrying U.S. visitor became a staple of continental humor—and of continental anti-Americanism. Stimulated by the vast highway construction which began in the 1950s, tourism at home became a booming activity marked by the growth of luxury motel chains and comfortable camping facilities, by the overrunning of such attractions as the major national parks.

Recreation and entertainment boomed apace. One of the most visible manifestations was the growth of popular music to a multi-billion-dollar recording and concert business, a substantial portion of which drew its support from a youth subculture whose depression-era equivalent had been almost penniless. The million-sale recording, once a comparative rarity, became a relatively common occurrence for any nationally successful artist or group. Rock festivals grossed hundreds of thousands of dollars, leading the cultural historian William O'Neill to observe that "the difference between a rock king and a robber baron was about six inches of hair."

By the 1960s, the nation had entered an athletics boom. Participant sports such as golf and bowling gained devotees in numbers that threatened to overwhelm available facilities. The major professional spectator sports went through periods of expansion and paid their stars astronomical salaries until every big-league team seemed to have at least one $100,000 player. Rival football and basketball leagues engaged in bidding wars for top college players. In 1972, the newly formed World Hockey Association wrote a check for a cool million in cash, only the first installment of an $8 million agreement, to secure the services of Chicago Black Hawks star Bobby Hull. In an even more ludicrous deal, one WHA team signed Boston Bruins player Derek Sanderson to a several-year multimillion pact; when Sanderson's performance was disappointing, the team gave him a million dollars *not* to play for it. Even journeymen athletes claimed upper-middle-class salaries and fringe benefits—early in 1973, a Yankee pitcher complained to a New York *Times* reporter about the difficulty of supporting a family on $40,000 a year—and fans flocked in ever-greater numbers and paid ever-higher prices to see them perform.

The arts experienced large-scale growth also, although the support given them was not so lavish. Several major cities invested hundreds of millions of dollars in opulent cultural centers for concerts, opera, ballet, and the legitimate theater. The noted Shakespearean director Tyrone Guthrie astounded eastern intellectuals by establishing a successful repertory company in Minneapolis, Minnesota. Classical recordings remained a sideline in the music business but were a bigger and more profitable area than ever before. Clearly, a growing percentage of Americans was drawn to the "highbrow" entertainments, perhaps from simple interest, perhaps from the same status-seeking that impelled corporations to sponsor radio and television presentations of the arts.

Education grew as a matter of necessity. A postwar "baby boom" inundated the elementary and high schools during the 1950s and hit the college campuses in the 1960s. The growth of affluence made it possible for many families without a college background to send their children to state-supported institutions of higher education. Enrollment pressures were met after a fashion with bond issues and sharply increased state and local taxes. Schools at all levels remained crowded as construction and staff additions usually failed to keep pace with growth; still, the educational system probably gained strength. Teachers from the lower grades to the universities possessed more impressive academic credentials and were usually able to demand better pay than ever before. Social critics could observe with justice that Americans remained much more prone to pay for entertainment than to underwrite learning, that high school teachers frequently drew lower salaries than garbagemen, that few college professors earned as much as utility infielders; nevertheless, the United States financed its educational system more generously than any other Western democracy, largely, no doubt, because America had a wider economic margin upon which to draw. Economic expansion provided a dividend that allowed both for indulgence in the pleasures of life and for fairly decent support of activities such as education, which gave the average taxpayer little tangible gratification.

The new prosperity appeared to be based largely upon the strength of big business. Throughout U.S. history, Americans have feared the power of corporate bigness while craving the benefits usually identified with economic concentration—mass production, efficiency, and technological innovation. During the depression, when private enterprise seemed to have failed badly, both popular and intellectual opinion condemned the inadequacy and social irresponsibility of business leaders. The affluence of the postwar era brought new perspectives. For one thing, the corporate managers themselves came to understand the importance of public relations and strove to present themselves as men with a sense of civic duty devoted to more than the maximization of profit. Few average citizens accepted such pretensions fully; still, the new rhetoric against the backdrop of general prosperity gave the corporations an image that was at the least neutral and probably a bit positive. David Lilienthal, once head of the Tennessee Valley Authority, a government enterprise which had earned the abiding hatred of the business community, wrote a volume proclaiming that big business had entered a new era; Lilienthal had abandoned none of his belief in the TVA, but having moved into the world of business himself, he had found many of its leaders surprisingly enlightened and constructive.

In *American Capitalism* (1952), John Kenneth Galbraith argued that concentration, even oligopoly, produced far more dividends than drawbacks. The large corporations might not be as socially concerned as they pretended and assuredly they employed legal and extralegal means to charge artificially high prices for a wide range of commodities from liquor to automobiles to breakfast cereal. But the hidden tax of price fixing was a small amount to pay for the technological progress that seemed to accompany relief from competitive pressure and that sustained economic growth and prosperity. Monopolistic big business was, in short, the cornerstone of American affluence and the most important component of postwar prosperity.

Without restraint, the giant companies might commit excesses which would do serious harm to the economy, but Galbraith argued in effect that bigness begat bigness, creating a system of countervailing powers which effectively prevented disastrous excesses. Large buyers checked the power of large sellers; big labor, on the whole, checked big business; organized agriculture had secured advantages against both; the state checked them all. Galbraith did not believe that America had achieved an economic utopia; not all groups were effectively represented within the system of countervailing power. Still, he conceded the essential beneficence of bigness and organization and waved good-bye to the older American dream of smallness and competition with no regrets.

The development of the labor movement illustrated the consequences, both good and bad, of countervailing power. In the immediate postwar years, it became apparent that the labor unions were too well entrenched in the positions they had captured during the New Deal and the war to be dislodged; antilabor efforts consisted in the main of preventing the spread of unionism, a task facilitated in part by the Taft-Hartley Act and even more by the disinclination of the established unions to lend more than token support to organizational drives in nonunion occupations. (It is probable, indeed, that the rank-and-file member was more opposed than was the average labor leader to the diversion of union dues for the organization of migrant farm workers or other unfortunates.) Occasional strikes might engender something resembling the militance of the 1930s, but it was a fair generalization that labor was recognized as a member of the "establishment." Consequently, it became a common practice to settle major strikes with generous hikes in wages and employee benefits funded by corresponding price increases; the unorganized public thus underwrote higher blue-collar living standards and handsome corporate profits. Such was the price of bigness, tolerable perhaps for the middle class, harder for the poor; but it was at the least a moot question whether any other system conceivable within the limitations of American traditions could perform as well.

CONSUMPTION AND CONFORMITY

In the years after World War II, social analysts began to discern important shifts in national values. Actually, these were changes of emphasis which had begun to develop as early as the 1920s but had been submerged by the depression and the war. The American character appeared unmistakably altered both by a prosperity dependent upon mass consumption and by the growing importance of large organizations, public and private. The affluent, organizational society that was reaching maturity by mid-century encouraged styles of life quite different from those of the late nineteenth-, early twentieth-century industrializing society. It was a fair generalization that by mid-century in most situations the key to individual success lay less in productive talent than in sensitivity to the attitudes of others, that the values of individualism were being supplanted by the virtues of adaptability.

David Riesman delivered the first and most important analysis of the change in *The Lonely Crowd* (1950). Riesman focused upon the urban and suburban middle classes, the pace setters of American society; his generalizations thus did not apply equally to all groups, but he was successful in locating an important new development in American life. The old dominant national character, Riesman argued, had been "inner-directed." The product of an industrializing economy and a psychology of scarcity, it had extolled hard work, saving, and individual gain as the primary virtues; the inner-directed man had been above all an individualist and a moralist who acted according to his values without regard for the opinions of others. His ethic was that of the expanding entrepreneur. The new American type was "other-directed." The product of a stage of economic development which accepted affluence and leisure as a matter of course, the other-directed man was motivated by an ethic of consumption and cooperation; his values were less deeply held and he was likely to take his cues to proper behavior not from any instilled morality but from the expectations of those around him. His virtues were those of the manager or organization man.

The economic facts of life actually dictated the new trend. "Hard work" in the grueling sense of the standard 50–60 hour week no longer existed for the average blue-collar employee, who instead had more spare time and greater purchasing power than ever. Nor was thrift any longer a virtue. Most people realized at least dimly that a wide distribution of purchasing power made the economy dependent upon consumer spending; Keynesian economists and government policy makers consciously acted upon this assumption.

One of the most pervasive economic developments of the postwar era was the growth of installment buying. Once a device used mainly for the purchase of homes and automobiles, the installment contract became the vehicle for all manner of purchases. The credit-card industry, practically nonexistent in 1939, became a business that touched the lives of practically every American. The first major credit-card companies, Diners Club and

American Express, existed mainly to perform a service for traveling executives and professionals, who patronized expensive hotels, restaurants, and gift shops; the card companies did little advertising, exercised a degree of selectivity in approving applications for accounts, and charged an annual membership fee.

By the 1960s, large banks were forming their own credit-card syndicates, organizing practically every enterprise within a community, and actively inducing applications from depositors. The bank credit card typically required no membership fee, was freely issued to anyone with a checking account and a passable credit record, and could be used for the most routine purchases; in some localities, enterprising bankers even arranged to have their cards used for payment of taxes or college tuition fees. Large retailing firms which maintained their own customer-credit systems likewise encouraged the maximum possible use of an account, even to the point of holding sales for cardholders only. By the end of the 1960s, middle-class America was immersed in a credit-card economy which, by permitting deferred payment for most necessities, made it possible to buy luxuries, large and small; many people were willing to pay the interest charges that accompanied such an arrangement. In all its forms, the expansion of credit was underwriting national prosperity.

Popular culture encouraged the assumption that every American was entitled to an upper-middle-class standard of living. Television, the most pervasive form of mass entertainment, inevitably gave the characters in its programs stylish clothing, expensive automobiles, and luxury apartments, always at least a cut or two above what the ordinary American could afford. This mode of unreality was carried to the breaking point when the glamorous black performer Diahann Carroll portrayed "Julia," a widowed nurse with a small child who nevertheless possessed a wardrobe and a hairdresser that in real life would have made her the envy of Fifth Avenue. The intent of the television producers was of course simply to make their characters as attractive as possible; it seemed natural to attempt to achieve the objective by presenting them as consumers of the finer things in life.

Adventure heroes of TV and the movies met the same requirements. On the level of pure, mindless entertainment, some of the most successful films of the 1960s were the James Bond adventures, in which the hero was not just capable of superhuman combat against the forces of evil in the manner of all make-believe heroes but was a consumer of breathtaking prowess, a cultured connoisseur of fine wines, high-powered automobiles, ultramodern gadgetry, and, of course, beautiful and expensive women. In earlier films of the genre, such characters were invariably villains. The archtypical tough-guy hero of the 1930s and '40s, portrayed by, say,

Humphrey Bogart playing such roles as Sam Spade in *The Maltese Falcon,* was far more likely to be shabby and deliberately uncouth, caring little for the appearance of his office, living quarters, or automobile so long as they were functional. Where Spade rejected the consumer ethic, Bond was a hero of consumption; both characters. were supremely entertaining because they incorporated the values of their eras. One other distinction was essential: Sam Spade, private eye, was a lone wolf who acted according to a personal, rigidly internalized code; James Bond, British intelligence agent 007, was an organization man.

Just as the imperative of consumption changed American life, so did the pervasiveness of the large organization. "The organization" actually took varied forms—the military forces, the government agencies, the rapidly expanding state universities, the business corporation were perhaps the most important—but all shared common characteristics, and at the managerial level, individuals moved from one to another with surprising ease. Social critics tended to focus their attention upon business. William H. Whyte in *The Organization Man* (1956), the most important critique of the organizational ethos, decried the conformity which corporate ladder climbing seemed to demand. Individuality, genius, daring—these may have been the qualities necessary to establish a large firm, but they did not appear necessary to keep it functioning; in fact, corporate bureaucrats discouraged such traits. Advancement hence depended more than ever upon an individual's ability to relate well to his co-workers and superiors; individualism, whether it took the form of abrasiveness or withdrawal, whether it was creative or not, appeared less likely to be tolerated than in the past. Organizational life was one of the major forces imposing an other-directed character upon America.

The organization not only rewarded other-direction; it behaved in an other-directed manner itself. Large personnel departments sought with varying degrees of sincerity and cynicism to convince employees that the organization cared for them. Advertising campaigns frequently stressed the corporate interest, real or imaginary, in the public welfare; in the early 1970s, for example, oil companies responded to the public concern over pollution with television commercials that sought to demonstrate a tender concern for the ecology and failed to mention a product at all. Of course, advertising usually touted some item, but the tendency was to emphasize the way in which possession or use of the item made the buyer more attractive to others and to ignore the possibility that the product was worth purchasing because of the benefits it delivered to the autonomous individual. Hence, the makers of an iron tonic which allegedly increased stamina and vitality pictured their patent medicine as a medium that would make the busy housewife more attactive to her mate ("my wife—I think I'll keep her"). In all cases, the truly crucial considerations were the perceptions of others.

Not surprisingly, the same trends influenced the practice of politics. Increasingly, a candidate sought to advance his fortunes by stressing, not his stand on the issues, but his personal qualities—youth, sincerity, good looks, experience, decisiveness, compassion, etc.; these were not necessarily trivial matters, but they were ideologically neutral. In 1952 the Republican party broke new ground by hiring the advertising firm of Batten, Barton, Durstine & Osborn to run its presidential campaign. Critics deplored the fact that a candidate for the highest office in the land was being merchandised "like a bar of soap," but thereafter politicians of both parties resorted to advertising agencies and media experts, who functioned as hired guns available to any candidate or ideology. One of the most widely read books on the campaign of 1968 was entitled *The Selling of the President.*

Candidates also looked with increasing openness to the polls for cues as to where to stand on the issues; political leaders of course had always shifted positions in order to identify with the public will but never before had such manipulative practices been so open and widespread. During the 1960s, men of substance in both parties became little more than media creations whose Gallup poll popularity standings were the political equivalent of the Nielsen ratings of television programs. Social critics might justly doubt that creative national leadership was possible in such an ethos.

Throughout the 1950s, intellectuals decried the growth of materialism and conformity. William Whyte argued that the organizational values were emasculating business leadership. Arthur Miller's powerful drama *Death of a Salesman* (1949) condemned the hypocrisy and self-deception of other-directed commercialism. On a less impressive literary level, Sloan Wilson's *The Man in the Gray Flannel Suit* (1954) was able to find self-realization only by partially disengaging from the organization, undertaking his own business enterprise, and voluntarily assuming the unattractive responsibility of supporting an illegitimate child. The intellectuals at least remained prone to extol the virtues of inner-direction.

There were, to be sure, arguments in favor of the other-directed character and the organizational ethos, though the best ones were seldom made. The worst were typified by Herman Wouk's widely read novel *The Caine Mutiny* (1952), with its conclusion that authority, however incompetent, however cowardly, however psychopathic, had to be obeyed; but Wouk's thesis was only an extreme variant of the increasingly common line that authority deserved respect simply because it *was* authority. A better argument was that organization and other-direction had been factors in the greatest distribution of abundance and the greatest growth of tolerance in American history. Sensitivity to others was a trait that was hardly altogether reprehensible while inner-direction in its starkest form was little more than egotistical self-aggrandizement. One might doubt that the other-directed corporation manager of the 1960s was really a more contemptible figure than the robber baron of the 1890s. The obvious need was to achieve a satisfactory synthesis of the two types. The ever-stronger critique of the culture of consumption and conformity and the increasingly visible deviations from it gave hope at the least for a healthy diversity.

THE GREAT LIBERATION

The older, inner-directed values of American life had demanded self-denial; the other-directed culture of consumption and leisure encouraged wide and immediate gratification. One result was the development of a mood of liberation which permitted the discussion and display of previously taboo behavior and led to a breakdown of the sanctions against it. Another result, connected to the first, was a quest for an alternative culture that would go beyond other-direction and the organizational ethic to the forging of a life style that would permit maximum self-exploration, fulfillment, and individuality.

One of the first indications of the new liberation was the success of *Playboy* magazine and its related enterprises. Established in 1954 on a shoestring by Hugh M. Hefner, *Playboy* became one of the legends of the postwar publishing world. The magazine itself featured nude women, risqué humor, conspicuous consumption, superior slick fiction, and social commentary. Its first major related enterprise, a string of nightclubs, featured scantily clad hostesses and waitresses. The operation prospered fantastically, branching out into resort hotels, foreign gambling casinos, films, books, music publishing, and records. The *"Playboy* life style," largely adopted by the publisher himself, was a bachelor's dream—beautiful girls, lavish apartments and beach houses, expensive cars, electronic gadgets, and executive jets. Seeking a rationale, Hefner wrote a rather tedious *"Playboy* philosophy" which he published in several installments of the magazine. By the end of 1972, after the demise of *Life* and *Look,* *Playboy* had the ninth largest circulation in the United States; and its textual material was probably of better quality than that of the eight higher-ranking publications.

The *Playboy* ethos represented something less than the triumph of uninhibited eroticism. The nightclubs functioned under strict "look but don't touch" rules which seemed positively conservative by the early 1970s. The magazine's models and the bunny style in general stressed cheerful wholesomeness rather than earthy sex appeal. Hefner himself, for all the unconventionality of his life, exhibited elements of Puritanism in his compulsive work habits and his need to write up a philosophical justification. Appealing to the safer adolescent fantasies, he attempted to give his enterprise both respectability and deeper meaning by seeking quality editorial content. Ironically, by the mid-1970s the sexual revolution was perceptibly moving beyond the *Playboy* culture. Hefner's empire suddenly became shaky as both his magazine and nightclubs began to lose customers to less inhibited competition. The response, an effort to imitate *Playboy*'s more daring imitators, resulted in a noticeable decline in the quality of the magazine; whether it would restore company profits remained uncertain. Whatever Hefner's future, to the cultural historian his most important achievement had been to demonstrate that sex could be packaged and marketed as an article of mass consumption.

The next important development was the collapse of old legal standards of literary pornography. As late as the 1950s, obscenity laws were so rigid and blue-nosed that they invited the contempt of thinking individuals. In 1959 Grove Press, armed with endorsements from distinguished literary critics, issued an unexpurgated edition of D. H. Lawrence's *Lady Chatterley's Lover,* a book which U.S. customs and postal authorities had banned for thirty years, although its author was possibly the most important English novelist of the twentieth century. When the postmaster general attempted to deny mailing privileges to the volume, Grove sued in the federal courts and won the case with ease.*

The basic principle established in the *Lady Chatterley* case was that four-letter language and vivid descriptions of sexual conduct were permissible as long as some serious literary or social purpose was served. In practice, the standard could be used to justify the publication of almost anything. Grove Press itself specialized in works of increasingly less merit. Many of its subsequent publications, such as the writings of Henry Miller, the memoirs of Frank Harris, and even *Fanny Hill,* deserved to be taken seriously, but the press's editors engaged in an unceasing search for "forgotten classics" of Victorian pornography, and the purpose of its list appeared to be more sexual titillation than literary value. As the bars fell, fiction in general became more sexually explicit, making sensationalism almost a necessity for the writer who wanted mass sales. Hard-core por-

---

* The federal attempt to ban the novel took on a peculiarly quixotic quality when, prior to determination of the case, the U.S. Supreme Court overruled a New York attempt to ban a film version of the story *(Kingsley International Pictures* v. *Regents* [1959]). It was hardly startling, therefore, that a federal district judge threw out the postal prohibition against the book and that the government decided against an appeal.

nography flourished, partly because it could take refuge behind court decisions that protected more serious literature, partly because most large cities could no longer muster the will to suppress it as long as its retailers displayed some circumspection and avoided sales to minors. There was, after all, no evidence that pornography caused sex crimes or antisocial behavior; and with every year a greater number of Americans seemed willing to tolerate the material, however they felt about the values implicit in it.

In the theater by the later 1960s, nudity and simulated sex seemed on the way to becoming obligatory parts of any production that attempted to be modish. *Hair,* a rock musical about youth and the counterculture, enjoyed a New York run that lasted well beyond the play's considerable merits, largely because of a scene in which the young performers totally disrobed. *Oh! Calcutta!,* a clever comedy review authored by a half-dozen leading writers, featured extensive nudity and became one of the most successful plays on Broadway.

Playwrights who sought greater profundity were less successful. One of the most interesting attempts, the Living Theater's *Paradise Now,* conceived of nudity as both therapeutic and revolutionary; the cast sought interaction with the audience, encouraging its members to cast off personal and political inhibitions along with their clothing. Other less memorable plays featured explicit displays of homosexuality, bestiality, sadomasochism, and occasionally even conventional heterosexual intercourse; one play, *Che,* went so far beyond the fringe that even in permissive New York it was closed down and its cast arrested for lewdness, obscenity, and consensual sodomy. Such efforts rarely achieved an erotic effect; indeed, many sought to depict sex as a disgusting existential necessity, a mood in its own way highly pornographic and subversive of healthy thinking.

The cinema moved in some of the same directions but in general avoided the worst excesses of the stage. As late as the 1950s, Hollywood had been shackled with a self-censorship system which forbade any treatment of controversial topics such as sexual deviation or drug addiction and which was so rigid in its depiction of conventional sexual mores as to assume that married couples invariably slept in twin beds. By then, films were beginning to grope for a new purpose; television had supplanted them as routine family entertainment, and audiences were declining. In order to hold the minimum numbers required for survival, the movies had to adopt strategies that were not feasible for television: the large-scale, lavish epic, the appeal to the youth market or to blacks (TV was aimed primarily at white middle-class adults), the low-budget "personal" film, the exploration of previously forbidden themes. Each strategy involved increasingly larger doses of sex.

The major film makers replaced the old censorship code with a rating system that attempted to classify releases in terms of audience suitability (G for general viewing, PG for parental guidance, R for restricted to adults and minors with an adult escort, X for adults only). The new practice fell short of perfection. Some of its ratings were questionable, and it engaged in censorship by "suggesting" deletions that would give a film the designation its distributors wanted. Still, it was far more enlightened than its predecessor. The ratings provided clear and ample warning to patrons who might find extreme explicitness offensive while giving screen writers and directors freedom to go beyond stifling old restrictions.

By the early 1970s, American film makers routinely depicted explicit conventional sex in films which sought adult appeal, and major stars—the most sensational example being Marlon Brando in *Last Tango in Paris*—performed roles which in the 1950s would have been deemed appropriate only for stag movies. The low-budget "underground cinema," most notably the efforts of Andy Warhol, claimed serious intellectual attention. "Sexploitation" films which made little pretense at artistry ran routinely in about every large city, and the ones made with some minimum of talent were big moneymakers. One of the best practitioners of the trade, Russ Meyer, became for a time a pop figure whose movies were shown at campus film festivals and subjected to lengthy critical analyses. Increasingly bold films from *I Am Curious (Yellow)*, which had some serious pretenses, to *Deep Throat*, which was pure pornography, not only drew large audiences but also became chic cultural events.

The main trouble with the rating system was that its administrators judged films almost solely on the basis of sexual content and verbal obscenity; huge doses of violence were permissible as long as they did not involve sex. Arthur Penn's *Bonnie and Clyde* interpreted a couple of depression-era bank robbers, contemptible thugs in real life, as beautiful young people trapped and ultimately destroyed by a situation they could not control; in the process, blood splattered across the screen in unprecedented amounts. The film was the beginning of a vogue; Hollywood effects men quickly developed a new skill—the simulation of violent death in all its ugly reality. A widely acclaimed John Wayne film, *True Grit*, rated G, featured a scene in which a helpless victim's finger was hacked off. Sam Peckinpah pursued his thesis that sadism was endemic in all men and that violence was the ultimate form of masculine self-realization in *The Wild Bunch* and *Straw Dogs*, both of which culminated in terrifying scenes of mass slaughter. *The Godfather*, considered by many critics one of the best American films ever made, reveled in bloody episodes. Stanley Kubrick's *A Clockwork Orange* sympathetically examined the tribulations of a fascistic young hoodlum while depicting as loathsome the behaviorists who attempted to program him against capricious brutality. The vogue of violence was understandable in a society which, through the medium of television news, watched Vietnam combat at the dinner hour every evening, witnessed domestic riots, and saw instant replays of political assassinations. Brutality, destruction, and death became a fixation not simply of the movies but of every area of American culture.

Because fiction was not a visual art, it had never possessed extensive inhibitions about violence, but even quality novels became more violent. Joyce Carol Oates' *them* (1969), winner of a National Book Award, began with murder and rape and ended with a long description of the Detroit race riot of 1967. A frail, scholarly woman obsessed with the relationship between love and violence, Miss Oates expressed her motivation with compelling brevity: "I am concerned with only one thing, the moral and social conditions of my generation." In the hands of a Stanley Kubrick or a Joyce Carol Oates, violence became a theme whose exploration yielded deep, if frightening, insights into the human condition. But, like sex, violence lent itself to exploitation, and writers and film makers most skilled in sensationalism for its own sake attempted to combine the two themes.

By the early 1970s, a reaction had developed against sexual excess. Many newspapers refused to run display advertising for X-rated films. A New York judge banned *Deep Throat* with the comment, "This throat deserves to be cut." In 1973 the U.S. Supreme Court issued its murkiest obscenity decision yet. By a 5–4 vote, the Court ruled that censorship henceforth would be a local matter to be decided by "community standards," although localities could not prohibit serious films or literature. The decision raised more questions than it answered—publishers and film makers held some projects in suspension and waited for the other shoe to drop as states and cities attempted either through formal definition or police action to define their standards. Some early incidents were reminiscent of old-fashioned repression; the Georgia Supreme Court, for example, upheld a ban on the distinguished Mike Nichols movie *Carnal Knowledge*. Whether the Supreme Court justices liked it or not, the question of obscenity would return to their chambers. And whatever the ultimate resolution, it was unlikely that either the artists or the exploiters would be pushed very far back toward the norms of the 1950s. Unhappily, the whole controversy revolved around the depiction of sexual behavior. The national tolerance of violence remained strong.*

* The most effective movement against violence involved television, the medium where it was least objectionable. Because the airwaves were federally regulated, TV programmers felt extremely vulnerable to the preachments of government officials and for a

Another sign of the new morality was the increasing openness of homosexuality. Literary figures such as Paul Goodman and Merle Miller discussed their own lives as homosexuals with candor. Others formed organizations such as the Gay Liberation Front and campaigned openly for an end to legal restrictions and social discrimination; some even established homosexual churches. Their adoption of the designation "gay" reflected an insistence that theirs was simply an alternative life style as capable of providing happiness and fulfillment as heterosexuality. Few Americans were prepared to go that far, but the country did appear ready to extend increased tolerance. In an important symbolic move, the trustees of the American Psychiatric Association voted in 1973 to drop the definition of homosexuality as a "psychiatric disorder."

A movement with deeper implications was women's liberation. The older values had always assumed a man's world; the American woman was typically a housewife and mother. If she worked, it was in a subordinate role at a low salary; and if on occasion she performed the same tasks as men, she was invariably paid less. Female participation in the professions, figured on a percentage basis, was actually smaller in the 1960s than in the 1920s. Sex was in fact a stronger determinant of discrimination than the color line—the average earnings of black men, while well below those of white men, were higher than those of white women. The older feminist movement, after the success of women's suffrage, had faded during the depression and World War II and had been all but obliterated by the impulse to restore the familial ethic after the war; two decades later, however, a new militant feminism was challenging not simply economic discrimination but a broad range of stereotypes and limitations.

Like any widely based movement, women's liberation had its share of extremists, some of them seeking to escape their sexual identity altogether, others paranoiacally blaming men for every problem the world had ever known (in effect, reversing the Adam-Eve myth), some forming "revolutionary" organizations such as SCUM (Society for Cutting Up Men) and WITCH (Women's International Terrorist Conspiracy from Hell). Predictably, the kooks and bra burners drew the most media coverage; they gained women's lib a degree of attention it might not otherwise have received but also left it open to ridicule.

season or two toned down the bloodless shootouts and circus-style fist fights which characterized the typical adventure series. One must question, however, whether children were deeply affected by watching Matt Dillon gun down an outlaw or observing Secret Agent James West effortlessly beat up half a dozen desperados; such ritualized play acting had been a staple of human entertainment in almost every era and society. It seems more probable that if television harmed impressionable minds, it was by showing violence that could not be suppressed because it was real and part of the daily news.

The mainstream of the movement stemmed from the publication of *The Feminine Mystique* (1963) by Betty Friedan and Friedan's subsequent founding of the National Organization for Women (NOW) to fight economic discrimination and challenge stereotypes which limited female opportunity. Even such moderate objectives, however, encountered widespread opposition, not just from conservatives but from many liberals. By the early 1970s, the women's movement had made some gains. The Civil Rights Act of 1964 prohibited discrimination on the basis of sex. The Department of Health, Education, and Welfare and other federal agencies administering economic assistance to educational institutions and businesses made the federal money dependent upon equal employment practices. Court decisions invalidated laws that placed special restrictions upon the work women could do. Nevertheless, discrimination was so widespread and pervasive that its elimination might require at least a generation—if it could ever be accomplished.

The new feminism failed to mobilize much of its potential support. Interest in it was great enough to sustain a large circulation magazine, Gloria Steinem's *Ms.*, established in 1972. But the movement, like *Ms.* itself, appealed mainly to middle-class intellectuals and professionals, not to working-class females, some of whom still felt a need for protective legislation which the feminists wanted to abolish as discriminatory. Moreover, it lacked a focus. Some feminists saw their cause as part of a larger liberal-radical "new politics"; others raised moral hackles by advocating abortion upon request. Such viewpoints drove many undecided women away. Nevertheless, the movement seemed unlikely to collapse, however bizarre its fringes or questionable its tactics; the conditions in American life that were undermining other values would keep it alive.

The loosening of old standards, perhaps their overthrow, was to be expected in a postindustrial society characterized by affluence, leisure, and consumption. More Americans than ever were able to expand their range of experience; engaging in once-forbidden behavior—or observing its simulation—was an alluring way of doing so. Moreover, old sexual mores were fairly certain to change as large families became an ever-greater economic burden and the contraceptive pill practically guaranteed freedom from unwanted pregnancies. It was logical that practices formerly condemned as promiscuous or perverse would win greater tolerance. It was equally logical that women would demand new opportunities as changing conditions made their former roles less necessary; in addition, the imperative of consumption provided a positive inducement for many housewives to become wage earners. Still, the new developments came with startling rapidity and outraged many individuals who could not adjust their values so quickly and feared that the Great Liberation was only the first step in a greater revolution.

THE COUNTERCULTURE

In 1968 young people flocked to movie theaters to see *The Graduate*. A supremely entertaining comedy-satire, the film dealt with the trials of Benjamin, an intelligent young upper-middle-class man who could not complete the rites of passage from college into the business-professional world. Inarticulate and unable to cope with the adult Babbittry and mendacity which surround him, he is alienated from his well-to-do, sumption-mad parents, although he thinks it natural to live with them, drive the car they have given him, and spend large quantities of their money. He is seduced by an older woman, the wife of his father's business partner, and she uses him coldly and ruthlessly, shunning his efforts to make their relationship more than physical. He falls in love with her daughter, whose freshness and honesty set her apart from her mother; ultimately, he overcomes every obstacle thrown in their path. In the end, after committing an act of comic sacrilege, he and his young lady flee the adult establishment, presumably for a happy and independent life.

The Graduate was a well-made movie, but the real secret of its appeal was the faithful way in which it projected the prejudices of the young to the screen. Its older characters were unfeeling, materialistic, hypocritical, and exploitative; its young protagonists, earnest, innocent, and virtuous. It became a classic expression of a cult of youth with deep appeal not simply to the under-thirty set but to many people who had reached middle age and felt impelled to question the meaning of their own lives. In a watered-down manner, it presented a view of America from the perspective of a youth subculture so large and influential that it could represent itself as an alternative way of life.

The first important sign of the new wave was the surfacing in the 1950s of the beat generation. A small but significant literary movement led by such writers as Jack Kerouac and Allen Ginsberg, its influence was mainly confined to college campuses and bohemian centers in large cities. The beats protested against the McCarthyite, gray-flannel-suit conformity of "square" American life and against the impersonal horror of modern technology as represented by Auschwitz or Hiroshima. Existentialists, they withdrew from the conventional world to practice self-exploration, seek intense, elemental experience, and assert an identity which they had made for themselves rather than accept roles thrust upon them by society. For many, self-definition was a religious experience akin to the discovery of God, and "beat" was a shortened version of "beatific."

The beat, or beatnik, typically dressed and behaved in a manner intended to signify defiance of the conventions of society. He practiced free love, used drugs, and was drawn to non-Western mysticism; his quest for experience might even lead him to commit personal acts of violence, although the Beat movement as a whole tended toward pacifism. He might seek, in Normal Mailer's phrase, to be a "white Negro," a man who forged his identity out of the alienation and desperation of living with insecurity and the imminence of death—a hipster, a "cool," sensual man of action who lived outside the norms of society. As a literary phenomenon, the beat generation passed quickly, but it established an intellectual basis for a larger subculture which would follow it.

By the mid-1960s, the term beatnik had fallen into disuse, but in many ways the style of life that the beats advocated was more attractive than ever to the middle-class young. The new extreme was the "hippie" culture, which, despite differences in name and nuance, was mainly an assertion of the beat style. The hippies rejected "straight" society, embraced poverty, used drugs, practiced free sex, and frequently lived in communes. They preferred to think of themselves as flower children who practiced the love ethic, but a strain of violence existed among them also. More consciously than the beats, the hippies were in revolt against materialism, science, and all the institutions of modern life. They sought simplicity and naturalness; at their best, they attempted to practice basic virtues of peace and love. Both the beats and the hippies in their fullest development were fringe movements relatively small in number; their importance stemmed from the way in which middle-class youth adopted large aspects of the hippie style and became in effect "fellow travelers" of the movement.

By the 1960s, demographics alone guaranteed that the culture of youth would be more powerful than ever, for a larger percentage of the population was young, products of the post–World War II "baby boom." Postindustrial society, moreover, had developed means of prolonging "adolescence" well beyond its traditional physiological definition, largely because the labor market could not absorb the young if they attempted to enter it at the ages common in the 1920s or '30s. Frequently, the jobs of postindustrial society required greater training, but education was also a means of putting the young in cold storage, even as advances in medicine and nutrition made them physiological adults at increasingly early ages.

The major storehouses were the colleges and universities, which through the 1960s seemed ready to burst with young people pushed into them with little sense of purpose other than the vague notion that a degree was essential to social and financial success. And as graduate programs grew apace, many campuses contained substantial groups of students in their middle or late twenties, adults who still functioned in many ways as adolescents. Add to this a substantial nonstudent hanger-on population which congregated around many large universities. The total effect in many college communities was that of a large, restless, purposeless community, excused from many of the norms of adult behavior and seeking a meaningful outlet for its energies. Mainly the children of the middle classes, they took affluence for granted. Products of middle-class child-rearing practices, they were accustomed to personal attention, permissiveness, and quick gratification of most of their wants.

In such circumstances, the adoption of a kind of semi-hippie life style was a logical, even an ideal method of differentiating the culture of extended adolescence from the adult world. It was rarely an exacting way of living. Popular youth slogans such as "Do your own thing" or "Make love, not war," whether or not they were good advice, hardly implied much self-sacrifice. A widespread use of marijuana might carry a small danger of arrest, but the drug itself, as nearly as researchers could determine, was nonaddictive and no more harmful than alcohol. Yet marijuana aroused the outrage of adults even as it gave the kids their own distinctive method of self-indulgence. A fascination with mysticism and the irrational provided a justification for rejecting the discipline of rational learning. A casual attitude toward sex, even if exaggerated and self-conscious, was the easiest and most pleasant way to resolve the tensions inherent in the contradictions which arose from adult physiques being assigned adolescent roles. The rejection of materialism was deceptive; the young pursued styles of consumption which differed from those of the adult world, but many of them accumulated possessions far more costly than their parents had owned at a comparable age. Many of them also took continued parental support for granted, much as did Benjamin in *The Graduate*.

Adult social critics disenchanted with the technological, organizational society found much of value in the youth culture. Theodore Roszak, perhaps the best interpreter of what he called the counterculture, found in its romanticism and striving for naturalness the fulfillment of a personal quest for faith. Charles Reich hailed it as the beginning of a new mood, Consciousness III, destined to displace an already obsolete Consciousness I (inner-directed, laissez-faire, social Darwinist) and the prevailing outlook of Consciousness II (other-directed, organizational, New Dealish). It was undeniable that in some respects, the counterculture or "Con III" presented at least possibilities of joyous self-expression which were attractive when contrasted with the impersonality and rigidity of the bureaucratized society. As it functioned, however, it was a logical extension of that society in more ways than its celebrants cared to admit.

Semi-hippie life was conformist in its patterns of dress and consumption, more so than middle-class suburbia. It sought to relieve adolescent anxieties by making poverty-style clothing obligatory; young people bought brand-new "prefaded" and "prepatched" jeans, "military surplus" garments manufactured especially for the commercial market, and machine-produced "handcrafted" accessories. Adolescents had always sought conformity—only the style was new. Horrified adults criticized a cult of the slovenly in which the beautiful and handsome dressed down to the level of the plain and homely, in which sex appeal and even sexual differences were minimized.

On college campuses, a variant of the same process affected old intellectual distinctions, as counterculturists assailed the traditional forms of higher learning. Here they could count on the support of many students who might not be drawn to other aspects of the counterculture but who felt alienated from the system into which they had been pushed. The *Yale Course Guide* characterized Charles Reich's "Individualism in America" as "the finest and most flexible course in Yale College," although it could find few enrollees who had bothered to attend many of the lectures. It noted that the previous semester's grade distribution had been 67 honors, 196 high pass, 29 pass, 0 fail, and 248 incomplete, although the requirements were so elastic that students could meet them by baking a loaf of bread for the instructor. "Perhaps the most cogent remark to be made about Mr. Reich's course," the *Guide* concluded with (one hopes) tongue-in-cheek intent, "is that he thinks kids are neat and what can be bad about someone telling you how the system and the older generation have warped and destroyed things for us?"

The counterculture tended to seek profundity in the most unlikely places. Popular music, for example, became a form of social and political criticism. (Even in this respect, however, the young were not unique; the blurring of the distinction between entertainment and politics was common to all of American society in the 1960s.) The trend began with the revival of folk music in the late 1950s by performers such as Joan Baez and Bob Dylan, a development which offended few adults, even when the themes of songs were radical. By the mid-1960s, however, folk music was being overshadowed by varieties of rock with lyrics all but unintelligible to the adult ear; their import was made clear enough, however, by the tendency of performers to indulge in vivid displays of cultural radicalism ranging from garish dress to sexual exhibitionism. Rock groups such as the Beatles and the Rolling Stones assumed stances as advocates of peace, freedom, and equality and engaged in musical dialogues on the merits of violent revolution. Advocates of the counterculture, such as Charles Reich, asserted that the new rock possessed "a complexity unknown to classical music" and "an ability to penetrate to the essence of what is wrong with society . . . that is perhaps the deepest source of its power."

The centrality of rock music to the counterculture was demonstrated by the popularity of open-air music festivals which drew enormous crowds. The most unforgettable, at Woodstock, New York, in August 1969, pulled a third of a million people, mostly young. They listened to rock, smoked marijuana, swam and cavorted in the nude, and in the main presented a picture of the youth wave in idyllic triumph. The "Woodstock Nation" was the counterculture's preview of the future, and few commentators noted the irony of a movement that purported to reject technology nevertheless finding its mode of expression in a music created by complex electronic amplification.

Actually, most devotees of Con III had hardly begun to break loose from Con II; the counterculture represented a true alternative life style only in the case of the relatively small number of genuine hippies. In general, the young who embraced the counterculture sought only a stylistic differentiation from the adult world which assigned them to extended adolescence. They also were conformist and consumption-minded; they accepted technology without question when it pleased them. True, they rejected impersonal bureaucracy and organization, but so did representatives of Con II and Con I. Their distaste for most forms of disciplined endeavor proceeded rather naturally from childhood patterns established by their Con II parents. Their free and easy attitude toward sex, drugs, and fashion were only exaggerated manifestations of the liberation that was sweeping through all of American society. Accepting abundance and leisure as normal, they were natural products of the affluent society which supported their existence.

Children of the middle class, they won a wide measure of tolerance from that social group; the most vehement reactions against them came from blue-collar workers, young as well as old, who were less secure economically and more likely to possess Con I inner-directed attitudes. Less an alternative to the old consciousness than an extension of it, the counterculture represented a stage in the evolution of the other-direction which shaped the lives of so many middle-class adults.

THE NEW LEFT

For many young people, the countercultural mode was more than an independent way of living; it was a highly visible manifestation of a larger attempt to change a society in which racism, poverty, and violence were pervasive. More than a revolt against "straight" personal morality, it was part of a protest against American social and political morality. The counterculture was inextricably connected to a New Left that combined youthful idealism with an attempt to revive the exhausted radicalism of an older generation.

It was beyond question that the "old left" was worn out by the late 1950s and early 1960s. The Communist party, driven from the liberal-labor coalition, had dwindled to a few thousand members, many of them FBI informers; the remaining true believers were a pathetic group of Stalinists, demoralized by Khrushchev's denunciation of their former hero and baffled by the emerging Sino-Soviet split. The Socialist party, much of its platform preempted by the New Deal, had become little more than an educational association. Its 1956 presidential nominee, Darlington Hoopes, polled less than 2,000 votes nationwide; in 1960 it declined to go through the motions of a White House campaign. Independent radicals of the 1930s were long gone and forgotten, their movements having collapsed during World War II. Young left-wingers surveyed a radicalism that had been smothered and discredited by the cold war, McCarthyism, postwar affluence, and Eisenhower complacency; yet they could rightly see that America still neither gave equal justice to its dispossessed nor fully practiced its ideals abroad.

A youthful radicalism began to surface at the end of the 1950s. For the most part, the student leftists were from well-to-do homes and had tolerant, liberal-minded parents who encouraged idealism and the questioning of existing arrangements. They were, Tom Hayden commented, "perhaps the first generation of young people both affluent and independent of mind." Their experience fostered a kind of primal innocence. Never having known deprivation and injustice, the young leftists were unable to accept these forces as eternal aspects of the human condition; conceiving of them instead as unnatural, the new radicals were intellectually prepared to mount a moral crusade for their total elimination. Taught to question the system, they were quick to assume that its flaws rendered it illegitimate. Vehement critics of American institutions, they were nevertheless well within one of the oldest American traditions—perfectionism—and they sought to purge evil from American society by reshaping it.

The two most important early intellectual sources of the New Left were C. Wright Mills and Paul Goodman. Mills, a widely read independent radical sociologist who died in 1962 at the tragically early age of forty-six, argued in such works as *The Power Elite* (1956), *The Causes of World War III* (1957), and *Listen Yankee!* (1960) that, behind the façade of interest-group democracy, the United States was controlled by a military-industrial power elite responsible for the cold war, the arms race, and an imperialist foreign policy. Goodman, a social critic of broad learning and far-ranging interests, attacked the "organized system" as a set of institutions that stifled creativity and free personality development. His books *Growing Up Absurd* (1960), *Compulsory Miseducation* (1962), and *Drawing the Line* (1962) were among the most avidly read pieces of social commentary in the early and mid-1960s. A communitarian anarchist, he advocated a decentralized, voluntarist, and communal society with institutions small enough to give the individual a meaningful voice in his own destiny; he sought reforms that would remove what he considered stultifying rigidities from education, and promoted sexual mores that would allow free play to all nondestructive impulses. If Mills first gave the New Left an essential diagnosis of American life and politics, Goodman gave it a basic program.

There were other important intellectual influences. Norman O. Brown, a psychoanalytic thinker, and Herbert Marcuse, an emigre German political philosopher who drew on Marx and Freud, both argued for the liberation of the instinctual urges, especially sex, as the lever of change in a capitalist society which was repressive and excessively rational. Frantz Fanon, Regis Debray, and Ernesto "Che" Guevara wrote analyses of Third World revolution which influenced radical thinking on both American foreign policy and domestic social change. Albert Camus and the French existentialists were read as advocates of the necessity for *action* against the system and thereby contributed to the development of a "cult of the deed" which repudiated gradualism or purely intellectual criticism.

The first signs of a militant student left appeared with the Cuban revolution. Castro and the movement he led were appealing in their early years, apparently nondogmatic, anarchic, and representing the triumph of the oppressed against domestic authoritarianism and Yankee imperialism. Exhilarated students went to Cuba to work in the sugar-cane harvests; in Castro and even more in his chief aide and ideologist, Che Guevara, the young left discovered charismatic exemplars of romantic revolution. The subsequent U.S. conflicts with Cuba immeasurably strengthened the New Left conviction that American foreign policy was dominated by economic imperialism.

The other basic source of student radicalism was a more unequivocal morality play, the sit-ins of the early 1960s. The tactic had been employed on occasion in the past, but it began on a large-scale basis in 1960 when a few black students attempted to integrate a Woolworth lunch counter in Greensboro, North Carolina. The movement quickly spread across the South, became biracial, and involved tens of thousands of young people. Calling for deep moral courage and idealism in the face of outrageous verbal abuse, jailings, and occasional beatings, it was an effort that stirred the admiration of all liberal-minded people.

In the fall of 1960 young sit-in veterans established the Student Non-violent Coordinating Committee (SNCC). An interracial group which organized sit-ins and voter-registration drives, SNCC quickly moved into the vanguard of the civil rights movement with a moral fervor that led a white historian-supporter, Howard Zinn, to describe its members as "the new abolitionists." In the summer of 1964 the organization undertook its most utopian project: it sent a few hundred students into Mississippi to register black voters for the fall political campaign. Here its millennial idealism ran into a solid wall of diehard segregationism. The results—three deaths, countless beatings, jailings, acts of intimidation, few black registrations—would change both the organization and the civil rights movement profoundly.

On the campuses, the new activism led to an upsurge in the membership of several leftist organizations; the largest and most important among them was the Students for a Democratic Society (SDS). Once an adjunct of the Socialist party, SDS established itself as an independent organization at a convention held in Port Huron, Michigan, in 1962. Its founding manifesto, "the Port Huron Statement," written largely by its president, Tom Hayden, became the first major declaration of New Left ideology. It reflected an alienation born of disillusioned innocence ("Not only did tarnish appear on our image of American virtue, not only did disillusion occur when the hypocrisy of American ideals was discovered") and stated an idealistic moral perfectionism ("We regard *men* as infinitely precious and possessed of unfulfilled capacities for reason, freedom, and love").

Its most memorable aspect was its advocacy of "participatory democracy"—"we seek the establishment of a democracy of individual participation, governed by two central aims: that the individual share in those social decisions determining the quality and direction of his life; that society be organized to encourage independence in men and provide the media for their common participation." As a principle, participatory democracy seemed admirable; as a working technique, employed as an alternative to representative government, it was less satisfactory. In practice, it allowed committed and articulate minorities to control a group decision-making process and it begged the question of expertise. Who could argue with the idea of giving the oppressed and underrepresented greater access to the political system, but who could believe them equally competent to participate in every decision that affected their lives?

The Port Huron Statement, other SDS broadsides, and New Left thought in general increasingly depicted the United States as undemocratic, militaristic, and imperialistic. The American system, as radical thinkers depicted it, was "corporate liberalism," a pseudo-liberal government dominated by the great corporations and employing technocratic methods, "coopting" the noncorporate groups by giving them symbolic concessions, and pursuing a foreign policy built around the expansion of capitalism. Corporate liberalism engaged in little positive suppression of radical dissent but rather sought to smother it through a surface tolerance that blandly refused to acknowledge cause for complaint; it followed, therefore, that radicals had to strive to demonstrate the system's true colors. In practice, about the only way to do so was to provoke violent repression; by creating situations in which those who held power would be compelled either to yield unconditionally or to resist with force, the New Left intended to demonstrate the fundamental fascism of the power structure.

SDS members and other young New Leftists participated in a variety of causes, including civil rights and the organization of the poor, but their main target was the student population and, ultimately, dominance of the universities. The Port Huron Statement depicted the universities as "an overlooked seat of influence," distributed throughout the country, open to all viewpoints, packed with a potential radical constituency, and crucial to the military-corporate system because of their educational and research functions. New Left theorists urged the young to think of themselves as an oppressed class, exploited by a system which denied them their biological maturity, restricted them socially and politically, and manipulated them for its own ends. As a Berkeley student leader succinctly put it, "Never trust anyone over thirty."

From the beginning, the New Left could count on a certain appeal to university students. In the large sense, the New Left was the major political manifestation of the counterculture; there were exceptions, to be sure, but most young radicals accepted the counterculture in toto. Free sex, for example, was an integral component of radical politics. Goodman, Marcuse, and others came close to saying that political repression was but a by-product of sexual repression. It was easy—and attractive—to move to the proposition that political liberation must be a by-product of sexual liberation, that sexual promiscuity was the ultimate in political subversion. New Left leaders differed among themselves on whether the revolution would be essentially cultural or political.

In its advocacy of university reform, the New Left invariably supported curricular changes designed to bring "relevance" to the campus. "Revelance" might mean social concern and immediacy, a breaking down of the ivy walls which kept the university sheltered from the real world, even (as became the case with some black or Chicano studies programs) the establishment of a base for social revolution. But to many students motivated less by political radicalism than by the intellectual aimlessness that stemmed from socially imposed attendance, it meant easier and more interesting courses, abolition of core requirements, slacker grading standards, and in general relief from the intensification of work which had characterized practically every level of American education after Sputnik. It also meant fewer restrictions from the university bureaucracy and a greater personalization of increasingly impersonal class procedures. On such issues, the New Left could recruit many supporters whose radicalism ran shallow, if it existed at all.

The student left received its greatest boost from the escalation of the Vietnam war in 1965. Rapid increases in draft calls shoved a hitherto remote issue to the center of consciousness of every male student and created difficult psychological tensions. By forcing serious consideration of a conflict that had been widely tolerated, the threat of the draft was a profoundly radicalizing force, and the New Left gained huge numbers of fellow travelers almost in ratio to the size of the draft calls. One result was greater militance; many young men seeking to avoid military service felt compelled to demonstrate *machismo*. In protest activities, especially those connected to the war, young people increasingly abandoned Gandhian nonviolence in favor of verbal abuse, rock throwing, street fighting, and malicious destruction ("trashing"). Always able to muster greater force, the authorities often quashed such protests with devastating ferocity, thereby providing New Left ideologists with proof that the system was fascistic and giving most demonstrators satisfaction that they were masculine as well as virtuous.

As was so often the case with American life by the 1960s, California provided an initial portent of the future. In the fall of 1964 student activists, some of them veterans of the summer Mississippi registration drive, organized a Free Speech Movement (FSM) in protest against administration attempts to restrict on-campus political activity at the University of California at Berkeley. On the single issue of free political activity, the FSM managed to mobilize majority support from both faculty and students, and the demonstrations that followed, including a mass occupation of the central administration building, nearly brought the university to a halt. The administration largely conceded the issue, but unrestricted political activity failed to bring peace to the campus. From the beginning, FSM leaders had condemned the "multiversity" as impersonal and computerized and had demanded sweeping reforms. Given new impetus by the war, allied with the growing population of Berkeley "street people," student leftists continued to be a significant force. After Ronald Reagan was elected governor in 1966, the situation became a classic example of left-right symbiosis; the conservative state administration and the radical students thrived on their mutual hatred. The most trivial issues could explode into violence. In 1969, demonstrations aimed at forcing the conversion of a university-owned lot into a "people's park" resulted in the death of one student, the wounding of many others, the saturation of the campus with tear gas, and the mobilization of the National Guard. The university, which had been possibly the greatest in the country, declined apace, crippled by arbitrary budget cuts and resignations by distinguished moderate and liberal professors.

Berkeley became a paradigm for the rest of the university world. After 1965, student demonstrations against the universities themselves became relatively common and usually involved an intermeshed mixture of causes—abolition of officer-training programs or defense-related research, alleged university exploitation of the poor in surrounding neighborhoods, demands for curricular relevance, and, on many occasions, sheer springtime exuberance. Since the university was central to their own lives, the young demonstrators fallaciously assumed that it was the central institution of society and demanded that it solve practically every social problem.

No institution was more vulnerable to confrontation politics than higher education. Before the 1960s, it had rested largely upon a consensus of genteel values to which the use of force was alien. Largely unguarded libraries, laboratories, and offices all served as hostages to militants willing, implicitly or explicitly, to threaten their destruction. Even so, campus sentiment was usually against the introduction of outside law-enforcement personnel, who were likely to attack long-haired demonstrators with a gusto that might better have been reserved for muggers and heroin pushers. University moderates remained attached to the ideal of their world as an intellectual sanctuary; and the radicals, although they really conceived of the university as a tool of the power structure, were quick to invoke the sanctuary ideal when their self-interest depended upon it.

Many faculties and administrations found themselves partially intimidated, partially persuaded to make whatever concessions they could. The main dividend of the student revolt was curricular change, the result of which was to water down the functions the university performed best—disciplined learning and the transmission of knowledge. The trend seemed destined to continue into the 1970s even as student militance declined; many universities facing downward enrollment pressures were prepared to do whatever was necessary to attract paying customers.

New Left achievements off the campuses were equally equivocal. Radical leaders could mobilize impressive peace demonstrations, and, as the Vietnam war progressed, radical ideas gained credibility among the intelligentsia. On the other hand, the New Left's aggressive counterculturism, its "antipatriotism" (peace demonstrators at times burned the American flag while displaying the Viet Cong banner), and its increasing propensity for violence all alienated many Americans who might have been attracted by a "straighter" style.

The organized New Left largely destroyed itself by practicing the exclusionist sectarianism to which absolutist movements so frequently fall victim. Although the New Left was much more than SDS, that organization had provided the most important leadership and ideological direction. By 1969, it was hopelessly splintered between a dominant Progressive Labor faction and several other groups which adopted such colorful names as Weathermen, Running Dogs, Mad Dogs, Crazies, and Up Against the Wall, Motherfuckers. The Progressive Laborites, whose ideology was vaguely Maoist-Leninist, undertook the truly romantic and hopeless task of organizing the blue-collar "proletariat." The other factions dissipated their energies in mindless violence which escalated from vandalism and street fighting to arson and bombing.

Convinced of the depravity of the establishment, possessing romanticized notions about guerrilla revolution, and certain of their own righteousness, some New Left leaders concluded that the end justified the means and endorsed terrorism as a revolutionary tactic. The new direction was wretched as a matter of morality and futile as a method of advancing the cause. Scattered bombings might frighten ordinary people, but they could not intimidate the government or the large corporations. A few activists who lacked the necessary expertise with explosives managed to kill themselves. Occasionally misdirected violence discredited the movement. In 1970, bombers accidentally blew up a physics laboratory at the University of Wisconsin and killed a young graduate student; from hiding they issued a statement to the effect that they had meant to destroy an army mathematics research center, but mistakes, however regrettable, were part of any revolution. As a set of attitudes, ideas, and life styles, the New Left had made an impact that could never be wholly reversed. As an organized force, however, it appeared on the wane, existing more to satisfy the apocalyptic fantasies of its adherents than to effect real change in the system.

THE UNDERDOGS: THE BLACK REVOLUTION, POVERTY, THE URBAN CRISIS

No group was more visibly excluded from many of the benefits of postwar progress than the Negroes. It was true that blacks achieved some important advances after World War II as prosperity fueled the growth of a Negro middle class, as Court decisions and administrative action chipped away at the once monolithic structure of segregation, as Congress passed civil rights acts, and as an increasing number of outstanding Negroes achieved national prominence. Such gains nevertheless had only a marginal effect upon the life of the average black and acted to spur demands for more tangible dividends. These demands could not be ignored because with every election the American Negro demonstrated greater political power and more impressive leadership.

Once heavily concentrated in the rural South, blacks migrated in great numbers to the urban North throughout the twentieth century. The reasons were fundamentally economic—Negroes were increasingly less needed as a source of cheap labor in southern agriculture, especially after the development of the mechanical cotton-picker, and the North held the promise of jobs, most abundantly during periods of war. The political consequences were far-reaching—with every year of the migration the black community was less a repressed, invisible force on the national scene and more a sizable voting bloc in the large urban states that were crucial in presidential elections. Within the large cities, Negroes were an important enough force that local machine leaders, usually Democratic, moved to organize them. The result was the severing of the black population from its post–Civil War Republican allegiance and its incorporation into the northern urban coalition that provided the hard core of support for Democratic New Deal and neo-New Deal liberalism. Blacks could not dominate the coalition—indeed, until the late 1960s their leading politicians occupied disproportionately subordinate roles within it—but they could claim benefits from it much more substantial than those they had received from their earlier Republican affiliation.

The most effective black political action was carried on by pressure group leaders who, while working through the Democratic party, waved the banner of independence and warned that the Negro vote constituted the balance of power in national elections. The most established vehicle of black pressure was the National Association for the Advancement of Colored People (NAACP), which during the 1940s and '50s concentrated on court action to break down the legal foundations of segregation. Moderate and gradualist in approach, the NAACP sought to achieve change by working within prescribed channels. Farther to the left during the 1940s were the ad hoc movements led by A. Philip Randolph for the establishment of a Fair Employment Practices Committee during World War II and the abolition of segregation in the armed forces after the war. Randolph, president of the Brotherhood of Sleeping Car Porters, advocated nonviolent mass demonstrations and, if necessary, civil disobedience. "Only power can affect the enforcement and adoption of a given policy," he declared, defining power as "the organized masses ... united for a definite purpose." His plans for a mass march on Washington helped force the adoption of the wartime FEPC in 1941 and his threat of a Negro draft-resistance movement was a factor in the initiation of military desegregation in 1948.

The development of massive resistance after the school desegregation decision of 1954 seemed to demonstrate that the NAACP approach had neared the limits of its effectiveness; from the mid-1950s on, the drive for racial equality found its major expression in direct action tactics. In 1955–56, a Negro boycott of the segregated bus system in Montgomery, Alabama, produced a charismatic new leader, Martin Luther King, Jr. An eloquent young minister who had been deeply influenced by the writings of Gandhi, King advocated techniques that would bring the average black into the civil rights movement on an active basis. Walking to work or establishing car pools rather than riding segregated buses, marching in mass demonstrations rather than reading of NAACP court victories, the ordinary Negro would throw off his passivity and through his participation make a deep commitment to the cause of equal rights. The commitment, moreover, would be particularly sacred because of its rigid pacifism and nonviolence.

In 1957 King established the Southern Christian Leadership Conference (SCLC), an organization primarily designed to mobilize southern Negroes against the monolithic structure of segregation that characterized the region. The SCLC, the Student Non-violent Coordinating Committee, and the Congress of Racial Equality (CORE) all undertook demonstrations—marches, sit-ins, freedom rides—built around the theme of nonviolence, although the leaders of the latter two organizations were inclined to regard the concept as an expedient tactic rather than a moral absolute. NAACP leaders complained that the newer groups were not only upstaging the older Negro movement but at the same time making exorbitant demands upon its financial and legal resources. Nevertheless, the philosophy of nonviolent direct action captured the imagination of black America.

King himself provided the crucial margin for the new technique's ascendancy. His well-developed intellectual rationale, his forceful character, and, above all, his unusual oratorical powers enabled him to eclipse other black leaders. It was typical that he became the central figure of the greatest Negro demonstration ever held—the 1963 march on Washington—although he had neither originated the plan nor supervised its execution. His eloquent "I have a dream" speech, a masterful statement of integrationist aspirations, became the episode by which the entire event was remembered and firmly established him as the spiritual head of the

Negro movement. He also achieved an international reputation; in 1964, only thirty-five years old, he was awarded the Nobel Peace Prize.

Biracial and idealistic, the civil rights movement of the late 1950s and early 1960s was primarily a religious phenomenon seeking to convert sinners by the force of moral example. The sight of peaceful young demonstrators—"black and white together"—singing "We Shall Overcome" or praying in the presence of potential or actual violence brought greater white support than ever before to the civil rights movement. At times, the movement received important gains from its willingness to stand in Christian witness against evil and bear the cross of suffering. At Birmingham, in 1963, when the police used dogs and fire hoses against peaceful demonstrators, and at Selma in 1965, when state troopers and mounted deputies attacked marchers with tear gas, clubs, and bullwhips, television news brought the scenes into practically every living room in America and thereby facilitated the development of waves of sympathy which contributed to the passage of civil rights legislation.

Such tactics, however, possessed grave limitations. To a large extent, nonviolent action was dependent upon media coverage; in order to get sustained attention, it had to "buy" television time with the leadership of a prominent figure such as King, or with some dramatic set of circumstances. If segregationist officials remained cool enough to make arrests in a peaceful, orderly fashion and keep brutality away from the cameras, they could usually win a war of attrition against civil rights campaigners; even if they made some concessions, they could frequently renege once the newsmen and television crews had moved on to another story. The sinners were in fact rarely converted, and episodes such as the brutal Mississippi summer registration program of 1964 convinced many disillusioned activists that the hard-core areas were beyond redemption.

Nonviolence eventually achieved legislative victories on such "conscience issues" as segregation and the right to vote, but it was less successful in delivering the Negro economic benefits. Realizing the limits of his earlier work, King sought to devote himself to the plight of the impoverished urban black. In 1966 he took his movement into Chicago and attempted to identify himself with the cause of better housing and increased economic opportunity for Negro slum dwellers, but he got little more than a paper agreement with local politicians and civil leaders. In 1968, the SCLC laid plans for a large "poor people's" encampment in Washington.

King meanwhile went to Memphis, Tennessee, to lend his support to striking black garbage workers. In an incident that indicated the decline of nonviolence, the first demonstration he attempted to lead ended in brick throwing, looting, and gunfire. He was preparing for another march when he was shot and killed from ambush on April 5, 1968. As stunned white national leaders sought to render to him posthumously a degree of honor they had denied him while he was alive, black populations across the nation observed his death with the most widespread rioting in American history.

The events were sadly symbolic. Black urban protest riots had begun in 1964 and had escalated with each passing summer. Perhaps the worst occurred in 1965 in the Watts section of Los Angeles; several days of looting, arson, and black clashes with police and National Guard troops resulted in 35 deaths, nearly 900 injuries, 3,600 arrests, and tens of millions of dollars' worth of property damage. During the summer of 1967, there were at least 150 serious outbursts, including especially violent ones in Detroit and Newark; President Johnson appointed a special commission, headed by Illinois governor Otto Kerner, to investigate the disturbances. Well before King's death, the tide of nonviolence was ebbing.

Perceptive observers did not need a presidential commission to discern the reasons, although the Kerner report was an important and useful document. The civil rights movement by the rapidity of its upsurge and by its surface victories had created expectations which outstripped its actual accomplishments. Court victories and laws could bring the Negro closer to equal opportunity and the exercise of fundamental rights, but they could not suddenly topple the whole massive and complex structure of discrimination or erase the effects of centuries of disadvantage. Such objectives as the right to vote in the South or the integration of various public accommodations in all parts of the country barely touched the basic problems of a bitter northern urban black proletariat whose foremost hope was to escape from poverty and squalor. This was the segment of the Negro community primarily responsible for the riots, and King's appeal to it had never been profound.

The violent militance of the frustrated black proletariat in turn stimulated the revival of one of the oldest intellectual themes of American Negro history—black nationalism and separatism. Especially appealing to the young, the new mood was captured by the slogan "Black Power." At no time was Black Power a coherent program; its meanings varied greatly once its users got beyond such common denominators as black pride, independence, and self-help. For groups such as SNCC and CORE, it meant the abandonment of nonviolence and interracialism. Among college students, it meant demands for Black Studies programs and, frequently, special black living and recreational accommodations. Among ideologists, it might mean control of the businesses, schools, and political offices in Negro communities. Among some extremists, usually influenced by Maoism or the Cuban revolution, it could mean guerrilla warfare against the white power structure and the justification of crime as a political act. To many Negroes, it meant simply the adoption of Afro fashions and approval of the concept that "black is beautiful."

Too diffuse and ambiguous to possess a programmatic consensus, partly an expression of a new black consciousness, partly a cry of angry frustration, Black Power was no more a panacea for the plight of the Negro than was NAACP legal action or nonviolence. It could wring some concessions from white officials fearful of violence, and rioting frequently did call attention to problems that had been ignored. But black militance, most likely to be identified with gun-toting revolutionaries, frightened many whites out of sympathy with what they once had envisioned as the aspirations of a peaceful, brutalized people. A substantial number of middle-class white liberals displayed sympathy for the Black Panthers and similar groups, but Black Power advocates were so prone to employ antiwhite rhetoric that Caucasians who supported them were eventually ridiculed as guilt-ridden and masochistic.

Black Power might render considerable psychological benefits to many Negroes, and some of its exponents enjoyed successes in organizing localities where blacks were dominant. By 1973, there were fifteen blacks in the House of Representatives, predominantly independent and of a higher caliber than any Negro delegation that had preceded them; most were the beneficiaries of a new black consciousness within their districts. Still, they constituted less than 3.5 percent of the entire House, and Black Power theorists had developed no practical alternative to coalition politics. In fact, in its actual working form, Black Power as often as not consisted of little more than demands for greater Negro influence within the traditional liberal coalition. Nevertheless, its more extravagant sloganeering, coming in the wake of the urban violence of the 1960s, stimulated a "white blacklash" which threatened to bring an end to an era of progress.

By the 1970s, urban rioting had tapered off, although no sensible observer could dismiss the phenomenon as a thing of the past; but the black revolution had not reverted to the ideology of nonviolence. Instead, lacking a leader with a mass national following, it was seriously fragmented. The gains of the 1960s could not be eradicated, and the Negro population would continue to wield considerable political clout. But whether the black revolution could achieve unity and a sense of direction remained uncertain.

The civil rights movement had been transformed into a black revolution less by resistance to segregation than by the fact of massive black poverty. But poverty was more than a black problem; despite the optimism that accompanied postwar prosperity, it was a national affliction. The struggle against poverty had been a persistent theme of American history from the turn of the century through the New Deal. The rationale for social-welfare reform and unionization of workers revolved largely around the need to deal with large-scale poverty. During the Great Depression, President Roosevelt defined the mission of the New Deal as assistance to "one third of a nation ill-housed, ill-clad, ill-nourished." His statistics were accurate; during the 1930s, poverty in one form or another came close to being a norm of American life. Only the most privileged escaped some sort of brush with it; the more ordinary people who were able to cling to middle-class status were likely to have less fortunate friends of relatives or to live themselves with fears of wage cuts and job layoffs.

World War II, it seemed, had begun a new era of sustained prosperity and plentiful jobs. By the late 1950s, most social commentators assumed that poverty was no longer a matter of concern. In *The Affluent Society* (1958), John Kenneth Galbraith characterized poverty as "an afterthought" rather than a "universal or massive affliction" and estimated the percentage of poor families as approximately 7⅔ percent; to be sure, he recommended social programs to alleviate the residue of poverty which he saw, but by his definition the problem was not a major one requiring a vast effort. Galbraith's solutions, typical of those advocated by liberals in the 1950s, involved simply a diversion of affluence from excessive private consumption into public spending for programs, such as education, designed to improve the quality of American life.

Not until the early 1960s did studies emphasizing the true dimensions of the problem win wide acceptance. Michael Harrington's *The Other America* (1962), written the author said from "a sense of outrage," was especially influential. Harrington and other commentators effectively established that poverty—defined as individual or family income below recognized levels of minimum subsistence—remained a large-scale American dilemma, affecting 20–25 percent of the population, 40–50 million people. They demonstrated, moreover, that a number almost as large lived in a state of deprivation only a step removed from poverty. The statistics, drawn mostly from government surveys, were irrefutable.

The nature of American poverty varied greatly. In some rural areas, the poor might live in barely imaginable misery on the edge of starvation. But poor people normally could get a subsistence diet, if not a good one, and could obtain some sort of shelter. In this, American poverty differed from that which prevailed in most of the rest of the world. Julian Marias, a Spanish philosopher who taught for several years in the United States, found himself unable to take the issue seriously because the poverty income line approximated the average income of his homeland. Even the poor American family was likely to have a television set and an old automobile; an Asian beggar would consider such possessions as evidence of wealth. The U.S. poverty standard was far below the middle-class norm, but it did not carry the immediate peril to survival characteristic of poverty in most other parts of the globe.

In the United States, moreover, the poor were largely invisible, tucked away in rural isolation or in the slum ghettos of the central city. As Harrington and others pointed out, clothes increased the invisibility. America did not have deprived masses dressed in filthy rags; it was easier to be reasonably well dressed than to obtain a good diet, decent housing, or adequate medical care. The majority of the poor were the wrong age to be noticed—either senior citizens with inadequate retirement incomes or children ranging from infants to young, unskilled, unemployed high school dropouts. Another large percentage consisted of mothers who had to spend most of their time caring for dependent children. At the beginning of the 1960s, the poor existed unorganized and unseen.

In part, it was true, the problem of poverty was insoluble because those at the bottom of the income scale would always consider themselves poor. It was true also that the American poor were caught up in a revolution of rising expectations just as were the more deprived masses of the Third World. A young black whose experience was limited to the ghetto or a poor white in an isolated area of Appalachia might assume that the exaggerated standard of consumption he saw on television really was the middle-class routine. Nevertheless, only the most callous could argue that a nation as wealthy as America should not attempt to provide its underprivileged with food that met good standards of nutrition, comfortable living conditions, and access to medical care. Moreover, it was in the enlightened self-interest of the affluent to provide the education and skills which would enable the poor to fend for themselves and break an increasingly expensive cycle of dependency.

The 1960s brought a large decline in the numbers of the poor, largely because of the economic boom which began in the middle of the decade and also because of the antipoverty programs undertaken by the Johnson administration. Census Bureau statistics estimated the numbers of the poor in 1960 at 39.9 million, approximately 22 percent of the population; of this total, 28.3 million were white (18 percent of the U.S. white population), 11.6 million nonwhite (56 percent of the U.S. nonwhite population). By 1972, the Census Bureau estimated the poor at 25.4 million, or 13 percent of the total population; 17.5 million were white (10 percent of the white population), and 7.9 million were nonwhite (32 percent of the nonwhite population). Yet, despite the reduction in numbers, poverty was both more visible and more expensive than ever.

The poor had become organized and self-conscious, not powerful enough to escape from poverty but able to gain federal antipoverty programs and increased public-assistance (welfare) payments. As a result, the cost of welfare programs, established by the states and financed on a matching basis by state and federal funds, steadily increased. For many states, the escalating expenditures created budgetary difficulties so severe that harassed governors and legislators talked despairingly of a welfare crisis. In New York City, welfare recipients totaled about 600,000 in 1965; by 1972, the number was up to 1.2 million. Yet the welfare system was a conspicuous failure which did nothing to alleviate poverty even as it placed an ever-heavier burden upon the taxpayer. In all but a few states, welfare standards were well below minimum subsistence levels. Benefits varied widely from state to state; in 1972, Mississippi doled out average family welfare payments of only $55 a month while New York paid its recipients $259 a month. Nationally, only about 40 percent of the poor could qualify for any benefits; complex regulations frequently had the effect of making need a secondary consideration. Perhaps worst of all, the system tended to perpetuate poverty by discouraging work—typically, a recipient would have his welfare benefit reduced by every dollar of earned income and thus stood to gain nothing by accepting a low-paying job. Welfare also broke up family structures—in most states, families with a male head of the household could not qualify for aid to dependent children; thus the father who wanted to stay with his family could do so on an open and full-time basis only at the cost of sacrificing public assistance. By every standard, the system was a monstrosity; yet after a decade of attention to the poverty problem, it remained intact. The United States had neither eliminated poverty nor devised a workable method of combating it.

Race and poverty were not exclusively urban problems, but in the great cities they were most visible and most explosive. Urban life with its crowding, uneasy pluralism and freedom from the harshest forms of repression constituted the perfect breeding ground for all the symptoms of poverty and discrimination; the urban-oriented news media focused an intense spotlight on the situation. Many sections of rural America were poorer, less free, and devoid of minority opportunities, but increasingly during the 1960s, America turned its attention to the urban crisis.

Throughout most of human history, urban life had been a difficult and dangerous proposition; in fact, the mid-twentieth-century American city deserved good marks for comfort, safety, and cultural amenities when compared with most of its historical prodecessors. Still, by the 1960s, there was a wide feeling that the quality of city life had dropped from an earlier high point, and the rising expectations of Americans at every social level made the drop all the less tolerable. The crisis had many dimensions ranging from increased pollution levels to sharply escalating costs for public services which seemed nevertheless constantly more inefficient. From the middle-class viewpoint, the cities were dirty, unhealthy, unsafe, inconvenient, and yet frightfully expensive; the poor felt the same problems, but with much greater intensity. The typical middle-class response was the flight to suburbia; the response of the poor might involve drug addiction and crime, in many cases, the latter being necessary to support the former.

Lower-income housing deteriorated rapidly during the 1960s, in part because federal and local tax systems made it profitable for owners of slum buildings to write off depreciation and discouraged improvements which would add to property valuations. When a dwelling finally became so miserable that it was condemned and demolished, any incentive for a private developer to replace it rarely existed; as a result, several large cities contained areas that looked almost as if they had been bombed out. Journalists who had covered World War II frequently compared sections of the south Bronx and Brooklyn to the cities of Germany at the time of the Nazi surrender.

The standard liberal solution, public housing, proved a failure. Typically, public housing units were high-rise apartment buildings with eligibility requirements that excluded all but the poorest and least stable elements of the population. It should not have been surprising that they became hotbeds of crime and vice, objects of vandalism, and terror-ridden prisons for the law-abiding citizens forced to live in them. Perhaps the most notorious such project, Pruitt-Igoe in Saint Louis, was finally partly demolished by despairing municipal officials. The urban slums continued to be a desperate problem in themselves and a breeding place for all the other problems that grew out of poverty.

Crime and drug addiction increased steadily. In a development paralleling the growth of New York's welfare rolls, the number of addicts in the city doubled from 60,000 in 1965 to 120,000 in 1972. The increase in addiction was the major cause of a sharply spiraling crime rate which placed mugging and burglary among the standard risks of urban life. Many cities that probably had been growing progressively safer since the early twentieth century experienced a reversal of the trend. Police forces demanded and usually received large increases in personnel and funding; in most cities, the number of arrests increased markedly. Yet crime continued to be the most serious concern of many urban citizens.

The crime problem persisted less because of Supreme Court decisions, although the Court was a bête noire of conservatives and law-enforcement officials, than because of the worsening slum life which generated crime and because of a breakdown of the criminal justice system at the state and municipal level. Badly overtaxed court dockets caused trials to be postponed for as much as a year, made convictions difficult, and encouraged plea bargaining, a process in which a felon would agree to plead guilty to a lesser offense and receive a light sentence. Prisons, moreover, were so overcrowded and brutalizing that judges hesitated to impose long sentences upon first or second offenders, and parole boards usually felt it necessary to err on the side of leniency. Until the slums were eradicated, until the courts could deal swiftly and justly with defendants, until penologists discovered workable methods of rehabilitation and obtained financing for them, crime would continue as a major aspect of urban life.

The urban crisis also involved a serious financial dilemma. The exodus of middle-class whites and the accompanying flight of many businesses to surburban settings meant serious losses in tax revenues. Efforts to make up the deficit by increasing taxes only stimulated the flight of the well-to-do. Many cities, especially those with nonexpandable boundaries, experienced precipitate population declines in the 1960s; those which did not were likely to have engaged in a reshuffle in which the incoming poor, many of them potential welfare recipients, were about equal to the departing middle class. Near the end of 1975, New York City required substantial federal loans to avert bankruptcy. If such trends continued, many cities would be increasingly dependent upon outside aid and face ultimate ruin.

MIDDLE AMERICA

Most Americans were *un*young, *un*poor, *un*black. They constituted a vast middle group, not monolithic to be sure, but increasingly alienated from the forces of change—the counterculturists; the New Leftists; the welfare recipients claiming ever-higher benefits; the blacks pressing for formerly white homes and jobs and underscoring their demands with militant behavior; the affluent, liberal-minded establishment which looked benignly upon these forces while displaying contempt for the Middle American and his values. Middle Americans differed vastly in ethnic background, worked in many occupations, and earned incomes that ranged from substandard to quite comfortable. On farms or in the towns and small cities between the Appalachians and the Rockies, their attitudes formed a broad consensus which defined the outer limits of political struggle and social behavior; only in the metropolitan areas were they likely to feel that they were an embattled minority. To describe

Middle America, Peter Schrag wrote, was like trying to describe America itself; but, for all their diversity, Middle Americans shared a respect for order and tradition and a fear of rapid cultural change.

It was easy to caricature such attitudes as the callousness of those who recently had joined the middle class toward the less fortunate. The intellectuals and the media with their tendency to focus on urban situations seized upon the blue-collar working class as the epitome of Middle America and tended to caricature it. The voguish and popular film *Joe* depicted its central character, a lower-middle-class factory worker, as ignorant, bigoted, fascistic, and ultimately homicidal in his hatred of counterculturists. In a somewhat lighter vein, the television series "All in the Family," which regularly drew more viewers than any other program on the air, gave America Archie Bunker, who differed from Joe only in refraining from murder. Like all caricatures, such characterizations exaggerated for effect, but they contained a strong dose of reality. "All in the Family" won its top rating by being closer to the truth than the patently synthetic situation comedies which previously had dominated TV programming. The Bunker family was so real that the show's stars, when interviewed, felt no compunctions about going beyond the scripts they had played and discussing authoritatively the Bunkers' religious or sexual life. The liberal intellectuals laughed at Bunker, but many viewers had feelings of positive identification toward him.

What the caricaturists ignored was that the urban blue-collar worker feared more than phantoms. Unlike the farmers and small-town Babbitts who shared his attitudes or the well-to-do liberals who ridiculed them, he existed on a tense and dangerous frontier of social change. Frequently living on the edge of an expanding black ghetto, he experienced the real problems that accompanied the outward push of the Negro population—racial tensions, street crime, declining property values, overcrowded and deteriorating schools, the prospect of his children being bused to an even worse slum school for the sake of racial balance. In 1969, when Samuel Lubell interviewed residents of white precincts along the shifting boundary of the black areas of Cleveland, he compared the experience to "inspecting a stretched-out war front." A housewife in Little Italy told him matter-of-factly about being pinned down by a black sniper and rescued by a neighborhood defense group which killed the gunman. Older residents who owned homes in blocks that were becoming black complained of being terrorized by youthful hoodlums and street gangs.

Detached social analysts might counter with the argument that blacks were no more prone to crime and violence than other poor and disorganized social groups and that most victims of black crime were other blacks, but few whites living along the edge of the ghetto could be expected to achieve superhuman objectivity. Their fears might lead them to racism but were also, however unfortunately, well grounded. Those who squarely faced the ugly crime statistics could not escape the fact that black arrest rates for robbery and violent crime were far higher than for whites; moreover, there was a sharp escalation of crime among young blacks. Nor could one honestly gainsay a growing tendency to consider crimes against whites a legitimate political act. Picked by fate to be actors in an American tragedy, the working-class urbanites who felt the pressure of black expansion were unwilling to accept their roles without bitterness

If Middle America could find specific grievances against the black revolution, its outrage at the counterculture and the New Left was more ideological. The working-class American, whether white, Anglo-Saxon Protestant, Jewish, or ethnic Catholic, possessed a set of deeply held values including patriotism, law and order, hard work, orthodox sexual behavior, and personal neatness. By the mid-1960s, all these values seemed under attack. The forces of change burned the flag and dodged the draft, broke the law and attacked the police, rejected the work ethic in favor of the hedonistic pursuit of leisure, engaged in promiscuity and homosexuality, and shunned haircuts or baths. The indictment was of course as exaggerated as that of the liberal intellectuals against Middle America, but it expressed the angry feeling of a group that considered *itself* the victim of discrimination and neglect.

Critics of the urban Middle American failed to realize that, unless he was a skilled craftsman or a member of a strong union, he frequently existed on the fringes of poverty himself and stayed off public assistance only through a diligent application of the work ethic. As often as not, he kept afloat by moonlighting; rarely did he have an income that permitted luxuries far beyond bowling and beer. His assets might be tied up in a modest house located in an older neighborhood and maintained or improved by his spare-time labor. No group was more pinched by tax increases, and only the poor were more vulnerable to inflation. People who had worked hard to acquire so little were likely to be highly sensitive to any threats that they perceived to their property or jobs.

Demanding little in the way of public services and generally receiving even less, they were likely to feel betrayed by a Democratic-liberal political-intellectual establishment which they had supported but which seemed more concerned with the plight of the poor. "My kids don't have a place to swim, my parks are full of glass, and I'm supposed to bleed for a bunch of people on relief," a bitter resident of South Boston told Peter Schrag. Referring to a demand by militant black welfarists for city-guaranteed credit accounts at New York's E. J. Korvette department store, an incensed ironworker told Pete Hamill: "I *work* for a living and *I* can't get a credit card at Korvette's. . . . You know you see that, and you want to go out and strangle someone."

Perhaps even more fundamental was a psychic rage at the upper-middle-class intellectuals who sneeringly rejected the Con I values of the working class, lampooned its speech patterns (frequently while upholding the legitimacy of black American dialect), and contemptuously labeled it as bigoted and authoritarian.* The open contempt of the intellectual establishment when paired with neglect from the political establishment could only lead to a sense of social and political alienation.

By the late 1960s, conditions were ripe for a massive Middle American backlash, and the first stirrings seemed to be appearing: massive labor-union demonstrations against black quotas and "peaceniks," indications of a taxpayer revolt against the universities and the welfare system, the northern support for George Wallace, the election of tough-guy mayors such as Charles Stenvig in Minneapolis or Frank Rizzo in Philadelphia, the wide approval for attacks upon liberal newsmen. Yet by and large such manifestations remained surface phenomena which did little to interfere with the objects of their wrath. However strong their bitterness, Middle Americans remained divided in their political attitudes. In 1968, the urban ethnics tended to support the most radical of announced presidential candidates, Robert Kennedy, out of a feeling that he understood their problems as well as those of the classes below; it was only after his death that many of them switched to Wallace. A constituency so volatile, so divided between traditional liberalism and potential fascism, was up for grabs, waiting for a leader who could go beyond demagogy to a realistic understanding of its anxieties and legitimate interests. By the mid-1970s, it was still waiting. More than the young, the poor, or the black, the uncommitted Middle Americans held the key to the future of American politics and society.

---

* The concept of "working class authoritarianism" has been especially promoted by Seymour Martin Lipset, who emphasizes the nonpermissive child-rearing practices of blue-collar families, and Robert E. Lane, who argues that the working class fears freedom and equality. Nevertheless, when one considers the behavior of many New Leftists, the vast majority from upper-middle-class professional families, it seems at the least debatable that the working class has any special claim to authoritarian attitudes.

TEN

The Promise Unfulfilled: John F. Kennedy and the New Frontier

CHRONOLOGY

1960–63

1960

MAY	John F. Kennedy wins West Virginia presidential primary
SEPTEMBER	Kennedy and Nixon begin series of television debates
NOVEMBER	Kennedy defeats Nixon by margin of .2 percent of popular vote

1961

JANUARY	House of Representatives decides by 5-vote margin to enlarge Rules Committee
MARCH	Kennedy proclaims Alliance for Progress
APRIL	Bay of Pigs invasion
MAY	Area Redevelopment Act; cease-fire in Laos and negotiations for coalition government
JUNE	Kennedy and Khrushchev meet in Vienna
AUGUST	Erection of Berlin Wall
OCTOBER	Taylor-Rostow mission to Vietnam

1962

MARCH	Manpower Development and Training Act
APRIL	Steel price controversy

JUNE	Kennedy advocates new economics at Yale
JULY	Laotian agreement signed at Geneva
AUGUST	Anti-poll tax amendment passes Congress
SEPTEMBER	Accelerated Public Works Act; federal troops enforce integration at University of Mississippi
OCTOBER	Trade Expansion Act; investment tax credit; Cuban missile crisis
NOVEMBER	Presidential executive order bans discrimination in federally owned or insured housing

1963

JANUARY	Kennedy requests tax reduction
JUNE	Kennedy requests civil rights legislation; Kennedy advocates Soviet-American détente at American University
SEPTEMBER	Senate ratifies Nuclear Test Ban Treaty
OCTOBER	United States and USSR negotiate wheat sale
NOVEMBER	Coup in South Vietnam—assassination of Diem and Nhu; Kennedy assassinated in Dallas, Texas

For four days in November 1963, a disbelieving, immobilized nation watched the unfolding of the most traumatic public occurrence since the death of Franklin D. Roosevelt. Given powerful immediacy by television, the assassination of John F. Kennedy was a searing emotional experience. The outpouring of grief was global in scope; the great and powerful of the world, including the imperious Charles de Gaulle, came to march in the funeral procession. The death of any President causes shock and mourning among the people whose national identity his office incarnates, but Kennedy's seemed especially terrible, for he had been shot down while still young, vigorous, and questing for the limits of his powers. His murder became a national tragedy burned into the consciousness of his generation.

The first memories of Kennedy's tenure were inevitably adulatory. At the level of popular romanticism, he became a figure of Arthurian legend, who for a time transformed the nation's capital into Camelot. The intellectuals, adopting him as one of their own, praised him as a statesman who had perceived and inspirationally articulated the needs of his countrymen, who had conducted American diplomacy with rare vision and restraint. Through the 1960s and into the 1970s, the popular view endured. Among the intellectuals, however, less than a decade after Kennedy's burial, it became fashionable to depict him as a failure, weak and incompetent in legislative leadership, immature and irresponsible in the life-and-death art of diplomacy.

The real man was neither Lancelot nor LeMay, and he had little patience with sentimentalism. As politician and diplomatist, he sought to attune himself to the realities of power and to exercise constructive, responsible leadership within the pragmatic limits as he perceived them. His understanding of the possibilities before him and his estimates of diplomatic alternatives may have been flawed—or perhaps his critics allowed the passage of time to mar their own comprehension of the world of the early 1960s. The historian who attempts a sober assessment cannot escape the depth and authenticity of a sentiment felt around the world on November 25, 1963, as the slain President was lowered into his grave, a conviction that the United States had lost not simply an attractive personality but also that the Western world had lost an invaluable asset.

JFK AND THE ELECTION OF 1960

In a sense, all of John Fitzgerald Kennedy's early life had been a preparation for politics, beginning perhaps with the day he had been christened with the name of his maternal grandfather, a former mayor of Boston. His father, Joseph P. Kennedy, a fabulously successful speculator who dabbled in all manner of risky enterprises, was the first chairman of the Securities and Exchange Commission and from 1937 to 1941 ambassador to Great Britain. A maverick among both businessmen and politicians, Joe Kennedy could neither win acceptance into the eastern financial establishment nor bring himself to give full support to Franklin D. Roosevelt's domestic and foreign policies. Heartily disliked in the end by Roosevelt and then by Truman, an admirer of Senator Joe McCarthy, he nevertheless remained a figure of influence within the Democratic party, especially among the old-line machine leaders.

Joseph Kennedy projected his thwarted political ambitions on to his sons. He encouraged them to discuss public issues with him, gave them the best education available, and transmitted a strong competitive drive to them. It was widely understood that he expected his eldest son, Joseph, Jr., to go into politics with the White House as the ultimate objective. When young Joe, by all accounts a man of great charm and ability, was killed in the war, his mantle descended upon the next oldest son, John. From his first run for Congress in 1946, John Kennedy was the bearer of the family's political aspirations, and it seemed natural for the rest of them to devote their time and talent to his advancement. He in turn considered it natural to appoint his younger brother, Robert, attorney general of the United States.

He was more than an extraordinarily good Irish-Catholic politician. At the conclusion of the 1960 campaign, Murray Kempton described him as more Harvard than Boston; the phrase was apt, for Kennedy's style was more that of the patrician than the ethnic politico. His schooling at Choate and Harvard was identical to that normally accorded the best sons of the Protestant elite—Joe Kennedy felt that parochial education would not equip his sons to compete in a Protestant world. His manner was reserved, his sense of privacy highly developed. Although he considered himself a man of action, he appears to have taken great pride in a second identity as an intellectual and man of letters.

In fact, it was as a writer that Kennedy first attracted wide national attention. In 1940, upon his graduation from Harvard, he published his honors thesis, *Why England Slept,* an analysis of British policy toward Nazi Germany in the late 1930s; the book was a best-seller. In the mid-1950s, while recuperating from a major back operation, he wrote *Profiles in Courage* (1956), a great commercial success and a Pulitzer Prize winner. In these works he came closer to developing a political philosophy than do most public figures. Both books expressed patrician, Whiggish reservations about democracy, the first blaming English appeasement more on popular apathy than incompetent leadership, the second eulogizing statesmen who had put their careers on the line defying popular sentiment for the sake of principle. Statesmen had to lead the masses, he seemed to be saying, but in a democracy political leadership was difficult and dangerous. One corollary was obscured—the realist in him knew that usually the aspiring statesman would have but one political life to give for principle and doubted that it was better to be right and out of office than to be cautious and stay in.

No one questioned Kennedy's physical courage. During World War II, he had sought combat duty, conducted himself heroically, and sustained a crippling back injury. When his back condition deteriorated and he faced the prospect of a life on crutches, he opted for a dangerous operation, fully aware that it might cost him his life (it nearly did). Even then, his back remained a source of nearly constant pain for the rest of his life. But during the 1950s, many questioned his political courage, especially on McCarthyism, an issue on which he maintained silence, probably out of deference to his father and out of fear of McCarthy's popularity among the Irish-Catholic ethnics in Massachusetts. With reason, many liberals wondered what principles could be more fundamental than those which McCarthy dragged through the mud, and from there it was but a short step to questioning whether Kennedy possessed any fundamental political principles at all or whether he had managed to establish his independence from his father.

Nevertheless, he was the most successful politician in the history of his state. Winning his first race for Congress with relative ease, he served three terms in the House and then moved to the Senate in 1952 with a victory in the face of the Eisenhower landslide over Henry Cabot Lodge, Jr., a hitherto unassailable figure in Massachusetts politics. By 1958, his position was impregnable and his reelection the most overwhelming in the annals of Massachusetts politics. There were two major reasons for his political rise: his organization and his "star quality." The rest of the Kennedy family constituted a formidable pool of organizational and campaigning skills; and the family fortune, estimated at some $300 million, easily provided whatever was needed to hire outside expertise, travel first class, buy media time and space, or obtain adequate campaign staff and material. (Upon losing the 1960 West Virginia primary, Hubert Humphrey remarked that he felt like a small independent grocer who had been squeezed out of business by a corporate chain enterprise.)

As always, however, the candidate's own appeal was critical, and for Kennedy the decisive element was less his routine New Deal–Fair Deal liberalism than his personal style. To the ethnics, he was the ultimate success story—wealthy, polished, and on the surface indistinguishable from the scions of the Yankee elite. To the young, he came to symbolize the vigor and idealism of a new generation. To many women, young and not so young, he was quite simply a sex symbol; during the campaign of 1960, many journalists were startled to notice, first, teen-age girls, then older women, jumping in excitement at his rallies, as if he were a rock star instead of a candidate for the Presidency. A southern senator humorously remarked that Kennedy seemed to combine the best qualities of Franklin D. Roosevelt and Elvis Presley.

Kennedy himself avoided the contagion of his charisma. He viewed his own life with an unusual detachment and seemed to grasp for opportunities to turn his wry sense of humor on himself. How had he become a war hero? asked a network television interviewer. It was absolutely involuntary, replied the candidate; they sunk his boat. Why had he been attracted to Hemingway's definition of courage as "grace under pressure"? The phrase reminded him of the name of a girl he had once dated. Was the Presidency a splendid misery? No, it provided a nice house, a conveniently located place of work, and a good salary. Such witticisms, tossed off so easily, reflected the supreme confidence of a man able to poke fun at himself precisely because he felt no private insecurity. In 1960, at the young political age of forty-three, he had no doubt about his ability to lead a nation.

Kennedy faced tough competition for the Democratic nomination in 1960. His challengers among his Senate colleagues—Lyndon Johnson of Texas, Hubert Humphrey of Minnesota, and Stuart Symington of Missouri—were men of ability; all of them had more impressive records as legislators. (Within the Senate, Kennedy was considered something of a lightweight.) Adlai Stevenson did not campaign for the nomination but he did nothing to discourage a draft. Kennedy had three handicaps; in order of importance, they were his religious affiliation, his youth and alleged inexperience, and his father's reputation. The last two cost him the support of some leading Democratic politicians, including Harry S Truman; neither, however, stirred mass emotions. Kennedy's major difficulty involved fears of a Catholic President; such apprehensions were deeply imbedded in the cultural and voting patterns of Protestant areas from Oregon to the Carolinas, from Wisconsin to Texas, and it was axiomatic among political leaders that a Catholic could never be elected President.* It was this specter that Kennedy would have to exorcise in order to be nominated.

The only way to do it was to demonstrate popular appeal in the presidential primaries, where the candidate's charisma and organization could be exploited to the fullest. In the first crucial contest, the Wisconsin primary, Kennedy faced Humphrey, who enjoyed great popularity in his next-door state. Kennedy polled 56 percent of the vote but ran badly in heavily Protestant areas; the effect was almost to turn a numerical victory into a defeat and to encourage Humphrey to stay in the race. The two men staged a final showdown in West Virginia. Facing an electorate that was 95 percent Protestant and heavily fundamentalist, Kennedy brought the Catholic issue out into the open, repeatedly affirmed his dedication to the principle of separation of church and state, and scored a landslide victory. After West Virginia, his candidacy was unstoppable; by the time of the Democratic convention, he had enough delegates to be nominated on the first ballot. His choice as a running mate was Lyndon Johnson.

The Republican contest was less suspenseful. From the beginning, Vice-President Richard Nixon was miles ahead of his only serious challenger, Governor Nelson Rockefeller of New York, who represented the party's "northeastern liberal" wing. Rockefeller possessed genuine talent, a magnetic campaign personality, and wealth which dwarfed even the

* This great truth rested of course on only one example, Alfred E. Smith in 1928. But as many historians have demonstrated, the religious issue was only one of many factors that doomed Smith's candidacy. His strident opposition to Prohibition and his ostentatiously urban provincialism were at least equally damaging. Most importantly, the Democratic party was the natural minority party of the nation in the 1920s, and the Republicans were reaping the benefits of economic prosperity. All things considered, Smith ran well; his margin of defeat was much slimmer than that of the Democratic candidates of 1920 and 1924.

Kennedy fortune. Nixon had hundreds of IOUs from Republican leaders across the nation whom he had helped in one way or another during his years as vice-president, and his following among the rank and file was broad and deep; most decisive was his identification with the Eisenhower administration and the acquiescence of the old general in his candidacy. Rockefeller had little chance and withdrew before the convention. Largely as a unity gesture, Nixon acceded to the New Yorker's demands for a moderately liberal platform. His selection for a vice-presidential nominee was Henry Cabot Lodge, Jr., who had been Eisenhower's ambassador to the United Nations after being defeated by Kennedy for the Senate in 1952.

The public reaction to the campaign that followed was perhaps best indicated by the fact that one of Kennedy's ardent supporters, Arthur Schlesinger, Jr., felt compelled to write a small tract entitled *Kennedy or Nixon: Does It Make Any Difference?* Although Kennedy had sought to identify himself with New Deal liberalism in contrast to the relative conservatism of Eisenhower and Nixon, although Kennedy was a critic of Eisenhower's diplomacy, which Nixon championed as near-perfect, many voters perceived little in the way of substantive conflicts between the two. Kennedy's liberalism was muted by the failure of the heavily Democratic Congress to pass Medicare or other significant reform legislation in 1959 and 1960. His foreign policy criticisms—such as his assertion that it had been foolish to guarantee the defense of Quemoy and Matsu and his remark that Eisenhower should have expressed diplomatic regrets for the U-2 overflight—made little impact because he retreated from them. (The average American, he concluded, could not be educated in the tumult of a national campaign.) Instead, he emphasized vague charges that the nation was losing ground in the cold war. Consequently, voter preferences hinged more on style than substance.

Kennedy sought to present an appearance of youth and vigor as the counterpoint to his charges that the Eisenhower regime was tired and complacent. His campaign theme was his determination to lead the nation to a "new frontier" of achievement. His following was strongest in metropolitan areas. There his style and sophistication was most appreciated, and he could count on especially enthusiastic support from the ethnic groups whose aspirations he embodied. Conversely, Nixon depicted himself with more than a bit of exaggeration as Eisenhower's right-hand man entitled to the Presidency by virtue of the unique experience he had gained serving next to the old hero. The traditional Republican groups—small town, Protestant, middle class—composed his natural constituency, and he felt most comfortable when campaigning away from the cities in the mid-American heartland. Although he appealed in the

Eisenhower manner to the virtues of moderation, he, like Eisenhower, considered himself a defender of the traditional values. (It was typical of the contrast between the two candidates that Nixon complained of the profanity which former President Truman used in his campaign speeches and that Kennedy, unable to suppress his disdainful amusement, suggested that the complaint might be better addressed to Mrs. Truman.)

Kennedy needed only to bring the Democratic Roosevelt coalition behind him to win the election. To do so, however, he had to face and overcome renewed doubts about his religion. Very early in the campaign, it became obvious that the West Virginia primary had not quelled the anti-Catholicism of many voters in other parts of the country, that in fact it was impossible to do so. Speaking to a gathering of Protestant ministers in Houston, Kennedy forcefully reiterated his views on the separation of politics and religion; the meeting itself was a triumph, and films of it became one of the TV staples of his campaign. Still, the old fears would not die, and much of the Houston achievement was undone when the Catholic bishops of Puerto Rico intervened (unsuccessfully, as it turned out) in the island's gubernatorial campaign.

Nixon unwittingly provided the device needed to still questions about the Democratic nominee's ability and experience when he accepted Kennedy's challenge to engage in a series of nationally telecast debates—actually press conferences in which the two men fielded questions from prominent journalists. Few rules of democratic politics are more fundamental than the injunction against giving publicity and exposure to a lesser-known challenger. Nixon had excelled as a college debater and had helped his career by engaging in a filmed impromptu argument with Khrushchev, but his confrontation with Kennedy was in no way comparable to either experience. Kennedy demonstrated that he could hold his own in exchanges with the vice-president, and, perhaps most importantly, he was a vastly superior television performer. Whether college judges would have declared him a winner was unimportant. The programs, the only such affairs in the history of presidential politics, drew huge audiences, and a majority of the viewers felt that Kennedy was the winner. The debates went far toward determining the election results.

One other incident swayed a substantial number of votes. In 1956, many Negroes had drifted back into the Republican party, and since Kennedy had no special identification with the civil rights movement, it was possible that they might vote for Nixon. But when a Georgia court sentenced Martin Luther King, Jr., to a prison term on a trivial charge, Kennedy intervened with state authorities to obtain his release; Nixon, hoping for southern support, remained silent through the whole affair. Negro leaders, many of whom harbored fundamentalist Protestant suspicions of Catholicism, then threw all their weight behind the Democratic nominee. King's father, admitting that he had opposed Kennedy on religious grounds, was foremost among those who recanted. ("Imagine," Kennedy purportedly remarked, "Martin Luther King having a bigot for a father.")

Kennedy's victory was among the narrowest in American history. He won 49.7 percent of the popular vote to Nixon's 49.5 percent and carried the electoral college 303–219. His strength in the urban and suburban North was decisive; he took the election by carrying seven of the nine largest states. The religious issue altered normal voting patterns. Kennedy ran poorly in many of the normally Democratic areas where anti-Catholicism was a traditionally strong force. On the other hand, the controversy cut both ways—Kennedy won very heavy majorities among Catholics who had defected to the GOP in the 1950s. At the least, he had proven that it was possible for a Catholic to reach the White House, and his conduct as President on church-state matters was so scrupulous as to make it doubtful that the Catholic bogey would ever again be a crucial issue in presidential politics.

In the immediate aftermath of the election, however, it was most apparent that Kennedy had sustained some reverses not usually associated with a presidential victory. The Democrats had lost twenty seats in the House of Representatives, almost all of them held by northern and western liberals. In 1959 and 1960, the Democratic party had failed to enact important reforms because of a lack of presidential leadership; now, the process of electing a Chief Executive ready to lead had come close to wiping out the liberal Democratic congressional margin. Kennedy himself, shaken by the closeness of the election, felt that he lacked a mandate from the people and prepared to move with caution.

THE POLITICS OF STALEMATE

Kennedy's situation in 1961 was somewhat similar to Truman's in 1949. Both men had campaigned on highly liberal platforms; both had been elected with less than 50 percent of the total popular vote; both faced Congresses of a moderate orientation—in each instance the House Democratic delegation numbered 263. Truman and Kennedy each managed a respectable record of enlarging established reform programs; they usually failed to squeeze new departures out of Congress. That two politicians so diverse in personality and modes of operation should compile such similar records can only suggest that enduring patterns were more fundamental than deficiencies of leadership. Neither Democratic President could break out of the reform stalemate which had developed with the end of the New Deal in 1938.

The first major legislative struggle revealed Kennedy's difficulties. He sought to increase the membership of the House Rules Committee, which regularly had blocked liberal legislation in the 1940s and '50s by refusing to report it for a floor vote. The administration used every appeal to party loyalty, every type of persuasion available to it; in addition, the respected old Speaker of the House, Sam Rayburn, made enlargement a matter of his personal prestige. Yet Rayburn and Kennedy between them could muster only a five-vote victory, the margin being supplied by a small group of moderate-to-liberal Republicans. The Rules Committee vote represented about the maximum support Kennedy could expect for reform measures and indicated that Congress would not indulge him with a "honeymoon" period. In at least one respect, moreover, the Rules struggle was futile; Kennedy's aid-to-education bill, which had no provision for help to parochial schools, was still blocked, this time by the usually liberal Catholic Democrats on the Rules Committee.

Although he established an elaborate congressional liaison unit, Kennedy could never count on the support of a majority, especially in the House of Representatives. His power as a legislative leader was largely limited to persuasion, and his own background had been insufficient to give him much standing with the powerful committee chairmen who made the fundamental decisions on Capitol Hill. As Vice-President Johnson privately remarked, the White House had the support of the minnows, but not the whales. The results could be anticipated: Kennedy could usually gain some improvements for established, ongoing programs such as the minimum wage, government assistance to housing, or unemployment compensation, and he could get modest legislation for less controversial issues, including water pollution control, combating juvenile delinquency, and aiding community health facilities. But the big, hard issues, such as aid to primary and secondary education or Medicare, continued to wither in Congress.

Kennedy's central domestic concern for most of his Presidency was the state of the economy. One of the major themes of his campaign had been criticism of the inflation-cum-recession stagnation which had characterized Eisenhower's second term. Now Kennedy faced the difficult task of promoting a high rate of economic growth while achieving price stability. The goal defied the maxims of economics; the President could count on little cooperation from Congress; the effort to restrain inflation of necessity would involve friction with pressure groups attempting to garner short-range advantages rather than long-range national benefits. In the circumstances, it was not surprising that his major achievements were educational.

When Kennedy became President, he had no special claim to expertise in economics. Although he had taken a course with Harold Laski at the London School of Economics, his academic background was thin, and as a congressman he had displayed little interest in economic theory. He was disposed to consider different economic problems as unrelated issues to be handled on the basis of political possibility. At the beginning of his tenure in the White House, he horrified the economists around him by tentatively deciding to ask for a tax increase as a mode of patriotic sacrifice during the Berlin crisis; apparently, he did not understand that such a move might seriously damage an already weak economy. Still, he was educable, and he drew on the best liberal economists in the country for advice—Walter Heller, whom he made chairman of the Council of Economic Advisers, John Kenneth Galbraith, Seymour Harris, Paul Samuelson, Robert Solow. His secretary of the treasury, C. Douglas Dillon, was a moderately progressive Republican who accepted the basic framework of Keynesian economics. A year and a half after he had entered the White House, Kennedy had developed a solid understanding of neo-Keynesian macroeconomics. He made his policy decisions accordingly and assumed the role of a public educator whose objective was to give the American people a sophisticated grasp of economic policy.

The President's first concern was economic expansion; in the recession economy of 1960, the gross national product had increased by an anemic 1.9 percent, and unemployment had averaged 5.5 percent. With ever-larger numbers of young people entering the labor force, the economy would have to grow faster just to maintain the 1960 unemployment rate, but Kennedy's ultimate goal was the achievement of full employment. In 1961, with unemployment peaking at 6.7 percent, he sought to stimulate growth and mitigate the worst effects of the last Eisenhower recession with a multifaceted legislative package: extended unemployment benefits, aid to dependent children of the long-term unemployed, area redevelopment programs, liberalization of social security benefits, an increased minimum wage with extended coverage, an emergency relief program for hard-hit grain farmers, stepped-up housing and slum-clearance efforts. All passed Congress in one form or another, although in some cases, such as the minimum wage, the administration had to settle for less than it requested. In addition, Kennedy used his executive authority to speed up expenditures in many previously authorized federal activities. To stimulate business, he proposed an investment credit, enacted in 1962, which would give corporations a generous tax break on new machinery and equipment. Recovery was already underway before these measures got through Congress, but there can be little doubt that they strengthened it.

Another approach was the expansion of foreign trade, a concept which combined possibilities for domestic growth with Kennedy's diplomatic vision of an economically united Atlantic community. For most of 1962, the administration's highest legislative priority was a bill that would give the executive wide authority to negotiate freer trade with foreign nations. Its passage as the Trade Expansion Act of 1962 was itself enough to encourage an upsurge in both exports and imports. American and European leaders began difficult negotiations in an atmosphere of high expectations and after years of effort would reach agreement on substantial trade liberalization. However, the effect on the domestic economy was at best marginal.

By mid-1962, Kennedy was fully converted to the "new economics." He used a commencement address at Yale as the occasion to launch a widely noted attack against such shibboleths of economic orthodoxy as the necessity of low government spending, the imperative of a balanced federal budget, and the dependence of prosperity upon business confidence in national economic policy. Roosevelt and Truman had in a rough way practiced Keynesian economics, but they had neither understood the doctrine as fully nor defended it so articulately.

With unemployment hovering at about 5.5 percent, the President prepared to take action. He considered asking for large increases in domestic spending, but rejected the idea as politically impossible—especially when piled on top of stepped-up military and space exploration expenditures. Instead, he decided to ask for a general cut in income tax rates, a move calculated to enhance consumer purchasing power. At the beginning of 1963, he made an unprecedented request for a $10 billion tax reduction. Realizing that the short-range effect would be to throw the federal budget far out of balance and substantially increase the national debt, he argued that the bill would create a long-term full-employment equilibrium which would deliver larger tax revenues to the treasury and in the end pay for itself while creating unprecedented prosperity. The argument was sound and sophisticated, but it impressed neither Congress nor the general public. Facing popular apathy and conservative outrage, Kennedy worked skillfully to persuade congressmen. Near the end of September, the measure passed the House of Representatives and went to the Senate, where after further delays it was expected to win approval.

Kennedy was more successful in restraining inflation, a problem he approached with extreme presidential activism. The basic principle he advocated was that corporations must hold the line on prices and that labor unions must permit price restraint by keying wage demands to increases in productivity. He used his power of persuasion to the fullest on Democratic labor leaders, and most of them responded to his efforts by keeping contract settlements at a level that left no excuse for price hikes. When steel industry leaders tried to raise prices after the administration

had persuaded the steelworkers union to agree to a noninflationary contract, the President cracked down hard. He denounced the corporation
executives with some of the harshest antibusiness rhetoric since the militant period of the New Deal, ordered antitrust investigations, threatened
to withhold government contracts, persuaded two of the smaller steel
companies to maintain price stability, and obtained a complete capitulation from the rest of the shell-shocked industry.

It is hard to say whether Kennedy's antiinflation tactics would have
continued to work over an eight-year administration. Some labor unions,
notably the Teamsters and the various dock workers' organizations,
rejected the guidelines from the start. Leaders of other unions were likely
to be under pressures from their memberships which would make each
consecutive moderate wage settlement increasingly difficult. Noncoercive
cajolery from above could hardly override potentially coercive constituency pressures from below. The long-term effectiveness of jawboning
was doubtful. By the same token, the technique of denunciation, dependent as it was upon shock effect, could be employed only sparingly; in fact,
it was used only in the steel controversy, and that single instance poisoned
relations between the administration and the business community.

The historian may doubt that Kennedy had found the magic formula
for combining long-term price stability with sustained economic growth.
Nevertheless, his accomplishments were substantial. Refusing to be
satisfied with the moderate economic recovery of 1961–62, he did much to
educate the nation on the necessity of achieving maximum performance
from the economy and the ways of obtaining it. During his three years in
the White House, the consumer price index was much more stable than it
had been during Eisenhower's second term. His record as an economic
manager was the best of any President in the post–New Deal era.

Part of the Kennedy program for economic growth involved an attack
against the structure of poverty. The initial moves assaulted the problem
in piecemeal fashion, but by 1963 the administration was arriving at a
coherent view of poverty and making plans for a general move on it. The
first important step was the Area Redevelopment Act of 1961, a bill that
liberal Democrats had gotten through Congress in the late 1950s only to
encounter Eisenhower's veto. It provided low-interest loans to bring new
industries into underdeveloped regions. The following year, the President
obtained legislation providing for accelerated public works and job-re-
training programs in chronically depressed areas. His early efforts tended
to focus upon the Appalachian region, largely because of his personal
observations of massive poverty in West Virginia during his presidential
campaign; Appalachia became the beneficiary of multiple federal programs, including much-needed highway construction.

The first attempts to deal with urban poverty were developed by a special presidential committee on juvenile delinquency, headed by Robert Kennedy; by the fall of 1963, it had established ten pilot programs aimed at slum children and characterized by the "community action" principle, the participation of the poor in planning and execution. For the poor in general, the administration revived the "food stamp" program of the New Deal era, which allowed those below a specified income line to buy food coupons at generous discounts. By mid-1963, the President had directed his advisers to go beyond these beginnings and prepare plans for a general attack on poverty.

Kennedy had to deal with one other major domestic issue, the Black Revolution. During the first two years of his Presidency, his support of civil rights, while genuine enough and frequently effective, was dispassionate and cautious. Convinced that he did not have the votes in Congress for major civil rights legislation, he initially decided to confine his legislative efforts to extension of the Eisenhower voting-rights bills and to a constitutional amendment prohibiting the poll tax as a requirement for casting a ballot in a federal election. Both efforts were relatively noncontroversial; the amendment, the twenty-fourth to the Constitution, cleared Congress in August 1962 and was ratified by the states in eighteen months.

Kennedy's use of his presidential authority took several forms. He actively recruited qualified Negroes for important executive positions, most notably Robert Weaver as home finance administrator, and appointed five blacks to federal judgeships, including Thurgood Marshall, who had been the chief counsel of the NAACP. He strengthened antidiscrimination machinery for the federal service and for plants doing government contract work. The Justice Department, under Robert Kennedy, enlarged its civil rights section and undertook a strong drive to enforce legislation already enacted. The administration dispatched marshals and troops to protect "freedom riders" from mob violence in Alabama and to enforce integration at the universities of Mississippi and Alabama. (The University of Alabama incident involved a farcical confrontation with Governor George Wallace, who had promised to block the registration of Negro students by "standing in the schoolhouse door"; he did so, only to be ordered to stand aside by the commander of his own National Guard, which had been mustered into federal service. For all its comic touches, the episode made Wallace the dominant political force in Alabama.) After the 1962 elections, the President signed a long-delayed executive order banning discrimination in housing owned or directly insured by the national government.

In 1963 the fire hoses and police clubs of Birmingham, along with some other instances of segregationist violence, pushed Kennedy further. Although he was afraid that neither the Congress nor the public was prepared for it, he decided to request a comprehensive civil rights bill. The controversial provisions provided for an end to discrimination in places of public accommodation, for wide Justice Department authority to initiate school desegregation cases, and for the withholding of funds from U.S.-assisted programs that practiced discrimination. The bill moved slowly but perceptibly. Kennedy lobbied effectively among Republican leaders in the House and Senate; by the time of his death, the legislation, which now contained a fair-employment provision, had reached the floor of the House. There it seemed assured of passage, but its future in the Senate was more doubtful. What could not be doubted was the President's own commitment.

Although his civil rights policies made him detested in much of the South and his actions in the steel case won him the enmity of business groups, Kennedy appears to have achieved a generally high popularity rating by the fall of 1963; he could look toward the 1964 election with confidence. After his death, his admirers were convinced that he would have gotten the tax cut and civil rights bills through Congress, presided over a full-employment economy, won an overwhelming victory in the 1964 election, and gone on to lead a new era of reform highlighted by passage of the long-overdue Medicare and education bills, more civil rights legislation, and a war on poverty. The proposition is too hypothetical to permit either absolute verification or total refutation. Still, the tax cut and civil rights legislation had at least 50–50 chances by November 1963, and in the upcoming election one can safely assume that Kennedy would have trounced Barry Goldwater, already widely expected to be the Republican candidate, and carried a militantly liberal Congress with him. In such circumstances, he might well have achieved much. As it was, his chief accomplishments at home were those of the educator who prepared the way for others.

THE COLD WAR, POWER, AND RESPONSIBILITY

When Kennedy took office, the cold war was at its worst and most dangerous point since the death of Stalin. The new administration faced difficult situations in Cuba, Laos, and Berlin; Khrushchev in the wake of the U-2 fiasco was at his most belligerent and truculent. Many informed observers felt that the nation had lost a sense of purpose and was experiencing a crisis of confidence, that America's standing and prestige had declined dangerously. Thus it was hardly surprising that the new President was a cold warrior; acceptance of the cold war was imbedded in the broad political consensus to which any serious national political figure subscribed. In 1961 the question was not whether there was or should be a cold war, but rather how to wage it.

As secretary of state, Kennedy selected Dean Rusk, an experienced diplomat, who had served in the State Department under Truman. Rusk was picked to head the department largely because he was less controversial than other possibilities such as Adlai Stevenson, Chester Bowles, or J. William Fulbright. Bland and reserved, Rusk would not be a lightning rod for administration critics in the manner of his mentor, Dean Acheson. Unfortunately, neither would he exercise Acheson's forceful leadership. He possessed, Roger Hilsman observed, both "an intelligence that highlighted complexities rather than ordering them" and "a great skill with the diplomatist's technique of using words that obscure rather than reveal." Gifted in the examination and analysis of policy problems, he might ask penetrating questions in discussion, but somewhat in the manner of an academician presiding over a seminar he masked his own opinion, even from his closest subordinates. His role as a policy advocate was confined to private communications with the President. In larger groups he seldom expressed firm opinions; Arthur Schlesinger, Jr., was struck by his "Buddha-like" demeanor at so many important policy meetings. He was, Schlesinger concluded, essentially "the ideal chief of staff, the perfect number-two man" incapable of exercising the leadership his post demanded.

The new secretary of defense, Robert S. McNamara, was a very different personality. President of the Ford Motor Company in 1960, once a teacher at the Harvard Business School, he combined the qualities of the corporate manager with those of the intellectual. His business success was based largely upon his skill as a cost accountant. Using cost-efficiency techniques, drawing upon new modes of strategic analysis, bringing in "whiz kid" intellectuals to evaluate service requests, strategic concepts, and logistic capabilities, McNamara brought an unprecedented degree of rationality and coordination to the Pentagon. In the process, he established more genuine civilian control over the day-to-day operations of the armed services than had ever existed. His managerial techniques would be less effective when applied to a range of political and diplomatic questions not easily comprehended by quantitative analysis.

Kennedy appears to have been impressed with McNamara and somewhat dissatisfied with Rusk. His central concern, however, was the maintenance of his grip on military and diplomatic policy. To this end he appointed McGeorge Bundy as White House coordinator for national security affairs. A quintessential representative of the northeastern establishment, a committed cold warrior, Bundy was a man of strong views and forceful administrative qualities. He and his staff constituted a diplomatic policy-making center that rivaled the State Department in access to the

President. But, under Kennedy at least, Bundy conceived of his role as the preservation of the President's options; he was not a surrogate secretary of state. Kennedy himself assumed that role.

The new President, like most of the Democrats in the 1950s, had criticized the Eisenhower administration for its reliance on massive retaliation and paper alliances, its overcommitment to right-wing governments, and its mishandling of the Third World. In his policies, his rhetoric, his very appearance, Kennedy sought to project an image of virility and idealism which would contrast with the tired anticommunism of Eisenhower-Dulles years. Thus his inaugural address sought a stance of enlightened toughness: America would pay any price, bear any burden to assure the success of liberty; would not negotiate out of fear but would never fear to negotiate; would support the revolutionary aspirations of the poor around the globe; would work for the freedom of man. One of his first acts was to establish a Peace Corps to do volunteer work in the underdeveloped world. Another early move was the initiation of the Alliance for Progress program designed to invigorate the sick economies of Latin America. During the long period of disorder in the former Belgian Congo, he refused to back right-wing secessionists and threw American support behind United Nations peacekeeping efforts.

Hoping at the same time to give an impression of American strength, Kennedy began an extensive military buildup—from the development of the elite "Green Beret" counterinsurgency forces to a large increase in strategic missile capability—with the aim of permitting varied responses to whatever communist challenges might appear around the world. He challenged the USSR to a space race and committed the nation to the objective of putting a man on the moon within the decade, a goal achieved in 1969 after the spending of many billions of dollars. Finally, he hoped to repair the Western alliance through personal consultation with European leaders and through legislation, the Trade Expansion Act of 1962, which would establish closer economic ties with the North Atlantic democracies.

These brave and hopeful beginnings were, however, quickly dealt a setback by a presidential decision that tarnished the idealistic image New Frontier diplomacy was attempting to achieve, called Kennedy's good judgment into question, and undercut his authority. Shortly after winning the election, Kennedy had been informed of the CIA-managed plan to stage an exile invasion of Cuba. The scheme appealed to his activist instincts, and the CIA was able to obtain support from the entire military establishment. The President approved the invasion with the proviso that there should be no direct U.S. military involvement in the landing itself; he was willing to give extensive clandestine aid to the anti-Castro exiles but believed that they alone should fight within Cuba. The outcome was a disaster. On April 17, 1961, a brigade of 1,400 exiles landed at a southern

Cuban inlet called the Bay of Pigs; with inadequate air and sea support, their situation was hopeless. It took the Castro regime only a couple of days to surround the force, decimate it, and cart the survivors off to prison. Eventually, they would be ransomed by a private, administration-encouraged campaign to buy medical supplies, agricultural equipment, and construction machinery for the Cubans.

The plan was so absurd that one wonders how intelligent men ever conceived it. Its controlling assumption was that the mere fact of landing would touch off an uprising by the Cuban people. In fact, as any objective Latin American specialist knew, Castro had mass support among the lower classes, the majority of the population; moreover, he had the militia and police strength to quash any rebellion, and he proved it by arresting tens of thousands of suspected subversives even as his troops overwhelmed the invaders at the Bay of Pigs. Kennedy publicly accepted full responsibility, although privately he was bitter at the intelligence and military advisers who had given him such firm assurances of success. But whatever the failures of those around him, the ultimate responsibility was indeed Kennedy's, and, unlike Eisenhower, he had no reservoir of prestige to draw upon. By giving the green light to a scheme so rash and badly prepared, he had stumbled badly and thereby impaired his ability to meet other crises.

In the meantime, Kennedy had been forced to come to grips with the perilous and deteriorating situation in Laos. Eisenhower had not hesitated to urge consideration of military intervention when he had outlined the situation to his young successor. Kennedy rather quickly decided, however, that U.S. military intervention in a tiny, landlocked nation on the border of Communist China would be both diplomatically dangerous and logistically untenable. Although the President made some threatening military gestures—the establishment of a few hundred marines in neighboring Thailand, the placing of several thousand others on alert, the movement of the Seventh Fleet into the South China Sea—his objective was to obtain a neutral Laotian government; the military muscle-flexing was designed to forestall a total communist takeover rather than to sustain the ineffective right-wing group which the United States had installed during the Eisenhower era. The communists, perhaps impressed by the possibility of U.S. intervention and doubtless convinced that their long-range position in Laos was strong, toned down their own operations. Agreeing to a cease-fire, they entered into talks for a coalition government; the eventual result was the establishment of a tripartite rightist-neutralist-communist regime headed by the neutralist politician Prince Souvanna Phouma. In July 1962, a fourteen-nation conference at Geneva sanctioned the arrangement; Laos had been officially removed from the cold war.

Actually, the agreement never went into effect. It was persistently violated by the Laotian Communists and by the North Vietnamese, who occupied much of the eastern part of Laos and used it as a supply route into South Vietnam. Later events would underscore the futility of attempting to isolate Laos from the rest of Indo-China. The Laos agreement might have worked as part of a larger neutralization scheme which would have included Vietnam, but the possibility was too hypothetical to merit serious consideration. The political center of gravity in Laos was neutral; such was not the case in either half of Vietnam. It is even *possible* that American disengagement in Laos encouraged the Vietnamese Communists to step up their efforts in the south. The Laotian "settlement" was little more than a fig leaf of respectability for a U.S. retreat.

More importantly, Laos represented a triumph of common sense over obsessive anticommunism. When a nation's power is overextended, strategic retreat is usually the only intelligent solution. Kennedy seemed to realize that the challenge to American interests in Laos was minuscule compared to the challenges facing the United States in Berlin and in Latin America. He knew that if circumstances inhibited him from open intervention in Cuba, a tiny country within America's historic sphere of influence, he should be wary of intervention in a nearly inaccessible nation on the other side of the world. He properly allowed these considerations rather than feelings of personal or national prestige to guide his course.

The most dangerous situation that the new President faced was the long-simmering Berlin crisis. By the beginning of 1961, both sides were locked into relatively rigid negotiating positions—Khrushchev by the unchecked flow of refugees which threatened to drain East Germany of its skilled workers and technicians, Kennedy by the realization that the maintenance of the freedom of West Berlin had become a symbol of American determination to protect all of Western Europe. If the status quo continued, the Soviet leader could anticipate the collapse of his East German puppet government. If the United States retreated in almost any fashion, the whole North Atlantic alliance might disintegrate. Some leeway existed for meaningful negotiation, but not much; even the Soviet suggestion that Berlin might be declared a "free city" appeared too dangerous for serious exploration. The result was a diplomacy of confrontation, a test of will. With both sides feeling that their most vital interests were at stake, the issue, unlike the Bay of Pigs or Laos, posed the actual terrifying possibility of nuclear warfare.

The ambience of an irrevocable conflict increased after Kennedy met personally with Khrushchev at Vienna in June 1961. Not accustomed to the crude truculence characteristic of Soviet diplomacy, Kennedy was shaken by Khrushchev's dogmatic Leninism, his imputation of aggressive intentions to the United States and West Germany, and his belligerent insistence upon signing a peace treaty with East Germany that would abrogate Western rights in Berlin. Hoping to arrive at some sort of sphere-of-influence understanding, Kennedy instead found himself being subjected to an ideological harangue.

A worried President left Vienna with premonitions of the apocalypse. Upon returning to the United States, he ordered greater military preparedness, called up selected reserve units for active duty in Germany, authorized an increased civil-defense program, and attempted to impress on the Russians his willingness to engage in nuclear warfare if the communists tried to seize West Berlin. But during and after his discussions with Khrushchev, he made it clear that his concern was simply to protect the existing American sphere of influence and that he would not interfere with any measures that the Soviet Union might take in the areas under its control. Ultimately, this distinction would allow for resolution of the crisis.

In mid-August, the situation seemed to worsen when the East Germans unexpectedly threw up barriers to halt free access into West Berlin; in a matter of days, they literally transformed the demarcation line into a wall which sealed off the Eastern sector. Movement from East to West, once as easy as taking the subway, became an experience akin to a prison break.* At first, Washington feared this was only the beginning of an orchestrated plan to seal off West Berlin, and the USSR encouraged such apprehensions. Soviet tanks frequently rumbled up to border check points to engage in dangerous confrontations with whatever allied armor might be brought up to face them. Even more ominously, the USSR quit a voluntary atomic test ban it had initiated during the later years of the Eisenhower administration and ostentatiously began to explode huge hydrogen bombs.

The United States for its part stood firm against any threat to the Western sector of the city. The administration ordered reinforcements to the American garrison in West Berlin, dispatched Vice-President Johnson to deliver a morale-boosting address, and recalled to duty as the President's personal representative in Berlin General Lucius D. Clay, remembered as the tough American commander during the blockade of 1948–49. In a variety of ways, the administration let the USSR know that U.S. intelligence had discovered that Russian nuclear missile strength was

---

* One of the most repugnant aspects of a common variety of historical revisionism is its selective morality. Consider Richard J. Walton's treatment of the Berlin situation: "Although one unreservedly and entirely sympathizes with those East Germans who were 'voting with their feet,' as Western propagandists happily put it, they obviously presented a serious problem to East Germany and Russia." Thus, "It was obvious that almost any government with the capacity to stop such a debilitating flow would eventually do so." Perhaps, but Mr. Walton's moralistic indictment of the Kennedy administration as counterrevolutionary would carry more force if he applied his demands for altruistic idealism to non-Western governments as well as to the United States.

much weaker than previously supposed, that hence America knew it was dealing from a position of strength. In fact, however, Soviet belligerence was probably a cover for embarrassment over the method Khrushchev had employed to accomplish his fundamental objective—ending the flow of refugees. Convinced by the fall that the Western powers would make no concessions regarding their position in Berlin, the Russian leader rescinded his year-end deadline for an East German peace treaty and agreed to protracted, ultimately inconclusive negotiations. Over the next several months, the Berlin crisis faded away, ending not with a bang but with a whimper.

THE MISSILES OF OCTOBER

The gradual resolution of the early crises Kennedy faced did not lead to an era of good relations with Moscow, only a lessening of tensions. The administration had sought to avoid overextension of U.S. power and had not attempted to interfere with the Soviet sphere of influence, but had expressed its determination to protect areas in which American interests and commitments were paramount. Hence, the retreat in Laos, the acquiescence in the building of the Berlin Wall, even the fatal limitations on American participation in the Bay of Pigs fiasco; hence also, the unyielding stance in West Berlin, the buildup and diversification of U.S. military forces, and the efforts at closer political and economic ties with Western Europe. But although Kennedy had stated his hope of arriving at a mutually agreed-upon line of demarcation when he had conferred with Khrushchev, it is doubtful that the Soviet leadership even understood, much less trusted, him. Before the cold war could begin to end, the two nations had to experience another crisis, this one the most perilous of the entire postwar era.

As early as August 1962, rumors began to circulate that the Soviet Union was installing offensive missiles in Cuba. Because U-2 intelligence flights revealed only short-range antiaircraft missiles, the administration at first disregarded the stories. On September 4, the Soviet ambassador in Washington delivered a confidential message from Khrushchev to the President in which the Russian leader pledged that no offensive weapons would be placed in Cuba, and the Soviet news agency issued a similar public declaration. Nevertheless, Republican politicians, especially New York Senator Kenneth Keating, took up the allegation. (Keating did not prove particularly helpful when he failed to identify his sources to the chief of the CIA.) Assuming that the Republicans were engaging in exaggerated campaign rhetoric, the administration was stunned when in October U-2 photos revealed the construction of medium-range (1,000 miles) and intermediate-range (2,200 miles) missile-launching sites, being built and guarded by several thousand Russians. Presented with the new information on October 16, the President immediately established an "Executive Committee" (Ex Comm) of leading military and diplomatic advisers to consider the U.S. response. His brother, the attorney general, and his trusted aide Theodore Sorensen acted as his own representatives. For five days, the group engaged in exhausting emotional debate while the President maintained a public façade of business as usual.

The Ex Comm then, and historians later, had to ask just why the missiles were being placed in Cuba. The Soviet motivation for such an audacious move was doubtless complex, but in retrospect four considerations, all considered by the committee, stand out: (1) The USSR hoped to compensate for its long-range missile weakness and redress the balance of power by installing shorter-range missiles in Cuba. (2) The missiles may have been a bargaining device. Perhaps the Russians hoped to trade them off for a favorable Berlin settlement. From a realpolitik viewpoint, there were important similarities between Berlin and Cuba; both were hostile enclaves within well-defined spheres of influence and hence natural subjects for reciprocal bargaining. A somewhat less likely possibility involving an exchange was the chance that the Russians hoped to force a withdrawal of U.S. atomic missiles from Turkey and Italy. (Actually, these missiles were considered obsolete and the administration already had ordered their evacuation.) (3) Having promised to defend Cuba, the USSR was attempting to display its reliability in a big way. (4) The Soviet Union had the grand objective of destroying American credibility by bringing powerful weapons into the back yard of the United States and by extending its influence through Castro into other Latin American nations.

The historian writing a decade later cannot go far beyond this speculation. Khrushchev's memoirs, apparently dictated from memory and possibly "doctored" by Soviet intelligence before being allowed to pass to the West, stress the need to protect Cuba, influence the rest of Latin America, and equalize the balance of power. The explanation is plausible, but the book is too suspect to be treated as definitive. Whatever their motivation, the Soviet leaders would not have taken so expensive and dangerous a step lightly; they must have expected major dividends.

As the Ex Comm considered these and less likely possibilities—for example, that Khrushchev hoped to precipitate an American attack on Cuba and seize Berlin while U.S. military energy was diverted—it concluded that the missiles must not remain. Because it seemed unlikely that diplomatic means alone could pry them out, the discussions moved to two alternatives: either a bombing raid against the missile sites to be followed probably by an all-out invasion; or some sort of limited military gesture, such as a blockade of the island, in conjunction with diplomatic pressure.

The bombing option had some forceful advocates, including former Secretary of State Dean Acheson, but it presented severe moral and military liabilities. Attorney General Kennedy was especially passionate in arguing that the United States could not undertake a Pearl Harbor-style attack against a small country, that to do so would bring procommunist regimes to power throughout the hemisphere, that his brother would go down in history as the American Tojo. Moreover, the consequences of an air strike were incalculable, for it would kill many Russians. Could the USSR take such a move without retaliation? A bombing raid would place the situation far up the escalator that led to World War III; it might put events beyond human control. The President had read Barbara Tuchman's *The Guns of August,* an account of how the Sarajevo crisis of 1914 had set off the chain of events which had precipitated World War I against the wishes, it seemed, of all sides; he did not want some future historian, he told his brother, to write in the same way of the missiles of October. In the end, the uncertainties of a blockade, a step much farther down on the escalator, seemed far preferable to those of a military attack; but if the Russians still refused to yield, the President was prepared to send the bombers.

On Monday, October 22, the President made a nationally broadcast speech in which he revealed the missile-site construction. "This secret, swift, and extraordinary buildup of Communist missiles in an area well known to have a special and historical relationship to the United States . . . is a deliberately provocative and unjustified change in the status quo which cannot be accepted by this country, if our courage and our commitments are ever to be trusted again by either friend or foe." Demanding removal of the missiles and destruction of the launching pads, he announced a naval "quarantine" against the introduction of any more weapons into Cuba. He added two chilling warnings: "Should these offensive military preparations continue, . . . further action will be justified. I have directed the Armed Forces to prepare for any eventualities." And: "It shall be the policy of this Nation to regard any nuclear missile launched from Cuba against any nation in the Western Hemisphere as an attack by the Soviet Union on the United States, requiring a full retaliatory response upon the Soviet Union." Having thus practically written his determination in blood, Kennedy hinted at a way out: "We are prepared to discuss new proposals for the removal of tensions on both sides—including the possibilities of a genuinely independent Cuba. . . ." U.S. destroyers moved into the waters around Cuba; an army division was poised for a possible invasion; the Strategic Air Command, on full war footing, kept many of its

B-52s in the air around the clock; and Polaris submarines left for the preselected areas from which they could hurl their atomic missiles at the USSR. Meanwhile, in Cuba the Soviet construction crews and technicians redoubled their efforts to finish the sites and make their weapons ready for action.

The rest of that week was a confusing mélange of public charges and countercharges, informal diplomacy, and private communications between Kennedy and Khrushchev at a pace so fast that conventional channels could not handle it. Soviet vessels carrying weapons did not challenge the blockade, but work on the missile sites proceeded at a frantic pace. On Friday the 26th, Kennedy received two letters from Khrushchev. One—long, rambling, and emotional—offered to withdraw the missiles in return for a no-invasion pledge; the administration was perfectly amenable to such a deal. But the second, obviously drafted by the Soviet foreign office, demanded a reciprocal withdrawal of U.S. missiles from Turkey; this Kennedy was unprepared to do—he firmly believed it would be taken as a retreat under pressure.

After discussions with the Executive Committee, he decided to ignore the second letter and accept the offer stated in the first; he also sent his brother to the Soviet ambassador to indicate informally that the United States had been planning all along to take the missiles out of Turkey. No one could say whether the gambit would work; the President set October 30 as the tentative date for a military solution. Meeting with Soviet Ambassador Anatoly Dobrynin on the evening of Saturday the 27th, Robert Kennedy did not mince words: "We had to have a commitment by tomorrow that those bases would be removed. I was not giving them an ultimatum but a statement of fact. He should understand that if they did not remove those bases, we would remove them." At that point, the planet was less than seventy-two hours away from World War III.

The next morning, Radio Moscow announced Khrushchev's acceptance of the Kennedy deal. In return for assurances that the United States would not invade Cuba or permit the overthrow of the Castro regime, the USSR would pull out its offensive weapons. That afternoon, the President and his brother met again, and Robert Kennedy recalled the end of their conversation: "As I was leaving, he said, making reference to Abraham Lincoln, 'This is the night I should go to the theater.' I said, 'If you go, I want to go with you.'"

A few weeks of anticlimactic mini-crises followed. Castro adamantly refused to permit onsite inspection, but the administration agreed to confirm the removal of the missiles by sea inspection. Russian captains secured the missiles to their decks, and the U.S. Navy examined them by sight from a distance. Eventually, forty-five medium-range missiles were removed; apparently, no intermediate-range weapons had been delivered before the quarantine. On the island the Soviet work crews bulldozed all that they had accomplished. The United States announced that it would guard against any new missile threat by instituting systematic U-2 reconnaissance. Castro made a final attempt to torpedo the agreement by refusing to return a group of bombers which the USSR had given him, but the United States was firm in its insistence that these also were offensive weapons, and after some Russian arm twisting, the Cuban dictator gave in. By Thanksgiving, it was over.

The United States, it seemed at the time, had won a great victory and Kennedy had scored an enormous personal triumph which made him in a sense the President of the entire Western world. In fact, however, the missile crisis had not brought unalloyed success. Kennedy had made a big concession in guaranteeing the survival of the Castro government; he had in effect renounced freedom of action in his own sphere of influence. If Khrushchev had been primarily concerned with protecting Castro, he had succeeded. If one places the dividends of the crisis on a balance sheet, it is hard to say with confidence who won. At the time, however, everybody *knew*, including the Russians, who made no secret of the fact that they felt humiliated. After Khrushchev was ousted from power in 1964, his successors would openly condemn his "adventurism," and Soviet military leaders would get huge increases in their defense budgets as they made determined steps toward the goal of parity or better with the United States in every category of warmaking. The appearance of a Soviet defeat overpowered any sober studies of the balance sheet.

At the time, only a few dissenters questioned Kennedy's tough handling of the missile situation, but by the late 1960s several revisionist historians and journalists, convinced by the Vietnam war that U.S. foreign policy was dangerously aggressive, had written critical accounts. In the aggregate, they charged that Kennedy had rashly chosen public confrontation over confidential diplomacy and that in any case he had overreacted to a situation which was not dangerous enough to require nuclear brinksmanship. Some analysts attributed the overreaction to politics, others to *machismo* impulses.

The revisionists assumed either that (1) the USSR would have negotiated withdrawal of the missiles without an ultimatum, or (2) the missiles could have remained in Cuba with no serious effect on the national interest. The first assumption usually begs the question of just what concessions would have been necessary to get the missiles back to Russia, but it is reasonable to assume that they might have been very large. Great powers do not engage in international pistol cocking for petty stakes. The second assumption imposes an unfounded degree of rationality upon the world of diplomacy. It is true that the Cuban missiles were mere additions to an already formidable Soviet capacity for nuclear holocaust. At best, however, such an argument is a half-truth. Both sides had the capacity to inflict fearsome devastation upon the other, but in the world of overkill, the Soviet Union could not win. Its armed long-range missiles were too few and unreliable to guarantee the destruction of America; conversely, the United States could have quite literally obliterated Russia. The Cuban missiles then would have made a real difference in the balance of power. For this reason, it is unlikely that they would have been crated up without the payment of a heavy diplomatic ransom.

Still, the Kennedy administration was willing to accept Soviet nuclear parity. Secretary McNamara in time became convinced that parity was the necessary point of departure for meaningful arms-limitation talks. Adopting McNamara's viewpoint, Presidents Kennedy and Johnson made no effort in the next several years to match the rapid Soviet long-range missile buildup. *The important thing about the Cuban missiles was not that they threatened nuclear parity, but that they were in the Western Hemisphere.* Neither Kennedy nor the country he led could have been taken seriously had the intrusion into a long-standing American area of influence been accepted. No one can speak with certainty about the Kremlin's long-range plans, but U.S. tolerance of the Cuban ploy would have at the least encouraged a degree of boldness in Soviet diplomacy.

At the height of the crisis, one of the participants wrote: "It is well known that if one tries to mollify a robber by giving him at first one's purse, then one's coat, etc., the robber will not become more merciful, will not stop robbing. On the contrary, he will become increasingly insolent. Therefore it is necessary to curb the highwayman in order to prevent the jungle law from becoming the law governing relations between civilized people and states." The writer was Nikita Khrushchev. From his frame of reference, the bandit was the United States, but the analysis may have been more self-revealing than he intended.

THE GREAT DETENTE

If the Cuban missile crisis had accomplished nothing else, it had brought the two great powers to the brink of the precipice. Having looked into the abyss, they now were eager to seek accommodation. One item that was both dramatic and negotiable was the frightening nuclear testing in which both nations had engaged; the USSR especially had been culpable of employing it as a terror tactic. By the end of 1962, the two countries, having just completed a series of tests, were ready to begin discussions.

In the negotiations that followed, the major stumbling block was the problem of inspection. Khrushchev at first made what was for him an important concession by stating his willingness to accept an agreement which would include three onsite inspections a year. Kennedy might have gone along if the decision had been his alone, but he was convinced that a treaty providing for so few inspections could never get through the Senate. In fact, talks with the Russians had hardly begun before Republicans and conservative Democrats were denouncing the very idea of a test-ban pact.

In order to counter such objections, Kennedy delivered one of the most notable addresses of his Presidency at American University on June 9, 1963. His central thesis was that whatever the distribution of blame and virtue in the cold war, it was to a great extent a situation that fed on *mutual* suspicion. A relaxation of tensions thus required a reexamination of attitudes on *both* sides. Moreover, despite their many differences, the two superpowers had a mutual interest in seeking peace and halting the arms race. The way to begin was by ending nuclear tests; a treaty to do so might not provide absolute security but it would give America much more security than a steadily escalating arms race. "We all inhabit this small planet," he declared. "We all breathe the same air. We all cherish our children's future. And we are all mortal."

In July an American delegation headed by W. Averell Harriman arrived in Moscow to negotiate an end to atomic testing. They quickly discovered that Khrushchev had reversed the Soviet position on inspection, which he now declared unacceptable. It remained possible, however, to work out a limited agreement which would terminate atmospheric tests, easily detectable without inspection. By the end of the month, work on the document was completed. Despite overwhelming public sentiment in favor of ending radioactive pollution of the atmosphere, Senate approval was by no means assured. There also existed a widespread distrust of Russia, and the military establishment especially tended to be dismayed by *any* form of conciliation. Kennedy won over the suspicious by pledging the continuance of underground tests and immediate resumption of open-air detonations if the USSR violated the treaty. In September the Senate gave its consent by a healthy margin of 80–19.

As Kennedy seems to have realized, the test-ban pact was only a modest step. The two major signatories continued with vast programs of underground experimentation, and two other nuclear powers, Communist China and France, refused to adhere to the treaty. Nevertheless, the agreement did much to alleviate a very important atmospheric danger, and it had a considerable symbolic value. Khrushchev talked grandly of following it up with a general nonagression pact, and the United States and USSR worked out some other small agreements—the establishment of a "hot line" communication system between the White House and the Kremlin, the sale of surplus American wheat to Russia. These steps down the escalator had not ended the cold war or the arms race, but they represented significant progress in that direction. In the fall of 1963, it was possible to hope that mankind was just beginning a journey toward a safer and saner world.

By then, however, one ominous shadow was increasingly prominent on the horizon—Vietnam. The U.S. interest in Southeast Asia was well established by the time Kennedy became President. The Japanese occupation of southern Vietnam in 1941 had triggered the events that led to Pearl Harbor. Afterward, the region had been caught up in the cold war with the United States funneling aid to the French struggle against the Viet Minh from 1950 to 1954 and then to the anticommunist government established in Saigon. When Kennedy took office, 2,000 American advisers were in South Vietnam attempting to organize the fight against the guerrillas. The administration accepted the ongoing policy without subjecting it to the hard reevaluation which marked Kennedy's handling of Laos. It surely is an exaggeration to say, as have Arthur Schlesinger, Jr., and other Kennedy admirers, that the President had no choice, but it is true that his room for maneuver was more limited than in Laos. It is also true that throughout the Kennedy administration other problems—Cuba, Laos, Berlin, the missile crisis, atomic testing—were all more urgent

It also appears that the policy makers in Washington did not until a very late date have a realistic picture of the Vietnamese situation. Diplomatic and military reports from officials emotionally committed to the South Vietnamese regime were radiant with optimism. In reality, the Saigon government of Ngo Dinh Diem was repressive, unpopular, and increasingly unstable; allied with the landowners and upper classes, it gave only lip service to U.S. suggestions for social and economic reform. Its army was ineffective and demoralized, gutted of much of its best leadership after the failure of a military coup in November 1960; moreover, U.S. advisers were training the South Vietnamese army for a Korean-style war and leaving them ill prepared to cope with the developing guerrilla rebellion. As a result of all these factors, the Viet Cong insurgency was constantly growing in strength and audacity.

In April 1961 Vice-President Johnson led a mission to Saigon and returned urging strong economic assistance and military aid programs to sustain what he considered a solemn U.S. commitment. In October 1961 another trip, headed by General Maxwell Taylor and White House national security aide Walt Rostow, produced a similar report. By naming a prominent military figure to lead the U.S. delegation, Kennedy had almost guaranteed an emphasis on the military dimension of the Vietnam problem. There were prominent dissenters within the administration—Chester Bowles argued for an attempt to neutralize all Southeast Asia; Averell Harriman, John Kenneth Galbraith, and Roger Hilsman all asserted in one fashion or another that the problem was primarily political, that the only way to solve it was to get rid of Diem. Still, Kennedy passed over their suggestions, perhaps because in the nature of things they could offer no solid, easily implemented alternatives to the Taylor-Rostow report. In late 1961 the United States began the dispatch of military advisers; by November 1963, there would be 16,000 of them in South Vietnam, most of them working in the field with Vietnamese combat units.

On the surface, the program seemed to be working. For a time, the Viet Cong was more cautious in its activity. The government attempted to mobilize the countryside by pulling the peasants into fortified "strategic hamlets" where they purportedly would be safe from Viet Cong terrorists. The reports that came back to the Pentagon, the State Department, and the White House all reflected the power of positive thinking. Some upon close analysis were ludicrous—it was claimed that 30,000 casualties were inflicted upon the Viet Cong in 1962, although its strength had been estimated at only 15,000 at the beginning of that year—but Washington was impressed. Only the dispatches of the American newsmen displayed an on-the-spot skepticism.

Suddenly, in the summer of 1963, there came the jolting realization that Diem was in serious trouble. His repression of his Buddhist political opponents had become so vicious as to create resentment throughout his country. Several Buddhist monks chose the ultimate protest of public suicide by self-immolation, events that unbelieving Americans watched on the evening news. As Diem remained unyielding, the opposition to him increased both in South Vietnam and in the United States. A number of South Vietnamese generals made discreet inquiries about U.S. neutrality in the event of a coup. Washington's reaction was equivocal; in effect, the United States would neither support nor oppose such a move. On November 1, 1963, after weeks of rumors, the blow came; the generals seized power and summarily shot Diem and his brother Ngo Dinh Nhu. Kennedy was stunned by the assassinations, but the new regime was presumably more in tune with popular opinion. Momentarily, it appeared that the Vietnamese situation might improve. Three weeks later, John F. Kennedy was shot and killed in Dallas, Texas.

Within a few years, historians and other intellectuals, mesmerized by the spectacle of disaster in Vietnam, would reduce an evaluation of Kennedy the diplomatist to the question of what he would have done in Southeast Asia. Revisionist critics were convinced he would have pursued about the same policy as his successor. As Richard Walton put it, he "pushed to its logical, tragic conclusion in Vietnam the course begun by Harry Truman and carried on by Dwight Eisenhower." Such statements are nonsense; at Kennedy's death, not a single American combat unit was fighting in Vietnam and not a single bomb was being dropped on the north; the 16,000 U.S. advisers of 1963, all of them professional soldiers, represented, to engage in comic understatement, a somewhat smaller contingent than the half-million man, draftee, full-combat situation of 1968. Kennedy had not left his successor with a no-exit road to disaster.

His admirers were convinced that he would have dealt with Southeast Asia in the same cool, restrained manner as he had handled Laos. Their case is convincing—Kennedy had demonstrated that he understood that American power was limited; moreover, his public and private statements on Vietnam in the months before his death made it clear that he did not contemplate a full U.S. combat role there. In a television interview on September 3, 1963, he had declared that the South Vietnamese government could win the war only with the support of its people. The United States could send equipment and advisers, but "in the final analysis, it is their war. . . . They have to win it, the people of Vietnam." Still, even knowledge of a President's *intentions* does not allow the historian to predict his *actions* at a later point in time. It is ultimately as impossible to say how Kennedy would have reacted to the circumstances of 1965 as to say how Franklin D. Roosevelt would have dealt with the Soviet Union after World War II. In either case, real circumstances might have overwhelmed intentions.

One can only measure Kennedy's performance on Vietnam against the world context at the time of his death. There can be no doubt that his Vietnam policy had failed. He had handled the problem rather absentmindedly, and the situation that he passed on to his vice-president was worse than the one he had inherited. All the same, by November 1963, Vietnam still was a minor concern, albeit a growing one; Kennedy had been preoccupied with problems which not only *seemed* but actually were greater at the time. In managing such difficult matters as Laos, Berlin, the Cuban missiles, atomic testing, and the whole problem of cold-war deescalation, he displayed a capacity for growth and a sense of balance which justly earned him the leadership of Western democratic civilization and carried the conduct of American diplomacy to its highest point in the twentieth century.

ELEVEN

LBJ, the Great Society, and the Little War

CHRONOLOGY

1963–68

1963

NOVEMBER   Lyndon B. Johnson sworn in as President after assassination of Kennedy

1964

JANUARY   Anti-U.S. rioting in Panama

FEBRUARY   Kennedy tax-cut bill passes Congress

MAY   Johnson calls for a "Great Society" at University of Michigan

JULY   Civil Rights Act of 1964

AUGUST   Economic Opportunity Act; Gulf of Tonkin incidents

NOVEMBER   Johnson swamps Goldwater in presidential election

1965

FEBRUARY   United States begins regular bombing campaign against North Vietnam

APRIL   Elementary and Secondary Education Act; Johnson calls for peace and economic development in Vietnam; U.S. Marines sent to Dominican Republic

JUNE   U.S. troop strength in Vietnam reaches 75,000

JULY	Medicare Act; Johnson announces major escalation of U.S. involvement in Vietnam
AUGUST	Civil Rights Act of 1965; Housing Act of 1965
OCTOBER	Congress passes immigration reform and antipollution legislation
NOVEMBER	Congress passes aid to higher education
DECEMBER	U.S. troop strength in Vietnam reaches 180,000

1966

JUNE	U.S. troop strength in Vietnam reaches 285,000
SEPTEMBER	Model Cities Act
OCTOBER	Johnson speaks to troops in Vietnam
NOVEMBER	Democrats suffer heavy losses in congressional elections
DECEMBER	U.S. troop strength in Vietnam reaches 389,000

1967

JUNE	U.S. troop strength in Vietnam reaches 463,000
NOVEMBER	Secretary McNamara nominated to head World Bank

1968

JANUARY	Tet offensive begins
FEBRUARY	U.S. troop strength in Vietnam reaches nearly 500,000
MARCH	Clark Clifford succeeds McNamara as secretary of defense; My Lai massacre; General Westmoreland requests 206,000 additional troops; Eugene McCarthy nearly defeats Johnson in New Hampshire presidential primary; Robert F. Kennedy declares candidacy for Presidency; Johnson announces partial bombing halt, withdraws from presidential race
APRIL	Assassination of Martin Luther King, large-scale rioting
JUNE	Assassination of Robert Kennedy; Congress passes tax surcharge
AUGUST	Rioting at Democratic convention in Chicago
OCTOBER	Johnson announces total halt to bombing of North Vietnam
NOVEMBER	Nixon narrowly defeats Humphrey

"This is a sad time for all people," said Lyndon B. Johnson, returning to Washington as President of the United States on November 22, 1963. "We have suffered a loss that cannot be weighed. . . . I will do my best. That is all I can do." The rhetoric was characteristically clumsy; the new Chief Executive was a doer, not a talker. During the next five years, Lyndon Johnson would lead America through an era of frenetic activity and bitter controversy, lifting the nation out of the despair of the Kennedy assassination only to leave it in a mood of even deeper despair. His ambitions were vast, his vanity overweening; the result was a record of major achievement and enormous failure. Johnson's chief enemy was himself; his insecurity led him into a crudeness, arrogance, secretiveness, and defensiveness that combined to deny him what he coveted most—the trust and love of the American people. Always, however, both his friends and his foes could agree on one proposition: He was larger than life.

LBJ

Born into a relatively poor Texas farm family in 1908, the young Johnson had discovered in politics a natural outlet for his driving ambition and shrewd intelligence—his father and both his grandfathers had served in the Texas legislature. Coming to Washington in 1931 as the legislative assistant of a Texas congressman, given the tutelage and patronage of his father's old friend Sam Rayburn, he soon demonstrated a talent for comprehending and wringing favors out of the complex bureaucracy that was thrown up during the early days of the New Deal. In 1935 Rayburn's sponsorship got him an appointment as Texas director of the National Youth Administration. Returning to his home state, he administered the program with a vigor and imagination that squeezed a maximum number of jobs for unemployed youth out of a minimum budget; in the process, he garnered favorable publicity and built an organization. In 1937, running as an unreserved supporter of the New Deal, he outpolled nine opponents to win a special election for a seat in the House of Representatives.

Johnson quickly became a friend and protégé of FDR—on the day of Roosevelt's death, the congressman tearfully told a journalist friend, "He was like a daddy to me." But with the changing temper of Texas politics it was difficult to be a New Dealer and continue to climb the political ladder. In 1941, running in a special senatorial election with Roosevelt's endorsement, Johnson was narrowly defeated by W. Lee "Pappy" O'Daniel, a right-wing demagogue previously best known as a hillbilly entertainer. Thereafter, Johnson developed a moderate-conservative image. In 1948 he tried again for the Senate, this time defeating the conservative governor of Texas, Coke Stevenson, by a margin of 87 votes out of nearly a million ballots. The victory, which Stevenson disputed with charges of fraud, brought Johnson the sobriquet "Landslide Lyndon."

The Senate was Johnson's element. With his instincts for power relationships, he quickly grasped that the body was run by the southern and "border state" Democrats rather than by the disorganized and in-dividualistic northern liberals. He cultivated the power structure so as-siduously that in 1951, he was elected Democratic whip and in 1953 Democratic leader. His rapid rise to power and his conservatism con-solidated his home-state power base, leaving him free to manage the Senate. In the next few years he would become a Washington legend.

Johnson's control of the upper chamber was never absolute, but few men in American history were more powerful legislative leaders. Ideo-logically, he based his influence on a bipartisan centrism which rejected excessive conflict with the popular Eisenhower. But the real source of his mastery over the upper house was his understanding of the nature of power and his fabled skill at the art of persuasion. The post of Senate Democratic leader was not exactly dictatorial, but it entailed substantial control over committee assignments and permitted some discretion in assigning office space or rendering many other small favors. After the Democrats captured Congress in 1954, Johnson set the Senate calendar and would not hesitate to impose marathon sessions on his colleagues if necessary to obtain passage of an important bill. He constructed an "in-telligence" system which outpaced any opposition in ferreting out the attitudes and plans of other senators and getting vote commitments from them. Finally, Johnson himself subjected waverers to "the treatment." Beginning as an exhortation to "come, let us reason together," Johnsonian persuasion usually developed into a monologue, anticipating and dispos-ing of arguments, appealing to the emotions, dangling rewards, frequently overwhelming the recipient. With these resources and with an inexhaust-ible reserve of energy, Johnson put his stamp on the Senate and began to win a reputation as the greatest legislator of his time.

Inescapably, his ambitions turned toward the White House. He hardly had become Democratic leader before his aides began to remind reporters that Texas was really a *western* state and that Johnson was hence not a traditional southerner. Presenting himself as a moderate, Johnson softened his previously tough position on racial problems and got the civil rights bills of 1957 and 1960 through the Senate. Although weak, the legislation was the first of its kind since Reconstruction and, given the indifference of the Eisenhower administration, was a considerable achievement. All the same, the senator was too much of a moderate to appeal to the liberals who dominated the Democratic presidential party. Beyond his ideological position, moreover, his style—that of the noveau riche Texan—was unlikely to appeal to many northern urbanites. Unwilling to risk the primaries, Johnson hoped to win the 1960 Democratic nomination on his reputation as Senate leader; instead, swamped by the Kennedy organization, he wound up as the running mate of a man he never had taken seriously as a senator.

In the close campaign that followed, Johnson played a key role in holding Texas and a portion of the South for the Democratic ticket. For the next three years, however, it seemed that this effort might be the last hurrah of a colorful, successful career. Like most of his predecessors in the office, he discovered that the vice-presidency was synonymous with powerlessness and obscurity. His relationship with Kennedy was good, and the President gave him occasional assignments, usually involving foreign travel, which allowed for episodic public visibility. But no one pretended that Johnson was a major adviser on diplomacy or even domestic politics. Some in the White House circle, including Robert Kennedy, treated the vice-president with contempt and hostility. Near the end of 1963, there were widely reported rumors, probably untrue, that Johnson was to be dumped from the ticket in 1964. Comedians who specialized in political humor could usually milk a laugh out of an audience by asking whatever had happened to Lyndon Johnson. Suddenly, on November 22, 1963, everything was changed.

The new President's characteristics were on the table for all to see; Johnson was not adept at self-concealment. First and foremost were his ostentatious provincialism and crudeness, traits that he flaunted, perhaps as a way of dealing with feelings of insecurity about his background and his legitimacy as an accidental President. His favorite social function, to which he frequently subjected unwary foreign leaders, was the Texas-style barbecue. After he underwent gall bladder surgery in 1965, he lifted his shirt at a press conference to display the scar. Inviting a group of female reporters for a ride around his ranch, he drove his Lincoln Continental at ninety miles an hour while drinking beer and delivering what one of his passengers described as a graphic description of the sex life of a bull. He outraged animal lovers when he allowed a photographer to snap him while he was holding a pet beagle off the ground by its ears. His private conversations tended to be filled with scatalogical references, and his grossness made even worldly men blanch. Annoyed at a journalist who wasted his time with an insignificant question, he said: "Why do you come and ask me, the leader of the Western world, a chicken-shit question like that?" On another occasion, he introduced the secretary general of NATO to reporters and then excused himself with the remark, "I'm going to have a piss." Such actions were typical, and many observers considered him the personification of backwoods vulgarity.

By the time he moved into the White House, Johnson had acquired a deserved reputation as a politician who sought as much power as possible and exercised it relentlessly. He wanted absolute control over every situation he had to manage. Few if any Presidents had given more attention to relatively minor details, whether the selection of bridges and highways to be bombed in North Vietnam or the choosing of subcabinet officials. He was obsessed with secrecy. Probably no President had ever before canceled a planned appointment to a governmental position because advance word leaked to the press; Johnson seems to have done so on several occasions.

Few Presidents had ever treated their subordinates with such abuse and contempt. He did more than drive his staff hard—any group of presidential aides must expect that—he resorted to tongue-lashings and gestures of disdain in the presence of outsiders. He made his vice-president, Hubert Humphrey, personally clear every use of the vice-presidential plane with him, seized opportunities to remind Humphrey of his total dependence, and forced him to behave with a demeaning servility. In short, he sought to dominate those around him by humiliating them. Nor was he above making ugly threats if he thought it necessary. One story —unfortunately very believable—had him warning an official who was about to resign in disagreement with an administration policy that if he did so, he would be pursued by two men for the rest of his life—the directors of the Federal Bureau of Investigation and the Internal Revenue Service. The wisest among Johnson's friends and advisers regularly turned down appointments that would have placed them under his control. His obsessive concealment and dictatorial capriciousness may or may not have been effective as a way of managing the executive branch, but they seriously impaired his effort to gain the public trust every President needs.

Concealed beneath Johnson's heavy-handedness was a remarkable subtlety in dealing with most persons and situations he could not dominate. A shrewd practical psychologist, he was the consummate personality analyst of twentieth-century American politics. Instinctively, he reached for the arguments which made strong-willed men reverse irrevocable decisions. He employed eloquent appeals to duty and patriotism, for example, in persuading Chief Justice Warren to head a special investigation into the assassination of President Kennedy or in talking Supreme Court Justice Arthur Goldberg into becoming U.S. ambassador to the United Nations. With other politicos, such as the wily old Senate Republican leader Everett McKinley Dirksen, he might use these appeals, but he also knew when to offer a trade and how far to compromise. He spent half his waking hours on the phone "wheeling and dealing" for support. In domestic politics especially, he practiced the art of the possible, usually with great success.

Despite his vicious bullying of those he could dominate, Johnson possessed a deep strain of sentimentality and generosity. He lavished gifts upon his employees—a new station wagon for his harassed and brow-beaten press secretary, for example, or a $26,000 sinecure for the husband of his favorite secretary. He had a genuine feeling for the plight of the underdog; he really believed in civil rights legislation, in the war on poverty, even in TVAs on the Mekong River. If he once had adopted the role of a conservative as a matter of political self-preservation, he was again able to be a liberal who still revered the memory of Franklin D. Roosevelt and admired Harry S Truman, while seeking to outdo them. Now that he was President of all the people, he wanted to lead them all to a better life. In turn, he wanted them to think of him as their benefactor; and above all, he wanted their love.

Outsized in his talents, energies, and emotions, unrivaled in his capacity for domination, manipulation, and self-pity, he overwhelmed most of the mortals who surrounded him and placed his own brand on five years of American history. One of his most loyal assistants, Jack Valenti, remarked that the President seemed to have extra glands. Musing over Johnson's bunkhouse language, his appetite for power, and his lofty ideals, Wilbur Cohen, his secretary of health, education, and welfare, described him as "a combination of Boccaccio and Machiavelli and John Keats." He was, Henry Cabot Lodge remembered, a giant in all his qualities: "His virtues seem huge and his vices seem like monstrous warts, almost goiters."

THE GREAT SOCIETY AND THE ELECTION OF 1964

The new President from the beginning radiated strength and deter-mination. He pledged himself to follow the policies of his predecessor and in the months that followed displayed great energy, talent, and shrewdness in doing so. It was undeniable that his advantages were great—the shock of Kennedy's assassination had generated an enormous wave of sympathy for his successor; the Kennedy administration had lobbied effectively and almost certainly would have obtained passage of at least the tax bill anyway. But Johnson was an even stronger legislative leader. Kennedy had been a lackluster senator in the eyes of his colleagues, while Johnson had been awesome. Kennedy had fairly rigorously separated his social and political lives; Johnson was incapable of doing so. He lived politics twenty-four hours a day and enjoyed a far greater rapport with the average congressman than Kennedy ever had possessed.

By mid-1964, he had completed the two major pieces of unfinished business that the Kennedy administration had left him. In February the tax-cut bill finally cleared Congress; its passage would set off one of the great economic booms of American history. The civil rights bill took longer, but here Johnson's conviction was strong and emotional. As vice-president, freed from his dependence upon Texas conservatives, he had quickly established himself as an eloquent spokesman for black aspirations and had achieved good relations with the Negro organizations. As a southerner, moreover, he faced political imperatives similar to those which Kennedy had met on the issue of aid to Catholic education—he could not compromise. The President ordered his Senate leader, Mike Mansfield, to suspend all other business until civil rights legislation had been passed; after a fifty-seven-day filibuster, he persuaded Everett Dirksen to provide the GOP votes necessary to end debate and allow for a vote. The resulting civil rights act of 1964 was the most comprehensive since Reconstruction and, observers believed, far tougher than any legislation Kennedy could have achieved. The major provisions included the strongest safeguards yet for the right to vote; a prohibition against discrimination by most places of public accommodation; various aid programs to assist school districts in the process of desegregation; a ban against discrimination in any federally assisted program; the outlawing of discrimination in most forms of employment on grounds of race, color, religion, sex, or national origin; and the establishment of an Equal Employment Opportunity Commission to enforce the employment provisions. The new law did not create a racial utopia, but despite difficulties of enforcement, it served as a large opening wedge in the drive to gain better opportunities for blacks and ultimately for women as well.

The President displayed his talents and energies in other ways. He personally negotiated the settlement of a critical railway labor dispute. He took what had been a hopelessly stalled bill to provide price supports for wheat and engineered its passage by marrying it to cotton supports for southern farmers and food stamps for the needy. By mid-1964, the transition from the Kennedy to the Johnson administration was nearly complete. Speaking at the University of Michigan on May 22, the President outlined his ambitions and enunciated the slogan by which he wanted his administration to be remembered. He proclaimed the goal of a "Great Society," characterized by abundance and liberty for all, by an end to poverty and racial injustice. For the cornerstone of the Great Society, he eagerly adopted the antipoverty program which the Kennedy administration had been preparing.

With a characteristic intensive lobbying effort, Johnson pushed the beginnings of a war on poverty through. Congress in whirlwind fashion. The result, the Economic Opportunity Act of 1964, was a milestone in the history of social legislation. A complex amalgam of educational and training programs (the Job Corps, Neighborhood Youth Corps, Adult Basic Education, and Work Experience and Training), loan programs for rural families and cooperatives and for urban small businesses, aid programs for migrant workers, and a "domestic peace corps" called Volunteers in Service to America (VISTA), the act was the foundation of what would become a massive new federal program. It was the most ambitious example of welfare liberalism to clear Congress since the New Deal; yet it had been rushed through with surprising rapidity and remarkably little debate. The achievement was a testimonial to Johnson's legislative skill, but it allowed little time for intelligent debate, careful analysis, or sober second thoughts. Instead, the atmosphere of exuberance that attended the initiation of the war on poverty did much to create expectations that could not be fulfilled.

Yet, while pursuing the most liberal legislative agenda in American history, Johnson took care to cultivate the image of a political moderate. He wooed the leaders of the business community by ostentatiously seeking their advice and praising their importance.* He sought to present himself as a tightfisted advocate of government economy by paring his first budget to just below $100 billion and by the ludicrous device of ordering a drastic reduction in the bright lighting in and around the White House. He used his Texas background to appeal to southern conservatives and moderates for votes or at least for a measure of tolerance. His objective was to create a climate of consensus so broad that it would fragment and isolate the ideological opposition. Like Roosevelt at the beginning of the New Deal, he had used an atmosphere of crisis to create something resembling a national will and to push innovative programs through Congress. It was a magnificent juggling act. It could not be sustained indefinitely, but the campaign and election of 1964 gave Johnson a magnificent opportunity to prolong it.

---

* Business leaders, John Maynard Keynes told Franklin D. Roosevelt in 1938, would respond to those political leaders who extended the same sort of attention and understanding that a patient master would give to a house pet which had been badly trained. "They are . . . much milder than politicians, at the same time allured and terrified by the glare of publicity, easily persuaded to be 'patriots,' perplexed, bemused, indeed terrified, yet only too anxious to take a cheerful view, vain perhaps but very unsure of themselves,

Since its narrow defeat of 1960, the Republican party had been floundering. The 1962 elections had failed to produce the normal midterm gain for the minority party. Richard Nixon had removed himself from serious contention for the 1964 nomination by losing his race for governor of California. The apparent front-runner, Governor Nelson Rockefeller of New York, had severe handicaps which even his wealth and crowd appeal could not overcome. As a moderate leader of the eastern establishment, he was regarded with suspicion by the midwestern-western conservative, middle-class hard core of the Republican party, and he greatly enhanced these suspicions by divorcing his wife of thirty-two years and promptly marrying a recent divorcee with several children. Nevertheless, he waged a hard campaign for the presidential nomination and effectively froze out other moderates such as Henry Cabot Lodge, Jr., or Governor William Scranton of Pennsylvania.

By 1964, Rockefeller's major challenger was Senator Barry Goldwater of Arizona. Since his election to the Senate in 1952, Goldwater had become nationally known as an important spokesman of traditional Republican conservatism with his book, *The Conscience of a Conservative* (1960), and with a nationally syndicated newspaper column. Personally one of the most sincere and likable men in America public life, he was nevertheless identified with an ill-tempered, reactionary movement that sought to refight the battles of the New Deal and take America back to the days of Calvin Coolidge. One of the significant political phenomena of the early 1960s had been the emergence of a radical right, disillusioned with the moderate conservatism of the Eisenhower administration and disgruntled with the liberalism of the Kennedy administration. In its most visible and extreme form, the radical right was exemplified by the John Birch Society and a few small paramilitary organizations such as the Minutemen; in a more general and less tangible form, the radical right represented the emotions, if not always the reason, of the firmest supporters of the Republican party.

Not given to the equivocation characteristic of most politicians, Goldwater spoke directly to these emotions. At one time or another, he had condemned the Tennessee Valley Authority, the graduated income tax, social security, and virtually the entire achievement of the New Deal and its successor reform movements. To this, he added a rhetorically militant anticommunism which made him sound like a militarist warmonger; without really meaning it, he would toss off such recipes for

pathetically responsive to a kind word.'' An overstatement, no doubt, but the moderate segments of the business community responded to Johnson's symbolic attentions in a way that demonstrated a deep hunger for some minimal recognition from a Democratic President.

World War III as, "Let's lob one into the men's room of the Kremlin." And what of the northeastern Republican establishment? "Sometimes I think this country would be better off if we could just saw off the Eastern Seaboard and let it float out to sea." Such remarks might delight a militant and frustrated minority, but to the general public they labeled Goldwater as an extremist.

The dedication and militance of Goldwater's following proved more than a match for the "softer" appeal of the politically handicapped Rockefeller. In the politics of nomination at any level, the committed minority, "extremist" or not, often exercises an influence out of proportion to its numbers; such was the case with the Goldwater movement. Rockefeller's supporters were, in the main, disspirited by their candidate's controversial personal life and in any event inclined toward moderation and political independence; Goldwater's supporters, on the whole, were devoted and frustrated Republicans in revolt against the political trends of a generation, convinced that across the country there existed a vast silent vote alienated from the post–New Deal political consensus and ready to return the nation to the faith of the fathers if only given the proper candidate. It was this enthusiasm which carried the decisive presidential primary—California—for Goldwater by a narrow margin and assured him the Republican nomination.

Meeting in San Francisco, the Republican convention degenerated into an orgy of right-wing vituperation. The pro-Goldwater galleries hooted and jeered when Rockefeller and other moderate Republicans attempted to speak. Network news commentators complained of an unusual amount of verbal abuse from the delegates. Triumphantly nominated on the first ballot, Goldwater chose as his running mate Representative William Miller, an upstate New Yorker so conservative that he was retiring from Congress because of a strong prospect of defeat in November. The candidate's acceptance speech was in keeping with the tone of the proceedings. In foreign policy, it asserted a militant anticommunism; at home, it depicted an America caught up in bureaucracy and collectivism, suffering from moral aimlessness and decay. In the keynote phrase of the speech, deliberately italicized by its writers, Goldwater declared: *"Extremism in the defense of liberty is no vice! . . . Moderation in the pursuit of justice is no virtue!"* From the beginning, the Goldwater campaign was a no-compromise defense of yesterday, attempting to bring out the hypothesized silent vote with the slogan, "A Choice, Not an Echo."

With such an enemy, Johnson needed no friends. Advocate of civil rights, champion of the Great Society, big spender and tax cutter, he could nevertheless depict himself as a moderate aligned with the reassuring forces of continuity. He could select as his vice-presidential candidate one of the most effective liberals in Congress, Hubert Humphrey, yet still appear to be in the center of the road. He could unleash bombers against North Vietnam on a retaliatory raid; yet Goldwater still seemed more the warmonger. It was easy to picture the Republican candidate as a dangerous radical and a positive threat to the complex fabric of social-political-economic relationships that had emerged from the New Deal and World War II.

To millions of Americans who were normally inclined toward the Republican party, Goldwater was thus anything but a conservative. When asked if the black riots of Summer 1964 might create a "white backlash" that would benefit Goldwater, Johnson replied that the "frontlash" of deserters from the GOP would overwhelm whatever backlash developed. At the highest level, he and Humphrey enjoyed a nearly solid phalanx of support from the Republican business and financial establishment. At a more prosaic, if ultimately more important, level, they would get the ballots of millions who had voted enthusiastically for Dewey, Eisenhower, and Nixon. Johnson was an energetic campaigner, often entertaining and effective with his Texas style ("Y'all come down and hear the speakin' "), but the dimensions of his landslide were more a measure of feeling against Goldwater than for the President.

On election day, Johnson and Humphrey polled 61.1 percent of the popular vote, a margin of nearly 16 million; they carried every state except five from the segregationist Deep South and Goldwater's own Arizona. Their party compiled its most impressive congressional majorities since the New Deal had reached high tide with the Roosevelt landslide of 1936. The Democrats controlled the Senate 68-32 and, most importantly, the House of Representatives, 295-140. It was at the least debatable that the millions who had voted against Goldwater had meant to endorse a new age of reform, but the Democratic victory had cleared the way for one.

Johnson understood the limitations of his mandate; he realized, he said, that his support was like the Rio Grande, broad but not deep. Thus he was determined to move rapidly, for he knew that as the Goldwater specter receded, American political patterns would move back toward stalemate. The President's objective was no less than the passage of reform legislation as extensive and far-reaching as that put through Congress by his idol, FDR. During the first half of 1965, one bill after another went up to the Hill, overwhelming congressmen who were resentful at "rubber stamp" demands, yet awed by the dimensions of the 1964 vote.

One of Johnson's top priorities was Medicare, an issue that had been deferred for two decades. The Medicare Act of 1965 provided substantial health-insurance coverage for persons over sixty-five as part of the social security system; the Republican alternative, a voluntary plan financed directly by small monthly payments from the participants, was simply incorporated into the legislation as a device which would cover doctors' fees and some other services not included in the basic plan. The law was much more restricted than the sweeping universal national health insurance which Harry S Truman had advocated twenty years earlier, but Johnson, who flew to Independence, Missouri, to sign the bill in Truman's presence, had gotten a law that would deliver real benefits to a large and needy portion of the population and would serve as an opening wedge for extension of health benefits. (In 1973, despite the Nixon economy drive, Congress would pass legislation providing for federal payment of the catastrophic expenses connected with serious kidney illness.)

The other major priority, aid to elementary and secondary education, moved through Congress about as quickly and smoothly as was possible for such an emotionally disputed piece of legislation. The President avoided the old church-state controversy by developing legislation that aimed assistance, in theory at least, toward children rather than schools. Almost every school district in the nation would receive some benefits, but the distribution formula reserved the greater aid for the underprivileged. The major purpose was the establishment of special programs for the educationally disadvantaged and the purchase of special equipment. An elated Johnson signed the bill in the old one-room Texas schoolhouse where he had begun his education. As with Medicare, the bill was more an opening wedge than a culmination. Although it provided real and important benefits, it skirted the old and pressing issues of classroom construction and teacher salaries; these would remain among the unresolved problems of the Great Society.

As Johnson shepherded these bills through Congress, he faced another crisis. The violence at Selma, Alabama, against marchers demonstrating for the right to vote showed that the civil rights bill of 1964 had been a beginning rather than an end. Although the President had not planned for more civil rights legislation, he moved quickly. On March 15, just a week after the Selma brutality, he went before Congress to make a personal appeal for voting-rights legislation, punctuating his condemnation of discrimination with the words, slowly and emphatically delivered, "We . . . shall . . . overcome." The events that followed resembled those of 1964—the cooperation of Dirksen, the voting of cloture in the Senate, the ultimate passage of the legislation by top-heavy majorities in both houses. Signed into law that August, the bill authorized the appointment of federal registrars in states and counties where a comparison of election and census statistics indicated a systematic denial of the right to vote. One of the first targets of the new federal action was Selma, Alabama. During the next year, federal registrars or the threat of their imposition extended the franchise to about 500,000 southern Negroes who had not voted before; by 1968, the total of new black voters had reached one million.

In addition to these three pieces of legislation, Johnson obtained in 1965 passage of other enactments that would have been considered amazing just a year or two earlier. The Immigration Act finally put an end to the infamous national-origins quota system that had been established more than forty years before and had effectively discriminated against Southern and Eastern Europeans seeking admission to the United States. The Housing Act authorized the largest and most expensive series of programs for low- and middle-income housing in American history. An aid bill for higher education provided important forms of assistance for students (loans and scholarships) and colleges (grants for libraries and teaching or research equipment). Other bills greatly enlarged the antipoverty and Appalachian development programs. Congress authorized a new cabinet Department of Housing and Urban Development. Social security benefits were hiked. The growing concern with the environment led to legislation to control water pollution. A highway beautification law, a pet project of Mrs. Johnson, established procedures for controlling roadside billboards and junkyards. Even "culture" received important help through the creation of a National Foundation for the Arts and Humanities. And on top of all these programs, the administration engineered a major cut in the excise taxes that had been in effect since World War II. The President suffered only two defeats—rejection of home rule for the District of Columbia and inaction upon his request for revision of the Taft-Hartley Act. It was doubtful whether the second really amounted to a defeat, for there was a wide belief that Johnson did not "push" Taft-Hartley revision as partial payment to Dirksen for Republican cooperation on civil rights and other issues.

The following year saw some more of the same, but it also brought some significant defeats. Among the administration successes were a higher minimum wage; auto and highway safety legislation; the establishment of a cabinet-rank Department of Transportation; and a "model cities" act which would provide extensive grants for housing, welfare, and mass transit to selected cities. However, these achievements were overshadowed by a failure to obtain reform of the unemployment compensation system and by the defeat of an "open housing" civil rights bill in Congress. Large segments of the public were already beginning to sour on Johnson, the Great Society, and the increasing social chaos which characterized the America of the mid-1960s. The Vietnam war was being rapidly escalated, and a serious inflation was gathering steam. In the congressional elections of 1966, the Democrats lost 47 seats in the House of Representatives, thereby bringing their delegation to its lowest point since the start of Eisenhower's second term and forfeiting the reform margin which had made the Great Society possible. The latest era of domestic innovation gave way to a period of stalemate and consolidation.

LBJ, AMERICAN FOREIGN POLICY, AND THE ROAD TO VIETNAM

American Presidents seldom make their way to the White House by displaying expertise in foreign policy. No Chief Executive demonstrated this maxim more vividly than Johnson. Until he reached the vice-presidency, his life had been almost entirely occupied by the intricacies of domestic political maneuver and compromise; acquaintances recalled that he tended to confuse Iran with Iraq, Indo-China with Indonesia. Still, inexperience, even a certain amount of ignorance, was not an impossible handicap; indeed, it might facilitate a salutary openness of mind and freshness of approach. More important in the end than any reservoir of knowledge or any special training were the President's own instincts, and these served both Johnson and the nation badly. As he personalized domestic politics, so he personalized diplomacy; as he crudely wielded carrot and stick with those around him, he attempted to do so with other nations; as he practiced secrecy on so many issues, he was furtive in determining foreign policy, eventually to the exclusion of dissenting opinion; as he so frequently resorted to emotional appeal on issues at home, he would do the same on issues abroad.

Johnson wanted to be remembered as a benefactor to the world in much the same way he sought to establish himself as a benefactor to the American people. His personal ambitions were to continue the process of détente with the USSR and to extend aid to the impoverished masses of the globe. At times, events conspired against him—in the summer of 1968, the Soviet military suppression of a liberal Czechoslovakian government forced the President to cancel a planned goodwill visit to Moscow and give up hope of completing arrangements for major arms-limitation negotiations.

But other impulses worked against these beneficent aspirations. Johnson was prone to view military-diplomatic challenges as personal in nature; he delighted in telling intimates of the way in which he had faced down Soviet Premier Kosygin during the six-day Arab-Israeli war of 1967 when Kosygin had employed the U.S.–Soviet hot line to display concern and probe American intentions. Nor was he immune to the traditional set of patriotic beliefs that America must never retreat under pressure, that a U.S. pledge, once given, had to be fulfilled at almost any cost. He saw no clash between the preservation of his personal authority and the interests of the nation; the two were identical. Realizing that power and prestige were fragile commodities, Johnson was cautious in making firm commitments, either domestic or diplomatic, but tenacious in following through on those he did make.

Vividly remembering the days of Senator Joe McCarthy, he feared that any Democratic President would be vulnerable to charges of "softness" and "no-win" policies toward communism. As benevolence might easily be mistaken for softness, it was essential to display strength and firmness in dealing with other nations, especially, it seemed, small, upstart nonwhite nations. Not a vicious bigot, Johnson nevertheless was, like many less provincial Americans, prone to overestimate the impression that displays of force and resolve would make on other people. Finally, once he had made a policy decision, he tended to identify emotionally with it, expect approval from all sides, dig in against criticism, and ultimately direct his rhetoric at self-reinforcement rather than persuasion.

Johnson's first diplomatic crises involved Latin America. In 1964, Panamanian rioters protested U.S. control of the Canal Zone, a privilege tendered by a sixty-year-old treaty that had been dictated by Theodore Roosevelt. Refusing to present the slightest impression that he had given in under pressure, Johnson resisted even discussion of renegotiating the agreement for months, and when talks were finally begun they dragged on inconclusively throughout his administration. In the spring of 1965 he sent the marines into the Dominican Republic to abort a revolution against an unpopular military government because communists appeared to be involved. It was the first such U.S. military intervention in Latin America since the administration of Calvin Coolidge.

Yet Johnson was not a blatant imperialist, and as a Texan he especially wanted to be liked by Latin Americans. In 1966 when large and enthusiastic crowds greeted him in Mexico City, he was elated that he had won a reception beyond that which even Kennedy could have expected had he been alive. It was true that no President could have conceded much to Panama in the face of violent demonstrations; nor should any Chief Executive have ignored warnings of communist or Castroite influence among the Dominican rebels. Johnson had at least been willing to negotiate with Panama, and his objective in the Dominican intervention was the establishment of a moderate government, not a restoration of military control.

Still, in dealing with Panama he had displayed stubbornness; with the

Dominican Republic, he exhibited lack of candor, overreaction, emotionalism, and self-pity. He first justified the Dominican intervention as simply a measure to protect American lives. Later, he declared falsely that the communists actually had taken over the revolution, patted himself on the back for possessing the courage to make a difficult decision, and commented that for having acted in the national interest he was being vilified by both the communist bloc and the Congress. The President could do as he wished with small Latin American republics, but in the larger world such attitudes could neither develop a successful foreign policy based on a realistic assessment of the national interest nor win broad and deep public support.

The Latin American events to some extent overshadowed the increasingly difficult situation in South Vietnam. Here, Kennedy had undeniably left a heritage which any administration would have experienced difficulty in handling. The death of Diem had solved nothing; the unstable and, it seemed, constantly changing, military-dominated governments that followed him displayed little in the way of either popular support or greater strength. To many outsiders, the South Vietnamese generals appeared corrupt, primarily interested in self-enrichment, and preoccupied with Byzantine intrigues against each other. Internal dissent remained nearly as high as it had been under Diem, and the Viet Cong gained strength by the month.

Nevertheless, during the first year or so of his administration, Johnson considered Vietnam to be a rather low priority. His main concern was the establishment of a record in domestic areas. It was in this period that Vietnam policy became largely a function of the Defense Department, "McNamara's War," some called it. As in the Kennedy administration, the problem was defined largely as military, in part because Johnson was impressed by Secretary McNamara's vigor, intelligence, and decisiveness, in part because Secretary of State Rusk was in fundamental agreement with the secretary of defense. Typical of most Americans with his faith in technology and his quantitative approach to problems, McNamara was convinced that the application of sufficient military power would inevitably crush the primitive communist insurgency. In the last analysis, nevertheless, the President was truly responsible for the ever-faster pace of escalation which began in early 1964 and continued through the first half of 1965.

Presidents, it is true, are frequently the prisoners of situations beyond their control. Such, Johnson argued, was the case with Vietnam—he was simply carrying through policies that his predecessors, Republican as well as Democratic, had set in motion; he was performing the unpleasant duty of enforcing a national consensus against communist expansion; he would

prefer a peaceful, negotiated settlement, but the other side's unreason-
ableness prevented such an alternative. There was a modicum of truth to
such explanations, but they did not go deep enough. Kennedy, Eisenhower, even Truman had all involved the United States in Indo-China,
but none had contemplated massive intervention; future events in Vietnam would prove, as the experience of Korea had demonstrated, that the
national anticommunist consensus could wear thin under the pressure of
casualty lists; it was also true that the stubbornness, although not the
determination, of the South Vietnamese was about as great as that of the
North. When Johnson became President, he faced some hard decisions on
Vietnam, and he had inherited a commitment that was not working well,
but it was neither gigantic nor irreversible. Deeper impulses, bound up
with his overall approach to military-diplomatic challenges, led him to
escalation.

As early as December 1963, Secretary McNamara was visiting Vietnam to pledge U.S. support and in January 1964 was warning Congress
and the public of the gravity of the situation. In February the President
made his own personal promises and delivered a thinly veiled warning to
North Vietnam by asserting that "those engaged in external direction and
supply" to the Viet Cong were playing a "deeply dangerous game." The
administration also flatly rejected a French proposal for an attempt to
neutralize all of Southeast Asia. In July 1964 the United States announced
that an additional 5,000 military advisers would be sent to assist the South
Vietnamese.

Then, in August 1964, the Southeast Asian involvement reached a
turning point far more momentous than most observers realized at the
time. On August 2, the *Maddox,* a U.S. destroyer on a patrol-intelligence
mission off the coast of North Vietnam in the Gulf of Tonkin, came under
attack by North Vietnamese PT boats; the vessel was not hit and managed
to inflict some damage on the attackers. There the incident might have
rested. Washington assumed that the North Vietnamese had attacked the
Maddox in the belief that it was providing cover for a nearby South
Vietnamese commando raid (apparently, it was not), and only the enemy
had sustained injury. But on August 4, the *Maddox* and a companion
destroyer, the *Turner Joy,* reported another attack, this one at night. There
was no doubt about the August 2 fight—it occurred in daylight, and the
North Vietnamese awarded decorations to the PT crews involved—but,
although there appears to have been no conscious attempt at deception,
the second incident was a much fuzzier case in which the attackers were
never visually sighted and the hostility was determined by an interpretation of radar and sonar readings. At the time, it seemed natural enough to
assume that another attack had occurred, but in calmer retrospect it was

possible to believe that the engagement had been only an illusion in the minds of worried men.

The President, nevertheless, did not hesitate. He had been outraged by the first incident, and now he ordered an air attack upon North Vietnamese naval installations and fuel storage tanks. A one-time-only operation, the raid incurred little disapproval. The most important consequence of the episode was a resolution which the administration pushed through Congress. The Gulf of Tonkin Resolution amounted to a blank check. It empowered the President "to take all necessary measures to repel any armed attack against the forces of the United States and to prevent further aggression." In the aftermath of a military battle, no matter how small or obscure, measured debate was impossible. The resolution passed the Senate, 88–2, and cleared the House, 416–0; without quite believing that the document would be used in such a manner, the Congress had given Johnson a functional declaration of war.

Nevertheless, Johnson seemed anything but a warmonger during the rest of the year. With the presidential campaign on, he assumed the image of a man of peace while characterizing his opponent as a simpleminded militarist itching to push the nuclear button. Whenever he mentioned Vietnam, he always affirmed the American commitment there, but in such a way as to make it appear that assistance would consist primarily of economic aid, military hardware, and advice by professional soldiers. "We don't want our American boys to do the fighting for Asian boys," he declared in what would become one of his most quoted speeches. In September the administration did nothing about a third Gulf of Tonkin incident as murky as the second; nor was there a reaction when Viet Cong saboteurs managed to sneak into the large American air base at Bien Hoa on November 1 and blow up five planes. A far more serious provocation, the bombing of a Saigon hotel used as a U.S. officers' billet on December 24, was also absorbed without retaliation. But the administration faced something far more ominous than these relatively minor attacks—the South Vietnamese government was losing the war and could be rescued only by massive U.S. intervention. Johnson had already increased the number of American troops in Vietnam by about 50 percent; still, the total was only 23,300 and, in the afterglow of his overwhelming election victory, withdrawal was an option that could be chosen and managed without serious loss of face.

However, the President was convinced that the Vietnam struggle possessed epochal overtones akin to those accompanying the crises which foreshadowed World War II. He believed in the domino theory without reservations; the fall of South Vietnam would mean the fall of all Southeast Asia. American withdrawal would destroy U.S. credibility throughout the "free world," encourage Peking and Moscow to expand elsewhere in Asia, the Middle East, or Europe, and thereby establish the basis for World War III. Johnson, Secretary Rusk, and other administration spokesmen regularly invoked the trauma of Munich and the conflagration to which it had led as the justification for fighting a "small" war in Southeast Asia. Seen from this perspective, a conflict which some had dismissed as a localized civil war took on a cosmic importance which would serve as the rationale for a boundless escalation. In its rhetoric and, one must believe, its genuine conceptualization, the administration pictured Vietnam as the ultimate testing ground in the struggle between American freedom and communist totalitarianism. The question thus was less whether to escalate than how.

The occasion presented itself in February 1965, when the Viet Cong attacked U.S. forces stationed at Pleiku, killing 8 Americans and wounding 100. The administration quickly ordered a retaliatory bombing raid against North Vietnamese military installations. Unlike the Gulf of Tonkin reprisal, this was only the beginning of a new air war; henceforth, aside from a few intermittent pauses for diplomatic negotiations, the bombers would fly north on a daily basis. The troop increases now began to be announced every few weeks, and the increments included full combat units, not just teams of advisers to work with the South Vietnamese army. By July, Johnson had increased U.S. troop strength by nearly 50,000 over the January figure to almost 75,000. As the buildup progressed, the President also held out the carrot. Speaking in Baltimore on April 7, he proposed an ambitious, if vague, plan for the economic development of Southeast Asia, North Vietnam included, once peace was achieved. In Hanoi, however, the communist leaders displayed little interest in the lure of a TVA on the Mekong River. Their perspective was broad and their confidence great—they had been fighting for twenty years and already had vanquished one Western power. Convinced that they were riding the wave of history, they were prepared to see the struggle through at almost any cost.

By early July, few observers could doubt that the North was on the brink of victory. The U.S. commander in Vietnam, General William Westmoreland, reported the grimmest of prospects: the South was losing men at the rate of one infantry battalion a week; the enemy was taking over at least one district capital each week; only a massive introduction of American ground troops could rescue the situation. On July 28, Johnson announced to the nation that the troop level would be increased once more, this time to 125,000, and he made it clear that this would be but the first in a series of step-ups, the limits of which he did not define, that the draft calls would be raised accordingly.

The President had in effect issued a declaration of war, but for a multitude of reasons ranging from domestic politics to global military strategy, the war was to be made as unobtrusive as possible. Troop increases would be achieved through higher draft quotas rather than through reserve call-ups. Taxes would remain low; there would be no economic controls; the Great Society would march on. Never mind that the creaking Selective Service System was shot through with unfairness, that as Walter Lippmann sagely observed, neither the French nor the British had been able to fight limited, faraway "imperial wars" with conscripts, that the economy could not absorb even a "small war" without severe strain, that the practitioner of consensus politics was gliding the nation into a war for which no consensus existed. Convinced that his course was in the national interest, Johnson was prepared to travel a long, hard road. In the summer of 1965 few Americans could imagine just how difficult and unending the trail would be.

THE AMERICANIZATION OF VIETNAM, THE VIETNAMIZATION OF AMERICA

The U.S. war effort was typically American in its continuation of McNamara's quantitative-technological approach. Large helicopters whisked troops from one combat area to another or evacuated whole villages to areas of government control; smaller medivac copters took the wounded to sophisticated field hospitals. Bombers and artillery laid waste to areas that the communists used as refuges; herbicides were dropped from the air to defoliate jungle hiding places and to destroy rice crops which might go to the enemy. In mobility and weaponry—and in numbers—the South Vietnamese and United States forces enjoyed an undeniable advantage. From the beginning, it was easy to believe that, as McNamara said at the conclusion of one of his inspection visits, there was light at the end of the tunnel. Yet the war, far from being won, sucked in ever-increasing numbers of Americans; by early 1968, U.S. troop strength had reached 500,000, and the conflict had degenerated into a frustrating stalemate with no end in sight.

The United States and the South Vietnamese had fallen into the self-defeating trap of trying to fight a guerrilla war with conventional methods; all too often, the result was to turn the battle against the Viet Cong into a fight against the people. The insurgents followed Mao Tse-tung's dictum that they should swim among the people as fish in the water. They were not necessarily welcomed in the villages as saviors; they ruthlessly employed terror against their opponents, drafted young men, levied taxes, and expropriated crops. Still, they were closer to the Vietnamese peasant and his aspirations than was the remote government in Saigon, which in the countryside was usually identified with the landlords and seemed even more brutal and exploitative than the VC. The policy makers were aware of these problems, and at a very early stage of American involvement, someone coined the slogan that the war was being fought to win the minds and hearts of the people. The phrase was a noble basis for a policy, but in practice it became a cynical joke.

The Viet Cong claimed to be fighting a "people's war"; whether or not that was true, the U.S.-South Vietnamese effort became one which undeniably alienated a large portion of the Vietnamese people. There was only one way to win the war—the tedious, dirty, extremely dangerous business of distinguishing the guerrillas from the people and hunting them out individually. Such a mission, moreover, could be successfully performed only by Vietnamese troops who possessed high motivation and represented a government that enjoyed the respect of the peasantry. Instead, the war was fought with methods that played into the hands of the other side. Villagers were forced off their ancestral lands to live in miserable relocation camps. Evacuated areas were declared "free fire zones," and all remaining inhabitants were presumed to be hostile. Support bombers were routinely called in to plaster villages that might contain only a few enemy troops. In the South alone, the bombing caused an estimated half-million civilian casualties. Foreign soldiers moved through the countryside, frequently destroying homes, crops, and livestock. The lavish use of military technology converted a counterinsurgency effort into a terror campaign epitomized by the comment of an American officer surveying a village that had been reduced to rubble in the process of recapturing it from the other side: "We had to destroy the town in order to save it." Few Vietnamese were willing to accept the probable destruction of their property and lives by foreigners as the necessary price of salvation from other Vietnamese.

The air war proved to be an equally futile application of technological overkill. By the end of 1968, the tonnage of bombs dropped on Southeast Asia was half again as large as the amount the United States had dropped in Africa, Europe, and Asia during World War II; yet far from bringing victory, the air war became almost a liability. Vast bombing campaigns were at best semieffective against the mobile, lightly equipped, heavily dug-in communist troops in the South. Attempts to close the supply routes from the North, collectively known as the Ho Chi Minh trail, were unsuccessful; air attacks might destroy some convoys and inflict damage upon many but could not cope with the multiplicity of roads, the frantic repair efforts, the horde of light vehicles and even bicycles which streamed south. The attacks against the North destroyed some industries, but China and the USSR vied for leadership of the communist movement by pouring supplies into Vietnam.

The American bombers, in fact, appear to have given the North Vietnamese a sense of national unity and purpose which they might not have otherwise achieved. Moreover, the raids were undertaken against the most sophisticated antiaircraft weaponry in the history of warfare, developed and supplied by the USSR. By the end of 1968, the United States had lost 900 planes over the North alone. Many of the pilots were captured and periodically displayed by Hanoi not simply for propaganda purposes but as a form of psychological warfare which was immensely effective in America. The great wave of sympathy in the United States for the prisoners would give the enemy powerful leverage in any negotiations.

The pilots were a unique breed among American combatants—they all were professionals and volunteers. U.S. ground troops, enlisted men especially, were likely to be draftees, the victims of an army system that rewarded its long-termers with noncombat duty; the field officers and noncoms might be more likely to have professional aspirations but tended to be short on experience. The army preserved morale by limiting Vietnam tours to twelve months, a policy which may have had its merits but which also provided maximum discontinuity of leadership at the fighting level. There was a great deal of truth to a graffito observed on a wall somewhere in Vietnam: "This is a war of the unwilling led by the unqualified dying for the ungrateful."

Thrown into a fearsome situation in a faraway land, surrounded by a strange and impenetrable people, the American combat soldier could easily and naturally react by developing a racist contempt for Vietnamese in general. He of all the participants in the war could hardly be expected to pursue the distinction between the people and the Viet Cong, existing as he did in constant peril and always knowing that any villager, male or female, might be prepared to kill him if he turned his back. The callous, indiscriminant use of military technology—the evacuations, the bombing, the defoliations—encouraged an anti-Vietnamese attitude; if the strategists were unable to devise methods which would differentiate the innocent from the enemy, how could the frightened foot soldier do so? Individual examples of brutality and murder against the population for whose minds and hearts the war was being waged were countless. Inevitably, such behavior escalated into episodes of mass murder. The worst occurred on March 16, 1968, when an American infantry unit moved into a small village called My Lai 4 and systematically gunned down more than 400 civilians, most of them old men, women, and children; although there was no engagement with the enemy, the official report of the incident listed 128 Viet Cong killed.

The My Lai massacre and the casualty report exemplified not simply the blurring of the distinction between the enemy and the people which the Viet Cong had sought. It also demonstrated the self-deceptive use of quantification which characterized the American management of the war. In the absence of a fixed front, the United States sought to measure success by numbers, most important by the number of enemy casualties, and the pressure on field commanders for a high kill-ratio was extremely great. Consequently, officers from the platoon level up employed the power of positive thinking when reporting the result of any mission. Another indicator of success was the amount of land area pacified or semipacified. here also optimism was pervasive, and favorable reports often were turned in for regions where the Viet Cong remained a threat. Most fundamentally, General Westmoreland's headquarters made it plain that bad news, whatever the reason for it, would be taken as a sign of failure. Careerists who wanted to get ahead discovered that optimism was more valuable than honesty and gave their superiors what they wanted. The result was a deluge of statistics, eagerly fed into computers which in turn produced impressive printouts demonstrating beyond question that the United States and the South Vietnamese were inflicting intolerable casualties upon the communists, gaining control of an increasing amount of territory, and moving toward an inexorable victory.

It all came apart at the beginning of 1968. On January 30, the Vietnamese New Year (Tet), the supposedly declining enemy launched a ferocious offensive. The attackers overran and occupied the old imperial capital of Hue for a period of weeks, using the time to slaughter every opponent they could ferret out. They established themselves in the Cholon district of Saigon, and a suicide squad managed to penetrate the outer defenses of the American diplomatic-military compound. A dozen other areas of U.S.–South Vietnamese strength came under heavy attack. After extremely difficult fighting, the Tet offensive was beaten back with heavy losses to the enemy—the estimate of 42,000 communist dead probably was fairly accurate—but the other side had scored an important psychological victory.

To call the North Vietnamese–Viet Cong victory psychological did not mean that it was illusory. The enemy had laid bare the organized mendacity which had permeated earlier official analyses of the war. The American command claimed triumph and boasted that it had inflicted extensive casualties; some of the war's strongest supporters even asserted that the communist defeat was a turning point, that the offensive was a desperate last gasp by a beaten foe. But most disinterested observers agreed that the Viet Cong and North Vietnamese, even if temporarily crippled, had displayed a continuing strength and determination which could not be eradicated with the existing level of U.S. troop commitments.

American military analysts privately agreed. At the beginning of March, General Westmoreland asked for an additional 206,000 troops; the request soon leaked to the press. It would be impossible to grant such an escalation without putting the nation on a full war footing. As the President agonized over the Westmoreland proposals, his subordinates engaged in vehement infighting to persuade him one way or the other, his party was torn with dissension, his nation was bitterly divided, and his dream of a Great Society was in shreds.

The war consumed no politician more fully than Johnson himself. He assumed an unprecedented degree of personal control over day-to-day military operations; the White House actually exercised the right of specific approval of bombing targets. His emotional commitment extended to his own family; one of his sons-in-law, a young marine officer, saw combat in Vietnam and purportedly exercised a profound influence upon his father-in-law; the other, a reservist, "volunteered" for Vietnam duty. When the President flew to Manila in the fall of 1966 for a conference of the anticommunist Southeast Asian nations, he insisted on making an inspection of the war zone, and, speaking to American troops at Camranh Bay, he exhorted the U.S. soldiers to "nail that coonskin to the wall." As the reaction against the war deepened, he appears to have felt increasingly defensive and persecuted. When prominent members of the administration developed doubts about the war, they might be eased out, as was Secretary McNamara at the end of 1967, or cut off from the information necessary for viable criticism. By the time of Tet, the administration was taking on the appearance of a band of pioneers who had drawn their wagons in a circle for a last stand against their attackers.

At home, the war placed an intolerable overload on the economy and sparked a serious inflation, which spelled failure for the administration hope of somehow squeezing the conflict into an already booming economy and creating the illusion that a "real war" was not being fought. Congressional sentiment was so strongly against higher taxes, the best antidote to inflation, that a request probably would have been futile. Johnson could get a tax increase only if he used the arguments of all-out war and, as he would later put it, "wrapped himself in the flag," but to do so would have been both politically and diplomatically dangerous. There was little left but intermittent and usually impotent jawboning against large wage and price increases.

Not until the beginning of 1967 did Johnson request a tax increase; not until the middle of 1968 did he finally get one passed after intricate negotiations with congressional leaders. The tax bill of 1968 imposed a surcharge of 10 percent upon the regular tax schedules; in order to obtain its passage, the administration slashed federal spending by $6 billion. In the meantime, the only solid attempt at curbing inflation was carried on by the Federal Reserve System in the form of a tight money policy which sent interest rates soaring to new highs. The resultant "credit crunch" of 1967–68 hit the average American especially hard by drastically slowing down home construction. The tax surcharge-spending cut combination of mid-1968, when it finally came, was too little and too late. The war had built inflation solidly into the economy with the usual difficult consequences for those who had to get along on low or fixed incomes. And for the first time in all the rounds of inflation since World War II, there were serious international monetary ramifications as the dollar's declining value made it ever less suitable as the Western exchange standard.

The war also closed in around the Great Society, obscuring the accomplishments of some programs, highlighting the deficiencies of others, subjecting many to economic malnutrition, claiming an ever-greater proportion of the President's time and attention, disrupting and demoralizing the reform coalition Johnson had put together in 1964–65. All large new government programs face initial problems of organization and execution. Some Great Society measures, such as the civil rights legislation and Medicare, functioned rather effectively from the beginning, but some of the poverty programs degenerated into boondoggles for patronage-hungry politicians or power-seeking militants and did so at a time when national discontent with welfare expenditures was rising. By 1967, the pressures of inflation and the demands of the war were bringing a halt to increases in appropriations for social programs and reducing the value of the money allotted to them. Many of the liberal Democrats who had enthusiastically supported LBJ the reformer were now livid in their opposition to LBJ the warmaker. Johnson's use of presidential power to escalate the war even did much to discredit the traditional liberal reliance upon a strong Chief Executive and big government.

On a pervasive, if not altogether tangible level, the war seemed to worsen every social strain in American life. Black militance, the New Left, the counterculture, student discontent, and the Middle American reaction against all these forces would have developed anyway, but the war magnified them. To the left, the war made America appear evil and repressive and justified a politics of violence. Male students facing the draft attempted to cope with an intolerable situation by demonstrating *machismo* in campus disruptions and justifying their actions with watered-down revolutionary ideology. The protests against the war somehow became the showcase of the intellectuals, the New Leftists, the young countercultur- ists, and the black militants, all of whom seemed more interested in flaunting their distinctive styles of behavior and demonstrating what they considered their moral superiority than in building an antiwar movement that would reach into Middle America. Working-class types, incensed at the sight of long-haired, pot-smoking demonstrators burning draft cards or the U.S. flag while others waved a Viet Cong banner, reacted predictably with hard-hat rallies in support of America, the status quo, and, almost incidentally, the Southeast Asian conflict.

Far more than any other force, the war socially polarized America and in the process speeded up the disruption of the old New Deal-Democratic coalition which Johnson had revived in 1964. Even so wise and respected an observer of the American scene as Walter Lippmann, whose experience included two world wars and the Great Depression, could remark that never before had American society faced so terrible a crisis. As the electoral year of 1968 began, all the forces of discord in American society seemed to be building toward an explosion, and the Tet offensive was but the first in a series of terrible shocks.

1968: THE TRAUMATIC YEAR

Tet left all those responsible for the war shaken in their optimism. With the military requesting a strength increase that would necessitate mobilization of the reserves, higher taxes, and economic controls, the civilian policy makers could not avoid a drastic reevaluation of what was happening in Southeast Asia. Formerly hawkish advisers such as Dean Acheson and McGeorge Bundy counseled a movement toward deescalation and negotiation with the North. Secretary Rusk suggested a cessation of the bombing campaign north of the 20th parallel as a concession which might permit meaningful talks with the enemy. The new secretary of defense, Clark Clifford, once a firm supporter of the war, became the leading figure in the struggle to wind it down. Johnson himself remained torn between his fear of displaying weakness and his genuine hope of being a bringer of peace, between his anger at the dogmatic intransigence of the communists and his growing realization that the country had turned irrevocably against the war. At times during the coming months he might be drawn to a military solution—at one point, Clifford was cut off from access to vital diplomatic communications—but the President had decided to work for a compromise peace.

The unpopularity of the war was brought home to Johnson in the most forceful way possible. On March 12, he nearly lost the New Hampshire Democratic presidential primary to the insurgent peace candidate, Senator Eugene McCarthy. Bucking the regular party organization with a legion of student volunteers, the hitherto obscure McCarthy polled 42.2 percent of the Democratic vote to Johnson's 49.4 percent, and Republican primary write-ins brought his overall vote total close to the President's. In the wake of the McCarthy showing, Robert F. Kennedy announced his candidacy for the nomination. Facing a formidable party revolt, worried that his health could not endure another four years in the White House, Johnson decided to end his political career and spend his remaining months in office pursuing a peace settlement. In a nationally televised address on March 31, he announced a suspension of the bombing of the North in all but the small panhandle area below the 20th parallel and declared: "I shall not seek, and I will not accept, the nomination of my party for another term as your President."

The North Vietnamese responded to the partial bombing halt by agreeing to engage in preliminary peace talks—or in effect discuss an agenda for serious discussion—but for a time it looked as if even this small beginning might go awry as the two sides haggled for more than a month before finally settling upon Paris as a conference site. The U.S. negotiating team, headed by the most experienced of all active American diplomats, W. Averell Harriman, was anxious to conclude an agreement but was hemmed in by rigid restrictions from Washington and by a North Vietnamese insistence upon a total bombing halt as the prelude to substantive bargaining. Thus, during the summer and fall, as the talks made no visible progress, the antiwar movement remained alienated from the administration and intensely suspicious that Washington was engaging in an election-year charade.

The bitterness of the antiwar forces represented only part of a larger pattern of trouble at home. Just four days after Johnson's renunciation of the Presidency, Martin Luther King, Jr., was assassinated in Memphis, and riots erupted in a hundred cities from Boston to San Francisco. In Washington, troops took up defense positions around the White House and the Capitol. Campus discontent and disruption continued to escalate with the paralysis of Columbia University attracting the greatest national attention. From street crime to the revolt of the ghetto to the revolt of the upper-middle-class young, American society appeared to be careening toward an instability that would have been incomprehensible four years earlier.

Having taken himself out of the running, Johnson was determined to control the choice of his successor and prepared to throw the Democratic nomination to Vice-President Humphrey, although, typically, he kept Humphrey guessing. In the meantime, most public attention focused on the struggle between the other two major Democratic contenders, Eugene McCarthy and Robert Kennedy.

Sensitive, philosophical, deeply moral, McCarthy had in the beginning offered himself to the antiwar movement almost as a human sacrifice.

Suddenly, he had become the instrument of the President's political destruction and the hero of the college kids who manned his campaign. Adopting the slogan "Be Neat and Clean for Gene," they shaved their beards, cut their hair, donned jackets and ties, and demonstrated that dissenters could function within "the system" so long as their objective was to persuade rather than to outrage. McCarthy himself, whimsical and detached, did not seriously seek the Presidency, but he reciprocated the loyalty of his workers and, having made a commitment when every other major Democrat had held back, he would not withdraw.

If McCarthy was soft and idealistic, Bobby Kennedy was tough and opportunistic; if McCarthy was primarily concerned with representing a cause, Kennedy was above all attuned to the realities of power. He had hoped for the vice-presidential nomination in 1964, then had resigned from the cabinet, moved to New York, and won election to the Senate. He detested Johnson, and the feeling was mutual—place the two men in a room together, Hubert Humphrey observed, and they became animals tearing at each other's throats. Yet Kennedy's toughness, opportunism, and power seeking overlay deeper commitments, above all to the memory of the assassinated brother whose political mantle had descended to him and to the cause of the underprivileged, whose plight he had come to understand during his years as attorney general. His brother's death had scarred and transformed his own life and left him with a reservoir of compassion and sensitivity which ultimately overrode whatever qualities of ruthlessness he possessed. Upon hearing of the death of Martin Luther King just before he was to speak at a black political rally in Indianapolis, he delivered an extemporaneous address that no other American politician could have made; reminding his audience that his brother also had been killed—by a white man—he quoted Aeschylus: "In our sleep, pain which cannot forget falls drop by drop upon the heart until, in our own despair, against our will, comes wisdom through the awful grace of God."

Yet he was above all a politician concerned with maximizing his support. He established a superb campaign organization, drew freely upon his family's resources, spoke reassuringly to working-class ethnics about the need for law and order, and maintained generally good relations with the old-line regular Democrats. Such tactics were self-serving, but they also were in line with the politics of inclusiveness which had built the post–New Deal Democratic party. McCarthy was a one-issue candidate whose appeal was limited mostly to the young and the professional-intellectual middle class; Kennedy could be greeted as a charismatic leader in the slums of Harlem, in the barrios of Los Angeles, in the white ethnic neighborhoods of Mayor Daley's Chicago, and in the hill country of West Virginia. His diverse followings required some political equivocation but also held out the hope that he could heal the divisions which threatened to destroy American society. In the District of Columbia primary, the only one in which he faced a direct contest with Humphrey, he took 62.5 percent of the vote. In Indiana, he polled 42 percent of the vote against the Humphrey-Johnson stand-in, Governor Roger Brannigan (31 percent), and McCarthy (27 percent). He won a solid 51.5 percent in Nebraska. His only primary defeat was to McCarthy in Oregon. On June 5, he won the primaries in South Dakota and California, thereby creating a real possibility that he could take control of the convention away from the White House. But a few minutes after delivering his victory statement in Los Angeles, Bobby Kennedy was murdered by a young Arab immigrant obsessed with the fringe issue of U.S. support for Israel.

The second Kennedy assassination in five years, the second major political killing of 1968, the event deepened the national mood of frustration and despair. Within the Democratic party, it practically sealed the nomination of Humphrey and intensified the anger of the antiwar forces. Although the McCarthy organization sought to discourage student demonstrators from coming to Chicago, militant peace groups prepared to turn the Democratic convention into a theater of confrontation; the Johnson administration and the Chicago police responded by girding for battle. The result was one of the most divisive conventions in the history of the party and certainly the most violent. Employing tactics that had become familiar, the peace demonstrators attempted to goad the local authorities into displays of fascistic brutality and were successful beyond their dreams. Enraged policemen ran amok, clubbing demonstrators, bystanders, and journalists indiscriminately. Mayor Richard J. Daley, the ultimate symbol of the "old politics" and white ethnic America, angrily defended his cops and allowed television cameras to capture him shaking his fist at Senator Abraham Ribicoff, who decried the brutality in the streets. When the convention closed, it was apparent that the police had won on the field of battle, but neither side had yielded an inch in its conviction of moral superiority even as both had behaved with primitive indecency toward the other. Almost as a sideshow, Humphrey received a presidential nomination that looked worthless.

The Democratic debacle opened the way for a major third-party effort by George Wallace of Alabama. Once just a vocal segregationist, Wallace had become a mouthpiece for all the grievances, real and imagined, of blue-collar Middle Americans, and in the immediate aftermath of Chicago, polls estimated his support at more than 20 percent of the electorate. His speeches were diatribes against black militants (a term which in his mind covered all organized Negroes), "beatniks" and hippies, "pointy-headed intellectuals and bureaucrats," crime in the streets, school integration, and high taxes; his panaceas were little more than affirmations of "law and order" and a militant anticommunist foreign policy. Kennedy had captured the support of much of the white working class by appealing in the last analysis to its better instincts. Wallace appealed only to its hatreds. Yet he was the strongest third-party candidate since Robert La Follette, Sr., in 1924. In a classic example of the symbiotic relationship between opposing extremist groups, militant blacks and long-haired New Leftists usually showed up at his rallies to heckle and disrupt, and the candidate shielded at the speaker's podium by bullet-proof glass pointed to them as living examples of the moral decay which afflicted modern America. Here, the aura of hatred and violence that characterized the politics of 1968 was at its worst, and one always expected the sound of gunfire or perhaps the thud of a grenade.

The Republicans, meanwhile, had turned back toward the center with the nomination of Richard Nixon, and Nixon ran a moderately conservative campaign, touching some of the same nerves as Wallace but in a more dignified way. He appointed himself spokesman for the "forgotten American" who worked hard and paid his taxes only to be victimized by inefficient bureaucracy, ill-advised spending programs, and rampant crime. Cautious in his statements about Vietnam, he nevertheless declared that he had "a plan" to end the war. His strategy, by and large, was to avoid the appearance of rightist extremism which had brought Goldwater down, mobilize the 45 percent or so of the electorate who usually voted Republican, and count on Wallace to draw large chunks of the labor vote away from the Democrats.

The outcome was closer than expected. Humphrey's campaign began badly and was miserably financed; antiwar hecklers hounded him relentlessly. Nevertheless, the components of the traditional Roosevelt–New Deal majority slowly began to come together. Organized labor engaged in a massive anti-Wallace, pro-Humphrey drive. Humphrey declared his independence from the Johnson administration by advocating a total halt to the bombing of North Vietnam. At the end of October, in the belief that the Paris negotiators had arrived at a formula for meaningful substantive negotiations, Johnson ended the bombing, thereby encouraging hopes for a quick settlement and giving Humphrey a powerful boost. The voting a few days later was reminiscent of the cliff-hanger of 1960. Nixon won the election with 43.40 percent against 42.72 percent for Humphrey and 13.53 percent for Wallace; the Republicans and their standard bearer had come back from defeats that supposedly had doomed them to obscurity.

The closeness of the Nixon-Humphrey race partially obscured the depth of Johnson's repudiation. In that faraway, hopeful fall of 1964, he had taken command of what seemed to be a national consensus and had rolled up more than 61 percent of the presidential vote; four years later, he hardly dared venture out of the White House, and his choice as a successor could muster less than 43 percent of the ballots. Like all Presidents, he brooded about the judgment of history; his achievements, he was convinced, were large and impressive, yet they—and he—were neither understood nor appreciated. He had brought legal equality to 20 million black Americans, had freed the elderly from the fears of financial disaster which accompanied illness, had enriched the education of millions of young people, had lifted 8 million people out of poverty, and had presided over an era of increased well-being for most Americans. But he also had plunged the nation into a disastrous war which had cost over 30,000 American lives since the escalation of 1965, had severely strained the American economy, and had left the nation divided and dispirited. It was the record of an enormous historical personality overcome in the end by the boundlessness of his aspirations and his ego, but able, one hoped, to spend his final years taking solace in the knowledge that the good he had done would outlive the evil he had unleashed.

TWELVE

Richard M. Nixon
and the Difficult Quest
for the Center

CHRONOLOGY

1969–73

1969

MARCH	U.S. troop strength in Vietnam peaks at 545,000
MAY	Abe Fortas resigns from Supreme Court
JUNE	Justice Department asserts right to conduct "internal security" wiretaps; Burger succeeds Warren as chief justice of the United States
JULY	Nixon proclaims doctrine of greater self-reliance for U.S. Asian allies
AUGUST	Family Assistance Plan introduced; Justice Department supports Mississippi request for delay in school desegregation
OCTOBER	Supreme Court orders immediate end to school segregation
NOVEMBER	Agnew begins attacks against media; Senate rejects nomination of Haynsworth to Supreme Court
DECEMBER	Draft lottery instituted; U.S. troop strength in Vietnam at 475,000

329

1970

APRIL   Senate rejects nomination of Carswell to Supreme Court; U.S. troop strength in Vietnam at 430,000; Nixon orders invasion of Cambodia

MAY   Kent State killings; Senate approves nomination of Blackmun to Supreme Court; Dow-Jones index reaches low point of 631

AUGUST   Arab-Israeli negotiations aborted by Soviet-Egyptian missile buildup

SEPTEMBER   Jordan expels Palestinian guerrillas, turns back Syrian invasion

OCTOBER   Nixon rejects findings of pornography commission

1971

JANUARY   Mass arrests of antiwar demonstrators in Washington; Nixon rejects decriminalization of marijuana; U.S. troop strength in Vietnam at 280,000

JUNE   Pentagon Papers case

AUGUST   New Economic Policy begins with wage-price freeze (Phase I); U.S. dollar cut loose from gold

NOVEMBER   Phase II of New Economic Policy begins; U.S. troop strength in Vietnam at 206,000

DECEMBER   Nixon appoints Powell and Rehnquist to Supreme Court; U.S. dollar devalued 8.5 percent; India-Pakistan war

1972

FEBRUARY   Nixon visits China

APRIL   Major communist offensive in Vietnam; United States resumes bombing of North

MAY   U.S. troop strength in Vietnam at 69,000; Haiphong harbor mined; Nixon visits USSR

JUNE   Burglars arrested in Watergate offices of Democratic National Committee

JULY   Democrats nominate McGovern; sale of wheat to USSR

AUGUST   Eagleton resigns from Democratic ticket; Senate ratifies Strategic Arms Limitation Treaty

SEPTEMBER   U.S. troop strength in Vietnam at 39,000

OCTOBER   Revenue Sharing Act; bombing of North Vietnam suspended; Kissinger and Tho reach abortive peace agreement

NOVEMBER   Nixon defeats McGovern in landslide
DECEMBER   Bombing of North Vietnam resumes

1973

JANUARY   Vietnam peace agreement

Few American politicians had possessed careers as long and bitter as had Richard Nixon. By 1968, he had been a nationally known political figure for twenty years. In 1972 he would equal Franklin D. Roosevelt's record of having been a candidate for President or vice-president five times. Like Roosevelt, he was hated by a substantial segment of the people; unlike FDR, he was loved by few. Passing from early triumphs through a period of defeat and near obscurity, he would come back to power and then on to one of the great electoral victories of U.S. history. Yet for all the ups and downs, emotional as well as political, that marked his career, for all the controversy he aroused, his political quest, like that of most politicians, was to preempt the broad center of American politics. His first term as President would in large measure be the story of his success.

THE MAN WHO CAME BACK

When Lyndon Johnson took the presidential oath on January 20, 1965, almost nobody imagined that four years later the central figure of the same ceremony would be Richard Milhous Nixon; at the time, only Barry Goldwater seemed more definitively out of the running for national office. Nixon's victory in the election of 1968 was the culmination of a remarkable political comeback. Made possible by the diverse reactions against the Johnson administration, it was also a triumph of perseverance on the part of a politician who had come up the hard way and had never quit struggling against long odds.

Nixon's early life, by all accounts, resembled that of a Horatio Alger character. His parents, the owners of a small grocery store–filling station in Whittier, California, worked long hours in order to cling precariously to a lower-middle-class status. Two of his brothers died in their teens after lingering illnesses, experiences both emotionally and financially traumatic for the family. In such circumstances, one learned the necessity of hard work and self-control at an early age; and Nixon's mother, a devout Quaker, provided a personal example of these virtues. A first-rate student and an effective debater, Nixon graduated second in his class at Whittier College and third in his class at Duke Law School. His reach appears to have exceeded his grasp only when he tried out for football at both schools and succeeded in demonstrating that his skills were verbal and intellectual rather than athletic. Nevertheless, football with its patterns of controlled aggression, organized struggle, and strategic planning appealed to him deeply, and his coach at Whittier was one of the genuinely inspirational figures of his life.

Unable despite an outstanding academic record to land a job with a major law firm, Nixon returned to Whittier near the end of the Great Depression and established a small, unrewarding legal practice. In partnership with some friends, he tried to set up a frozen-orange-juice business, but the underfunded enterprise soon folded. At the beginning of World War II, he moved to Washington where he worked briefly as a lawyer for the Office of Price Administration; the experience gave him a lasting distaste for the federal bureaucracy with its miles of red tape and, he felt, mediocre personnel. Enlisting in the navy, he served out the war in the Pacific. When he returned home in 1946, he found himself presented with his first break—an unexpected opportunity to go into politics.

Acting on the recommendation of the president of Whittier College, a group of Republican businessmen offered to back Nixon for the House of Representatives against the Democratic incumbent, Jerry Voorhis, a fourth-termer widely respected in Washington. Several other prospects had shied away from what was presumed to be the futility of opposing him, but for Nixon, the decision seems to have come easily. Life had always been a difficult struggle, and returning from the service, he had no established business or law practice. Voorhis, like many strong Democrats, turned out to be beatable in the Republican year of 1946, and Nixon attacked with every weapon at his disposal. Seizing upon an issue that was just beginning to surface, he pinned a Red label upon Voorhis, who actually was anticommunist and a member of the House Committee on Un-American Activities. Whether the charge was decisive or not, it became the most memorable feature of the campaign. On election day, Nixon and many other aspiring young Republicans celebrated a GOP sweep.

As a congressman, Nixon continued to push the communist issue. As a member of the Un-American Activities Committee, he became one of Whittaker Chambers' strongest supporters when Chambers made his first charges against Alger Hiss, and Hiss's eventual downfall contributed mightily to Nixon's reputation. In collaboration with South Dakota Senator Karl Mundt, he sponsored a sedition bill which never passed Congress in its original form but was substantially incorporated into the McCarran Internal Security Act of 1950. It was in that year that he ran for the Senate against Helen Gahagan Douglas, a glamorous entertainer who had served effectively in the House of Representatives. With the Korean war underway and McCarthyism building toward its peak, charges of procommunism could be especially devastating. The Nixon organization circulated a "pink sheet" which scurrilously compared Mrs. Douglas's voting record to that of a radical New York congressman known to have close communist connections. "Helen Gahagan Douglas is pink right down to her underwear," Nixon declared in one speech. He won the election by a decisive margin. In the minds of most Democrats, he was irrevocably stamped as a ruthless demagogue, but many Republicans could view him as one of the party's bright young stars. A youthful, aggressive conservative from a populous state, he fitted the GOP ticket well as Eisenhower's running mate in 1952.

Nearly forced off the ticket by charges of corruption leveled at his acceptance of a secret fund, Nixon fought back. His "Checkers" speech may have drawn ridicule from committed Democrats, but it probably established him as an asset to the ticket. He sought an identity with the average Middle American—earnest, hard-working, trying to get ahead, concerned about communism, cherishing his family. Once it was clear he had survived the episode, his visibility and his value to the party were greater than ever. His partisan rhetoric might at times border on the indecent, as when he accused the Democrats of "twenty years of treason," but it roused the GOP faithful.

As vice-president, Nixon was second only to Eisenhower as a party spokesman and was by far the most active Republican campaigner in 1954, 1956, and 1958. Yet his relationship with the President was cool. The old general, he believed, treated him like a junior staff officer. Nixon himself subsequently revealed that he felt engaged in a political tightrope act during Eisenhower's heart attack in 1955, and he sought to avoid the slightest appearance of assuming any presidential function. Nevertheless, as the 1956 nominating convention approached, there were rumors that he might be dumped from the ticket. The President in fact privately suggested that Nixon might want to leave the vice-presidency and take a cabinet post in order to establish himself as a serious national figure. No human being cognizant of Eisenhower's precarious health and possessing an ounce of ambition would have taken the offer, and the President apparently did not feel strongly enough about it to force Nixon out.

The second term quickly developed into a preparation for the 1960 campaign. Journalists began to write of a "new Nixon," more moderate and statesmanlike than the old model. The vice-president made highly publicized trips abroad. On a Latin American tour, he was assailed by communist demonstrators; at a trade exposition in Moscow, he engaged in a vociferous ideological debate with Premier Khrushchev. The film footage of these incidents was more valuable than finely spun gold in an anticommunist era. With Eisenhower acquiescing in his candidacy, with a new moderate identity, with strong rank-and-file backing, he was a natural choice for the Republican presidential nomination in 1960. His hairline loss to JFK indicated that he could muster a substantial following across the political spectrum. Still, he was a defeated politician without a tangible power base, and the worst was yet to come.

His race for governor of California in 1962 was a disaster in which he was handily defeated by the incumbent, Edmund G. ("Pat") Brown. The morning after the election, physically and emotionally drained, he called a press conference. With whirring cameras recording every word and gesture, he launched into a bitter diatribe against the reporters who had been covering him: "Just think how much you're going to be missing. You won't have Nixon to kick around anymore." Shortly afterward, he moved to New York and began a lucrative law practice. In the spring of 1964 he discreetly offered himself to Republican leaders as the moderate alternative to Barry Goldwater. In the main, the collective reaction was surprise and amusement; there were no takers. Goldwater himself publicly remarked of his would-be rival: "He is sounding more and more like Harold Stassen every day." The astute Washington journalist Robert Novak opined that, "Dick Nixon had come to the end of the line."

Out there, somewhere, however, beyond the reach of the television cameras or the ken of the big-city journalists, he still had a constituency, and in the wake of the Goldwater fiasco he set about to rebuild it the only way he knew—with hard work in the service of the party. In the congressional elections of 1966, he emerged as the GOP's chief fund-raiser and campaigner. He traveled 30,000 miles, spoke in 82 congressional districts, left innumerable local politicians feeling they owed him a favor, and reaped a large proportion of the credit for the Republican gains in the election. Far more than the usually remote politicos of the eastern Republican establishment, he identified with the GOP rank and file and embodied its values. Beginning with New Hampshire, he scored one victory after another in the 1968 Republican primaries and gathered delegate commitments throughout the West and Midwest. Meeting with Senator Strom Thurmond and other southern Republican leaders, he successfully put across the conviction that he was a right-of-center candidate who sympathized with the problems of the South. His first-ballot nomination was indicative of his standing within the party, and his narrow

November victory as a minority President was an equally accurate measure of his precarious standing with the whole electorate.

The man who was inaugurated on January 20, 1969, had traveled an even longer and harder road than do most seekers after the White House. To a large extent, he was a self-made President who had won the office through effort and perseverance. He was acutely aware that he was not a national hero like Eisenhower or a man such as John F. Kennedy whose appeal rested so heavily upon style, sophistication, and wit. He knew of Eisenhower's private skepticism about him and Kennedy's somewhat less private disdain of his lack of "class." He not only had worked hard; he had fought his way to the top with more than the usual amount of political kicking and gouging. Even so professional and detached a politician as the old Democratic Speaker of the House, Sam Rayburn, had loathed him and had characterized him as an "evil" man. To a large extent, the future of his Presidency would depend on his ability to restrain the ugly instinct for the jugular which he had displayed so frequently during the first decade of his political career.

His resiliency was ideological as well as electoral. At heart, Nixon was a conservative who deeply believed in the traditional values of self-help, individualism, small government, patriotism, and Victorian social behavior. But like almost all successful politicians, he was a pragmatist-opportunist who would subordinate his personal preferences to the necessities of the moment as he understood them, whether it meant changing a position to win an election or arriving at the detached conviction that the national interest required an understanding with the hated Red Chinese. Whenever possible, he would follow his values, but he would not let them become a trap.

Yet this intensely practical man possessed streaks of melodramatic romanticism. His experience had taught him that political friendships were fragile and transitory, that he could trust only a few close associates. He transmuted this rather grubby lesson of practical politics into a self-image as a loner who pondered the great problems of state in solitude before descending the mountain to deliver his judgment. Realizing that luck had played an important role in his career, he liked to think of himself as a man of destiny who had emerged as a leader after years of travail. His only autobiographical work, published in 1961, depicted his life as a series of crises which he had faced and overcome. He idealized no foreign leader more than General Charles de Gaulle. On occasion, his personal quest for grandeur became ridiculous, as when he outfitted the White House police in uniforms that might have been purchased from a theater company ending a run of *The Prisoner of Zenda*. Even more than most Presidents, he appears to have been outraged by demonstrators, interpreting their presence outside the White House or at his inauguration as a variety of lèse majesté.

Clearly, these attitudes had developed as compensation for a deep insecurity which they nevertheless could not wholly conceal. Nixon's critics charged him with paranoia, but he was surely correct in believing that he had many political enemies. What was remarkable was his apparent fear that he could not cope with them. His televised speeches were frequently lackluster and unconvincing; his televised press conferences, on the other hand, he usually handled with skill and mastery. Yet he preferred the speech, a situation that was under his total control, to the press conference, an ordeal to which he submitted with increasing rarity. And his near abrogation of public meetings with the press was only the most visible manifestation of the extreme isolation he imposed on himself, not simply from reporters but also from the cabinet, the Republican party leadership, and most of the White House staff. As a modus operandi, this aloofness possessed about the same virtues and vices as had Eisenhower's rather similar management of the Presidency; it gave the Chief Executive time to concentrate on matters of high policy but also insulated him from many sources of opinion and irritated many politicians and officials who were resentful of having to deal with White House subordinates. The unassailable Eisenhower could conduct his office in such a manner, but in this as in other ways Nixon was prone to forget that he did not have Eisenhower's standing as a public hero.

THE POLITICS OF LAW AND ORDER

Although Nixon had been elected with a minority of the total popular vote, he and his advisers felt that the prospect of developing a Republican majority was good. The goal could be reached by bringing slightly more than half the Wallace voters into the GOP fold, and it was possible to appeal to them without alienating many regular Republicans. The most ambitious advocate of such a ploy was Kevin Phillips, campaign strategist, author of *The Emerging Republican Majority* (1969), and, during the first year of the administration, a special assistant to the attorney general. What Phillips sought was no less than the preemption of Middle America through cultural appeals, use of the segregation issue, and positive economic programs such as aid to parochial schools. The administration did not follow Phillips's program to the letter, and, as is the case with almost all administrations, its policies were at times inconsistent and self-contradictory. Nevertheless, from the beginning it followed a reasonably coherent design of playing to the grievances of the South and the blue-collar Middle American.

One major aspect of this strategy was a new approach to civil rights. The objective was not to undertake a naked reversal of Johnson administration policies but rather to keep a low profile. The administration would not push hard for any civil rights objective and would above all refrain from any display of punitive attitudes toward those who resisted integration. On the other hand, it would vocally oppose busing children for the sake of integration; here was an issue with great clout in the North as well as the South, and Wallace's strength in the northern industrial states tended to peak in the areas that felt threatened by court-ordered transportation.

The administration rejected the policy of cutting off federal funds to school districts that resisted desegregation; instead, it proposed special financial aid to ease the difficulties of change. When Mississippi lawyers went before the U.S. Supreme Court to plead for delays in integration, government attorneys filed supporting arguments; it was a stunning symbolic reversal of the federal role. The White House refused to back the Equal Employment Opportunity Commission when that body asked Congress for the power to issue enforceable cease-and-desist orders against employers it considered guilty of discrimination; the commission had to settle for the authority to sue in the federal courts. Programs initiated during the Johnson administration to bring more blacks into lily-white construction unions languished, ignored and forgotten. When the Voting Rights Act of 1965 came up for renewal, the attorney general testified, unsuccessfully, in favor of amendments that would have crippled it. The President himself repeatedly stated his opposition both to busing and to proposed federal programs that would push low-income housing, and blacks, out of the central cities into white middle-class suburbs. Civil rights leaders, insurgent liberal bureaucrats, even the U.S. Civil Rights Commission, denounced the new policies, but White House strategists were aware that Nixon could obtain few votes in such circles whatever his course and that his moves were very popular with the constituencies he sought to cultivate.

The second important line of action was the use of what analysts were beginning to call "the social issue," a broad-gauged appeal to Middle America at the level of cultural politics, not too different from Wallace's denunciation of beatniks and pointy-headed intellectuals. By attacking New Left revolutionaries, hippie counterculturists, pornography, and elitist intellectual critics of America (and the administration), by adding large doses of patriotism, by ostentatiously affirming the old morality and the work ethic, the President and his advisers appealed to the tradition-oriented. Nixon had adopted the slogan "Bring Us Together" after noticing the phrase on a hand-lettered sign at a campaign rally, but the thrust of his strategy ran in the opposite direction. Cultural issues were real and important, but rather than seeking measured debate on them, the administration used them for manipulative purposes. It *wanted* to engage in a theater of confrontation with the dissenting elements in American civilization in the belief that support could be most easily built by making enemies.

One of the most visible symbols of the Middle American strategy was the attorney general, John Mitchell, the President's 1968 campaign manager and most influential political adviser. Under Mitchell, the Justice Department pursued a rigid yet extremely selective policy of "law and order." It declared war on crime and stressed tough drug-law enforcement with methods which included tedious customs searches and midnight raids by plainclothesmen against the homes of suspects. For the District of Columbia, it sponsored and obtained passage of a bill which permitted no-knock raids and allowed judges to impose "preventive detention"—denial of bail—on persons with previous arrest records. Mitchell argued that such methods were effective, but libertarians with good reason questioned the statistics used to justify the claim and assailed the administration's contempt for individual rights.

The Justice Department was equally tough against domestic radicals. Mitchell claimed, and exercised, the right to impose "internal security" wiretaps without court approval until the Supreme Court ruled against the practice in 1971. The department also obtained conspiracy indictments against several groups of radicals, in some cases attempting to magnify misdemeanors such as draft board vandalization into major felonies, in other cases basing the prosecution simply on the assertion that the accused individuals had planned to commit crimes. Resting usually upon the testimony of paid informants, the prosecutions failed to produce a single conviction, although they were successful in subjecting the defendants to immense personal and financial stress. In the spring of 1971 the administration nipped a mass antiwar attempt to tie up District of Columbia traffic by arresting almost anyone who looked like a demonstrator, some 12,500 people in all, whether engaging in disorderly conduct or not. When Daniel Ellsberg leaked the secret Pentagon Papers to the New York *Times* and other newspapers, Mitchell obtained a temporary restraining order against their publication, a case of prior censorship without precedent in modern American history. After the Supreme Court ruled against the government,* U.S. attorneys secured an indictment against Ellsberg and an associate under the Espionage Act.

* Voting against the government position were Justices Hugo Black (appointed by Roosevelt), William O. Douglas (Roosevelt), William Brennan (Eisenhower), Potter Stewart (Eisenhower), Byron White (Kennedy), and Thurgood Marshall (Johnson). Voting to sustain the federal restraining order were Chief Justice Warren Burger (Nixon), Harry Blackmun (Nixon), and John Marshall Harlan (Eisenhower).

In other areas, law and order was not as rigorous a proposition. The Justice Department sought no indictments in the shooting of students at Kent State University in 1970 during an antiwar demonstration. Only a few weeks after the Kent State incident, the President accepted a hard hat from New York construction union leaders whose men had roamed through lower Manhattan beating up students, and he sensed nothing untoward in praising their patriotic zeal. The government secretly pursued the investigation and prosecution of Ellsberg with illegal methods, which when they came to light would impel the trial judge, a Republican appointee, to throw the case out of court. The administration applied pressure and persuasion to the federal parole board to get the convicted labor racketeer Jimmy Hoffa out of prison before the 1972 election. Hoffa and his Teamsters Union predictably responded with a declaration of political support. After a military court-martial sentenced Lieutenant William Calley to life in prison for commanding the infamous My Lai massacre, the President responded to what appeared to be a groundswell of Middle American support for Calley. He suspended the requirement of military law that Calley begin serving the sentence immediately, allowed him to live comfortably in his Fort Benning apartment while appeals made their leisurely way through the military justice system, and promised to review the final decision personally. The administration of justice had become a political weapon to a degree unexperienced in twentieth-century America.

The chief rhetorician of the social issue was Vice-President Spiro T. Agnew. Hardly known outside his home state of Maryland before being picked for the vice-presidency, Agnew was little more than a subject for jokes about his obscurity until the fall of 1969, when he emerged in spectacular fashion as the administration's verbal hatchet man. He first attracted notice in October by calling the organizers of a Washington antiwar demonstration "an effete corps of impudent snobs who characterize themselves as intellectuals." The next month, he tore into network television news programs (in a speech televised without charge as an important event by the networks being attacked), decried the "instant analysis" of presidential speeches by commentators, and asserted that coverage was in general biased and slanted against the administration. A follow-up address made similar accusations against leading newspapers.

The Agnew speeches against the media were part of a carefully orchestrated campaign to intimidate the world of professional journalism and discredit it with the public. The administration harassed newspaper reporters by attempting to subpoena their confidential notes as evidence in federal prosecutions; in several parts of the country, state and local officials followed Washington's lead. Journalists resisted, arguing that their notes were protected by the First Amendment guarantee of freedom

of the press; and in fact if notes of confidential interviews were subpoenaed on a large scale, the result would be the destruction of investigative
reporting and hence severe limitations upon the flow of information to the
public. Most newspapermen were convinced that the administration's real
objective was news management. Unable to obtain relief in the courts,
they struggled for state and federal laws to protect them and raised a
protest so loud that the Justice Department backed away from free-
wheeling application of the tactic.

Television, the most pervasive of the news media, was also the most
vulnerable. The White House launched an effort, aborted only by the
Watergate scandal, to transform the independent Public Broadcasting
System into a Gaullist-style government mouthpiece. It attacked one of its
harshest newspaper critics, the Washington *Post,* by organizing challenges
to the renewal of the federal licenses of two Florida television stations
owned by the *Post.* It ordered an FBI investigation of Daniel Schorr, a CBS
television correspondent it considered particularly unfriendly. Agnew
himself, while piously disclaiming any suggestions of censorship, observed
ominously that the airwaves were subject to public regulation. The
television networks did not fold up, but they displayed signs of intimidation. The quality of news documentaries declined noticeably, and the
"instant analyses" which followed presidential speeches reached new
levels of timidity. The Federal Communications Commission, dominated
by the Republicans, scuttled a CBS attempt to establish a series of "loyal
opposition" programs in which the Democrats could reply to administration positions; thereafter the networks refused even to let the Democrats
buy time. When a guest on ABC's "Dick Cavett Show" spent about ten
minutes criticizing the administration's support for development of a
supersonic transport plane, the White House demanded, and got, the full
ninety minutes of a subsequent show to defend the SST. "We are now faced
with an almost complete Republican strangle hold on network television,"
complained Democratic National Chairman Lawrence O'Brien in the fall
of 1970.

Agnew himself suddenly became the GOP's hottest property. He had,
many observers believed, touched the nerve ends of Middle America. As a
speaker at party fund-raising functions, he was more in demand than any
Republican except the President, and, unlike Nixon, he did not have to
concern himself with presidential inhibitions against divisive rhetoric.
Less an impassioned orator than a clever speaker, Agnew attracted a
broad audience for his denunciations of "creeping permissiveness" and
"radical liberals" by turning his addresses into epigrammatic events,
spiced with bizarre alliterations designed to amuse and attract attention.
The process achieved the ultimate when one speech included the phrases
"troubadors of trouble," "nattering nabobs of negativism," and "hysteri-

cal hypochondriacs of history." But Agnew was no comedian. In his inimitable way, he voiced the hostilities of many people who were not traditional Republicans. His pronouncements made him both a favorite of the party faithful and a major politician whose appeal reached out far beyond the GOP fund-raising dinners and rallies into blue-collar and lower-middle-class constituencies.

The Mitchell-Agnew approach to politics dominated the administration's handling of the Supreme Court. One of Nixon's campaign promises, designed to appeal both to the South and to Middle America in general, was that he would fill Supreme Court vacancies with "strict constructionists" * who would take a hard line against crime and disorder. When the President took office, one crucial vacancy awaited his decision and another quickly developed.

In the summer of 1968 Earl Warren had announced his resignation as chief justice, doubtless partly motivated by the expectation that President Johnson would appoint a like-minded successor. Johnson had nominated Justice Abe Fortas, a dedicated libertarian, but in doing so he aroused the wrath of southern Democrats and the nearly united opposition of Republicans. In a dramatic demonstration of LBJ's lame-duck status, the Senate thumbed its nose at the man who once commanded it and refused to act on the nomination. In May 1969, as Nixon still pondered the choice of a successor to Warren, *Life* magazine broke the story that Fortas had accepted an annual income supplement of $20,000 from a foundation controlled by a financier who had been convicted of stock fraud. Such behavior was improper, although probably less so than the financial dealings which Nixon himself had defended in the celebrated "Checkers" speech of 1952. Nevertheless, the administration applied heavy pressure to get Fortas off the Supreme Court, and on May 15 the jurist submitted his resignation.

A week later, Nixon filled the chief justiceship with Warren E. Burger, a federal judge and native of Minnesota. Promptly confirmed by the Senate, Burger quickly established himself as a moderate conservative who usually would vote to uphold the clear precedents established by the Warren Court but not to break new ground. Convinced that the Court had overextended and overworked itself, he invited congressional limitations upon its jurisdiction and lobbied for the establishment of a special appellate tribunal which would screen out many of the cases that burdened the justices.

Fortas's seat remained vacant for thirteen months as Nixon tried to

---

* "Strict constructionism" in theory had a very fuzzy meaning. Mr. Justice Black, one of the most consistent liberals on the Court, called himself a strict constructionist. To the public at large, however, it meant conservatism; and to the South it had possessed a special meaning since the days of John C. Calhoun.

fill it with two southern conservative federal judges—first, Clement F. Haynsworth, Jr., of South Carolina, then, G. Harrold Carswell of Florida. Both men were rejected by the Senate. Haynsworth was turned down on the basis of his hostility to labor unions and the civil rights movement and because of a possible economic conflict of interest more serious than the circumstances which had driven Fortas from the Court. The Carswell appointment went under partly for ideological reasons but mainly because the nominee's reversal-studded record demonstrated an undeniable lack of competence. (One of Carswell's strongest backers, Nebraska Senator Roman Hruska, found himself reduced to the lame argument that, after all, the vast mediocre segment of the American legal profession was entitled to some representation on the highest judicial body in the country.)

During the prolonged controversy, Nixon displayed some of his worst characteristics. He petulantly argued that the Senate was usurping the powers of the Presidency by refusing to rubber-stamp his choices; after Carswell's defeat, he accused the opposition of bigotry against southerners. To the relief of all concerned, his third selection, Federal Judge Harry Blackmun, possessed solid credentials and unquestioned integrity; he won rapid confirmation. Natives of the same state, Burger and Blackmun were nearly identical in outlook; they voted together so often in Court decisions that journalists soon dubbed them "the Minnesota twins."

In December 1971 Nixon made his third and fourth appointments, Deputy Attorney General William H. Rehnquist and Lewis F. Powell, a distinguished Virginia lawyer. Powell, a conservative in the Burger-Blackmun mold, faced no opposition. Rehnquist also won confirmation, although he was known as a dogmatic right-winger and had been closely associated with the Justice Department's unsavory civil rights and civil liberties policies. The result was the emergence in 1972 of a reasonably cohesive four-man Nixon bloc on the Supreme Court, frequently joined by Kennedy's most conservative appointee, Byron R. White, to form a majority in cases on civil liberties and equal legislative representation. In these areas, the net effect was to back away from the more liberal positions of the Warren Court by qualifying and trimming them but not by reversing them outright. In racial decisions, the Court remained firmly integrationist, and it outraged many conservatives by striking down most of the restrictions on abortion. Still, its day in the vanguard of the libertarian movement had come to an end.

The President employed the social issue in a somewhat more dignified fashion than Agnew and other Republican orators, but he also ostentatiously affirmed traditional values. When a select commission on obscenity reported its conclusion that pornography was a relatively harmless phenomenon, Nixon rejected the finding as a "morally bankrupt" endorsement of smut. When a commission on drugs decided that marijuana was no more harmful than alcohol and suggested an end to legal penalties for its possession, the President refused to consider the recommendations. Vetoing a bill to establish a nationally subsidized system of day-care facilities for the children of working mothers, Nixon unstintingly praised old concepts of motherhood and family togetherness. Arguing in favor of work requirements for welfare recipients, he asserted the dignity of all labor, right down to the sweeping of floors or the emptying of bedpans.*

The management of radical dissent was a tougher problem. Many of the administration's policies—its conspiracy prosecutions, Agnew's rhetoric, the excruciatingly slow winding-down of the Vietnam war—stirred a resentment that inevitably and appropriately focused upon Nixon. The President's own critiques of the radical left were less inflammatory than Agnew's, but at times his emotions overcame him. On May 1, 1970, the day after he had made an impassioned speech justifying his decision to invade Cambodia, he allowed a reporter with a tape recorder to catch him in an emotional denunciation of antiwar college students as "bums." Three days later, Ohio National Guardsmen shot and killed four students while trying to break up an antiwar demonstration at Kent State University. The effect was to reawaken a slumbering campus militance and plunge many of the nation's leading institutions of higher education into chaos. Nixon of course could not be held responsible for the actions of Ohio Guardsmen, and to his credit he made an effort, albeit fumbling and ineffective, to engage in a dialogue with some of the young demonstrators who descended upon Washington. But he also demonstrated insensitivity with a remark that the Kent tragedy exemplified the way in which protest could escalate into violence. Even here, he represented the mood of his constituency; opinion polls demonstrated little national remorse over the shootings, great indignation at the campus disruptions.

Underneath the divisive rhetoric and policies, the administration took some steps that were more constructive than most of its critics admitted. The White House decisively reversed the Johnsonian policy of escalation and disarmed a peace movement which now found itself reduced to protesting the slow rate of troop decreases. The President used his executive authority to initiate a long-overdue reform of the Selective Service System. By employing a national lottery which established an individual's birthday as the basis for the order of induction and by elim

* The illustration was typical of so much of Nixon's rhetoric in its tendency to somehow cheapen genuinely noble sentiments by expressing them in a banal and ludicrous fashion.

inating most deferments, Nixon gave the draft uniformity, fairness, and predictability; moreover, he proclaimed the eventual goal of an all-volunteer army, and achieved it by 1972. Before Cambodia and Kent State, the universities had calmed noticeably, and the upsurge of indignation that came in the spring of 1970 would not be sustained over the long run.

Nixon's attitude toward social reform combined traditional Republican fiscal conservatism and a more pragmatic conviction that the Great Society had been guilty of promising too much too fast. Determined to hold down rapidly escalating federal expenditures for social programs, the President used his veto power freely; yet he appeared receptive to new approaches, even those which would cost money. For a time at least, he was strongly influenced by Daniel Patrick Moynihan, a respected academician hitherto connected with the liberal wing of the Democratic party. Serving as Nixon's adviser on urban problems, Moynihan adopted British Tory reformism as a model approach and rejected the millennial aspirations of the Great Society in favor of more modest, and more attainable, objectives. In a famous memorandum on racial problems, he argued that civil rights laws and social programs had produced notable increases in the standard of living of black Americans, doubted the feasibility of new legislation, and suggested a policy of "benign neglect." He also developed—and Nixon supported—the most innovative program in the history of American welfare liberalism, the Family Assistance Plan.

Basically, the FAP would have junked the existing welfare system in favor of a minimal guaranteed income determined by the number of individuals within a needy family; unlike the existing welfare system, it thus encouraged a father to stay with his wife and children. It required recipients to register for jobs, but, more importantly, it contained a strong work incentive. The FAP was a bold formulation which extended the hope of breaking through the welfare dilemma, but its cost, initially at least, would have been greater than that of the established system. Many liberals criticized the meagerness of the subsidy—the 1969 proposal would have provided only $2,400 in benefits for a family of four with no outside income—and found fault with other details. Still, the FAP was a promising beginning in the quest for an alternative to the universally criticized existing welfare procedures; its ultimate failure was both unfortunate and illogical. Criticized by Republican conservatives more outraged by the concept of a guaranteed income than mollified by the work provisions, attacked by Democratic liberals who proposed politically impossible levels of income maintenance, rather haphazardly supported by a White House preoccupied with other concerns, the FAP died a slow death in Congress. Moynihan himself eventually left his White House job to become ambassador to India. One of Nixon's most remarkable initiatives in the end came to nothing.

The administration responded to the rising wave of concern about environmental pollution. Its policies were not entirely consistent—Nixon sought unsuccessfully to subsidize the construction of a supersonic transport plane, although most ecologically minded people were convinced that the SST would be a disaster in terms of noise and air pollution and energy consumption. Presenting the control of water pollution as an urgent necessity, the administration proceeded to recommend funding for sewage treatment facilities below the level already authorized by Congress. Nevertheless, Nixon accepted pollution as an urgent problem, put his signature on laws to control it, used his executive power to establish a strong new Environmental Protection Agency, and appointed as its head William D. Ruckleshaus, a firm administrator and a sincere environmentalist. The SST aside, the White House's differences with liberal Democrats on ecological issues amounted to little more than an argument over the pace of cleanup and regulation.

In order to assist financially straitened state and local governments, the administration recommended a program of federal revenue sharing, a system of no-strings-attached federal grants to state and local governments, supplementing rather than replacing existing federal aid programs. The program was ideologically ambidextrous—conservatives could support it as a means of rejuvenating those governmental levels closest to the people; liberals could accept it as a way of providing support for many undernourished services traditionally financed by the states. The opposition likewise wore no ideological label. Some analysts and commentators, conservative and liberal, argued against separating spending privileges from the responsibility of taxing; some questioned the premise that state and local governments were more responsive to the needs of their citizens, especially the underprivileged, than was the federal establishment. Nevertheless, the White House put together a sustained nonpartisan lobbying campaign and obtained passage of revenue sharing in 1972. One could doubt that the program would have a profound effect upon the federal-state distribution of power, but it was a bold and possibly constructive innovation.

As the 1970 elections approached, the social polarization that had been mounting through the 1960s reached a peak, characterized by bombings, including the fatal episode at the University of Wisconsin, and by what amounted to a state of warfare between police and black militants in several cities across the country. There was a wide belief that radical and liberal students, galvanized by the Kent State shootings, would play large and perhaps decisive roles in many of the congressional contests. In this atmosphere, it was rather natural for the Republicans to turn to the social issues as the basis for fighting out the elections.

With 35 Senate seats being contested and 25 of them held by

Democrats, the White House perceived an opportunity to win, if not an actual GOP majority in the Senate, at least an ideological majority of conservatives inclined to support the President. The stress on ideology was so strong, in fact, that the administration threw its support in the New York senatorial contest to Conservative party candidate James Buckley against the liberal Republican incumbent, Charles Goodell, whom Agnew sneeringly described as "the Christine Jorgensen of the Republican party." The chief figure of the Republican campaign, Agnew crisscrossed the nation with the assertion that the Democrats were the party of riot and radicalism, permissiveness and pornography, the Republicans the party of law and order. Carried into overstatement by the enthusiasm of the party faithful, he handed the Democrats an issue most of them could meet; they simply made less extreme affirmations of traditional values and engaged in symbolic demonstrations of patriotism. In Illinois, for example, Democratic senatorial hopeful Adlai E. Stevenson, III, began wearing a tiny American flag in his lapel and reminding his audiences of his service as a tank commander during World War II—while also denouncing the divisive tactics of the GOP. In the closing weeks of the campaign, the President stumped the country making speeches similar to Agnew's. His final address, an emotional arm-waving performance, poorly filmed and edited for television, hurt the Republican cause. The Democrats responded with a talk by their 1968 vice-presidential candidate, Edmund Muskie, who presented a calm, firm refutation of the opposition, and thereby established himself as the probable carrier of his party's standard in 1972.

The results demonstrated the limitations of a law-and-order political strategy when it was not accompanied by more affirmative appeals. The Democrats gained 9 seats in the House and, for all their vulnerability in the Senate races, lost only 3 seats in the upper chamber. Victories of candidates such as Buckley in New York and the Independent Harry F. Byrd, Jr., in Virginia brought the President somewhat closer to his ideological majority, but in all the outcome was a disappointment. A fundamental reason for it was that the administration attempt to appeal to Middle America on the basis of social-cultural issues had not been accompanied by tangible benefits but by an economic policy that pinched and frightened many Middle Americans.

THE ECONOMICS OF STAGFLATION

The Democrats had countered the social issue in part by attacking on another front. Lawrence O'Brien called administration economic policy "Nixonomics," a system in which "all things that should go up—the stock market, corporate profits, real spendable income, productivity—go down, and all the things that should go down—unemployment, prices, interest rates—go up." The description was partisan but fundamentally accurate. By the fall of 1970, prices were increasing at the most rapid rate since the Korean war; yet the economy was in a recession, and unemployment was rising as fast as prices on the economic charts. For many voters, the social issue had become an ideological luxury.

Even Nixon's bitterest enemies had to admit that Johnson had passed along a difficult economic legacy. During 1968, prices had gone up 4.7 percent and neither the tax surcharge nor Federal Reserve tight credit policies had instituted a downswing. Yet the 1968 economy was in a boom, and unemployment had averaged only 3.5 percent, a rate that translated into substantially full employment. The new administration thus faced the enormously difficult and delicate task of controlling inflation while maintaining prosperity. It was in truth a task for which the American political economy remained unprepared. Tax adjustments, as the history of LBJ's surcharge demonstrated, were politically slow and difficult. Credit crunches could not be maintained over an extended period, and indeed the American economy was so dependent on credit at all levels that some analysts suspected that high interest rates actually fueled inflation. Giant corporations and labor unions, moreover, possessed a large degree of independence from government policy and market forces in raising prices and wages. Finally, inflation had become to some extent a problem that pervaded capitalist and mixed economies throughout the world. Neither conservative nor liberal economists could offer easy answers to the situation; in fact, they could offer no certain solutions at all. Neo-Keynesian economists no longer spoke optimistically of fine-tuning an economy to price stability and full employment.

The President's major economic advisers—Arthur F. Burns, whom he soon appointed chairman of the Federal Reserve Board; Paul McCracken and Herbert Stein, his successive chairmen of the Council of Economic Advisers—were moderates who accepted much of the New Economics and agreed that inflation had to be subdued without a drastic wringing-out of the economy. They rejected wage and price controls as unworkable in a nation not at total war, and Nixon himself still distastefully remembered his experience with the OPA. They foreswore "jawboning" as a technique which had been ineffective. The administration "game plan," as the President liked to call it, was to engineer an economic slowdown by cutting government spending and encouraging tight money policies by the Federal Reserve.

The result was what O'Brien and other Democrats called Nixon-omics, stagflation, or "the worst of all possible worlds." The economy curved downward into a recession, albeit the mildest of the post–World War II era, and unemployment climbed inexorably, reaching 6 percent by the end of 1970. Inflation surged on at an annual rate of more than 5 percent. The stock market, a force to which Republicans tended to be especially sensitive, plummeted disastrously. The Dow-Jones index had stood at 985 shortly after Nixon's election, and bullish investors had iced the champagne for a breakthrough at the symbolically magic 1000 level. Instead, the road was down—all the way to 631 in May 1970, before the Federal Reserve began to ease credit and thereby contribute to a steady recovery. The economy, to be sure, remained basically strong. Most families could maintain or better their standard of living, but the less secure felt a tightening, and many of them were among the Middle Americans Nixon had hoped to coopt for the Republicans. The 1970 election results made clear the need for a new economic strategy.

Over the next several months, pragmatic necessities ate away at the President's conservative convictions. Deciding that the rapid rise in unemployment had become a more critical problem than an inflation which in any case was not yielding to recessionary medicine, he presented Congress with a stimulative budget "balanced at full employment." This meant that in reality the budget was not balanced; rather government expenditures were proposed at a level that would have equaled total federal revenues had full employment, with its additional tax dividends, prevailed in the economy. The concept had been advocated as far back as World War II by such men as Henry A. Wallace and Leon Keyserling. The new departure seemed all the more pronounced when Nixon proclaimed, "I am now a Keynesian."

Fiscal policy, however, required lead time—at least a year to get appropriations through Congress and sufficiently disbursed to have an impact upon the economy. As the situation continued to deteriorate, the President opted for more drastic action. Nixon was especially influenced by his new secretary of the treasury, John B. Connally, the former governor of Texas. A conservative preparing for a move into the Republican party, Connally was nonetheless a pragmatic activist unwilling to remain passive in the face of impending disaster. On August 15, 1971, the President went on television to make a dramatic announcement. Employing authority previously given to him over his protests by the Democratic Congress, he proclaimed a ninety-day freeze of wages and prices as Phase I of a comprehensive control program. Phase II, introduced in November, established firm guidelines for increases in prices, wages, dividends, and interest rates. Phase II was loosely enforced at the small business level but fairly successful in dealing with the giant corporations and unions. Under it, economic conditions improved only marginally, but many people felt that Nixon had staved off a serious crisis and welcomed the small relief his new approach gave them.

One aspect of the President's new economic policy attracted minimal popular attention, but was all the same vitally important. The administration suspended the convertibility of the dollar into gold and thus announced the beginning of the end of the dollar-based international monetary system which the United States had established at the end of World War II. The step had become necessary because America had for years sent surpluses of dollars overseas; these surpluses, attributable to foreign economic and military aid until 1971, became an intolerable glut when the United States began to run an international trade deficit. Foreign central banks with no trading use for their dollar holdings began to present them for redemption in gold at the official price of $35 an ounce. By mid-1971, the vaults at Fort Knox were in danger of being emptied.

Nixon's decision to cut the dollar loose was the first in a series of steps designed to bring international trade, especially with strong exporters like Germany and Japan, back into some semblance of balance. No longer redeemable in precious metal, American dollars would find their true international value by "floating" in relation to other currencies and thus, it was hoped, arrive at a fairer and more realistic rate than that assigned by the old rigid system. After some months of negotiation with other nations, the process was facilitated by an official 8.5 percent devaluation of the dollar in December 1971. Another devaluation of 10 percent would follow in February 1973. These official reductions were accomplished within the context of the float system, and in actuality the value of the dollar declined even more sharply in relation to the two strongest international currencies, the Japense yen and the German mark. In a sense, the United States was paying the final installment on the price of victory in World War II. Having compelled the Germans to concentrate on capitalism, having taught the Japanese to make cars and transistor radios instead of war, all the while providing military protection for them, America now formally relinquished its once unchallenged economic supremacy.

It was easier of course to give up supremacy in the marketplace than lives on the battlefield, and devaluation was a long overdue necessity. By giving the dollar a realistic exchange value, it promised to rejuvenate many U.S. industries which had been stung by foreign competitors selling products at artificially cheap prices. Because of devaluation, a Ford Pinto or Chevrolet Vega could undersell a Volkswagen Beetle, American steel was a better buy than Japanese steel, the U.S. electronics and textile industries could hope not simply for survival but for revival. There was one important disadvantage to devaluation—it added to inflationary pressures by increasing both domestic and foreign demand for U.S.

products and by more or less automatically raising the prices for commodities, such as Middle Eastern oil, which had to be purchased abroad. Nixon thus had found no painless remedies for U.S. economic difficulties, but here as in most of his other dealings with the international community, he had grudgingly accepted the necessities of his time instead of fighting them or hiding from them. This acceptance was prime requisite of statesmanship.

RETRENCHMENT AND RETREAT: NIXON, KISSINGER, AND AMERICAN DIPLOMACY

Foreign policy, the President declared, was his strong suit; if necessary, the federal bureaucracy could run the domestic affairs of the country without White House supervision; a successful foreign policy required an activist Chief Executive. In large measure, Nixon was correct, and his handling of diplomacy was the most successful aspect of his administration. Here, indeed, he compiled a record that was genuinely distinguished.

The President had shed the dogmatic anticommunism that once was his trademark. Perhaps, as some of his critics would charge, he never had regarded anti-Sovietism as more than a useful political vehicle; perhaps his view of the world had matured during his years out of office. It was doubtless also true that he realized both rationally and instinctively that the world scene provided the best setting for his heroic aspirations and that the ebbing of the cold war required any statesman who wanted to be a mover and shaker to go beyond the formulas of the past. Nixon was determined to be his own secretary of state in the fullest sense, right down to the establishment of what amounted to a separate department of foreign policy in the White House. To head up the State Department he selected William Rogers, a close friend and associate who had been attorney general under Eisenhower; Rogers would preside over a large and increasingly demoralized bureaucracy which would handle the routine matters of diplomacy and concern itself with problems not of pressing interest to the White House. The job of managing the most urgent concerns of foreign policy would be carried on in intimate contact with the President by the staff of the National Security Council, headed by Henry Kissinger.

Kissinger's personal history symbolized Nixon's determination to bypass the established diplomatic channels. A German-Jewish refugee who had come to the United States as a young teen-ager, Kissinger still spoke with a Central European accent. His career had been essentially that of a highly regarded academic analyst whose participation in the real world of politics and diplomacy as a consultant to the Kennedy and Johnson administrations, as an adviser to Nelson Rockefeller, had been peripheral. Possessing a tragic view of history—the result no doubt of his own experiences as well as of intellectual conviction—he was above all a classical realist in his approach to foreign policy, convinced that power rather than ideals must be the ultimate factor in dealings among nations.

A man of great talent and energy, far more loyal to his chief than most bureaucrats, Kissinger was the ideal choice to head a compact policy-making staff which could give the President policy evaluations and alternatives with far greater dispatch and secrecy than the unwieldy, leaky structure of State; he became one of Nixon's most trusted advisers. He was not, as some believed, a quiet evangelist who converted his boss to a realistic, nonemotional approach to world politics; he and Nixon were in substantial agreement on policy questions. But he gave the President's impulses a philosophical coherence they had not previously possessed. Beyond this, he served as the chief executioner of presidential policy aims, frequently managing diplomatic negotiations in which for one reason or another the President could not be personally involved. As Henry Brandon put it, Nixon was the architect; Kissinger was the contractor who put the design together and frequently was given great discretion in doing so.

Both men accepted the proposition that the bipolar power struggle between the United States and the Soviet Union, the dominant fact of the post–World War II world, was winding down and being replaced by a much more complex configuration of political and economic power. The European Common Market nations, Japan, and China had all acquired sufficient military or economic strength to play independent roles in the world. The United States, on the other hand, had become a tired super-power, overextended in its commitments, strained in its finances, preoccupied with critical social problems at home. As they saw it, these facts of life dictated a retreat of American power from its most advanced positions and a toning down of U.S. commitments appropriate to the retrenchment in military spending and capability which was certain to be a theme of the 1970s. The problem was to manage the transition in a way which would assist, rather than abort, the birth of the new balance of power and would avoid the sacrifice of any important national interest.

In its larger outline, the task held little promise of grandeur, an obstacle which Nixon met by defining his objective as "a generation of peace," but it was vitally necessary. It was also terribly difficult because it had to be done under the pressure of the Vietnam war. The prime example of the overextension of U.S. power, Vietnam was wrecking the morale, reputation, and political support of the military. It was creating neo-isolationist pressures, sometimes moderate and little different in basics from the Nixon-Kissinger outlook, sometimes extreme and irrational in the hope of escaping from the world. This latter mode of isolationism could only gather strength as the war continued. Therefore, the administration's most important task was to disengage from Southeast Asia as quickly as possible.

During the presidential campaign, Nixon had proclaimed that he had "a plan" to end the war; the claim was at the least considerably exaggerated but it did demonstrate a recognition of the necessity of withdrawal. However, the President was equally determined to get out of Vietnam "with honor"; to his mind, the departure from Southeast Asia was at best an unseemly necessity to be carried out without abandonment of allies or the appearance of surrender. The North Vietnamese and Viet Cong held to negotiating positions which did nothing to ease Nixon's dilemma. Doubtless encouraged by the strength of antiwar sentiment in the United States and convinced of the inevitability of American withdrawal, accustomed to war against Western imperialism as a way of life, they displayed little serious interest in a compromise solution. Instead, they periodically displayed captured American pilots and sought to increase pressure on the administration by making it clear that the POWs, for whom Americans felt enormous sympathy, would go home only when the United States concluded an acceptable peace agreement.

On the other side, the South Vietnamese government, headed by General Nguyen van Thieu, opposed any peace agreement and did everything in its power to keep the United States enmeshed in the fighting. In Nixon's mind at least, the Thieu government had become a separate constituency whose demands for support had to be balanced against the public demand for withdrawal. To make matters even more complicated, Nixon correctly perceived that many of those Americans who wanted disengagement shared his concern with national honor and prestige. Ultimately it was this ambiguity in the public mind, more than the demands of Saigon, that allowed him to operate a slow withdrawal.

The President satisfied his constituencies and defied the North Vietnamese with a mixture of approaches which effectively dulled the cutting edge of domestic protest while providing protection for South Vietnam. He reformed the draft and began to cut back troop strength, but did so with deliberation. On a trip to the Far East in July 1969, he held a press conference at Guam and announced that while the United States would honor its Asian treaty commitments, it would henceforth expect its allies to assume the burden of their own defense. The administration announced a policy of "Vietnamization," the gradual replacement of American combat forces with adequately trained and equipped South Vietnamese, who eventually would be able to stave off the communist threat themselves. To those who argued that his prolongation of the war would result in mounting American casualties and would leave American prisoners to rot in Hanoi's prisons, the President replied that he was protecting the integrity of U.S. commitments and moreover was maintaining a presence in the South to force the return of the prisoners. To underscore his determination, he pointedly ignored the periodic mass antiwar demonstrations which were becoming regular episodes of Washington life.

The strategy worked rather well. During its first year in office, the administration managed to pull some forces out of South Vietnam; by the end of 1969, total U.S. strength was down from 545,000 to 475,000, by mid-April 1970, the number was down to 430,000. On April 20, 1970, Nixon went on television to announce plans for a phased withdrawal of another 150,000 Americans over the next twelve months. Many antiwar leaders complained that the administration was moving too slowly, but with draft pressures easing and with deescalation clearly underway, Nixon was succeeding in buying time for his diplomatic objectives. Then came the invasion of Cambodia.

The North Vietnamese army had long moved with relative impunity through the small, neighboring neutral country, using it as an attack route, a supply depot, and a privileged sanctuary. Clandestine air attacks had accomplished little, and the U.S. military had long requested authorization to pursue the enemy across the border. The possibility became even more enticing, and more necessary, after right-wing Cambodian generals, led by Lon Nol, overthrew the neutralist chief of state, Prince Norodom Sihanouk, in March 1970. Lon Nol was pro-American, and Washington had encouraged his coup. Nevertheless, his ascendancy was a mixed blessing; he had no more power to drive out the communists than had Sihanouk, while they with a determined effort would be able to destroy his shaky government and take over the country. Thus in the spring of 1970 even as Nixon pursued his policy of deescalation, he was forced to give ever greater consideration to bringing the ground war to Cambodia.

On April 30, just ten days after his deescalation announcement, the President again used television to announce his decision. He was at his emotional worst, declaring that the United States could not be a "pitiful, helpless giant," announcing incredibly that the objective of the operation was the capture of no less than the headquarters of the communist command (COSVN). The announcement seemed to portend a wholly unexpected enlargement of the conflict. Whatever his reasons, Nixon had launched what appeared in calmer retrospect as a limited mission designed to disrupt communist supply lines and by his rhetoric had magnified that action into a major event of the war. Perhaps he really intended to establish a long-term U.S. military presence in Cambodia; if so, subsequent events destroyed the possibility.

The antiwar movement experienced an angry rebirth, four students at

Kent State became civilian casualties of the incursion, and campuses across the nation erupted. The public as a whole was puzzled, and leading Democrats and liberal Republicans, fearing that "tricky Dick" was deceiving them, began to introduce legislative resolutions designed in one fashion or another to end the war. Whatever the President's original intentions, the Cambodian operation came to an end in eight weeks, having achieved the limited objectives that had provided its primary rationale. It was the last large-scale campaign in which American ground troops played an important role. By September 1972, the effective beginning of the presidential election campaign, only 39,000 Americans remained in Vietnam. Given heavy U.S. air support, the Lon Nol government managed to survive, although it never controlled much of the country it purported to rule.

As the ground war became a Vietnamese affair, the United States stepped up its bombing role, not only in Cambodia and South Vietnam but also against the North. In theory at least, air attacks against the North had remained suspended since President Johnson had proclaimed a halt in the closing days of the 1968 campaign. The United States, however, had always reserved the right to strike back in "protective reaction" at antiaircraft fire aimed across the border at aircraft on missions in Laos or South Vietnam. However justified the doctrine may have been in theory, in practice it developed into a cover for limited offensive bombing raids against military installations and staging areas in the southern part of North Vietnam. In April 1972 the North Vietnamese undertook a major invasion of the South. Nixon responded with drastic steps—the resumption of an open, full-scale bombing campaign against the North and the mining of Haiphong harbor. The move was a brutal application of raw power and a real gamble which threatened to reverse improving relations with the USSR and China, but it helped force the North Vietnamese into more serious negotiations. Hanoi discovered that its big communist allies would not give it a blank check and that the South Vietnamese with heavy U.S. air support were strong enough to contain the attack launched against them. Bypassing the long-stalled Paris negotiations, the communists engaged in private meetings with Kissinger.

By October, Kissinger and his North Vietnamese counterpart, Le Duc Tho, had reached a secret agreement which provided for a cease-fire in place, international supervision of the truce, negotiations for a coalition government, free elections, withdrawal of the remaining U.S. troops, and release of all prisoners; both men placed their initials on the paper, and the United States suspended the bombing of the North. Then came a great anticlimax—the South Vietnamese refused to accept the peace plan, and Nixon upheld their veto. The communists, angry, desperate, and fully cognizant that the presidential election was only a couple of weeks away, began to leak details of the accord. Kissinger replied with a bravado performance, a long press conference in which he made the entire document public, explained it at length, declared "peace is at hand," and asserted that only a few clarifications were necessary.

In fact, the whole agreement was on the verge of coming unstuck. The communists began to come up with a host of "interpretations" which the United States found unacceptable. After Kissinger and Le Duc Tho met again in December and failed to make headway, Nixon ordered a resumption of full-scale bombing, including the use of awesome B-52s. Essentially a terror tactic, this latest escalation of the air war drew widespread protests, but it brought the communists back to Paris. The Nixon administration by this point was ready to accept the essential October draft and overrode objections from Saigon. In January 1973 the United States and the North Vietnamese signed an agreement little different from the earlier one. For Americans the terms would bring the final contingents of military personnel out of the South and the prisoners back from the North, reciting canned eulogies of their president in front of the TV cameras as they stepped back into U.S. jurisdiction; it would bring Kissinger and Tho the Nobel Peace Prize. But it would not bring peace to Vietnam; there a shadow of war would continue.

Having presided over a slow retreat, the President had finally achieved his peace with honor. Whether it had been worth a four-year continuation of the war was at least debatable, but it was undeniable that Nixon for all his strategy of delay had found the will and means to extricate America from a disaster which had been costly in blood and treasure—50,000 Americans killed, $146 billion poured into the quagmire—and prohibitive in its erosion of the national morale.

DETENTE AND ITS LIMITS

The process of disengagement from Vietnam facilitated—and was facilitated by—the recognition of other realities. Nixon and Kissinger sought to take the United States out of other cold-war entanglements that they did not consider vital to the national interest. This was not a new quest; to some extent, every administration since the end of the Korean war had pursued it, but never before had it been done on such a sustained and systematic basis.

Nixon and Kissinger wanted not just episodic relaxations of tension or a few unrelated agreements but a large number of interlocking arrangements which in sum would amount to a genuine détente. Their essential hope was to subordinate ideology, still a strong factor in the thinking of all sides, to the pragmatic self-interest of both the communist and the Western nations. They believed that rivalries limited by realistic calculation would in the end be more favorable to world peace than modes of thinking which resorted heavily to abstraction and idealism. The new multipolar world which they saw developing would still be characterized by competition among the major national states, but the struggle for advantage would exist at a manageable level, contained by rational statesmen and by a viable balance of power.

The most surprising approach to reality came in the administration's policy toward China. Mainland China had become the most ideological regime in the world; its propaganda and official pronouncements were vituperative and uncivilized by the standards of traditional diplomacy. Shunning normal diplomatic contacts, it had effectively shut itself off from the world. During the mid-1960s, it had been wracked by a chaotic cultural revolution. On the surface at least, its government appeared unremitting in its hatred of the United States. A good many American politicians had accepted the Chinese attitude and used it to their own advantage, Nixon among them. But an American public, sickened by Vietnam, was ready for a new approach, and cautious explorations revealed that the Red Chinese were receptive.

The new China policy emerged slowly. Washington allowed free trade and travel in 1969 and 1970, but few observers realized how far the secret discussions between the two nations had gone until July 1971, when the President announced that he had accepted an invitation to make a state visit to Peking. The announcement was followed up by an act heretofore unthinkable—U.S. support for the seating of Communist China in the United Nations. In the space of a few months, mainland China had joined the family of nations, with the endorsement of a Chief Executive who once had been among its most vociferous enemies. The development, one that Nixon had contemplated well before his association with Kissinger, was the most indelible symbol of his new maturity as a diplomat.

The President's trip in February 1972 became a television spectacular, undertaken in a breathless "Gee Whiz" mood which not only sold China to the American public, but made the trappings of Maoist culture a middle-class fad. The Gallup poll reported that in 1966 Americans had most frequently described the Chinese Communists as "ignorant," "warlike," "sly," "treacherous"; however, in the wake of the presidential visit, its opinion takers found that the most frequent adjectives had become "hard-working," "intelligent," "artistic," "progressive," and "practical." It was not surprising perhaps that a *naif* such as the actress Candice Bergen could return from a carefully supervised tour of the mainland prattling about the pervasive respect for human dignity she had encountered, but serious journalists such as James Reston, Harrison Salisbury, and even Joseph Alsop came out of China full of praise.

The White House encouraged such attitudes because it wanted the new policy to be thought morally good and successful. But one can be certain that neither the President nor his chief foreign policy adviser had illusions about human dignity in China. Their broadest objective was to bring an isolated and ostracized nuclear power into the international community in the hope that it might be induced to follow at least some of the rules connected with established diplomatic practice and behave in a more responsible fashion. They also realized that their declaration that the United States no longer considered China an international leper would give them more leverage in their push for détente with the Soviet Union.

Embroiled in a serious dispute with China, Russia sought a relaxation on other fronts. What had first surfaced as an ideological controversy took on an ominous character when troops of the two great communist powers fought pitched battles along their border. Russian military officials and diplomats began to sound out their American counterparts on the desirability of a preemptive strike against China's nuclear manufacturing facilities. The USSR began a vast military buildup along the Chinese boundary. From the Soviet point of view, Russia's national interests were far more imperiled by Chinese belligerence than by the nonaggressiveness of the West. Moreover, China's challenge to the USSR's claim to moral and ideological leadership of the communist world may well have stirred more bitterness than any ideological hostility the Soviet leaders perceived from the capitalist powers. As with the military threat, the danger was pressing and immediate; hence some sort of understanding with the West was required, not out of good will but out of the USSR's need to protect itself.

Nevertheless, the road to détente was difficult. Even with the best of faith on both sides—a condition not invariably present—there remained hard questions about the new boundaries of U.S.–Soviet competition. In its approach to détente, the United States insisted upon the principle of the "linkage" of all areas of conflict into a general commitment to world stability and, in effect, the status quo. The Soviet Union could hardly be expected to agree to so sweeping a proposition. Russia inflexibly insisted on the status quo in its own sphere of influence—after invading Czechoslovakia in 1968, party leader Leonid Brezhnev had proclaimed the "Brezhnev Doctrine," which asserted the right of unilateral intervention in any "socialist," i.e., Soviet bloc, state threatened by "counterrevolution." Nevertheless, the USSR would not abandon its outward thrust for influence. John F. Kennedy's characterization of Khrushchev's attitude in 1961 remained apt: "What's mine is mine. What's yours is negotiable."

The détente that Nixon and Kissinger sought could never be as sweeping as they wished. At best, the Russians would cooperate in the establishment of a friendly atmosphere, would move with greater caution, and would be more willing to compromise. One could not expect, however, that they would give up their probes into the noncommunist world. The problem thus was one of differentiating legitimate Soviet attempts to enlarge the USSR's influence from those that were illegitimate. Was the denominator the method employed? Did the distinction hinge instead on the geographical area involved? Or was it necessary to develop some formula which combined these and possibly other factors?

In 1970, for example, U.S. intelligence assembled information that pointed firmly toward the probability that the Soviet Union was building at top speed a base for its atomic submarines in Cuba. If the facility were completed, it would allow a substantial Russian nuclear presence in the Western Hemisphere, as potent and more mobile than the missile installations that had brought the two nations to the brink of war in 1962. In the U.S. view, the Russians were violating the Kennedy-Khrushchev agreement which had resolved the missile crisis; the Soviet leaders apparently hoped to present the Americans with a fait accompli. After strong protests, carried out confidentially for the most part, the USSR ceased construction, claiming that it never had been putting up a military base anyway.

The Cuban episode was probably little more than a tentative probe, perhaps simply the staging of a "concession" to be recalled in future negotiations, but Soviet ambitions in the Middle East were far more serious. Here was an area that had been a prime target of Russian imperialism long before the communist revolution and was now more important than ever. Its strategic significance remained great but was overshadowed by its economic importance. The Middle East provided 80 percent of Europe's oil requirements, even more of Japan's; by the beginning of the 1970s, Arab oil was becoming crucial for the United States. The Russian drive for control of the area thus ultimately involved the threat of being able to sever the economic lifeline of much of the noncommunist world.

A dozen years after the Suez debacle, the Western position was more tenuous than ever, primarily because of the continued Arab-Israeli conflict. This bitter antagonism had given the USSR a foothold in a region which otherwise would have been more unreceptive than almost any part of the world to communism. In 1967, their arsenals overflowing with Soviet weaponry, the Arab governments, led by Egypt's Nasser, withdrew the 1956 concession of Israeli access to the Gulf of Aqaba, expelled United Nations peacekeeping forces, and trumpeted to the world their intention of destroying Israel in a holy war. The Israelis, conditioned by the Nazi holocaust, took the threat of destruction seriously. Without waiting for an Arab attack, they launched a devastating blitzkreig against the military forces of Egypt, Jordan, Syria, and Lebanon. In less than a week, the Jewish state inflicted the worst military humiliation in modern Arab history and in the process occupied vast areas—the strategic Golan Heights of Syria, the city of Jerusalem, all of Jordan west of the Jordan River, and the entire Sinai Peninsula right up to the Suez Canal.

The Six-Day War changed the map of the Middle East but altered little else. Psychologically unable to accept defeat at the hands of the Jews, Nasser and other Arab chieftains resorted to the most durable theme of Third World demagoguery, anti-Americanism, and charged that it actually had been the American air force which had wiped out their armies. Whipping up anti-U.S. sentiment, they refused to negotiate with Israel and accepted a massive resupply of arms from the USSR. The events demonstrated conclusively that the Soviet Union had no interest in a Middle East settlement; indeed, if some diplomatic magician were able to bring peace to the region, the likely result would be a rapid ebbing of Russian influence and a mellowing Arab attitude toward the West. To prevent such a prospect, the Soviet Union was prepared to give billions of rubles worth of arms to the Arab nations and run considerable risks.

When Nixon took office, a spasmodic "war of attrition" was still in progress along the Suez Canal. The Russians poured thousands of military advisers into Egypt and began to fly defensive missions themselves against Israeli air raids. The essential administration policy was to provide Israel with sufficient means of self-defense while trying to play an "even-handed" role as a mediator in the hope of achieving some sort of peace agreement that would reduce Soviet leverage in the area and restore some measure of American influence. In theory, the policy was admirable. In practice, it was rather clumsily applied and insufficiently cognizant of the irrational hatred which underlay the Middle Eastern struggle.

By mid-1970, the State Department felt that it had established a basis for negotiations, and the warring parties along the canal agreed to a cease-fire. Then the whole mediation effort collapsed as the Egyptians and Russians moved vast numbers of SAM antiaircraft missiles into the cease-fire zone, creating a defense more formidable than that which protected North Vietnam. The United States in turn felt practically forced to respond with increased aid to Israel. As a result, Soviet standing among the Arabs was enhanced, the American position worse than before. In September 1970, when Jordan's King Hussein, who still leaned uneasily toward the West, moved against Palestinian guerrillas who had used his nation as a base for terrorist activities, Syria with tacit Soviet support unsuccessfully attacked Jordan. The episode raised even further doubts about Soviet intentions. The Middle Eastern situation seemed somewhat brighter in the summer of 1972 after Nasser's successor, Anwar el-Sadat, ordered the Soviet military delegation out of Egypt, but he did not rupture his military alliance with the USSR. The "expulsion" of the Russians, whatever its motives, would prove to be only the prelude to another war which threatened to advance the cycle of Soviet rise and U.S. decline in the Arab world.

Détente was not without its benefits, however, One of the most dangerous areas of Soviet-American confrontation, Berlin, calmed considerably. With U.S. encouragement, West German Chancellor Willy Brandt pursued a policy of *Ostpolitik* directed toward an accommodation with the communist world. West Germany signed goodwill treaties with the USSR and Poland, recognizing for the first time the Oder-Neisse line as the Polish boundary. Brandt sought friendly relations with East Germany, and by June 1972 had worked out in direct negotiations with the USSR and the major Western powers a new agreement regularizing the status of Berlin. In all these cases, the West Germans appeared to have made the major concessions, but these amounted to little more than a recognition of reality. In the last analysis, of course, nothing would prevent the Soviet Union from precipitating new Berlin crises should it choose to do so; but the 1972 agreement gave the West a firmer legal position and provided a symbolic embodiment of the normalization of relations.

Another area of progress was arms limitation. Nixon and Kissinger not only accepted the McNamara doctrine of "parity" as the only basis for an arms agreement but actually altered it to "sufficiency," a euphemism for a willingness to let the USSR, feeling menaced as it did by both the West and China, have a numerical superiority so long as the American nuclear arsenal was sufficient to withstand an enemy first strike and destroy the aggressor. The administration negotiated some agreements that had only minimal practical effect—the mutual renunciation of biological warfare, the banning of atomic weapons from the ocean floor (not from oceangoing submarines)—but its major attention went into the Strategic Arms Limitation Talks (SALT).

The limitation of nuclear weapons presented terribly complex and difficult problems both in diplomacy and internal politics. The American and Soviet leaders had to satisfy their military forces that no sacrifice of security was involved. Nixon, moreover, faced a growing revulsion against high military expenditures. Convinced that any unilateral move toward arms reduction would deprive the USSR of an incentive to negotiate, he successfully pushed through Congress the authorization for a limited antiballistic missile (ABM) system and resisted pressures for the withdrawal of troops from Europe. An agreement, finally achieved in 1972, put limitations on some varieties of nuclear weapons and on the hideously expensive ABMS, but, welcome as it was, it remained no more than a small beginning in a domain where the opportunities for proliferation were still great and the technology so complex that statesmen were forced to weigh the requirements of national security against their instincts rather than against any firm certainty. Stopping the arms race in a balance-of-power world was an increasingly difficult proposition; yet the necessity on both sides to see to domestic needs and scale down international tensions dictated the effort.

Nixon's diplomacy was not always constructive. In December 1971, when India and Pakistan went to war over the independence of East Pakistan (Bangladesh), the United States followed a policy incomprehensible in terms of either morality or national self-interest. Nixon emotionally supported Pakistan, largely it seemed because he had gotten along well with the Pakistani rulers and detested the Indian leadership. Yet in fact India, strongly backed by the USSR, had ample cause for war in the genocidal policy which the Pakistani army had carried on in Bangladesh; India enjoyed the bulk of American public support and proved itself easily the more powerful nation. As the Indian army won a quick and decisive victory, the administration engaged in helpless fulminations in an attempt to prop up a discredited regime which had displayed a Nazi-like talent for mass slaughter.

But this was the exception to an otherwise commendable record. Nixon and Kissinger would not transform the world into a peaceful utopia nor would they end the cold war, but they were successful in winding down old hostilities and making the planet a somewhat safer place for human life. Everything seemed to come together in 1972; first the China trip, then a visit to Moscow carried off in an atmosphere of cordiality even after the resumption of bombing against North Vietnam, the signing of the SALT agreement, a large wheat sale to the USSR, and, finally, Kissinger's "peace is at hand" announcement. It was not coincidental that all these events were occurring in an election year.

REELECT THE PRESIDENT

By 1972, Nixon's carefully orchestrated foreign policy was producing one triumph after another. Even the application of the bombing-mining policy against North Vietnam won heavy popular support. At home, it was true, the glow of success was not nearly so warm. The labor unions in particular grumbled about Phase II economics; still, the economy was swinging up from the low point of stagflation and the price situation seemed to be showing some improvement. Nixon himself had an unshakable hold on the loyalties of most Republicans. To beat him, the Democrats would have to nominate an unusually attractive individual with broad appeal. As always, however, the Democratic party was in disarray; a half-dozen major candidates were fighting for the nomination. The winner of such a free-for-all would not necessarily be the person with the broadest appeal to the whole electorate but rather the one with the most fervent following and best organization within the party.

One of the most formidable and charismatic of the Democratic contenders, although he had no real chance to be nominated, was George Wallace, back in the party after his independent candidacy of 1968. Wallace's appeal was, if anything, greater than ever, for his campaign focused upon what could be the most explosive social issue of the 1970s, the busing of children over long distances to achieve racial balance in the schools. His vote totals demonstrated how large the number of alienated Democrats had become. In Michigan, where busing was an immediate issue, he overwhelmed the labor-liberal establishment with a runaway first-place finish in the presidential primary. By then, however, he was out of the race, partially paralyzed by a bullet from the gun of a would-be assassin whose mind had reached the farthest extreme of alienation.

The Democratic center produced three candidates, all from the Senate: Henry Jackson, Hubert Humphrey, and Edmund Muskie. Jackson of Washington was an old-style cold-war liberal with especially close ties to the labor movement. His main problem was that much of the support that might gravitate toward him was preempted by Humphrey. Reelected to the Senate in 1970, the Minnesotan could count on the affection of the older segment of all the elements of the classic New Deal coalition, but he remained out of touch with most young liberal-minded people. Muskie seemed at the beginning of the year to be the far-ahead front-runner. As Humphrey's running mate in 1968, as the major party spokesman in the 1970 congressional campaign, he had made strong impressions as a voice of calm and reason in an era of political passion, a man of Lincolnesque qualities who could unite a divided country. Straddling most of the issues, he hoped to win nomination on the basis of these traits and little else. But seething emotions lay just beneath his calm exterior. In the New Hampshire primary campaign, he betrayed his temperament; in the midst of a speech denouncing a publisher who had printed defamatory accusations against him and his wife, his voice choked and the television cameras picked up what seemed to be tears. Quickly falling from front-runner to almost everyone's second choice, he was ground under by opponents more vivid in image and appeal.

The two remaining Democrats represented the left wing of the party. One of them, Mayor John V. Lindsay of New York, a former insurgent Republican who had just switched allegiance, failed to develop a substantial candidacy. Lindsay was quickly finished off by the other left-wing

Democrat, Senator George McGovern of South Dakota. McGovern had been running hard without being taken seriously since the beginning of 1971. He did, it was true, have an identification with the Kennedy family, having served under JFK in the early 1960s before being elected to the Senate, and he had moved into presidential politics in 1968 after the assassination of Robert Kennedy by declaring himself a stand-in candidate for the slain senator. A soaring idealist, he advocated sweeping social reforms at home and urged a nearly unconditional disengagement from Vietnam in a manner which implied withdrawal from most of the rest of the world as well. He had gained some prominence by chairing a committee that had reformed the rules for choosing delegates to the Democratic convention, but at the beginning of 1972 he was the least known of the major Democrats. It was a small liability, for he had surrounded himself with shrewd organizers and his style and policy positions made him all but irresistible to advocates of the "New Politics."

A somewhat fuzzy and doubtless overused term, the New Politics denoted essentially a style of reform which differed from New Deal liberalism. The New Politics rejected the organized groups of the New Deal coalition—the political machines, the big labor unions, the old Negro organizations—as flabby and complacent. In the broader sense, it renounced the concept of pluralist liberalism, the notion that reform and prosperity could be achieved through the competitive interplay of organizations which represented workers and minority groups; pluralist liberalism, the New Politics asserted, overlooked the plight of the unorganized.

The New Politics was heavily moral in tone, but not in the old sense of obsession with liquor or vice; it conceived of issues like war or poverty as moral issues. To its spokesmen, Vietnam was not a grievous miscalculation of the national interest, it was a moral obscenity which was first of all a crime against the Vietnamese people, North and South, and secondly a crime against the American youth conscripted to fight it. Similarly, the quest of the poor for a decent income was not a movement for economic betterment but a moral imperative in an affluent society which had too long neglected its underprivileged citizens. In the end, the New Politics was an appeal to those who considered themselves in one way or another on the margins of American society—the poor, the minorities, the young, the activist women, the intellectuals. Not coincidentally, these were the same groups that had benefited from the McGovern convention reforms. The common denominator was not deprivation—McGovern's campaign was surprisingly well financed—but a certain degree of alienation which left the devotee of the New Politics suspended between revulsion at the establishment on the one hand and the guerrilla terrorism of the extremist radicals on the other.

Seeking to mobilize the unorganized in a moral cause, the New

Politics required above all else a charismatic leader, not necessarily a spell-binding orator with an electric presence but an individual who radiated earnestness and commitment. The candidate's personality could provide the impetus for an ad hoc grass-roots organizing campaign, for extensive television appeals which focused on the qualities of the individual as much as the issues, for direct-mail fund-raising efforts. These were techniques that required the energy, idealism, and skills most frequently found among the educated young, who adopted McGovern as their candidate.

At its best, the New Politics gave the old system a healthy infusion of dedication and made it confront causes which had too long been swept under the carpet. At its worst, however, it could be a politics of exclusion, so confident of its righteousness that it would reject compromise and become a movement which would attempt to seize power from the establishment rather than settle for a share of power. The Kennedys had been the most successful American politicians of the 1960s because they had moved with ease between the world of the old and new politics, realizing that in a two-party democracy exclusion, whatever moral gratification it might bring, could only throw strength to the other side. A New Politics that failed to temper its moral absolutism with conciliation and compromise faced the danger of becoming a Goldwaterism of the left.

McGovern's swift rise began with the New Hampshire primary, in which he ran a strong second to Muskie; many observers pronounced him the moral victor. It was the first of a string of primary victories and near victories engineered by sound organization and dedicated young volunteers, carefully packaged for the media to make it appear that the McGovern camp was always polling better than expected, never worse. As with the Republicans in 1964, the June California primary was decisive. McGovern defeated Humphrey, his only serious remaining opponent, 44.3 percent to 39.2 percent, and thereby cleared the way to a certain nomination.

Yet just beneath the surface of the South Dakotan's amazing surge, there lay serious political liabilities which would become increasingly visible. His strategy for winning the nomination had been to preempt the activist left wing of his party while his centrist opponents whipsawed each other to their political doom. But the Democratic left, for all its affluence, intelligence, organizational skill, and moral fervor, remained a minority of the party and a very small minority of the entire electorate. To have any chance of winning in November, McGovern would have to broaden his support by moving back toward the center. Such a move faced two obstacles—the long primary season had already identified the senator as the candidate of the left, and his original constituency would block efforts at compromise and accommodation.

Hubert Humphrey had almost won the California primary by launching a frontal attack on some of the more extreme positions with which McGovern had identified himself, including both an ill-conceived guaranteed income plan which would pay every American citizen $1,000 a year but contained no credible financing explanation, and a proposal to cut some $30 billion out of the defense budget. The Democratic National Convention and its immediate aftermath made the image of McGovern as a lightweight radical indelible beyond any possibility of change.

Insisting on total compliance with the convention representation rules which the McGovern committee had put together after the 1968 fiasco, the McGovernite majority refused to seat the Cook County, Illinois, delegation headed by Chicago Mayor Richard Daley, still the embodiment of evil to many insurgent Democrats but also one of the most powerful members of his party. The episode, the most deeply symbolic of the convention, exemplified the way in which the politics of morality might become the politics of exclusion. The Daley group, it was charged, had been improperly chosen—a somewhat lame accusation since it had won a primary election against insurgent challengers—and failed to give proper representation to women, the young, and blacks. It was this last charge that stuck in the consciousness of all who followed the convention. The insurgents had handed the Republicans an issue by insisting on rigid, compulsory quotas and had alienated not just Daley but all the groups of the old-time New Deal Democracy who envisioned him as a cultural representative. Where, they demanded, were the quotas for the Irish? The Italians? The Poles? The Hungarians? The Middle Americans? Mike Royko, a columnist who usually acted as a gadfly to the Daley machine, wrote a cutting public letter to the head of the Chicago insurgents: "Your reforms have disenfranchised Chicago's white ethnic Democrats."

Other convention incidents hurt McGovern. Some of the insurgents, acting against their candidate's wishes, insisted on debating previously forbidden issues such as abortion and homosexuality. When McGovern attempted to keep a line open to the regular Democrats by giving the vice-presidential nod to the young Missouri Senator Thomas Eagleton, many of his own followers rebelled. Considering Eagleton a member of the out-group (he originally had supported Muskie) and demanding an open convention, they staged a protracted, ultimately futile, floor fight and kept McGovern from delivering his acceptance speech until 2:48 A.M. McGovern discussed the chairmanship and vice-chairmanship of the Democratic National Committee with incumbent Lawrence O'Brien and Pierre Salinger, both men of national reputation with close ties to the Kennedy family, but at the insistence of his supporters he acquiesced in a woman and a black man unknown outside their home states and hardly qualified to lead what was becoming an increasingly uphill campaign.

With all this behind him, McGovern was hit by an extraordinary piece of bad luck. Investigative reporters following up an anonymous tip discovered that vice-presidential candidate Eagleton had been hospitalized for brief periods in 1960, 1964, and 1966 for psychiatric depression and that on two of these occasions he had undergone electroshock treatment. McGovern's first impulse was to keep Eagleton on the ticket; he stood behind his running mate "a thousand percent," he announced. Eagleton himself, making his first campaign tour, seemed to receive wide public sympathy. Nevertheless, McGovern was quickly subjected to intense pressure from his staff, from many supporters, and from key financial contributors. The situation worsened when syndicated columnist Jack Anderson printed a story, for which he could never provide documentary evidence, that Eagleton had a record of several arrests for drunken driving. Within a week, McGovern had changed his mind, but unable to bring himself to tell Eagleton directly, he made his feelings known to reporters and allowed his new chairwoman of the Democratic National Committee to declare that Eagleton's resignation from the ticket would be "a noble thing." Refusing to be forced out by indirection, Eagleton met personally with McGovern and only then, leaving no doubt that he was acting at McGovern's request, resigned from the ticket. The attempt to replace him was both comic and humiliating. Five leading Democratic politicians refused the offer; finally, R. Sargent Shriver, Kennedy in-law, former head of the Peace Corps, ex-ambassador to France, came on the ticket.

The episode damaged McGovern by making him appear wobbly and indecisive. Among those already alienated from him, he became an object of scorn. The Rhode Island Democratic chairman, one of the old ethnic Democrats who had been pushed aside by the insurgents, told reporters that he backed McGovern "a thousand percent." The phrase, noted Joseph Kraft, now carried much the same connotations as the Godfather's "make him an offer that he can't refuse." The Eagleton affair hurt McGovern, but, contrary to the subsequent lamentations of many of his disciples, it was not the decisive factor in losing him the election. Rather, it was the most prominent of several events in which he seemed to display what Carl Rowan would subsequently call a "marshmallow" character not suited to the Presidency.

He talked of crawling to Hanoi, if necessary, to secure the release of American prisoners. His slogan "Come Home America" was a thinly veiled appeal to neo-isolationism. He attempted to back away from his $1,000-a-person guaranteed-income proposal. He sent Pierre Salinger to Paris to negotiate for the release of American prisoners with the North Vietnamese delegation at the peace talks, then denied knowledge of the mission when it failed. McGovern supporters argued that their candidate rather than Nixon would appeal to the large alienated vote that had gone to Wallace in the primaries, that as his ideals became clear his support would increase rapidly. But it was more accurate to say that McGovern was precisely the kind of politician who alienated the Wallace voter, as well as many independents and regular Democrats.

Against such an opponent, the President had little to fear beyond his own blunders. To avoid the possibility of any serious mistake on the campaign trail, he became a practically invisible candidate. The Republican presidential drive was almost entirely the effort of the vice-president and a host of "surrogates." Most of Nixon's few speeches were made over the radio, a tactic which guaranteed that practically nobody would hear them. He refused to be smoked out even when McGovern larded his speeches with vicious personal attacks, including a comparison of the Chief Executive to Adolf Hitler. Concerned with piling up as big a popular majority as possible, Nixon's managers used the slogans "Re-Elect the President" and "Four More Years" as devices which implied support of the government with no reference to the personality or even the name of the man who headed the GOP ticket. Successful in casting doubt on McGovern's decisiveness and in identifying him with the forces of political and cultural radicalism, the Republican campaign managed to gloss over issues such as the revelation that the Russian wheat sale was poorly negotiated, inflationary, and possibly corruptly managed, or the discovery that burglars caught in the offices of the Democratic National Committee had ties to the White House.

The election results demonstrated both Nixon's effectiveness in building an electoral coalition and McGovern's failure as a candidate. The President took 60.7 percent of the popular vote to his opponent's 37.5 percent. He won 49 states and 521 electoral votes against McGovern's victories in Massachusetts and the District of Columbia for 17 electoral votes. His plurality in the popular vote was nearly 18 million. The Democrats, not repudiated as a party, ran strong in other races, winning several statehouses, maintaining firm control of the House, even picking up two seats in the Senate; the bulk of the landslide was doubtless an anti-McGovern vote rather than an enthusiastic endorsement of the incumbent. Nevertheless, no matter how one interpreted the totals, they added up to one of the most impressive victories in the history of presidential politics. As the majorities rolled in on election night, the winner must have recalled that it was ten years to the day since he had told reporters that they wouldn't have Nixon to kick around anymore.

THIRTEEN

Uncertain Tomorrows

1973–75

1973

JANUARY	Phase III economic policy—most controls ended
FEBRUARY	U.S. dollar devalued 10 percent; Senate authorizes "Watergate Committee"
APRIL	Magruder, Gray, Dean, Haldeman, Erlichman, and Kleindienst all leave the administration
MAY	Richardson becomes attorney general, Cox appointed special prosecutor; Ellsberg case dismissed
JUNE	Phase III½ economic policy—wage-price freeze; Magruder and Dean testify before Watergate Committee
AUGUST	Phase IV economic policy—controls reinstituted
OCTOBER	Yom Kippur War; Agnew resigns; Richardson, Ruckleshaus, and Cox dismissed from administration
NOVEMBER	Saxbe nominated as attorney general, Jaworski appointed special prosecutor
DECEMBER	Ford sworn in as vice-president

1974

JANUARY	Egypt and Israel agree on Sinai disengagement; Egil Krogh sentenced in Ellsberg break-in; Herbert Porter pleads guilty to Watergate-related offenses
FEBRUARY	House Judiciary Committee begins impeachment hearings; Herbert Kalmbach pleads guilty to illegal fund raising

APRIL	Dwight Chapin convicted of perjury; Nixon agrees to pay back taxes, releases White House transcripts; Mitchell and Stans acquitted of illegal fund raising
MAY	Kleindienst pleads guilty to false testimony; Israel and Syria conclude disengagement agreement
JUNE	Colson pleads guilty to obstruction of justice
JULY	Erlichman found guilty of obstruction of justice; Nixon meets with Brezhnev in Moscow; Supreme Court orders Nixon to hand over White House tapes to Jaworski
AUGUST	Nixon resigns; Ford becomes thirty-eighth President, selects Rockefeller for vice-president
SEPTEMBER	Ford issues pardon to Nixon; John Dean begins prison sentence
NOVEMBER	Heavy Republican losses in congressional elections

1975

JANUARY	Haldeman, Erlichman, and Mitchell convicted in Watergate coverup trial
MARCH	Ford signs tax-cut bill
APRIL	Cambodia and South Vietnam fall to communists
MAY	*Mayaguez* incident
JULY	Soviet-American space project; European Security Treaty
AUGUST–OCTOBER	United States, Egypt, and Israel reach second Sinai agreement

It has become almost an axiom of twentieth-century American politics that enormous presidential triumphs have a way of coming apart, perhaps because the winner mistakes votes cast *against* the loser as components of an overwhelming and unlimited personal endorsement. The victors of the three greatest landslides of the twentieth-century Presidency before 1972 had all in one way or another overreached themselves—Harding with fumbling economic policies and a tolerance of corruption, Franklin Roosevelt with the attempt to pack the Supreme Court, Johnson with the escalation of the Vietnam war. Nixon would repeat the pattern, more disastrously than ever. He would suffer the most precipitous loss of confidence in the history of the presidential office, would face impeachment, and would see even his impressive diplomatic achievements on the verge of evaporation. His fall from power would come at a time when America faced not only national and international crises but also a series of quiet yet implacable revolutions which threatened drastic alterations in the lives of almost every citizen.

THE SEVENTH CRISIS

Nixon and his advisers were convinced that the election outcome was a mandate for an activist conservatism. The President's new budget drastically cut many established social programs. Horrified state and local officials discovered that, in violation of what they had taken as firm commitments, the administration expected revenue sharing to substitute for older federal programs, not to supplement them. For example, one of the key aspects of the war on poverty, the community action agencies, would be phased out of the federal budget to be picked up, if at all, by the localities; but in fact police and fire departments, even tax reductions, could usually exercise priority claims on revenue-sharing money. The President ordered the impoundment of funds that Congress had appropriated for a variety of reform measures; other Chief Executives had exercised the power but never on so wide a scale. He placed a right-wing Republican in charge of the Office of Economic Opportunity with orders to dismantle the agency. He freely vetoed social welfare legislation he thought too expensive.

Many congressmen, outraged by the President's refusal to expend funds they had appropriated and by his determination to destroy an agency they had established, accused him of dictatorial rule. The federal courts ruled against some impoundments and prevented the actual abolition of the OEO, if not its emasculation. But, for all the fury on Capitol Hill, Congress could seldom muster the votes to override vetoes; its impotence could only serve to confirm Nixon's belief that he was carrying out the mandate of the people.

Economic policy moved in a similar direction. The President junked Phase II controls in favor of a predominantly voluntary Phase III policy, hoping that a return to the conservative ideal of a fundamentally free market would in some unexplained fashion contain inflationary pressures and enhance economic stability. Instead, with the economy booming, prices shot up. The second devaluation of the dollar came just a month after the introduction of the new system. With consumers in revolt and Congress ready to pass legislation mandating price and wage controls, Nixon declared a temporary price freeze (Phase III½) in June 1973, followed in August by a Phase IV control system not unlike the Phase II apparatus which had been discarded at the beginning of the year but much less effective. Phase IV, discontinued in April 1974, could do little more than put a drag on an accelerating inflation which now derived much of its impetus from a worldwide shortage of basic necessities ranging from petroleum to protein. Perhaps a tighter, more consistent administration economic policy could have moderated the price upsurge, but the basic force behind it could not be suppressed by Washington or any other world capital.

By mid-1973, however, almost everything the administration was undertaking had been submerged by the realization that it was deeply enmeshed in the worst scandals in American history, "the worst" because they involved massive illegality and abuse of power not for personal profit but for political aggrandizement. Involving extortion of campaign contributions, burglary, domestic espionage, assorted "dirty tricks," and obstruction of justice, the scandals demonstrated that the administration had attempted to subvert the American political process itself. The revelations and Nixon's response to them constituted at first a serious embarrassment to a law-and-order regime, and ultimately destroyed it.

In June 1972 Washington police had apprehended five burglars in the offices of the Democratic National Committee at the plush Watergate business-apartment complex. Even before the election, police and investigative journalists had uncovered ties between the Watergate conspirators and a White House consultant, E. Howard Hunt, Jr., who in turn had worked with White House aide G. Gordon Liddy. Two weeks after the Watergate episode, John Mitchell, who had resigned as attorney general to head the Committee to Re-Elect the President (CRP), quit the campaign, citing difficulties with his wife, who had called reporters to complain of "all those dirty things" in which her husband had become involved. Hunt and Liddy were arrested and indicted, but there the trail seemed to end.

Mitchell asserted that he had no knowledge of the break-in and implied that his wife had psychological problems. Other CRP officials issued equally steadfast denials. The President told a news conference that his special counsel, John W. Dean, III, had made a thorough investigation which had established that no White House official was involved. The attorney general, Richard Kleindienst, asserted that a mammoth FBI effort had uncovered no wrongdoing at higher levels. As the campaign got underway, Vice-President Agnew declared that the burglars had probably been hired by the Democrats themselves. Efforts to make a campaign issue of the Watergate affair were lost in the uncertainty which still surrounded the incident and in the national recoil from McGovern.

Nixon was hardly inaugurated, however, before the coverup began to become uncovered. The Watergate trial judge, John Sirica, a tough law-and-order conservative, a second-generation immigrant, an Eisenhower appointee, embodied the values to which the Nixon administration had appealed, and he was determined to apply them impartially. When the defendants remained silent and entered guilty pleas, he meted out "provisional" sentences as harsh as the law would allow—with the admonition that the final terms would be lenient for those who decided to tell the truth and be cooperative. The Democrats, with an election over and their congressional majorities still large, resolved to move ahead with a Senate investigation. Headed by Senator Sam Ervin of North Carolina, the Select Committee on Presidential Campaign Activities was authorized in February 1973 to probe not just the Watergate break-in but any improprieties connected with the 1972 campaign; of the three Republicans who sat on it, only one was a down-the-line administration loyalist.*

As the committee prepared to begin public hearings, one of the Watergate burglars, James McCord, offered to tell all. White House counsel John Dean, afraid that he was being set up as a scapegoat, began to talk freely with federal prosecutors. Stories spread that involvement extended as far as the President's two chief aides, H. R. Haldeman and John Erlichman, that former Attorney General Mitchell was deeply implicated. Acting FBI director, L. Patrick Gray, his Senate confirmation already in deep trouble, resigned, admitting that he had destroyed Watergate-related files given to him by Dean.

It became known that a team of burglars led by Hunt and acting on White House orders had broken into the office of Daniel Ellsberg's psychiatrist in an attempt to gather information which might be used to discredit the man who had leaked the Pentagon Papers, that illegal wiretaps had been used on Ellsberg, and that the judge in Ellsberg's espionage trial, Matthew Byrne, had been offered the directorship of the FBI while the trial was in progress. On May 11, 1973, Byrne pronounced the government's case hopelessly "tainted" and declared a mistrial.

By that time, on April 30, the White House had announced the resignations of Haldeman, Erlichman, Dean, and Attorney General Kleindienst, who felt forced to quit because so many of his close associates were under suspicion. Praising Haldeman and Erlichman as devoted public servants, Nixon made it clear that he had fired Dean.

The new attorney general, Elliot Richardson, enjoyed wide respect, but the Senate nevertheless required as the price of his confirmation the naming of an independent special prosecutor. Richardson met the demand; acting with apparent presidential approval, he promised to name a lawyer of unquestioned integrity and allow him to function with

---

* The Nixon stalwart, Florida Senator Edward Gurney, was himself driven from public life. Indicted for irregularities in the raising of campaign contributions, he was forced to withdraw from his 1974 campaign for reelection. The following year, however, he won acquittal on charges of conspiracy and bribery.

no restrictions whatever. His choice was Archibald Cox, an eminent Harvard law professor who had served as solicitor general under Kennedy and Johnson. Cox immediately set about building a large staff and gave it a mandate as broad as that of the Senate committee. The Ervin and Cox operations shared information extensively and together constituted the most formidable group of investigators that had ever looked into the dark recesses of any administration, Cox gathering evidence for the quiet legal processes of the courtroom, Ervin and his colleagues accumulating information and arguments for the political processes upon which Nixon's ultimate fate depended.

Over the next months, the Presidency itself began to look like "a pitiful, helpless giant," trapped in quicksand and pulled down ever deeper by its struggles. Amid revelations of extensive domestic espionage activities, which John Mitchell would later call "the White House horrors," several more officials resigned. Mitchell and former Secretary of Commerce Maurice Stans were indicted for fraud, obstruction of justice, and perjury stemming from the alleged acceptance of a large campaign contribution from a shady financier. Cox subsequently uncovered numerous instances in which the CRP had accepted illegal corporate donations given in the hope or expectation of government favors.

The Senate committee began public hearings in May and did not conclude them until September. Its first important witness, former CRP official Jeb Stuart Magruder, not only admitted his own role in the Watergate conspiracy and coverup but implicated practically every important person around the President. He was followed by John Dean, who in general reinforced Magruder's testimony and asserted that Nixon himself had known of the coverup at least as early as September 1972. A young middle-level ex-White House assistant, Gordon Strachan, swore that he had destroyed incriminating documents on orders given by H. R. Haldeman. Mitchell, Erlichman, and Haldeman denied most of the accusations, although Mitchell said that he had withheld information on the "White House horrors" for fear of damaging the President's reelection chances. Erlichman arrogantly defended the President's right to order burglaries in the interests of "national security" and to dig into the personal lives of his opponents. Two other high White House officials, Charles Colson and Dwight Chapin, refused to appear before the Ervin panel, invoking their Fifth Amendment privilege against self-incrimination.

New developments kept the Presidency in a state of siege. A minor witness revealed that the President had systematically bugged his own offices and telephone conversations. Tapes existed which should either verify or disprove Dean's allegations against Nixon, and, since the President's every move was routinely logged, it was easy to pick out possibly relevant conferences and phone calls. Claiming executive privilege, the need for confidentiality and national security, Nixon refused to hand over the recordings to either Cox or the Ervin Committee. In the meantime, investigators discovered that the federal government had spent millions of dollars on improvements for the President's private homes at Key Biscayne, Florida, and San Clemente, California. They raised questions about the wheeler-dealer financing arrangements that had gone into the purchase of the San Clemente estate. Someone discovered that Nixon had skirted the fringes of legality in using Internal Revenue loopholes to parlay his income-tax payments down to a point lower than that of the average assembly-line worker. The President and those around him issued denials and pleas for trust, but their responses to the specific accusations were shifting and evasive.

Then in August, the news surfaced that Vice-President Agnew had come under investigation for totally unrelated instances of corruption dating back to his career in Maryland politics and continuing into the years he had spent a heartbeat away from the Presidency. Agnew issued an across-the-board denial and for a time received wide praise for his forthrightness. But a beleaguered White House displayed no inclination to assist him, and the reason was soon obvious. The vice-president's blunt disavowals of guilt had been only a smokescreen behind which he and his attorneys were maneuvering for the best deal they could get. In October Agnew resigned the vice-presidency, pleaded guilty to one count of income-tax evasion, and received a $10,000 fine and a three-year probation. The Justice Department agreed to no further prosecution but made public a long summary of evidence which would have justified some fifty counts of tax evasion, bribery, conspiracy, and extortion. The administration's chief advocate of law and order, its most vociferous enemy of permissiveness, was suddenly a self-confessed felon who had been saved in all probability from multiple convictions, much larger fines, and a prison sentence only because he held the nation's second highest office as a bargaining tool.

By the fall of 1973, the White House tapes had become the issue upon which trust in the administration rested. Special Prosecutor Cox had obtained a court order from Judge Sirica for nine key conversations; the Ervin committee was demanding equal access. The President's struggle to withhold the tapes had both convinced many people of their vital importance and increased public doubts about his innocence. Few could imagine that he was acting simply out of an abstract concern for the constitutional separation of powers. A U.S. court of appeals sustained both the public mood and Cox's legal arguments by upholding Sirica's subpoena for the tapes. The administration began to maneuver for some way out between a contempt of court citation and complete capitulation.

The President offered to make the tapes available to the respected but elderly Mississippi Senator John Stennis, who would listen to them and authenticate summaries of them. Ervin accepted the compromise, but Cox refused, commenting that no trial judge could accept such material as evidence. Somehow convinced that with decisive action he could rid himself of Watergate and related issues once and for all, the President ordered the dismissal of Cox. But neither Richardson nor his new deputy, William Ruckleshaus, were willing to renege on the promises of independence Cox had received. On the evening of October 20, all three men were fired; Washington journalists called the episode the "Saturday night massacre."

The aftermath revealed that the White House had been almost hermetically sealed off from public opinion. Congressmen were deluged with letters and telegrams demanding impeachment; the President's chief of staff, General Alexander Haig, aptly characterized the outcry as "a firestorm of criticism." The House Judiciary Committee began an impeachment investigation; Republican congressional leaders warned the President that he could not expect unquestioning support. The Democratic leadership decided to move rapidly with the confirmation of the vice-president-designate (the first under the Twenty-fifth Amendment to the Constitution), House Minority Leader Gerald Ford. It was imperative, their reasoning ran, to have a Republican first in the line of succession in order to avoid any appearance of attempting to reverse the 1972 election.

The President's imperiousness suddenly gave way to pragmatism. Seventy-two hours after the Saturday night massacre, he unexpectedly offered the tapes to Sirica. The White House asserted, however, that two of the conversations had not, after all, been recorded. Moreover, after a delay of a month, the President's attorneys came forth with the admission that one of the remaining seven tapes contained an inexplicable 18½-minute gap. Court-appointed experts subsequently determined that the gap had been caused by at least five separate erasures; the finding all but ruled out any possibility of an accident. The President, his support badly eroded, made the minimal concessions that might stave off impeachment. As attorney general, he nominated a maverick Republican senator, William Saxbe of Ohio; as the new special prosecutor, Leon Jaworski, a conservative Democrat and former president of the American Bar Association.

Although it was a national trauma, the public airing of the various scandals that had come to be lumped together under the term "Watergate" was a good thing for the country. The contribution of the Ervin committee was especially great. Cox, as a prosecutor seeking indictments, had to be wary of pretrial publicity. The Senate panel, on the other hand, welcomed publicity as fulsomely as any other group of politicians and got live television coverage for most of its sessions. The result was to provide a coast-to-coast theater of political ideals and ethics in which the administration's adversaries were no longer obscenity-screaming hippies but impeccably bourgeois senators.

Ervin and his colleagues, behaving with varying degrees of indignation and courtliness, represented the most traditional ideals of elementary decency and constitutionalism, not some far-out radical or countercultural cause. They demonstrated that Nixon had surrounded himself with operators who were ruthless, unprincipled, and authoritarian in their attitude toward opposition, possessed by a paranoia which made them distrustful even of one another, and convinced that they were exempt from the rule of law and the norms of political behavior. One result was a reassessment of other issues. In 1970, for example, the public had thought the Kent State shootings justified and the Justice Department had disposed of them with a perfunctory investigation. In 1973 Attorney General Richardson ordered a reopening of the investigation, and Gallup pollsters found that the public mood had shifted to a 55–31 conviction that the killings were unjustified.*

In the wake of the Saturday night massacre, Nixon, embattled and widely distrusted, had to respond to an unforeseen crisis. In October, Egypt and Syria launched an attack against Israel. The war had hardly begun before the Russians began a massive resupply operation, and Soviet military advisers appeared to have been deeply implicated in planning and launching the war. Caught by surprise on their high holy day, Yom Kippur, the Israelis faced the most difficult situation of their national history. Their military superiority was based on blitzkreig tactics which assumed possession of the initiative. The Soviet Union had given the Arabs vast quantities of highly sophisticated antiaircraft and antitank missiles which would inflict heavy losses upon a counterattack. Nevertheless, Israel struck hard and successfully, throwing the Syrians back to a defense line 25 miles from Damascus, then smashing through the Egyptian lines, crossing the Suez Canal, and encircling a 20,000-man Egyptian army corps before an UN-mandated cease-fire went into effect.

Another military victory for Israel, the war was a diplomatic disaster for the West. It left the United States quarrelling with most of its allies and

*Eight Ohio guardsmen were subsequently indicted under the federal civil rights statutes but were acquitted in November 1974. A suit for civil damages undertaken by parents and injured students was also unsuccessful. Neither trial yielded firm evidence of a conspiracy to shoot students but rather confirmed the impression that the ill-trained guardsmen were primarily guilty of panic and overreaction in a difficult situation.

brought the Soviet-American détente to the point of disintegration. With the Israelis unable to wrap up the war in a few days, the United States was forced to sustain them with a large military supply airlift. When the Russians threatened intervention to bail out the trapped Egyptians, the United States warned against it and staged a military alert to underscore American determination. Yet American policy did not involve unlimited support of Israel; attempting to be honest brokers, Nixon and Kissinger restrained the Israelis and prevented the total destruction of the Egyptian armed forces. Nonetheless, most of the Arab nations embargoed oil shipments to the United States. At every point, U.S. policy ran into opposition from Japan and the Western European nations, petrified by the threat of an Arab oil boycott. The Europeans called on Israel to meet Arab demands, publicly protested and privately hampered the U.S. supply effort, and objected to the American military alert; for their efforts, they got only reduced oil shipments at higher prices from the Arab producers and poisoned relations with the United States.

The only winner seemed to be the Russians, who had no real interest in Middle Eastern peace or even a total Arab victory. By unreservedly supporting the Egyptians and Syrians, they had enhanced their influence in the Arab world and had created a situation in which the NATO alliance was at an even lower ebb than after the 1956 Suez debacle. Nixon and Kissinger warned that continued Soviet bad behavior might bring an end to détente, but considering the stakes involved, it was unlikely that the Russians would be impressed. It was in fact Kissinger alone, flying from one Middle Eastern capital to another, who assumed the burden of trying to put together a compromise peace settlement. If he failed, the result might eventually be a Soviet grip on the oil spigots of the Persian Gulf and the consequent "Finlandization" of Western Europe and Japan. Yet the whole history of the Middle East since World War II argued against success.

Kissinger responded with a virtuoso performance. Assuming the role of mediator, he eased the USSR out of the truce negotiations and spent weeks shuttling between Cairo and Jerusalem in the winter, Damascus and Jerusalem in the spring. The results were hailed by an anxious world as if he had achieved the millennium. Actually, they were so sparse that they hardly justified long, exhausting effort on an ambassadorial mission by the secretary of state of the United States. The warring sides agreed to prisoner exchanges, troop disengagements in which Israel gave up some territory but retained strong defensive positions, and small UN buffer forces to oversee the cease-fire. The Arab nations lifted their semieffective oil embargo but refused to reduce prices so high that they threatened the eventual economic ruin of the major industrial nations.

The major issues of the Middle East—Israeli occupation of Arab territory, Arab nonrecognition of Israel, the homeless status of the Palestinian Arabs, the future of Jerusalem—all remained unresolved with no solution in sight. The uneasy peace was further threatened by periodic acts of Palestinian terrorism and Israeli reprisal. Superficially, the United States had achieved better relations with the Arab powers, but it had done so only by obtaining concessions from Israel and offering economic aid to Egypt, including atomic reactors, to be used ostensibly for peaceful purposes only. Kissinger's accomplishment, such as it was, remained fragile, and it was hard to imagine a durable Middle Eastern peace as long as the Arab governments allowed Palestinian extremists a veto over their foreign policies.

Whatever the credit due the U.S. role in the Middle East, Nixon received none of it. Kissinger was extravagantly hailed as a miracle man, but the President was already so discredited that his authority continued to ebb. Many skeptics questioned the military alert he had ordered, although ample evidence existed in the public record to justify it. (Ironically, the alert actually had been initiated by Kissinger, ratified by a small committee drawn from the National Security Council, and only then relayed to the President for his approval.) Nixon did not improve his position by subsequently boasting of his coolness in a dangerous confrontation and by lashing out at the press in a manner reminiscent of 1962. Back of Watergate existed growing doubts about his personal stability. Moreover, by producing a cutoff of Arab oil, the Yom Kippur War had added to the President's domestic problems by accelerating a long-developing energy crisis and adding to dangerous inflationary pressures.

Even before the fall of 1973, America's energy supplies had been on the verge of running short. In many states, natural gas companies had refused to accept new customers; spot shortages of heating oil and gasoline had appeared in a number of areas. The emerging energy crisis was partly the product of unplanned economic growth, partly a result of state and federal policies that held the price of most energy sources below what the market would bear, partly a consequence of the noncompetitive structure of the energy industries, partly an unhappy by-product of environmental regulations that sought to cleanse the air and preserve the landscape. Fundamentally self-sufficient in petroleum as late as the end of the 1960s, the United States was importing a third of its supplies by the end of 1973.

The major oil-producing nations, banded together in the Organization of Petroleum Exporting Countries (OPEC), already had formed an effective international cartel that was dictating higher prices to the large multinational oil corporations. The Arab decision to use oil as a political weapon against the West facilitated huge OPEC price increases that threatened the economies and financial stability of the industrialized nations from Japan to West Germany; in this respect, the non-Arab OPEC nations, especially Iran and Venezuela, appeared more militant than the Arabs. In ideology and outlook, OPEC represented the wrath of the Third World striking back at Western imperialism. But in fact, the OPEC nations already were quite prosperous and frequently unable to absorb the flow of foreign payments coming to them. The OPEC cartel did its most grievous injury to genuinely impoverished countries unable to pay for the most basic petroleum needs—fertilizer was one of the essential commodities derived from oil. Observers of the international scene perceived the existence of a Fourth World threatened with disaster by the policies of the Third.

The United States was far better equipped than the other industrial nations to ride out the energy crisis that emerged full-blown in late 1973. The country experienced higher prices and some economic setbacks but not the serious reverses some pessimists had expected. Inconvenience was great—on the East and West coasts, long lines were for a time commonplace at gasoline stations—and price gouging was widespread. Administration management of the crisis was generally ineffective. Allocation regulations were ill conceived and price regulations poorly enforced. Shrinking from rationing, the administration threw that responsibility back to the states, most of which did nothing. A few of the hardest hit developed plans of their own, but in most cases the rationing of gasoline and fuel oil was done on an informal, often arbitrary, basis by the dealers themselves. Only a mild winter and the leakiness of the Arab embargo prevented chaos. The President proclaimed a goal of energy self-sufficiency by 1980, but no expert believed that objective was possible. Expensive oil imports threatened to be a grave strain on the American economy for years to come.

Fuel and food became the leaders in a price upsurge that appeared increasingly ominous. During 1973, the cost-of-living index rose 9.4 percent; in early 1974 inflation progressed at a double-digit rate with no easing in sight. Alarmists saw it as the prelude to a global depression. Worldwide commodity shortages, some real, some artificial, made part of the price increase unavoidable. But at least some of the upsurge was the product of a widespread "catchup" psychology that was beyond the restraint of a White House widely discredited by Watergate and too obsessed by it to devote full attention to economic problems. The Saturday night massacre had given the administration only the briefest of respites from the scandals closing in around it.

The White House had intended to dismantle the office of the special prosecutor entirely, but it succeeded in no more than a momentary disruption. At Cox's urging, its staff remained on the job; when public opinion forced retention of the post, Leon Jaworski was able to take over an ongoing operation that did not have to begin anew. Mild-mannered but tenacious, Jaworski was a conservative who genuinely believed in the rule of law; moreover, as he approached the end of a distinguished legal career, he must have been personally determined to head off any accusations that he was too soft with the President. The special prosecutor's office missed scarcely a beat in moving against those involved in the Watergate incident and related irregularities.

The fading of the Ervin committee from public attention signaled only a new phase of congressional involvement. The House Judiciary Committee began to consider the procedures for an impeachment investigation. In February 1974, the groundwork laid, the committee received authorization from the House to proceed. The Ervin panel had aroused and educated the public. The Judiciary Committee was embarking upon a high constitutional process not easily countered by administration public-relations efforts. Watergate had been taken a step farther from the opinion polls.

Almost everything seemed to go wrong for a beleaguered President attempting to stave off the inevitable. Consistently, the public-opinion surveys found that only a quarter to a third of the electorate approved of Nixon's overall performance as Chief Executive. There were, of course, many reasons for the low rating but only one issue for which the White House could not produce a coherent defense.

One former member of the administration or the CRP after another was indicted for or found guilty of Watergate-related crimes. Herbert Porter, one-time CRP scheduling director, pleaded guilty to lying to the FBI. Egil Krogh, once a top-White House aid, admitted complicity in the Ellsberg break-in. Herbert Kalmbach, the President's personal attorney, entered a guilty plea to charges that he had used illegal methods to raise campaign funds. The federal grand jury looking into Watergate issued indictments against Mitchell, Haldeman, Erlichman, Colson, and three other White House figures, charging them all with obstruction of justice in attempting to cover up high-level involvement. In addition, the grand jury submitted a large folder of evidence on presidential involvement to the House Judiciary Committee. Dwight Chapin was convicted of perjury. The Internal Revenue Service assessed the President himself $284,000 in unpaid taxes and penalties and noted an additional tax deficiency, beyond the statute of limitations, of $148,000. The only note of hope was the acquittal of Mitchell and Stans in their campaign-contribution case.

In the meantime, Nixon was rejecting demands for important tapes from the Watergate Committee, the Judiciary Committee, and Jaworski. At the end of April, he sought to stave off another showdown by dramatically releasing the transcripts of forty-eight conversations that touched upon Watergate. "My actions were directed toward finding the facts and seeing that justice was done fairly and according to the law," he claimed in a nationally televised speech. "It will be totally, abundantly clear that as far as the President's role with regard to Watergate is concerned, the entire story is there." He was, he asserted, providing "all the additional evidence needed to get Watergate behind us and to get it behind us now."

The new transcripts solved nothing. They were riddled with phrases such as "unintelligible," "expletive deleted," and "material unrelated to presidential actions deleted." The White House refused to verify the transcripts by releasing the tapes themselves. Critics noted in addition that several key conversations known to have taken place were missing. Finally, the White House version of the tapes itself demonstrated that Nixon had at the very least temporarily sanctioned the Watergate coverup and other questionable activities. The President countered that he only had been playing for the time needed to examine his options. Even to many of the administration's defenders, they displayed a moral tone that Senate Republican Leader Hugh Scott characterized as "deplorable, shabby, disgusting, and immoral." The transcripts thus satisfied no one and reduced Nixon's defenders to the argument that they fell slightly short of producing the "smoking gun," the solid, incontrovertible evidence that would warrant his removal from office.

Events continued to close in on the administration. Former Attorney General Kleindienst pleaded guilty to having lied to the Senate Judiciary Committee when he had denied that Nixon had intervened to quash an antitrust prosecution of International Telephone and Telegraph, an important campaign contributor. The President in fact had ordered the case dropped and had, with his silence, approved Kleindienst's perjury. Although he had committed a serious offense, Kleindienst was allowed to plead guilty to a misdemeanor and given a suspended sentence, apparently on the theory that it was enough of a disgrace to be the first holder of the office of attorney general ever convicted of a crime. Next, Charles Colson pleaded guilty to obstruction of justice in the Ellsberg case; admitting that he had disseminated false and slanderous information that might have interfered with Ellsberg's right to a fair trial, he claimed that the President had encouraged him to do so.

Then the public discovered that the Watergate grand jury had secretly named Nixon a coconspirator in the coverup and had not issued an indictment only because Jaworski, who believed that a sitting President was immune, had refused to approve it. One of the Watergate prosecutors revealed another apparent gap in one of the tapes the White House had released to it. Investigative journalists uncovered information that the President possibly used campaign contributions for the personal benefit of himself and his family. John Erlichman was found guilty of perjury and violations of civil rights in the burglary of Ellsberg's psychiatrist.

The President responded with a dual strategy. First, he attempted to project the image of a statesman grappling with vital national problems. In June he toured the Middle East, then went to the Soviet Union for a summit meeting with Brezhnev. The trips were personally exhilarating and gave the President a few more percentage points of temporary popularity in the polls, but they could not permanently increase his prestige. Devoid of any lasting accomplishment, they were little more than public relations extravaganzas, forgotten as quickly as most such pseudo events. Second, beneath the appearance of statesmanship was the tough and increasingly difficult strategy of "stonewalling it," adamantly refusing to produce the tapes that would answer the unresolved question of presidential involvement in the coverup. By the end of July, the stonewall was beginning to crack under the combined assaults of the House Judiciary Committee and the special prosecutor.

The Judiciary Committee had moved with elaborate slowness in the face of White House stalling tactics and Republican demands for scrupulous fairness. Arguing that executive privilege allowed the President alone to decide what evidence could be released, Nixon refused to obey eight separate subpoenas for tapes and other documents. The President's attorney, James St. Clair, demanded and received unusual privileges, including the right to call his own witnesses and cross-examine others; still, White House spokesmen characterized the proceedings as a "kangaroo court." In order to placate the Republican minority and especially the GOP waverers, committee chairman Peter Rodino rolled with the administration tactics and accepted one delay after another. In order to avoid a diversionary legal battle, the committee did not attempt to enforce its subpoenas in the courts.

By mid-July, the committee was ready to begin public debate. It released ten volumes of evidence which in the opinion of both its majority and minority counsels warranted impeachment. Arguing the case for the President, the deputy minority counsel could only assert that the committee should weigh against the evidence of wrongdoing the possibility that the President might not be convicted in the Senate, and the fact that his ejection from office would be divisive. The argument was not persuasive. At the end of July, the Judiciary Committee voted to recommend three articles of impeachment to the House. The charges were obstruction of justice, abuse of power, and contempt for constitutional procedures by Nixon's rejection of the committee subpoenas. Six of the committee's seventeen Republicans voted for the first article, seven for the second, two for the third. Political observers agreed that adoption of the articles by the House appeared certain, conviction in the Senate very possible.

Nixon in the meantime had attempted to cope with an even greater danger—a legal time bomb that Leon Jaworski had set ticking. Jaworski had obtained one subpoena after another for evidence held by the White House, at times getting what he wanted, at times encountering the administration stonewall. By May, the issue had come down to a subpoena for tapes of sixty-four key conversations that the President, asserting executive privilege, failed to produce. The Supreme Court agreed to take the case on appeal from Jaworski. On July 24, just as the Judiciary Committee was beginning its impeachment debate, the Court ruled unanimously in favor of the special prosecutor, declaring that the specific need for criminal evidence outweighed a sweeping assertion of executive privilege. The White House had previously hinted that it might disregard an adverse ruling, but in the circumstances such a course would have guaranteed Nixon's impeachment. Attorney St. Clair announced that the President would comply, and indications of a long delay were squashed when Judge Sirica ordered transferral of the material in ten days.

On August 5, as the entire House was preparing rules for debate of the impeachment resolutions, the White House released a portion of the subpoenaed material. The release, transcripts of three conversations between Nixon and Haldeman, demonstrated conclusively that the President had been actively involved in the Watergate coverup as early as six days after the break-in. Admitting that he had been mistaken both in his actions and in withholding the evidence even from his attorneys, Nixon still insisted that his offenses were not grave enough to warrant removal from office. But most Republicans, confronted with a "smoking gun," felt betrayed. Nixon's supporters on the Judiciary Committee now joined in the call for impeachment. The House vote, it was clear, would be practically unanimous; conviction in the Senate was nearly certain. The President's closest advisers privately urged him to resign. On the evening of August 8, Nixon went before the television cameras to announce his resignation, effective at noon of the following day. Still refusing to admit criminal guilt, he had nevertheless come to realize that he could no longer function as President. It was the last "historic first" of his administration.

In a sense, it was not surprising that Nixon displayed little remorse, not even after his successor, Gerald Ford, took his own political life in his hands and gave him a blanket pardon. His years in the White House had after all been marked by developments that many observers considered constructive—revenue sharing at home, détente abroad. But, however important and lasting these accomplishments, Nixon had also exhibited a moral obtuseness and an above-the-law attitude that was subversive of constitutional government. At the end, his retention in office had become incompatible with the principles of American republicanism.

AN UNEXPECTED PRESIDENT, AN UNCERTAIN FUTURE

At the beginning of 1973, nobody would have envisioned Gerald Ford as Nixon's successor. A veteran of a quarter-century in the House of Representatives, Ford had risen to the post of minority leader because of his popularity and a certain plodding competence, but not, it was universally recognized, because of any qualities of brilliance or unusual gifts of leadership. His selection for the vice-presidency appeared to be a move to enable Nixon to escape ouster in two ways: Ford's influence in Congress would be useful to the White House and his widely acknowledged lack of qualifications for the Presidency would reinforce the natural reluctance of legislators to vote for impeachment. Nixon's talent for self-destruction overcame these considerations. The country found itself with a President nobody had really wanted attempting to grapple with a profound set of crises at a turning point in American history.

Ford's early life embodied the American success ethic in a way both similar to and yet crucially different from Nixon's career. Psychologists might trace Nixon's open sense of insecurity to the difficult circumstances of his childhood. On the surface, Ford's childhood might seem even harder. He was the product of a broken home, bearing the surname of his stepfather, never actually meeting his natural father until he was in college. But Ford appeared to have overcome whatever neuroses the experience might have instilled in him. Nixon had struggled vainly to make his small college football team; Ford had been a star lineman at the University of Michigan. While Nixon had clawed his way to Congress and eventual fame, Ford had come to the House of Representatives as a protégé of the revered Arthur Vandenberg. Ideologically, both men were conservatives with an abiding faith in traditional values. The difference between them was personal. Both had worked hard to get ahead, but success had come a bit more easily to Ford, and one sensed in him an inner solidity that few had ever perceived in Nixon.

From his first term in the House, Ford had established himself as a Republican in the Vandenberg mold. He supported an activist foreign policy but held to the right on domestic political issues. Personally popular on both sides of the aisle, he was also tough enough to be involved in the overthrow of two House Republican leaders. When GOP Presidents were in the White House, Ford was a loyal lieutenant. Against Democratic Presidents, he tended to be a rough partisan who nonetheless usually played by the established rules. Congress watchers agreed that he was an effective minority leader.

To the extent that any wide perceptions of Gerald Ford existed in the fall of 1973, they derived from his public image as an oppositionist, the leader of a minority out of touch with new developments in American life and increasingly frustrated with the directions in which the nation was going. (Demanding the impeachment of Supreme Court Justice William O. Douglas in 1970, Ford cited the fact that Douglas had written an article for the avant-garde, erotic-oriented *Evergreen Review* as proof of the jurist's moral unfitness.) Lyndon Johnson, utilizing his gift for malicious abuse to the fullest, had coined the most frequently quoted characterizations of the Republican House leader: "Gerry Ford played too much football without a helmet" and "Gerry Ford is so dumb that he can't walk and chew gum at the same time."

Ford, however, established his conventionality as a political asset. For ten years the country had suffered Presidents who were secretive, devious, and rather openly neurotic. The new Chief Executive cultivated an image of openness and candor and compared himself to Harry S Truman as a leader who would be honest with the people and let the chips fall where they might. The image was tarnished when, only a few weeks after taking office, Ford granted an unconditional pardon to his predecessor, but critics quarreled less with the decision—few really wanted to put Nixon on trial and send him to prison—than with its abrupt timing. The Nixon pardon was soon forgotten, and Ford was successful in putting himself over as a calm, self-possessed national leader.

Nevertheless, the Republican party faced a nearly hopeless situation in the months after Nixon's resignation and pardon. Opinion surveys revealed that even during the depths of the Great Depression a greater percentage of Americans had been willing to identify themselves with the GOP. The Democrats swept the 1974 congressional elections, winning huge "veto proof" majorities on Capitol Hill. The new Democratic freshmen were predominantly aggressive young liberals identified with the tone and approach of the New Politics, determined to reform a creaking Congress and impose an era of legislative government on a nonelected Chief Executive.

Disorganized and weakly led, the new Congress proved to be less a threat to the President than an asset. The freshmen Democrats, although successful in deposing a few aged or reactionary committee chairmen, appeared more interested in being reelected than in imposing a tone of moral rectitude upon the government. Congress was neither veto-proof nor dominant, and Ford, pushing the Truman analogy as hard as he could, managed to put across the impression of an activist Presidency pursuing the public interest even as he followed policies that were essentially a continuation of Nixon's.

The most dramatic event of Ford's first year in office was the final collapse of anticommunist resistance in Indo-China. Here the President attempted to carry out commitments the Nixon administration had made and ran into a solid wall of frustration. Resentment against the Vietnam involvement in Congress and among the public had grown rather than diminished since ultimate U.S. disengagement. With Congress demanding an end to every vestige of American support for the anticommunist regimes of Southeast Asia and refusing to vote the full aid that Nixon had promised, the fall of Cambodia and South Vietnam was guaranteed.

The Cambodian situation was especially tragic. Since the American invasion of 1970, the entire country had been ravaged. The U.S.-backed government of Lon Nol was corrupt and ineffective in a manner reminiscent of Chiang Kai-shek's rule in China. By early 1975, Lon Nol's area of control had dwindled to the capital city of Phnom Penh, which was besieged by the enemy and able to maintain only airplane contact with the outside world. At the beginning of April, Phnom Penh fell. Yet as bad as the Lon Nol government had been, its overthrow failed to bring deliverance to the Cambodian people. The shadowy new Khmer Rouge regime slaughtered its opponents ruthlessly and attempted to resuscitate Cambodian agriculture by engaging in a reign of terror that forced millions of people into the countryside, where thousands died. Prince Norodom Sihanouk, in whose name the insurgents had waged war, found himself forced to watch developments from afar with little prospect of ever again becoming the effective ruler of his country.

The collapse of South Vietnam came with a stunning suddenness. Until the spring of 1975, the South's resistance had been more effective than most observers would have predicted. Still, General Thieu's government, with its widespread corruption and spotty military leadership, possessed serious long-term liabilities. As the North openly violated the truce agreement and engaged in a massive buildup, as the U.S. Congress balked at further aid to South Vietnam, Thieu's position became daily more precarious. In the field his troops, long accustomed to almost unlimited resources, found themselves held to two grenades per patrol. A shortage of artillery shells permitted most batteries to fire only a few rounds per day. A shortage of spare parts grounded many aircraft. For the

first time in the history of post–World War II Vietnam, Western-supported forces found themselves outgunned.

In March, after suffering some tactical reverses, Thieu ordered a
general strategic retreat from the sparsely populated Central Highlands.
His objective of establishing a more compact defense perimeter was
sound, but his army possessed neither the organization nor the leadership
for such a tricky maneuver. The retreat quickly degenerated into a rout
that rolled down inexorably toward Saigon with tens of thousands of
leaderless troops and panic-stricken civilians fighting for available transportation. Many of the refugees died along the way. Of those who made it
to Saigon, it seemed in the final days of the war that all were clustered
around the American embassy fighting for a place on the evacuation
helicopters that were putting an end to the U.S. presence in Vietnam.
Most were beaten back by marine guards in an unhappy scene that
symbolized the ultimate degeneration of the goal of winning minds and
hearts. Those who were finally able to get to America encountered vocal
hostility and widespread indifference.

Most Americans were fed up with Vietnam, convinced that the
United States no longer had any responsibilities there, and content to
blame the country's fall on the cowardice of its troops. It was undeniable
that many of the South's wounds were self-inflicted but equally undeniable that any army equipped as generously as its foe would not have fallen
apart. Southeast Asian nations interpreted the communist victory as a
sign that America was abandoning the region and moved toward accommodations with the communist world. What was decisive was less the
outcome of the long Vietnamese struggle than the circumstances of that
outcome. Failing to deliver on aid commitments, the United States
seemed unreliable, and the hurried evacuation of Saigon made the defeat
seem more an American debacle than it was. Thailand and the Philippines, once close allies of the United States, were most conspicuous in the
move toward neutrality.

It was against this backdrop that the Ford administration reacted
when a Cambodian naval patrol seized an American merchant ship, the
Mayaguez, in international waters. After a brief and futile attempt at
establishing diplomatic contact, the President ordered U.S. Marines to
retake the ship and rescue the crew. In the midst of a bloody battle on an
island outpost, the crew was returned from the mainland. Thirty-nine
Americans lost their lives; an equal number of merchant seamen were
rescued. The incident, involving as it did the recovery of American citizens, did little to reassure Southeast Asian governments—Thailand in
fact ostentatiously protested the use of military bases on its soil for the

operation. Still, the affair had a significance beyond the vague duty of a government to protect its citizens. It demonstrated that the United States remained capable of reacting to provocations and boosted the morale of a citizenry that emotionally approved the President's decision. However, it did little to meet long-range problems of American diplomacy.

Nothing exemplified these problems more graphically than the growing American isolation in the United Nations, whose General Assembly was controlled by a Third World more open than ever in its feelings of hostility toward the West. Even those underdeveloped nations being exploited by the OPEC cartel derived vast emotional satisfaction from OPEC's success in draining wealth from the old imperialists and those who shared their culture. The influence of OPEC and the predominance of Islam in the Third World made Israel the main target of the new hostility. But Israel was merely the most exposed outpost of Western liberal democracy, the ultimate object of an attack voiced by a numerical majority of the UN. Created with such great hope by the United States at the end of World War II, used as an effective tool in the cold war for twenty years, the United Nations suddenly had become a diplomatic Frankenstein monster; and the United States was about as powerless as the shocked doctor had been when his creation had gotten out of hand.

As Vietnam became a bad memory, one might have expected that American foreign policy would recover a sense of purpose and a certain stability. Instead, it appeared to become more purposeless and unstable than ever. This development was in part the result of the deep demoralization that Vietnam had created, in part the natural consequence of the division of the government between a Republican President and a Democratic Congress. Perhaps most fundamentally, however, the lack of purpose was inherent in the Ford-Kissinger continuation of the Nixon-Kissinger foreign policies after they had passed the point of productive return.

Whatever his private visions, the secretary of state seemed increasingly intent upon making diplomacy an exercise in illusion, in creating impressions of accomplishment without the substance. That he did so was perhaps understandable. His use of the technique in the Vietnam negotiations had brought him international acclaim. Moreover, he doubtless considered it part of his assignment to enhance the political prestige of the President he served. Yet pursuit of the illusion of success foreclosed efforts to build mass support for a foreign policy based on hard interests and realities. It encouraged false hopes and failed to prepare the American people for the facts of international life in an increasingly unfriendly world.

In its approach to the major immediate problem it faced, the Middle

East, the administration oscillated between military threats and professions of friendship toward the oil-producing Arab nations. Acting as a mediator between Jews and Arabs, it followed a "step-by-step" approach that sought to create momentum toward a final peace settlement. In practice, the approach consisted of wringing territorial concessions out of a reluctant Israel without giving the Israelis much in the form of either Arab concessions or U.S. guarantees. In August 1975 Kissinger persuaded and cajoled the Israelis into another modest fallback in the Sinai. In return, the United States offered impressive economic and military assistance, but, limited by public and congressional misgivings, the administration could not give Israel what it wanted most—ironclad military guarantees. The second Sinai agreement provided only for a small number of American civilians to monitor early-warning stations for both Israel and Egypt. Theoretically, at the end of the tunnel solutions would develop to all the impossible problems that plagued the region. Actually, the administration was continuing a bipartisan policy of equivocation and postponement that dated back to the Truman years, hoping that in some undefined way a mood of peace would develop in one of the most hate-ridden areas of the world.

For the long range, the question of relations with the Soviet Union remained crucial. Here, Ford enthusiastically adopted the Nixon policy of détente, but difficult questions about the meaning and utility of the policy loomed larger than ever. In the absence of significant accomplishment, the administration more than ever rationalized détente as the establishment of a congenial atmosphere, symbolized by media events, such as periodic summit meetings or the 1975 joint Soviet-American space mission. In mid-1975, just after the space spectacular, the United States, the USSR, and the European nations signed a European Security Treaty at Helsinki. The main effect of the vaguely worded pact was the legitimization of the boundaries that had emerged from World War II and tacit endorsement of Soviet imperialism in Eastern Europe. In return, the West received only Soviet affirmations of basic freedoms in a manner weaker than the guarantees Roosevelt had obtained at Yalta thirty years earlier. No one expected the USSR to cease efforts to extend its influence—as the treaty was signed, the Soviet Union was strongly supporting an effort to establish a communist dictatorship in Portugal. Kissinger privately confessed his misgivings about the agreement, but publicly the administration represented it as a triumph. The areas of contention between the two superpowers remained unsolved, plastered over by an administration that felt a political interest in creating an illusion of achievement, largely ignored by a Democratic opposition that felt an obligation to thunder to the left of any Republican President.

Americans appeared more alienated from world affairs than at any time since the 1930s. The dominant public mood toward the imperial responsibilities that the United States had shouldered since World War II was a blend of weariness, cynicism, and fear. Its most pervasive consequence was the rapid transformation of neo-isolationism from a reasoned critique of the overextension of American power in Vietnam to a mass impulse that shrank from *any* international commitment. The specter of a new Vietnam seriously inhibited U.S. freedom of action in areas central to American interests. In other parts of the globe, an activist foreign policy was impossible.

One force behind neo-isolationism, especially strong within the liberal wing of the Democratic party, was a revulsion at the moral compromises that had characterized a generation of American foreign policy. Congressional committees investigating clandestine CIA operations uncovered involvement in foreign coups d'etat and assassination plots. The evidence left little doubt that these activities had been carried on with the knowledge of the White House at least since the days of Eisenhower. To the new critics of American foreign policy, it was irrelevant that conspiracies, coups, and assassinations remained common in most non-Western political cultures. The effect was to discredit both U.S. diplomacy and the "imperial Presidency."

Many liberal leaders decried the CIA conspiracies as an affront to American values and sought reforms that would end them once and for all. Convinced that the Presidency had managed foreign policy both stupidly and immorally, they demanded a much greater role for Congress, which they represented as the repository of decent American values. The liberals were expressing an American trait as old as the first Pilgrim settlement—the quest for moral perfection and the urge to separate from a tainted world. Yet to withdraw from any seamy foreign involvement would be to withdraw from a sizable portion of a planet that had become smaller and more interlinked than ever. The separatist impulse begged the difficult question of how a perfectly moral nation could protect and advance its interests in an immoral world.

Many observers proclaimed the end of the American empire and the imperial Presidency with a sense of gratification. The very phrases evoked a sense of sin in a national psyche that connected the imperial ethos with despotism, exploitation, and militarism. Yet the American empire, for all its sins, had been among the most benign in human history; and its withdrawal from the world scene created temptations for its increasingly adventuristic Soviet counterpart. More importantly, the American empire still constituted the main bulwark of support for a Western liberal democracy that faced multiple challenges from without and a crisis of confidence from within; and the sustenance of liberal democracy remained the most enlightened form of American self-interest.

At its bicentennial, a chastened American nation was in retreat from the excesses of empire and would surely in the near future avoid the hubris that had led to the tragedy of Vietnam. Whether it could avoid an equally quixotic quest for moral perfectionism was unclear. It was reasonably certain, however, that any dismantling of the American empire could only open opportunities for other empires even less committed to the values the perfectionists cherished.

The Ford administration also followed the Nixon policies on domestic issues and waged a duel with an opposition Congress dominated by different viewpoints and priorities. The nation faced a three-cornered economic crisis from which it seemed there was no escape: recession, inflation, and the energy dilemma. Neither economists nor politicians had devised a credible formula for dealing with all three at the same time. Ford adopted the traditional Republican stance that inflation was the most serious problem and had to be fought with conservative fiscal and monetary policies at the risk of increasing the already high unemployment rate. Price stability, so the reasoning ran, would guarantee the return of a healthy prosperity; a temporary increase in unemployment was the unavoidable cost of a sound recovery.

The need to cope with the energy crisis added a serious complication. Ford, like Nixon, was committed to substantial energy self-sufficiency; not crippled by scandal, he was determined to work for the tough measures the goal required. At bottom, this meant accepting much higher prices for energy as a means of both encouraging conservation and facilitating expensive domestic exploration and production. Ford's fight against inflation was thus complicated by an acceptance of inflation in one key sector of the economy. Moreover, high energy prices would absorb purchasing power from other sectors of the economy and inevitably dampen economic recovery. From the standpoint of national security, the administration plan made sense; but it could promise little more than a slow and painful economic recovery.

The Democratic opposition in Congress considered unemployment as the most urgent problem and sought to combat it with expansionary spending programs. Ford acquiesced in periodic extensions of eligibility for federally subsidized state unemployment compensation programs and in a moderate tax cut, but he was determined to hold the federal deficit down. He freely vetoed bills that mandated high spending, and he almost always made the veto stick.

As the nation reached the second anniversary of the 1973 Arab oil embargo, the Democrats had failed to develop a coherent energy policy. It remained unclear whether this failure would be a political liability or a political asset. A bill sponsored by the Democratic House leadership to promote conservation by placing a large federal tax on gasoline was defeated, largely by defections from younger Democrats who had only a precarious hold on their constituencies. Thereafter, the party position on energy amounted to little more than advocacy of low prices and an apparent wish that the issue would go away. At the end of 1975, the President reluctantly signed a compromise energy act that included a number of conservation provisions but actually established lower prices for domestic crude oil that would extend well into 1977. The effect inevitably would be to increase national dependence on foreign oil. Politically, the Democrats were gambling that the American voter wanted cheap gasoline above all else. The position might rightly be termed irresponsbile, but many observers considered it good politics. Essentially, it reflected the mood of a country that had not yet come to grips with the energy crisis and its ramifications.

Yet the energy situation was at the core of America's economic difficulties, responsible for the greater part of the inflation-recession syndrome that wracked the economy. To do nothing was to make the United States ever more vulnerable to continuous rounds of OPEC gouging that could only perpetuate stagflation and possibly set off a worldwide depression. There was no easy way out. Even the best scenario for the years ahead envisioned sacrifice and a reduced standard of living. The American nation had known greater peril, it is true, but it faced difficulties of historic dimensions. Either Gerald Ford or his successor had to provide the leadership needed to develop a national will that could surmount the most serious threat to America's interests since Pearl Harbor.

THE END OF AFFLUENCE?

The central theme of American life in the 1950s and '60s was the accelerating growth of material affluence; the central theme of the 1970s and beyond threatened to be the reversal of that trend. The experience was in varying degrees common to all the advanced capitalist and mixed economies of the Northern Hemisphere but was most pronounced in the United States. Figured in constant dollars on a per capita basis, the disposable personal income of the average American in 1971 was 162 percent of the 1950 figure; he could afford more than half again as many consumer goods. The "standard-size" automobile took on proportions once reserved for limousines; air conditioning became a necessity and convenience foods a growth industry; downright exotic products like microwave ovens and trash compactors began to appear in hundreds of thousands of American homes. Ever-increasing levels of affluence were taken for granted.

This condition provided a reference point for most of the developments that shook American society in the 1960s. Only in a land of luxury could poverty become a moral issue. The urban riots featured widespread looting which amounted to a black demand for sharing the wealth. Many of the young who assailed materialist decadence themselves constituted a vast economic market with their own expensive consumption patterns. Prophets of leisure proclaimed the demise of the Puritan ethic and the emergence of a society that was rejecting competition and elitism in favor of a relaxed self-realization. Assembly-line workers no longer accepted high pay and fringe benefits as adequate compensation for long hours and tedious work. Young, long-haired blue-collar types with no memories of the Great Depression or World War II increasingly set the tone of industrial labor relations and expressed their protests against the accepted norms of mass production with individual acts of defiance such as absenteeism and sabotage. In 1973 the United Auto Workers made the abolition of compulsory overtime work the salient issue of contract negotiations with the industry; in the grim days of the 1930s, the very idea of a company having to compel overtime would have been scarcely conceivable.

The environmental movement, perhaps in the long view the most significant product of the 1960s, was at once a product of affluence and a reaction against it. Americans slowly began to realize that one by-product of the rush to riches was widespread poisoning of the air they breathed and the water they drank, that some of the most attractive areas of their country were being ruined by garish development. Almost everyone agreed that the trend had to be halted; if continued unchecked, massive pollution could become a serious danger to human life and would threaten the ecological balance that constituted the chain of existence for many species other than man. In 1972, a prestigious group of scientists and technocrats based at the Massachusetts Institute of Technology published a study which envisioned a Malthusian disaster before the year 2100 if human population, depletion of natural resources, and the attendant pollution continued to increase at late-twentieth-century rates. Based on computerized projections, the study was superficially impressive but probably overwrought; nevertheless, it highlighted grave problems which required much more serious and comprehensive attention than they hitherto had received.

At one level, environmentalism was a badly needed public health effort to clean up poisoned air and water; at another level, it was a conservation movement attempting to save man's habitat from needless and possibly irreversible despoliation. In a very real sense, it was a drive against the worst excesses of affluence from smog-ridden cities to oil-soaked beaches to the condominiums and resort hotels which brought commercial ugliness to areas of natural beauty; its spokesmen ran the gamut from those concerned with little more than achieving breathable air to those who hoped somehow to abolish modern technology. In all its forms, however, environmentalism possessed a fundamental assumption —if affluence were responsible for many of the threats to the environment, it could also provide the economic margin for achieving a better life; the nation, in short, was rich enough to pay for clean air and water and unspoiled surroundings.

The energy crisis which closed in on America in the winter of 1973–74 provided an initial challenge to this assumption. It would, for a time at least, require the suspension of many antipollution regulations and provide a green light for such enterprises as strip mining, coastal oil drilling, and the construction of a massive oil pipeline across the Alaskan wilderness. Still, it was possible to argue that the energy crisis was something of an aberration, the product of abysmal government planning and of an unforeseen oil cartel. In the long run, it could be overcome through the development of untapped resources and the creation of new forms of energy. The national interest demanded self-sufficiency, and ultimately self-sufficiency could be achieved with clean energy. The solutions would be expensive, but the affluent society, so the reasoning went, could afford it.

Yet most of the environmentalists also argued, quite reasonably, that pollution was an inescapable by-product of the economic growth which had produced affluence, that the essential first step in the establishment of a livable planet was the attainment of zero growth in population and in the economy. This assumption did not go unquestioned. Critics observed that it usually failed to distinguish between different types of economic growth and dismissed out of hand the possibilities of regulating growth in such a way that it would be compatible with environmental needs. Still it was hard to deny that growth had been a powerful stimulus to pollution and that regulation would be very difficult.

The United States was approaching zero population growth in the early 1970s—changing moral values and economic realities encouraged small families and the singles life—but zero economic growth was a different story. Federal social-economic policy, popular expectations of an ever-better standard of living—all were based on the assumption of economic expansion. Zero growth would for the foreseeable future mean perpetual recession and growing numbers of unemployed. To stop growing meant in reality to move backward and embrace a revolution of diminishing expectations. It also implied an explosive social politics in which money for liberal reforms could no longer be skimmed off the top of the expansionary increase, and one group could wrest benefits only at the expense of another. No administration could advocate such policies. The only realistic alternative was to discover ways of making protection of the environment compatible with economic growth. Otherwise, the ecologists would find themselves regarded as hair-shirted oddballs proclaiming the end of the world.

Even without a stoppage of growth, even without an energy crisis, Americans faced indications that they were reaching the outer limits of affluence. Western Europe and Japan, with their own affluence, relatively small military burdens, and revalued currencies, could compete for basic commodities in international markets. The less happy side of U.S. success in rehabilitating the noncommunist industrial nations after World War II, the situation demonstrated that strong allies could also be rivals in the scramble for the finite resources which served as the basis for rising living standards.

If all the signals pointed toward an end of affluence, they did not portend the disappearance of abundance. They indicated instead an end to the excesses of the 1960s and the beginning of an era in which people could still live decently but would find many commodities they had taken for granted, from cheap energy to cheap beefsteak, more expensive. In general they would have to make do with less at higher prices—small 4-cylinder automobiles instead of big V-8s, thermostats set lower in the winter, soyburger instead of sirloin. The transition was sure to hurt some groups more than others, but as nearly as forecasters could imagine, it was unlikely to cause real deprivation. Instead, the United States appeared to be settling on an economic plateau characterized by high prices, slower growth rates, and some belt tightening; still, the average American could expect a better material life than that of the citizens of most of the rest of the world, who likely would be landing on their own plateaus also.

As the nation moved toward the bicentennial of its birth, it had cause for neither self-flagellation nor self-congratulation. Having surmounted the challenges of the 1930s and moved forward into a new world, it had discovered that a success beyond the dreams of most Americans in 1939 entailed new problems and discontents; nonetheless, few wished to return to the unhinged decade of depression and militarism from which the contemporary United States had emerged. That America had faced its 200th anniversary with a discredited political leadership was cause for sorrow; that the system had struck back at those who transgressed its ethics was cause for rejoicing. It remained an open question whether the country possessed the strength and foresight to deal with the fundamental challenge of finding methods that could combine a decent level of prosperity with the measures necessary to assure a livable environment.

American historians invariably feel obligated to close their books with optimistic affirmations of the national promise. But the mid-1970s were years of uncertainty which held out both the hope of a better America and the possibility of a nation experiencing a qualitative decline in its way of life along with the quantitative drop which was bound to occur. Historians, able only to provide perspective, could not predict the nation's response; future generations would judge it.

Selected Bibliography

General

Samuel Lubell's *The Future of American Politics* (3d ed., rev.; New York: Harper, 1965) is essential to an understanding of American politics since the New Deal. Other significant contributions are V. O. Key, *The Responsible Electorate* (New York: Knopf, 1966); David Mayhew, *Party Loyalty among Congressmen 1947–1962* (Cambridge, Mass.: Harvard University Press, 1966); and James MacGregor Burns, *The Deadlock of Democracy* (Englewood Cliffs, N.J.: Prentice-Hall, 1963), and *Presidential Government* (Boston: Houghton Mifflin, 1965).

On presidential elections, see the appropriate essays and documents in Fred Israel and Arthur Schlesinger, Jr., *History of American Presidential Elections* (4 vols.; New York: Chelsea House, 1971); and consult Robert Divine, *Foreign Policy and U.S. Presidential Elections, 1940–1960* (New York: New Viewpoints, 1973).

On the Presidency, see especially Richard Neustadt, *Presidential Power* (New York: Wiley, 1960); Arthur Schlesinger, Jr., *The Imperial Presidency* (Boston: Houghton Mifflin, 1973); and James David Barber, *The Presidential Character* (Englewood Cliffs, N.J.: Prentice-Hall, 1972).

Two valuable books on economic policy are Robert Lekachman, *The Age of Keynes* (New York: Random House, 1966), and Herbert Stein, *The Fiscal Revolution in America* (Chicago: University of Chicago Press, 1969).

Foreign policy surveys are invariably attuned in mood and chronology to the cold war. John Spanier, *American Foreign Policy Since World War II* (5th ed., rev.; New York: Praeger, 1975), is something of a classic by a cold warrior and realpolitiker. Other important nonrevisionist interpretations are Norman Graebner, *Cold War Diplomacy* (Princeton, N.J.: Van Nostrand, 1962); Louis Halle, *The Cold War as History* (New York: Harper, 1967); Seyom Brown, *The Faces of Power* (New York:

Columbia University Press, 1968); Adam Ulam, *The Rivals* (New York: Viking, 1971); Robert Osgood et al., *America and the World: From the Truman Doctrine to Vietnam* (Baltimore: Johns Hopkins University Press, 1970). Various styles of revisionism are expressed in William Appleman Williams, *The Tragedy of American Diplomacy* (rev. ed.; New York: World, 1962); Ronald Steel, *Pax Americana* (rev. ed; Viking, 1970); Richard Barnet, *Intervention and Revolution* (New York: World, 1968), and *Roots of War* (New York: Atheneum, 1972); Gabriel Kolko, *The Roots of American Foreign Policy* (Boston: Beacon, 1969); Walter La-Feber, *America, Russia, and the Cold War* (3rd ed.: New York: Wiley, 1975).

Other significant sources include *Historical Statistics of the United States* (Washington: U.S. Government Printing Office, 1958), its *Supplement to 1962* (Washington: U.S. Government Printing Office, 1963), and the annual editions of *The Statistical Abstract of the United States.* Especially helpful for the more recent years are many of the publications issued by the Congressional Quarterly, Inc., and articles in the serious magazines.

Chapter 1: America in 1939

The literature on the New Deal is very extensive. A. L. Hamby, ed., *The New Deal: Analysis and Interpretation* (New York: Weybright & Talley, 1969), provides a sampling of major viewpoints. Important interpretations are William Leuchtenburg, *Franklin D. Roosevelt and the New Deal* (New York: Harper, 1963); and Arthur Schlesinger, Jr.'s monumental *The Age of Roosevelt* (Boston: Houghton Mifflin), three volumes of which have been completed: *The Crisis of the Old Order* (1957), *The Coming of the New Deal* (1959), and *The Politics of Upheaval* (1960). Edgar Eugene Robinson, *The Roosevelt Leadership* (Philadelphia: Lippincott, 1955), the work of a Hoover conservative, has had little influence. Left revisionist assessments, on the other hand, have drawn great attention. See especially Paul Conkin, *The New Deal* (New York: Crowell, 1967); Howard Zinn, ed., *New Deal Thought* (Indianapolis: Bobbs-Merrill, 1966); and Barton Bernstein's essay in Bernstein, ed., *Towards a New Past* (New York: Pantheon, 1968). Jerold Auerbach subjects these and lesser efforts to a stiff counterblast in "New Deal, Old Deal, or Raw Deal: Some Thoughts on New Left Historiography," *Journal of Southern History* (February 1969). For social and cultural history, consult Caroline Bird, *The Invisible Scar* (New York: David McKay, 1966); and Charles Alexander, *Nationalism in American Thought, 1930–1945* (Chicago: Rand McNally, 1969).

The most important biographical treatments of FDR are Frank Freidel, *Franklin D. Roosevelt* (4 vols. in progress; Boston: Little, Brown, 1952–); James MacGregor Burns, *Roosevelt: The Lion and the Fox* (New York: Harcourt, Brace, 1956), the first volume of a two-volume biography; and Rexford Tugwell, *The Democratic Roosevelt* (Garden City, N.Y.: Doubleday, 1957).

Various aspects of the New Deal receive treatment in Christiana Campbell, *The Farm Bureau and the New Deal* (Urbana: University of Illinois Press, 1962); Richard Kirkendall, *Social Scientists and Farm Politics in the Age of Roosevelt* (Columbia: University of Missouri Press, 1966); Sidney Baldwin, *Poverty and Politics: The Rise and Decline of the Farm Security Administration* (Chapel Hill: University of North Carolina Press, 1967); Jerold Auerbach, *Labor and Liberty: The LaFollette Committee and the New Deal* (Indianapolis: Bobbs-Merrill, 1966); Milton Derber and Edwin Young, eds., *Labor and the New Deal* (Madison: University of Wisconsin Press, 1957); Irving Bernstein, *The Turbulent Years* (Boston: Houghton Mifflin, 1970); Sidney Fine, *The Automobile under the Blue Eagle* (Ann Arbor: University of Michigan Press, 1963); and Ellis Hawley's indispensable *The New Deal and the Problem of Monopoly* (Princeton: Princeton University Press, 1966).

Among the most significant books on politics and political personalities are James Patterson, *Congressional Conservatism and the New Deal* (Lexington: University of Kentucky Press, 1967); Donald McCoy, *Landon of Kansas* (Lincoln: University of Nebraska Press, 1967) and *Angry Voices: Left-of-Center Politics in the New Deal Era* (Lawrence: University of Kansas Press, 1958); J. Joseph Huthmacher, *Senator Robert F. Wagner and the Rise of Urban Liberalism* (New York: Atheneum, 1968); and Bernard Sternsher, *Rexford Tugwell and the New Deal* (New Brunswick: Rutgers University Press, 1964).

Other important approaches to the period are James Patterson, *The New Deal and the States* (Princeton: Princeton University Press, 1969); Otis Graham, *An Encore for Reform: The Old Progressives and the New Deal* (New York: Oxford University Press, 1967); Richard Kirkendall, "Franklin D. Roosevelt and the Service Intellectual," *Mississippi Valley Historical Review* (December 1962); and William Leuchtenburg, "The New Deal and the Analogue of War," in John Braeman et al., *Change and Continuity in Twentieth-Century America* (Columbus: Ohio State University Press, 1964).

On foreign policy in the 1930s, see John Wiltz, *From Isolation to War, 1931–1941* (New York: Crowell, 1968); and Selig Adler, *The Uncertain Giant, 1921–1941* (New York: Macmillan, 1965). Adler's *The Isolationist Impulse* (New York: Free Press, 1957) is a good introduction to its subject. See also Manfred Jonas, *Isolationism in America, 1935–1941* (Ithaca:

Cornell University Press, 1966); John Wiltz, *In Search of Peace: The Senate Munitions Inquiry, 1934–1936* (Baton Rouge: Louisiana State University Press, 1963); Wayne Cole, *Senator Gerald P. Nye and American Foreign Relations* (Minneapolis: University of Minnesota Press, 1962); Warren Cohen, *The American Revisionists* (Chicago: University of Chicago Press, 1967); and Robert Divine, *The Illusion of Neutrality* (Chicago: University of Chicago Press, 1962). Julius Pratt, *Cordell Hull* (2 vols.; New York: Cooper Square, 1964), provides coverage from the viewpoint of the secretary of state. Lloyd Gardner, *Economic Aspects of New Deal Diplomacy* (Madison: University of Wisconsin Press, 1964), provides a revisionist perspective. For the Asian situation, see Armin Rappaport, *Henry L. Stimson and Japan* (Chicago: University of Chicago Press, 1963); and Dorothy Borg, *The United States and the Far Eastern Crisis* (Cambridge, Mass.: Harvard University Press, 1964). On the challenge of fascism in Europe, see Arnold Offner, *American Appeasement: United States Foreign Policy and Germany, 1933–1938* (Cambridge, Mass.: Harvard University Press, 1969); Alton Frye, *Nazi Germany and the American Hemisphere, 1933–1941* (New Haven: Yale University Press, 1967); and Richard Traina, *American Diplomacy and the Spanish Civil War* (Bloomington: Indiana University Press, 1968).

Chapter 2: Toward the Inescapable: The Pull of War

Robert Divine, *The Reluctant Belligerent* (New York: Wiley, 1965), provides a good brief overview; see also Donald Drummond, *The Passing of American Neutrality, 1937–1941* (Ann Arbor: University of Michigan Press, 1955). William Langer and Everett Gleason, *The Challenge to Isolation* (New York: Harper, 1952) and *The Undeclared War* (New York: Harper, 1953), are semiofficial accounts but nonetheless authoritative and essential. James MacGregor Burns, *Roosevelt: The Soldier of Freedom* (New York: Harcourt, Brace, 1970), and Robert Sherwood, *Roosevelt and Hopkins* (New York: Harper, 1948), are valuable both for this and the following chapter. Charles Tansill, *Backdoor to War* (Chicago: Regnery, 1952), is an isolationist critique, as are Charles A. Beard, *American Foreign Policy in the Making, 1932–40* (New Haven: Yale University Press, 1946) and *President Roosevelt and the Coming of the War, 1941* (New Haven: Yale University Press, 1948). Bruce Russett, *No Clear and Present Danger* (New York: Harper, 1972), reflects a rather extreme variant of contemporary neo-isolationism.

For the debate within the United States, see Walter Johnson, *The*

Battle Against Isolation (Chicago: University of Chicago Press, 1944); Wayne Cole, *America First* (Madison: University of Wisconsin Press, 1953); Mark Chadwin, *The Hawks of World War II* (Chapel Hill: University of North Carolina Press, 1968); Bernard Donahoe, *Private Plans and Public Dangers: The Story of FDR's Third Nomination* (Notre Dame: University of Notre Dame Press, 1965); Herbert Parmet and Marie Hecht, *Never Again: A President Runs for a Third Term* (New York: Macmillan, 1968); Warren Moscow, *Roosevelt and Willkie* (Englewood Cliffs, N.J.: Prentice-Hall, 1968).

Some of the books cited for chapter 1 remain relevant. Important problems connected primarily with the European war receive attention in John Haight, *American Aid to France, 1938–1940* (New York: Atheneum, 1970); Warren Kimball, *"The Most Unsordid Act": Lend-Lease, 1939–1941* (Baltimore: Johns Hopkins University Press, 1969); Theodore Wilson, *The First Summit* (New York: Scribner's, 1969); Raymond Dawson, *The Decision to Aid Russia* (Chapel Hill: University of North Carolina Press, 1959). On U.S.–Japanese relations, see Herbert Feis, *The Road to Pearl Harbor* (Princeton: Princeton University Press, 1950); Paul Schroeder, *The Axis Alliance and Japanese-American Relations, 1941* (Ithaca: Cornell University Press, 1958); Robert Butow, *Tojo and the Coming of the War* (Stanford: Stanford University Press, 1961); Walter Millis, *This Is Pearl!* (New York: Morrow, 1947); and Roberta Wohlstetter, *Pearl Harbor: Warning and Decision* (Stanford: Stanford University Press, 1962).

Chapter 3: Total War and the Pursuit of Total Peace

The literature on World War II is so great that a selected bibliography cannot pretend to list all the important books. A good brief account is Peter Young, *A Short History of World War II, 1939–1945* (New York: Crowell, 1966). Sir Basil Liddell Hart, *History of the Second World War* (New York: Putnam, 1970), was the final work of an influential strategic thinker and historian. A. Russell Buchanan, *The United States and World War II* (2 vols.; New York: Harper, 1964), is primarily an account of American military participation.

Each side of course had its official historians. The huge multivolume series, *The United States Army in World War II*, projected for some sixty volumes, provides in-depth coverage for about every aspect of its topic. Even more impressive in its way is Samuel Eliot Morison, *History of United States Naval Operations in World War II* (15 vols.; Boston: Atlantic Monthly, 1947–62), severely abridged as *The Two-Ocean War*

(Boston: Little, Brown, 1963). For the Russian front, consult Alexander Werth, *Russia at War, 1941–1945* (New York: Dutton, 1964), and Alan Clark, *Barbarossa* (New York: Morrow, 1965). Grand strategy is explored in the critical Hanson Baldwin, *Great Mistakes of the War* (New York: Harper, 1950); Samuel Eliot Morison, *Strategy and Compromise* (Boston: Little, Brown, 1958); Kent Roberts Greenfield, *American Strategy in World War II* (Baltimore: Johns Hopkins University Press, 1970); and Greenfield, ed., *Command Decisions* (Garden City, N.Y.: Doubleday, 1959).

The two most important American generals are covered in Stephen Ambrose, *The Supreme Commander: The War Years of Dwight D. Eisenhower* (Garden City, N.Y.: Doubleday, 1970), and in Forrest Pogue's multivolume *George C. Marshall* (3 vols., in progress; New York: Viking, 1963–), now complete through the war years. Eisenhower, *Crusade in Europe* (Garden City, N.Y.: Doubleday, 1948), Omar Bradley, *A Soldier's Story* (New York: Holt, 1951), and Douglas MacArthur, *Reminiscences* (New York: McGraw-Hill, 1964), are probably the most important of the American military memoirs.

The work on wartime diplomacy is about equally extensive. There are many books on the Big Three statesmen. For Roosevelt, see especially the Burns and Sherwood volumes cited for chapter 2. Robert Divine, *Roosevelt and World War II* (Baltimore: Johns Hopkins University Press, 1969), is a bit thin both in size and analysis. Gaddis Smith, *American Diplomacy during the Second World War* (New York: Wiley, 1965), focuses on FDR's approach to diplomacy and criticizes it from a moderate anti-Soviet perspective. For Churchill, see Alan Moorhead, *Churchill* (Boston: Houghton Mifflin, 1955); Trumbull Higgins, *Winston Churchill and the Second Front, 1940–1943* (New York: Oxford University Press, 1957); and Churchill's own *History of the Second World War* (6 vols.; Boston: Houghton Mifflin, 1948–53). Isaac Deutscher, *Stalin: A Political Biography* (2nd ed.; New York: Oxford, 1967), and Adam Ulam, *Stalin: The Man and His Era* (New York: Viking, 1973), are major treatments, but in many respects the most compelling books are those of Soviet dissidents, especially Roy Medvedev, *Let History Judge* (New York: Knopf, 1972), and Alexander Solzhenitsyn, *The Gulag Archipelago* (2 vols.; New York: Harper, 1973–75).

William McNeill, *America, Britain, and Russia* (New York: Oxford University Press, 1953), and Herbert Feis, *Churchill, Roosevelt, and Stalin* (Princeton: Princeton University Press, 1957), are classic surveys of World War II diplomacy. Gabriel Kolko, *The Politics of War* (New York: Random House, 1969), is a major effort by a neo-Marxist revisionist. John Gaddis, *The United States and the Origins of the Cold War, 1941–1947*

(New York: Columbia, 1972), explores the war and its immediate aftermath from a perspective best described as postrevisionist. See also John Snell, *Illusion and Necessity: The Diplomacy of Global War* (Boston: Houghton Mifflin, 1963), and William L. Neumann, *After Victory: Churchill, Roosevelt, Stalin, and the Making of the Peace* (New York: Harper, 1967).

Significant treatments of specific topics are Anne Armstrong, *Unconditional Surrender* (New Brunswick: Rutgers University Press, 1961); Robert Divine, *Second Chance: The Triumph of Internationalism in America during World War II* (New York: Atheneum, 1967); Herbert Feis, *The China Tangle* (Princeton: Princeton University Press, 1953); Barbara Tuchman, *Stilwell and the American Experience in China* (New York: Macmillan, 1971); Russell Buhite, *Patrick J. Hurley and American Foreign Relations* (Ithaca: Cornell University Press, 1973); Tang Tsou, *America's Failure in China, 1941–50* (Chicago: University of Chicago Press, 1963). Arthur Morse, *While Six Million Died* (New York: Random House, 1967); and Henry Feingold, *The Politics of Rescue* (New Brunswick: Rutgers University Press, 1970), examine the diplomatic ramifications of the slaughter of the European Jews. For Russian-American relations, see Robert Jones, *The Roads to Russia: United States Lend-Lease to the Soviet Union* (Norman: Oklahoma University Press, 1969); the excellent George Herring, *Aid to Russia, 1941-1946: Strategy, Diplomacy, the Origins of the Cold War* (New York: Columbia University Press, 1973); John Snell, ed., *The Meaning of Yalta* (Baton Rouge: Lousiana State University Press, 1956); Diane Shaver Clemens, *Yalta* (New York: Oxford University Press, 1970).

Chapter 4: Organizing for Victory

The domestic side of World War II is just beginning to draw attention. Until recently no acceptable general survey existed. Now there are three: Richard Lingeman, *Don't You Known There's a War On?* (New York: Putnam, 1971); Richard Polenberg, *War and Society* (Philadelphia: Lippincott, 1972); Geoffrey Perrett, *Days of Sadness, Years of Triumph* (New York: Coward, McCann, 1973). Burns, *Roosevelt: The Soldier of Freedom,* is useful also. Jim Heath, "Domestic America during World War II: Research Opportunities for Historians," *Journal of American History* (September 1971), provides a guide to work that has been done and opportunities that need to be exploited.

Albert Blum, *Drafted or Deferred* (Ann Arbor: Bureau of Industrial Relations, 1967), surveys selective service. Richard Hewlett and Oscar

Anderson, Jr., *A History of the United States Atomic Energy Commission: The New World*, 1939–1946 (University Park: Pennsylvania State University Press, 1962), covers the Manhattan project. For economic mobilization, see Eliot Janeway, *The Struggle for Survival* (2nd ed.; New York: Weybright & Talley, 1968); Herman Sommers, *Presidential Agency: OWMR* (Cambridge, Mass.: Harvard University Press, 1950); Joel Seidman, *American Labor: From Defense to Reconversion* (Chicago: University of Chicago Press, 1953); and David Brody, "The Emergence of Mass-Production Unionism," in John Braeman et al., *Change and Continuity in Twentieth-Century America* (Columbus: Ohio State University Press, 1964). Agricultural problems receive attention in Walter Wilcox, *The Farmer in the Second World War* (Ames: Iowa State University Press, 1947); Bela Gold, *Wartime Economic Planning in Agriculture* (New York: Columbia University Press, 1949); and Dean Albertson, *Roosevelt's Farmer: Claude R. Wickard in the New Deal* (New York: Columbia University Press, 1961). On the Office of War Information, see Roger Burlingame, *Don't Let Them Scare You: The Life of Elmer Davis* (Philadelphia: Lippincott, 1960); and Sydney Weinberg, "What to Tell America: The Writer's Quarrel in the Office of War Information," *Journal of American History* (June 1968).

On civil liberties, see Francis Biddle, *In Brief Authority* (Garden City, N.Y.: Doubleday, 1962); and C. Herman Pritchett, *The Roosevelt Court* (New York: Macmillan, 1948). For the Japanese-American controversy, see Morton Grodzins, *Americans Betrayed* (Chicago: University of Chicago Press, 1949). For the position of the Negro, see Richard Dalfiume, *Desegregation of the U.S. Armed Forces: Fighting on Two Fronts, 1939–1953* (Columbia: University of Missouri Press, 1969); Herbert Garfinkel, *When Negroes March* (Glencoe, Ill.: Free Press, 1959); Louis Ruchames, *Race, Jobs, and Politics* (New York: Columbia University Press, 1953); Louis Kesselman, *The Social Politics of FEPC* (Chapel Hill: University of North Carolina Press, 1948); Harvard Sitkoff, "Racial Militancy and Interracial Violence in the Second World War," *Journal of American History* (December 1971).

Among the more significant political studies are Roland Young, *Congressional Politics in the Second World War* (New York: Columbia University Press, 1956); Davis Ross, *Preparing for Ulysses: Politics and Veterans during World War II* (New York: Columbia University Press, 1969); John Moore, "The Conservative Coalition in the United States Senate, 1942–1945," *Journal of Southern History* (August 1967). For Willkie and the Republicans, see Donald Bruce Johnson, *The Republican Party and Wendell Willkie* (Urbana: University of Illinois Press, 1960); Ellsworth Barnard, *Wendell Willkie: Fighter for Freedom* (Amherst:

University of Massachusetts Press, 1966); Donald McCoy, "Republican Opposition during Wartime, 1941–1945," *Mid-America* (July 1967). For the independent and democratic liberals, see Alonzo Hamby, "Sixty Million Jobs and the People's Revolution: The Liberals, the New Deal, and World War II," *Historian* (August 1968); and the early chapters in Edward L. and Frederick H. Schapsmeier, *Prophet in Politics: Henry A. Wallace and the War Years, 1940–1965* (Ames: Iowa State University Press, 1970).

Chapter 5: The Ashes of Victory: The Cold War

All the general foreign policy surveys cited at the beginning of this bibliography are helpful, as are the books by Gaddis, McNeill, Herring, and Kolko listed for chapter 3.

Herbert Feis's work moves into the postwar period with *Between War and Peace: The Potsdam Conference* (Princeton: Princeton University Press, 1960); *The Atomic Bomb and the End of World War II* (Princeton: Princeton University Press, 1966); *From Trust to Terror: The Onset of the Cold War, 1945–1950* (New York: Norton, 1970). Revisionist counterpoints are provided by Lloyd Gardner, *Architects of Illusion* (Chicago: Quadrangle, 1970); D. F. Fleming, *The Cold War and Its Origins* (2 vols.; Garden City, N.Y.: Doubleday, 1961); Gabriel and Joyce Kolko, *The Limits of Power* (New York: Harper, 1972); Gar Alperovitz, *Cold War Essays* (Garden City, N.Y.: Doubleday, 1969); Thomas Paterson, *Soviet-American Confrontation* (Baltimore: Johns Hopkins University Press, 1973). The revisionists are criticized in Arthur Schlesinger, Jr., "Origins of the Cold War," *Foreign Affairs* (October 1967); Robert J. Maddox, *The New Left and the Origins of the Cold War* (Princeton: Princeton University Press, 1973); Robert W. Tucker, *The Radical Left and American Foreign Policy* (Baltimore: Johns Hopkins University Press, 1971). Lisle Rose, *After Yalta* (New York: Scribner's, 1973), is a brief post-revisionist survey; and Rose, *Dubious Victory* (Kent: Kent State University, 1973), is the first volume of a lengthier study.

For leading policy makers, see Richard Haynes, *The Awesome Power: Harry S Truman as Commander-in-Chief* (Baton Rouge: Louisiana State University Press, 1973); Robert Ferrell, *George Marshall* (New York: Cooper Square, 1966); Gaddis Smith, *Dean Acheson* (New York: Cooper Square, 1972). Important memoirs are James Byrnes, *Speaking Frankly* (New York: Harper, 1947); Dean Acheson, *Present at the Creation* (New York: Norton, 1969); George Kennan, *Memoirs* (2 vols.; Boston: Little, Brown, 1967–72); Charles Bohlen, *Witness to History* (New York: Norton, 1973).

On the atomic bomb, consult, in addition to the Feis study and other more general works cited above, Gar Alperovitz, *Atomic Diplomacy: Potsdam and Hiroshima* (New York: Random House, 1965); Walter Schoenberger, *Decision of Destiny* (Athens: Ohio University Press, 1969); Len Giovannitti and Fred Freed, *The Decision to Drop the Bomb* (New York: Coward, McCann, 1965); Robert Butow, *Japan's Decision to Surrender* (Stanford: Stanford University Press, 1954). John Gaddis discusses the evolution of cold war attitudes in "Was the Truman Doctrine a Real Turning Point?" *Foreign Affairs* (January 1974).

For European issues, see John Gimbel, *The American Occupation of Germany* (Stanford: Stanford University Press, 1968); Bruce Kuklick, *American Policy and the Division of Germany* (Ithaca: Cornell University Press, 1972); Hadley Arkes, *Bureaucracy, the Marshall Plan, and the National Interest* (Princeton: Princeton University Press, 1973). For the Far East, Tang Tsou, *American's Failure in China,* remains indispensable. See also Glenn Paige, *The Korean Decision* (New York: Free Press, 1968); David Rees, *Korea: The Limited War* (New York: St. Martin's, 1964); John Spanier, *The Truman-MacArthur Controversy and the Korean War* (rev. ed.; New York: Norton, 1965); Alan Whiting, *China Crosses the Yalu* (Stanford: Stanford University Press, 1960); Matthew Ridgway, *The Korean War* (Garden City, N.Y.: Doubleday, 1967).

Chapter 6: The Fair Deal

For accounts of Truman and his administration, see *Truman's Memoirs* (2 vols.; Garden City, N.Y.: Doubleday, 1955–56); Jonathan Daniels, *Man of Independence* (Philadelphia: Lippincott, 1950), valuable for its narrative of HST's pre-presidential career; Margaret Truman, *Harry S. Truman* (New York: Morrow, 1972), a sometimes revealing personal memoir. Cabell Phillips, *The Truman Presidency* (New York: Macmillan, 1966), is a competent, if too selective, journalistic survey; Merle Miller, *Plain Speaking* (New York: Putnam, 1974), is based on a series of oral interviews a decade after Truman left the Presidency; but Bert Cochran, *Harry Truman and the Crisis Presidency* (New York: Funk & Wagnalls, 1973), is pedestrian. The most complete scholarly study is Alonzo Hamby, *Beyond the New Deal: Harry S. Truman and American Liberalism* (New York: Columbia University Press, 1973). Richard Kirkendall, ed., *The Truman Period as a Research Field* (Columbia: University of Missouri Press, 1967), is a valuable guide to the historiography of the Truman years, and Kirkendall, ed., *The Truman Period as a Research Field: A Reappraisal, 1972* (Columbia: University of Missouri Press, 1973), is actually a wholly different book with new contributors.

On politics and political issues, see Susan Hartmann, *Truman and the 80th Congress* (Columbia: University of Missouri Press, 1971); Irwin Ross, *The Loneliest Campaign: The Truman Victory of 1948* (New York: New American Library, 1968); Richard Davies, *Housing Reform during the Truman Administration* (Columbia: University of Missouri Press, 1966); Stephen Bailey, *Congress Makes a Law: The Employment Act of 1946* (New York: Columbia University Press, 1950); Allen Matusow, *Farm Policies and Politics in the Truman Administration* (Cambridge, Mass.: Harvard University Press, 1967); R. Alton Lee, *Truman and Taft-Hartley* (Lexington: University of Kentucky Press, 1966); Arthur McClure, *The Truman Administration and the Problems of Postwar Labor* (Rutherford, N.J.: Fairleigh-Dickinson University Press, 1969); Grant McConnell, *The Steel Seizure of 1952* (University: University of Alabama Press, 1960); Barton Bernstein, "The Truman Administration and Its Reconversion Wage Policy," *Labor History* (Fall 1965), is perhaps the most important of several articles Bernstein has written on postwar reconversion.

Radical opponents of the Truman administration are covered in Karl Schmidt, *Henry A. Wallace* (Syracuse: Syracuse University Press, 1960); Norman Markowitz, *The Rise and Fall of the People's Century: Henry A. Wallace and American Liberalism, 1941–1948* (New York: Free Press, 1973); Curtis MacDougall, *Gideon's Army* (3 vols.; New York: Marzani & Munsell, 1965); David Shannon, *The Decline of American Communism* (New York: Harcourt, Brace, 1959); Joseph Starobin, *American Communism in Crisis, 1943–1957* (Cambridge, Mass.: Harvard University Press, 1972). For the Dixiecrats, see V. O. Key, *Southern Politics* (New York: Knopf, 1949). For the Republicans, see James Patterson, *Mr. Republican: A Biography of Robert A. Taft* (Boston: Houghton Mifflin, 1972); Athan Theoharis, *The Yalta Myths* (Columbia: University of Missouri Press, 1970); Ronald Caridi, *The Korean War and American Politics* (Philadelphia: University of Pennsylvania Press, 1968).

On civil rights, see Donald McCoy and Richard Ruetten, *Quest and Response* (Lawrence: University of Kansas Press, 1973); William Berman, *The Politics of Civil Rights in the Truman Administration* (Columbus: Ohio State University Press, 1970); Dalfiume, *Desegregation of the U.S. Armed Forces;* Harvard Sitkoff, "Harry Truman and the Election of 1948: The Coming of Age of Civil Rights in American Politics," *Journal of Southern History* (November 1971). Barton Bernstein, ed., *Politics and Policies of the Truman Administration* (Chicago: Quadrangle, 1970), contains an essay on civil rights by Bernstein and two essays on civil liberties by Athan Theoharis. On civil liberties, loyalty-security issues, and the origins of McCarthyism, see Alan Harper, *The Politics of Loyalty* (Westport: Greenwood, 1969); Athan Theoharis, *Seeds of Repression: Harry S. Truman and the Origins of McCarthyism* (Chicago: Quadrangle, 1971);

Richard Freeland, *The Truman Doctrine and the Origins of McCarthyism* (New York: Knopf, 1972); Earl Latham, *The Communist Controversy in Washington* (Cambridge, Mass.: Harvard University Press, 1966); Richard Rovere, *Senator Joe McCarthy* (New York: Harcourt, Brace, 1959); Robert Griffith, *The Politics of Fear* (Lexington: University of Kentucky Press, 1970); Daniel Bell, ed., *The Radical Right* (Garden City, N.Y.: Doubleday, 1963); Michael Paul Rogin, *The Intellectuals and McCarthy* (Cambridge, Mass.: MIT Press, 1967).

Chapter 7: The Ike Age

Herbert Parmet, *Eisenhower and the American Crusades* (New York: Macmillan, 1972), is the first good history of the Eisenhower administration. Charles Alexander, *Holding the Line* (Bloomington: Indiana University Press, 1975), is an important contribution. James L. Sundquist, *Politics and Policy: The Eisenhower, Kennedy, and Johnson Years* (Washington, D.C.: Brookings, 1968), is a basic guide to the major domestic issues. Gary Reichard, *The Reaffirmation of Republicanism* (Knoxville: University of Tennessee Press, 1975), is a model study of presidential-congressional relations. See also Dean Albertson, ed., *Eisenhower as President* (New York: Hill & Wang, 1962); Heinz Eulau, *Class and Party in the Eisenhower Years* (New York: Free Press, 1962); Samuel Lubell, *Revolt of the Moderates* (New York: Harper, 1956); Robert Donovan, *Eisenhower: The Inside Story* (New York: Harper, 1956); J.W. Anderson, *Eisenhower, Brownell, and the Congress: The Tangled Origins of the Civil Rights Bill of 1956-57* (University: University of Alabama Press, 1964); Daniel Berman, *A Bill Becomes a Law* (New York: Macmillan, 1962); David Frier, *Conflict of Interest in the Eisenhower Administration* (Ames: Iowa State University Press, 1969); Aaron Wildavsky, *Dixon-Yates* (New Haven: Yale University Press, 1962).

The Eisenhower administration produced a remarkable number of memoirs, including: Eisenhower, *Mandate for Change* (Garden City, N.Y.: Doubleday, 1963) and *Waging Peace* (Garden City, N.Y.: Doubleday, 1965); Richard Nixon, *Six Crises* (Garden City, N.Y.: Doubleday, 1962); Sherman Adams, *Firsthand Report* (New York: Harper, 1961); Emmet John Hughes, *The Ordeal of Power* (New York: Atheneum, 1963); Arthur Larson, *Eisenhower: The President Nobody Knew* (New York: Scribner's, 1968); Ezra Taft Benson, *Crossfire* (Garden City, N.Y.: Doubleday, 1962); Lewis Strauss, *Men and Decisions* (Garden City, N.Y.: Doubleday, 1962).

For the new conservatism, see in addition to Arthur Larson's *A*

Republican Looks at His Party (New York: Harper, 1955), Clinton Rossiter, *Conservatism in America*, preferably the first edition (New York: Knopf, 1955); the second edition (New York: Vintage, 1962) renounces some of the basic attitudes reflected in the first. Peter Viereck, *Conservatism Revisited*, was a pioneering statement when it first appeared in 1949; a second edition (New York: Free Press, 1962) contains new material lamenting the failure of the New Conservatism. William F. Buckley, Jr., first gained attention with *God and Man at Yale* (Chicago: Regnery, 1951) and *Up from Liberalism* (rev. ed.; New York: Arlington House, 1968).

On the Warren Court, see Alexander Bickel, *Politics and the Warren Court* (New York: Harper, 1965); Archibald Cox, *The Warren Court* (Cambridge, Mass.: Harvard University Press, 1968); Philip Kurland, *Politics, the Constitution, and the Warren Court* (Chicago: University of Chicago Press, 1970); Arthur Goldberg, *Equal Justice* (Evanston: Northwestern University Press, 1972).

Chapter 8: Caution at the Brink

Several of the books cited for chapter 7 remain relevant here. Serious scholarly work on the diplomacy of Eisenhower and Dulles is inhibited by the unavailability of State Department records which may not even begin to be accessible until the 1980s. Nevertheless, for this and succeeding administrations there are a number of worthwhile studies based on printed sources.

Dulles has been examined in Andrew Berding, *Dulles on Diplomacy* (Princeton: Van Nostrand, 1965); Louis Gerson, *John Foster Dulles* (2 vols.; New York: Cooper Square, 1968); Richard Goold-Adams, *The Time of Power* (London: Weidenfeld & Nicholson, 1962); Townsend Hoopes, *The Devil and John Foster Dulles* (Boston: Little, Brown, 1973). G. Bernard Noble, *Christian A. Herter* (New York: Cooper Square, 1970), deals with the brief tenure of Dulles' successor. For Southeast Asia, see Melvin Gurtov, *The First Vietnam Crisis* (New York: Columbia University Press, 1967); and Ellen Hammer, *The Struggle for Indo-China* (Stanford: Stanford University Press, 1966). On the Suez situation, see Herman Finer, *Dulles Over Suez* (Chicago: Quadrangle, 1964); and Hugh Thomas, *Suez* (New York: Harper, 1967). For Cuba, there are Theodore Draper, *Castro's Revolution* (New York: Praeger, 1962); Ramon Ruiz, *Cuba: The Making of a Revolution* (Amherst: University of Massachusetts Press, 1968); Hugh Thomas, *Cuba* (New York: Harper, 1971). David Wise and Thomas Ross cover *The U-2 Affair* (New York: Random House, 1962).

Chapter 9: Cultural Revolutions

John Brooks, *The Great Leap* (New York: Harper, 1966), is a thoughtful survey of American culture since the 1930s. Ronald Berman, *America in the Sixties: An Intellectual History* (New York: Free Press, 1968), is an important work by a critic unwilling to abandon the traditional values of liberal culture. William O'Neill, *Coming Apart* (Chicago: Quadrangle, 1971), contains several rewarding chapters on American culture in the 1960s.

In addition to the books mentioned in the text on middle-class life, see Robert C. Wood, *Suburbia: Its People and Their Politics* (Boston: Houghton Mifflin, 1959); and Scott Donaldson, *The Suburban Myth* (New York: Columbia University Press, 1969). For the great liberation, see Philip Nobile, ed., *The New Eroticism* (New York: Random House, 1970); J. Anthony Lukas, "The Alternative Life Styles of Playboys and Playmates," *New York Times Magazine* (11 June 1972); and Charles Rembar's perhaps prematurely titled book, *The End of Obscenity* (New York: Random House, 1968).

On women's liberation, see William Chafe, *The American Woman* (New York: Oxford University Press, 1972); Robin Morgan, ed., *Sisterhood Is Powerful* (New York: Random House, 1970); Caroline Bird, *Born Female* (New York: David McKay, 1969); Mary Ellman, *Thinking About Women* (New York: Harcourt Brace, 1969); Kate Millett, *Sexual Politics* (Garden City, N.Y.: Doubleday, 1970); Elizabeth Janeway, *Man's World, Women's Place* (New York: Morrow, 1971); Midge Decter, *The New Chastity and Other Arguments against Women's Liberation* (New York: Coward, McCann, 1972).

For the counterculture, see Bruce Cook, *The Beat Generation* (New York: Scribner's, 1971); Theodore Roszak, *The Making of a Counter Culture* (Garden City, N.Y.; Doubleday, 1969) and *Beyond the Wasteland* (Garden City, N.Y.: Doubleday, 1972); Bennett Berger, "The New State of American Man—Almost Endless Adolescence," *New York Times Magazine* (2 November 1969); The Editors of *Rolling Stone, The Age of Paranoia* (New York: Pocket Books, 1972). Philip Nobile, ed., *The Con III Controversy* (New York: Pocket Books, 1971), dissects *The Greening of America*. Richard King, *The Party of Eros* (Chapel Hill: University of North Carolina Press, 1972), admirably explores the meeting ground between the counterculture and the New Left by examining the social thought of Norman O. Brown, Paul Goodman, and Herbert Marcuse. See also Brown, *Life Against Death* (New York: Random House, 1959);

Marcuse, *Eros and Civilization* (New York: Random House, 1955) and *One-Dimensional Man* (Boston: Beacon, 1964); for Goodman, see in addition to the books mentioned in the text, *The Community of Scholars* (New York: Random House, 1962) and *New Reformation* (New York: Random House, 1970), a critique of the New Left as it had developed by the end of the 1960s.

Jack Newfield, *A Prophetic Minority* (New York: New American Library, 1966), is a good, sympathetic survey of the early movement; and see Massimo Teodori, ed., *The New Left: A Documentary History* (Indianapolis: Bobbs-Merrill, 1969), for its commentaries, chronology, and bibliography, as well as for its well-chosen documents. The best introduction to C. Wright Mills is *Power, Politics, and People* (New York: Oxford University Press, 1963), a collection of articles edited by Irving Louis Horowitz. Histories of organizations include Howard Zinn, *SNCC: The New Abolitionists* (Boston: Beacon, 1972); Alan Adelson, *SDS: A Profile* (New York: Scribner's, 1972); Kirkpatrick Sale, *SDS* (New York: Random House, 1973). New Left concepts and objectives are examined in Terrence Cook and Patrick Morgan, eds., *Participatory Democracy* (New York: Harper, 1971); Irving Howe, ed., *Beyond the New Left* (New York: McCall, 1970); Seymour Lipset and Philip Altbach, eds., *Students in Revolt* (Boston: Houghton Mifflin, 1969); Immanuel Wallerstein and Paul Starr, eds., *The University Crisis Reader* (2 vols.; New York: Random House, 1971).

Among the many studies of the Black Revolution, the following are fundamental: Charles Silberman, *Crisis in Black and White* (New York: Random House, 1964); Anthony Lewis, *Portrait of a Decade* (New York: Random House, 1964); the Kerner Commission's *Report of the National Advisory Commission on Civil Disorders* (Washington: U.S. Government Printing Office, 1968); David Lewis, *King: A Critical Biography* (New York: Praeger, 1970); Stokely Carmichael and Charles Hamilton, *Black Power* (New York: Random House, 1967); Harold Cruse, *The Crisis of the Negro Intellectual* (New York: Morrow, 1967); August Meier and Elliott Rudwick, eds., *Black Protest in the Sixties* (Chicago: Quadrangle, 1970). Paul Jacobs, *Prelude to Riot* (New York: Random House, 1967), discusses Watts; and Fred Graham, "Black Crime: The Lawless Image." *Harper's* (September 1970), is a candid discussion.

The major ingredients of the urban crisis, race, crime, and poverty have all received extensive attention. For poverty, see in addition to Michael Harrington's *The Other America* (New York: Macmillan, 1962), Dwight MacDonald, "Our Invisible Poor," *New Yorker* (19 January 1963); Ben Seligman, *Permanent Poverty* (Chicago: Quadrangle, 1970); Frances Fox Piven and Richard Cloward, *Regulating the Poor* (New York:

Pantheon, 1971); Lee Rainwater, *Behind Ghetto Walls* (Chicago: Aldine, 1970); Thomas Sowell, *Race and Economics* (New York: David McKay, 1975); Anthony Downs, *Who Are the Urban Poor?* (New York: Committee for Economic Development, 1970). For crime and violence, consult Ramsey Clark, *Crime in America* (New York: Simon & Schuster, 1970), and a number of reports prepared by the National Commission on the Causes and Prevention of Violence; Hugh Davis Graham and Ted Robert Gurr, eds., *Violence in America: Historical and Comparative Perspectives* (New York: New American Library, 1969); Jerome Skolnick, *The Politics of Protest* (New York: Simon & Schuster, 1969); James Campbell, Joseph Sahid, and David Stang, *Law and Order Reconsidered* (Washington, D.C.: U.S. Government Printing Office, 1970); *Final Report: To Establish Justice, To Insure Domestic Tranquility* (Washington, D.C.: U.S. Government Printing Office, 1970). The urban situation as a whole is treated in Nathan Glazer, ed., *Cities in Trouble* (Chicago: Quadrangle, 1970); and Edward Banfield, *The Unheavenly City* (Boston: Little, Brown, 1970). James Wilson and Robert DuPont, "The Sick Sixties," *Atlantic Monthly* (October 1973), attempt to tie the social and cultural crises of the decade to the postwar baby boom.

Middle America receives coverage in Samuel Lubell, *The Hidden Crisis in American Politics* (New York: Norton, 1970); Louise K. Howe, ed., *The White Majority* (New York: Random House, 1970); Peter Schrag, "The Forgotten American," *Harper's* (August 1969); Bill Moyers, *Listening to America* (New York: Harper, 1971); Richard Scammon and Ben Wattenberg, *The Real Majority* (New York: Coward, 1970); Michael Novak, *The Rise of the Unmeltable Ethnics* (New York: Macmillan, 1972).

Chapter 10: The Promise Unfulfilled: John F. Kennedy and the New Frontier

James MacGregor Burns, *John Kennedy: A Political Profile* (New York: Harcourt, 1960), is a real rarity, an "authorized" but nonetheless objective and excellent campaign biography. Theodore H. White, *The Making of the President, 1960* (New York: Atheneum, 1961), is an excellent account of the presidential campaign. Arthur Schlesinger, Jr., *A Thousand Days* (Boston: Houghton Mifflin, 1965), and Theodore Sorenson, *Kennedy* (New York: Harper, 1965), are part memoir, part history. Bruce Miroff, *Pragmatic Illusions: The Presidential Politics of John F. Kennedy* (New York: David McKay, 1976), provides a revisionist view of this era; Aida DiPace Donald, ed., *John F. Kennedy and the New Frontier*

(New York: Hill & Wang, 1966), is a collection of interpretive articles. Tom Wicker, *JFK and LBJ* (New York: Morrow, 1968), contains perceptive interpretations of both presidents.

For domestic problems, Sundquist, *Politics and Policy,* cited for chapter 7, remains essential. See also Jim Heath, *John F. Kennedy and the Business Community* (Chicago: University of Chicago Press, 1969); Grant McConnell, *Steel and the Presidency—1962* (New York: Norton, 1963); Seymour Harris, *The Economics of the Kennedy Years* (New York: Harper, 1964); Walter Heller, *New Dimensions of Political Economy* (Cambridge, Mass.: Harvard University Press, 1966).

For Kennedy's foreign policy, the best source is Roger Hilsman, *To Move a Nation* (Garden City, N.Y.: Doubleday, 1967). Richard Walton, *Cold War and Counterrevolution* (New York: Viking, 1972), offers revisionist interpretations. On Berlin, see Jack Schick, *The Berlin Crisis, 1958-1962* (Philadelphia: University of Pennsylvania Press, 1962); and Robert Slusser, *The Berlin Crisis of 1961* (Baltimore: Johns Hopkins University Press, 1972).

U.S. economic diplomacy is treated in John Evans, *The Kennedy Round in American Trade Policy* (Cambridge, Mass.: Harvard University Press, 1971). For Southeast Asia, see Kenneth Hill, "President Kennedy and the Neutralization of Laos," *Review of Politics* (July 1969), and the volumes on Vietnam listed for the following chapter. The Cuban missile crisis is examined in Elie Abel, *The Missile Crisis* (Philadelphia: Lippincott, 1966); Robert Kennedy, *Thirteen Days* (New York: Norton, 1969); Graham Allison, *Essence of Decision* (Boston: Little, Brown, 1971); Robert Divine, ed., *The Cuban Missile Crisis* (Chicago: Quadrangle, 1971).

Chapter 11: LBJ, the Great Society, and the Little War

Lyndon Johnson's own version of his Presidency is contained in his memoir, *The Vantage Point* (New York: Holt, Rinehart, 1971); Rowland Evans and Robert Novak, *Lyndon B. Johnson* (New York: New American Library, 1966), is excellent journalism; Eric Goldman, *The Tragedy of Lyndon Johnson* (New York: Knopf, 1969), is a compassionate, yet critical, examination. Sundquist's *Politics and Policy* remains fundamental for domestic issues, but see also Marvin Gettleman and David Mermelstein, eds., *The Great Society Reader: The Failure of American Liberalism* (New York: Random House, 1967). The 1964 election is covered in Theodore White, *The Making of the President, 1964* (New York: Atheneum, 1965); and Robert Novak, *The Agony of the G.O.P., 1964* (New York: Macmillan, 1965).

Johnson's Latin American policy receives attention in Jerome Slater, *Intervention and Negotiation: The United States and the Dominican Revolution* (New York: Harper, 1970). Most attention, of course, has been devoted to Vietnam, which serves as the focus of Tom Wicker's critique in *JFK and LBJ*. George Kahin and John Lewis, *The United States in Vietnam* (New York: Dial, 1967), and Bernard Fall, *The Two Viet Nams* (2d rev. ed.; New York: Praeger, 1967), are good introductions. Chester Cooper, *The Lost Crusade* (New York: Dodd, Mead, 1970), and Townsend Hoopes, *The Limits of Intervention* (New York: David McKay, 1969), are critical accounts by administration insiders. *The Pentagon Papers* are available in three separate editions, all published in 1971: the 12-volume official version (Washington, D.C.: U.S. Government Printing Office), the 4-volume "Senator Gravel Edition" (Boston: Beacon), which includes some classified material expurgated from the official version, and the single-volume New York *Times* edition (Chicago: Quadrangle). Frances Fitzgerald, *Fire in the Lake* (Boston: Little, Brown, 1972), and David Halberstam, *The Best and the Brightest* (New York: Random House, 1972), are critical of American intervention. Raphael Littauer and Norman Uphoff, eds., *The Air War in Indochina* (rev. ed.; Boston: Beacon, 1972), is a careful investigation of the bombing campaign. Seymour Hersh, *My Lai 4* (New York: Random House, 1970), recounts the tragedy which visited that hamlet. The best account I have seen of the experience of the ordinary American soldier in Vietnam is Arthur Hadley, "Goodby to the Blind Slash Dead Kid's Hooch," *Playboy* (August 1971).

For the tumultuous events of 1968, see Theodore White, *The Making of the President, 1968* (New York: Atheneum, 1969); Jack Newfield, *Robert Kennedy* (New York: Dutton, 1969); David Halberstam, *The Unfinished Odyssey of Robert Kennedy* (New York: Random House, 1968); and, on the Chicago riots, Daniel Walker et al., *Rights in Conflict* (Washington, D.C.: U.S. Government Printing Office, 1968), a report submitted to the National Commision on the Causes and Prevention of Violence.

Chapter 12: Richard M. Nixon and the Difficult Quest for the Center

Nixon's autobiographical *Six Crises* (Garden City, N.Y.: Doubleday, 1962) provides insights into his character and outlook. Earl Mazo and Stephen Hess, *Nixon: A Political Portrait* (New York: Harper, 1968), is an authorized biography. Other accounts and analyses are Gary Wills, *Nixon Agonistes* (Boston: Houghton Mifflin, 1970); Bruce Mazlish, *In Search of Nixon* (New York: Basic, 1972), an attempt at psychohistory; Jules Witcover, *The Resurrection of Richard Nixon* (New York: Putnam, 1970);

Rowland Evans and Robert Novak, *Nixon in the White House* (New York: Random House, 1971). From 1970–75, John Osborne published annual editions of his *New Republic* White House columns under the basic title, *The Nixon Watch* (New York: Liveright). Jules Witcover, *White Knight: The Rise of Spiro Agnew* (New York: Random House, 1972), profiled Nixon's then heir-apparent. Daniel Moynihan discusses his concerns and viewpoints in *The Politics of a Guaranteed Income* (New York: Random House, 1972) and *Coping* (New York: Random House, 1973). For Kevin Phillips and administration political strategy, see in addition to Phillips's book, cited in the text, his article, "How Nixon Will Win," *New York Times Magazine* (6 August 1972). Richard Harris's books *Justice: The Crisis of Law and Order in America* (New York: Dutton, 1970) and *Decision: The Carswell Nomination* (New York: Dutton, 1971) assail some of the seamier administration activities. The volumes by Lubell and Scammon and Wattenberg, cited for chapter 9, are important for an understanding of the political forces the administration attempted to harness. Initial assessments of the Nixon-Kissinger foreign policy are Robert Osgood et al., *Retreat from Empire?* (Baltimore: Johns Hopkins University Press, 1973); and Henry Brandon, *The Retreat of American Power* (Garden City, N.Y.: Doubleday, 1973). Marvin and Bernard Kalb, *Kissinger* (Boston: Little, Brown, 1974), analyzes the President's right-hand man. Stanley Karnow, "China Through Rose-Tinted Glasses," *Atlantic Monthly* (October 1973), is a sober critique of the euphoria which followed the China trip.

Chapter 13: Uncertain Tomorrows

By mid-1975 the Watergate episode had already spawned a voluminous literature. Three books published by the staff of the New York *Times* provide considerable source material and a basic account of events: *The Watergate Hearings* (New York: Viking, 1973), *The White House Transcripts* (New York: Viking, 1974), and *The End of a Presidency* (New York: Bantam, 1974). A volume by the staff of the Washington *Post, The Fall of a President* (New York: Dell, 1974), contains articles that go beyond its title to a consideration of the entire Nixon administration. Theodore H. White's *Breach of Faith* (New York: Atheneum, 1975) is likely to be considered the definitive account. Marcus Raskin, *Notes on the Old System: To Transform American Politics* (New York: David McKay, 1974), provides a radical interpretation of the growth of presidential power. For Nixon's successor, see Jerald terHorst, *Gerald Ford and the Future of the Presidency* (New York: Third Press, 1974).

On the problem of pollution, see Paul Erlich, *The Population Bomb* (New York: Ballantine, 1968); Barry Commoner, *The Closing Circle* (New York: Knopf, 1971); Donella Meadows et al., *The Limits of Growth* (New York: Universe, 1972); and Peter Pasell and Leonard Ross, *The Retreat from Riches: Affluence and Its Enemies* (New York: Viking, 1973).

Ira Sharkansky, *The United States: A Study of a Developing Country* (New York: David McKay, 1975), provides an interesting analysis of the uneven rate of political and economic development and the consequences to politics and public policy.

Index

DATE DUE

JE 2 7 '83			
JY 2 0 '83			
MY 4 '84			
MY 6 '85			
GAYLORD			PRINTED IN U.S.A.